Voices on Voice

Voices on Voice

Perspectives, Definitions, Inquiry

Edited by
Kathleen Blake Yancey
University of North Carolina at Charlotte

National Council of Teachers of English
1111 W. Kenyon Road, Urbana, IL 61801-1096

Manuscript Editors: Robert A. Heister, Mimi L. Mukerjee
Humanities & Sciences Associates

Production Editor: Michael G. Ryan

Interior Design: Tom Kovacs for TGK Design

Cover Design: Barbara Yale-Read

NCTE Stock Number: 56347–3050

Library of Congress Cataloging-in-Publication Data

Voices on voice : perspectives, definitions, inquiry / edited by
   Kathleen Blake Yancey.
      p. cm.
   Includes bibliographical references (p.) and index.
   ISBN 0-8141-5634-7
   1. English language—Rhetoric—Study and teaching. I. Yancey,
Kathleen Blake, 1950–
PE1404.V64 1994
808'.042'07—dc20   94- 21168
                                                          CIP

Contents

Introduction: Definition, Intersection, and Difference— Mapping the Landscape of Voice

Kathleen Blake Yancey
University of North Carolina at Charlotte

One of the more frequent metaphors employed in rhetoric and composition is voice. Working from an analogy to the spoken context, we use the metaphor of voice to talk generally around issues in writing: about both the act of writing and its agent, the writer, and even about the reader, and occasionally about the presence in the text of the writer. Sometimes we use voice quite specifically: to talk about the writer composing text, in the process addressing both a fictionalized audience constructed by the text and a human audience that is itself re-creating text and writer. Sometimes we use voice to talk specifically about what and how a writer knows, about the capacity of a writer through "voice" to reveal (and yet be dictated by) the epistemology of a specific culture. Sometimes we use voice to talk in neo-Romantic terms about the writer discovering an authentic self and then deploying it in text. These three specific conceptions of voice seem at odds with each other, and they are at odds too with still other interpretations of voice. Voice, then, can and does have several competing references, not all of them necessarily compatible with each other, nor with these three.

When I first began exploring the topic of voice—and as I sought to identify what voice is, or to determine what voice seemed to mean to various writers, or to outline what the metaphor of voice could mean—I encountered the first of several paradoxes: the more I seemed to know about it, the less certain I became, and the less I actually knew. In some cases, my confusion arose because of the absence of a simple definition. "Voice"—sometimes singular in the reference, sometimes plural, and often both—could on the one hand refer to an unstated

This work was supported in part by funds from the Foundation of the University of North Carolina at Charlotte and from the State of North Carolina, to whom the author expresses her thanks.

commonplace hovering somewhere outside the text, or could on the other hand draw tentative definition from assumptions and references within the surrounding text, if the reader were sensitive enough to construct them properly. In other cases, my confusion arose because of the definitions themselves, which argue rather than explain. The features such definitions emphasize lay the foundation for the new argument, which (of course) is that voice is exactly *not* what is claimed by the prior definitions. The aims in these definitions aren't to locate voice historically or semantically but to provide a reason for rewriting what exists. These definitions confuse precisely because they are incomplete and ahistorical. As I searched for a definition of voice, then, what I found was a concept signifying different things to different people, a floating signifier changing from one text to the next (Crowley 1989).

But I also found that as I continued to look, I began to discern patterns among the discussions on voice, points of agreement as well as points of contention, places where compositionists came together as well as those where we parted company. When relativized one to another, these places furnish a starting point for understanding what voice may and may not be, and a starting place for this collection of essays as well. It is the purpose of this introductory essay, therefore, to construct just such a map: to locate places of intersection and difference in the landscape of voice, as a means of guiding the reader both to the territory of voice and to the territory of text within.

Voice in the Oral Rhetorical Context

The metaphor of voice has its most immediate reference in our physical voice, the medium that enables talk, through which we speak to each other and through which we learn about ourselves, language, and the world. In the oral context, we acquire language as we interact with others, in ways that we think of as "natural" and self-correcting. As individuals, we speak in voices uniquely ours—Maya Angelou's will never be mistaken for Richard Nixon's—and in individual voices that are remarkably consistent over time and occasion. Our spoken voice is said to be so individualized that each human has his or her own voiceprint, the speaking analogue to fingerprints.

It's hardly surprising, therefore, that spoken voice is sometimes thought of as synonymous with an individual. Moreover, since voice brings with it certain obvious parallels to the written context—for example, a speaker articulating a message intended for another—voice provides a convenient metaphor for both the writer and the act of composing. Like all metaphors, it moves from what we know, often intuitively, to that which we seek to describe. At the same time, voice seems to bring to writing and the text a quality we don't have otherwise: the individual human being composed of words in the text.

Expressionism and Voice

As Pam Gilbert (1991) points out, using the notion of the individual human voice to talk about writing allows us to humanize or personify the text; this personification anchors conceptions of voice put forward by "expressionists" like Donald Graves, Donald Murray, and Peter Elbow. Donald Graves (1983), for instance, talks about voice as the "driving force" of composing, not in the sense of its being a component of composing, like revising or planning, but in the sense of its infusing the act of writing, of its being the "dynamo in the process" (227). Graves also defines voice in a second way, as "the imprint of ourselves on our writing" (227), here referring not to the writer composing, but to a writer's textual presence. And in a seeming third reference, Graves uses voice to talk about the writer. He notes that, like the writer him- or herself, voice is not static, but developmental: "new voices," similar but not identical, "fit the changing person" (228).

Like Graves, Peter Elbow locates voice as both a starting place and a (developing) style: In talking about teaching, he notes, "I can grow or change. But not unless I start out inhabiting my own voice or style. . . . In short, I need to accept myself as I am before I can tap my power or start to grow" (Elbow 1986, 204). Seen this way, voice is both inherent and emerging, a force within that when tapped motivates and evolves, and it is a source of "power."

Others—Donald Murray, Donald Stewart, and Ken Macrorie—suggest that development of this personal voice leads to what they identify as a crucial feature of successful discourse: authenticity. As Irving Hashimoto (1987) explains, some of these proponents of voice bring to their advocacy a "kind of evangelical zeal" (70), especially in their linkage of Platonic truth to the vision of the individual writer, a truth that is not so much a function of a historical moment or the result of shared knowledge, but a function of a stable individual's seeking to square the writing with the self. When the self is so found and so revealed in text, authenticity results. Not surprisingly, expressionists locate the pursuit of such truth, and its accompanying authenticity, as an appropriate (if not the appropriate) goal in writing.

At the extreme, advocates of expressionism argue that students, when left alone, develop a "natural," even transcendent, voice. Janine Rider (1990), for instance, contends that in order for students to develop a "voice which has validity," they must learn first to "speak their own minds": "By allowing a student his own voice first, we allow creativity and imagination, and we expand the possibilities of our language and our ways of knowing" (182–83). Moreover, Rider asserts, we "begin not with students' language but with their souls, first giving them the confidence to bare those souls in their own voices, and then teaching them the tricks to help make those voices heard" (184). Here, students' voices are genuine and truthful and godlike. Even so, writers use "tricks" after truth is discovered, presumably to translate it to others. The assumptions here seem contradictory: the writer will "naturally" develop a voice that is at once faithful to him- or herself and concurrently a means to revelation, but must also learn "tricks" to communicate with others.

Such individuation of knowing and of composing, of course, comes at a cost. Precisely because voice is a metaphor, it brings with it a matrix of relationships and assumptions, some of which may be confounding rather than illustrative. Such is the case here, where the expressionist application of the metaphor rests on three debatable assumptions. First, the expressionist notion of voice rests on an idealized and stable self learning to write arhetorically: not for a reader, nor for any necessarily particular task. Not unlike Jerzy Kosinski's (1971) figure Chauncey Gardiner's learning to talk, the expressionist writer learns to compose acontextually, without particular purpose or audience. Second, the expressivist notion of voice posits a writer developing "naturally," somewhat as do toddlers in an oral context, but without any component to supply "motherese." Toddlers learn because their caregivers talk back to them: these conversationalists provide the first of multiple voices the child will mimic and appropriate. Removed from such a rhetorical context, the expressivist writer is denied the response that helps infuse and shape meaning. Third, the expressionist notion of voice rests on the possibility of fixing voice in time, before it comes into contact with other voices or with other discourses. Given the synthetic nature of language, however, it seems unlikely that either voice (or time) can be so frozen.

Nonetheless, through the metaphor of voice, the expressionists have brought a powerful metaphor into our discourse on composing and the composer. First, by means of this metaphor they have located something so intuitively obvious that virtually all writing teachers recognize it, even if it is a pre-postmodernist notion: the medium employed by the writer to create his or her presence in text. If there weren't something named by the metaphor of voice, arguments concerning it would have fallen into silence and/or been silenced by others long ago. We wouldn't be having this (written) discussion. Second, expressionists have made explicit an inextricable connection between voice and authority, one that all writers on voice will claim. For expressionists, such authority means three things:

- the right to speak, which is a given (Elbow);
- a source of individual truth leading to authenticity; and
- the ability to speak, which is developed naturally, acquired as a matter of course if allowed to develop outside of intimidating and overly conventionalized discourses.

As we shall see, the connection of voice to authority is a key point of intersection among competing versions of voice.

Voice vs. Voices

Expressionists talk about voice in both the singular and the plural, often shifting from one to the next and back as the reference—to composing process, text, presence in text, revised persona or narrator—changes. Nonetheless, the one-to-one correspondence between an individual and his or her voice is what expressionists value; it is the writer trying to get "right" with him- or herself. Others value voice in a similar way: as a vehicle for expression of the self, but they see voice as a plural rather than a singular. Thus, Joseph Harris (1987), in describing the rhetorics of Roland Barthes and William Coles, talks in collectivist terms of both self and voice as "amalgam of other selves, voices, experiences" (161; qtd. in Frey 1990, 50). The "I" writing is not singular, but plural, a fluid composite of cultural voices and individual selves within the writer.

In a like move, Jane Tompkins (1987) writes of "two voices" inside, one "the voice of the critic who wants to correct a mistake. The other is the voice of a person who wants to write about her feelings" (169). Alice Walker (1990) speaks of a double vision, rooted in a dual community: the linguistic community of the United States; as important, the local community of the African American extended family. Joan Didion (1990) writes of multiple selves, the selves she was yesterday, the self she is now, the self she will be tomorrow. For these writers, voice is not singular, but multiple, a medium created through the weaving of different strands of self—or selves—into the fabric that at best only pretends to be whole. In this view of voice as a multiple construct—articulated within these pages by Toby Fulwiler, Gail Cummins, and Doug Minnerly—authority derives from the acknowledgement of multiplicity and the use of it, the playing off of one voice inside the self against another, the use of one to complement the other. These writers don't seek to square writing with the self, but with the selves, and such writing may not be "squared" at all.

Voices within Text

Multiple voices are not necessarily intentioned, however, by the writer. Sometimes they may simply be perceived by the reader in a text. Such is the case in Carl Klaus's reading of E. B. White and in Laura Julier's reading of Joan Didion. Klaus and Julier track the diverse voices they read: sometimes the voices composing an author, sometimes authorial voices made possible by the voices of others, sometimes authorial voices that claim their place by representing and then pushing aside the voices of others. In the act of re-creating text, the reader's task is also constructing such voices. In so doing, Peter Elbow claims, readers respond as much to the voice/s and their sound in the text as to its focus; they respond to what he calls the "audible" voice. According to Elbow (1981), a text is felicitous to the extent that it evokes "resonance" in the reader: "If I experience resonance, surely, it's more likely to reflect a good fit between the words and my self than a good fit between the words and the writer's self; after all, my self is right here, in contact with the words on the page, while the writer's self is no-where to be found" (300; see also chapter 1, this volume). From this perspective, voice is created as much by the reader as by the writer and the text; no longer is it controlled exclusively by the writer, nor is it here a means of seeking truth. It is rather a means of speaking to another, of trying to create a resonance between the reader and an audible voice carried in text.

Bakhtin, Voice, and Appropriation

Mikhail Bakhtin's thinking has also recently infused many of the current discussions on voice. As glossed by Charles Schuster (1985), Bakhtin's paradigm of communication includes three participants: the speaker, the listener, and the "hero," who "interacts with the speaker to shape language and determine the form" (595). Together, these three elements create a "dialogue" in which all three "speak, listen, and influence each other equivalently" (596). Change to each—speaker, listener, and hero—in the course of communication is thus one of its primary effects. Moreover, in effecting such change, all elements rely on the word, but it is a word that is hardly neutral. Rather, it is a word already "inhabited" by other voices. As Bakhtin narrates, "The word enters his (the speaker's) context from another context, permeated with the interpretations of others. His own thought finds the word already inhabited" (1986, 202). Accordingly, in order for the writer to develop a voice out of such words, he or she must learn to "populate it with his own intention, his own accent, when he appropriates the word, adapting it to his own semantic and expressive intention" (1981, 293–94). Appropriating the word, making it his or her own, thus is the task of the writer seeking to create a voice out of the voices of others, out of the heteroglossia that is language.

Appropriating the voices of others is not, however, a recent idea, having been identified, for example, by poets like Wordsworth as both the chief problem and the task of the poet. The difficulty: wrestling from a language already populated with and by meaning, another meaning. Sometimes, as in the case of Anne Sexton's "Cinderella"—a poem that retells the Cinderella story along feminist and modern lines—one text provides the hero for the next. The poet uses the old story to tell the new: Sexton's new Cinderella is predicated on the reader's knowledge of the first, and is thus a case of direct, deliberate, and conscious appropriation.

Such conscious appropriation isn't limited to modern poets or to obvious signs, of course. As Walter Jackson Bate suggests in *The Burden of the Past and the English Poet* (1970), the poet's task is double: (1) the rewriting of myth, and (2) the rewriting of a particular poet, of that poet whose prior appropriation of the language seems to make new creations impossible. In this view of literary history, the Romantics rewrite Milton, the Victorians, the Romantics (Miyoshi 1969). Thus it is that critics like M. H. Abrams and Harold Bloom "read" Wordsworth not just as formulating a response to, and emulating, Milton—"Almost every sentence of the prospectus rings with echoes of Milton's voice in *Paradise Lost*" (Abrams 1971, 21)—but as seeking quite consciously to rewrite the seventeenth-century poet and *thereby* take his own place in the poetic tradition. In other words, poetry requires such appropriation: Wordsworth, in Abrams's interpretation, sees himself as the "latest in the line of poets inspired by the 'prophetic Spirit,' and as such has been granted a 'Vision' (lines 97–98) which sanctions his claim" to rewrite, re-mythologize "Milton's Christian story in the scope and audacious novelty of his subject" (28). The poetry is not just about its story, but about the story of being a poet. As important for our purpose, poets show us one way of thinking about voice and sources of authority. They remind us that for some writers, voice is created quite deliberately by reference to others, by making them anew. In this view of voice, authority derives from a mix of knowledges, a "knowing that"—of who the others are—and a knowing how—of how to contextualize and appropriate them for new purposes.

Another version of the "appropriation" problem has been articulated by some of the more modern poets; they see the problem in another frame, not so much as connected to the poets who came before, but as a function of the language itself, of the authority and oppression it reifies. In "When We Dead Awaken: Writing as Re-Vision," Adrienne Rich (1979b) talks of the patriarchy that the language encodes and supports and of how it must be changed in order for other experiences to be known, given that language articulates knowing. According to Rich (1979a), the woman seeking to find herself in written discourse finds only an appropriated woman, one created by men: "looking for her way of being in the world . . . [S]he comes up against something that negates everything that she is about: she meets the image of Woman in books written by men. . . . [W]hat she does not find is that absorbed, drudging, puzzled sometimes inspired creature, herself, who sits at a desk trying to put words together" (487).

It is within the structures of patriarchy that the woman poet must work, but Rich holds out hope that even these "foreign" structures may allow new ways of knowing and being, citing Mary Daly's suggestion that women seek out "new space" on the boundaries of patriarchy as a place to write themselves, to find a voice (495). This, she says, will enable the act of renaming that is writing. Appropriation for Rich is intimately connected to authority and to voice: the woman writer who is not careful will be appropriated, and thus silenced. She will have no voice, and thus no existence as woman. Alternatively, she can seek to appropriate the voice of others to create a new voice, in the process establishing her authority.

These writers, however, remind us how conscious such appropriation is for them, how authority for them comes from the deliberate struggle with those who wrote before, from the struggle with a language that itself brings with it its own structures, its own ways of representing and indeed creating the world. They contend that it is out of a somewhat stable schema of reality and authority that the writer must work, seeking places of instability and exploiting those to appropriate others' voices. How and if and when one appropriates consciously is also the subject of much discussion in rhetoric, the hero—in Bakhtinian terms—of much current rhetorical debate. In speaking of students and their writing during the undergraduate curriculum, for instance, David Bartholomae, in "Inventing the University" (1985), suggests that as a student develops, he or she "must learn to try on a variety of voices and interpretive schemes" (135). In so doing, the student "has to appropriate (or be appropriated by) a specialized discourse, and he has to do this as though he were easily and comfortably one with his audience, as though he were a member of the academy or an historian or an anthropologist or an economist." In other words, this student "must learn to speak our language" (135).

In making his case, Bartholomae traces the (inappropriate) voices at hand for the struggling student seeking to sound "academic"—that of the teacher, that of a parent, that of an elder. Bartholomae argues that it is these struggling students particularly who need to "invent" themselves by "approximating" the discourse they seek to enter, and he identifies the moment of beginning as the most difficult, the time when it is hardest to establish the necessary authority: "They begin with a moment of appropriation, a moment when they can offer up a sentence that is not theirs as though it were their own" (145). By such approximations, says Bartholomae, students will learn to write "their way into a position of privilege" (157). For Bartholomae, authority and voice come through conscious appropriations called "approximations," through which a writer composes him- or herself.

Peter Elbow takes a different view of the relationships between appropriation and authority and voice. In "Reflections on Academic Discourse: How It Relates to Freshmen and Colleagues," Elbow (1991) suggests that there is no academic discourse per se—that different disciplines have within themselves varieties of discourse—and that even if there were a monolithic "discourse academic," we should nonetheless continue to write a discourse "that tries to render experience rather than explain it," "to tell what it's like to be me or to live my life" (136). In so doing, Elbow makes a radical proposition, that "we take a larger view of human discourse" (137), that we—teachers and students—refuse to be appropriated by others' notions of discourse, that we exercise our authority to resituate a discourse that renders. Elbow also takes issue with the kinds of signs of voice cited as inappropriate by Bartholomae—use of the "I" in referential discourse, for instance, or "hopefully" performing not hope but anxiety—suggesting that discourse within the academy is itself fraudulent, only pretending to be objective: "Academic discourse tries to be direct about the 'position'—the argument and reasons and claim. Yet it tends to be shy, indirect, or even evasive about the texture of feelings or attitude that lie behind that position" (145).

Moreover, Elbow contends that the voice we create in such writing does us no favor: "the price we pay for a voice of authority" makes us sound "like an insecure or guarded person showing off" (148). Asking students to assume such a voice, in any event, would be counterproductive, since it is "definitely alienating for . . . [them] to be asked to take on the voice, register, tone and diction of most academic discourse. If we have to learn a new intellectual stance or take on difficult intellectual goals, we'll probably have better luck if we don't at the same time have to do it in a new language and style and voice" (145). Rather, Elbow suggests, we should focus our efforts on helping students appreciate the "intellectual practices of an academic discourse," on helping the writer understand voice as a means of developing a "relationship with various live audiences" (153).

Given articles like Robert Connors's foreword to Gregory Clark's *Dialogue, Dialectic, and Conversation* (1990) and journals like the February 1992 issue of *College Composition and Communication* (*CCC*), Elbow's argument that we can rewrite the conventions of discourse and thus rewrite voice itself is cogent. Connors takes on many voices in his foreword to Clark's work, voices conforming to and voices working against the conventions governing such a piece.

> Greg takes us in this book on a quick but extremely useful tour of the Zone that we're trying to learn to live in now. Exhilarating, yes. But scary, very scary. This social constructionist deal doesn't solve too may problems for us, does it? It was kinda comfortable back in the lab and the garret, no? Kind of warm, nice boundaries to the experiment, nice boundaries to the self? (xi)

Here, the boundaries of self and voice and voicing and conventions are confused, are testimony to and embodiment of the issues they articulate. Here, a new way of working within the genre of "the Foreword" is unfolding, one oral, informal, and dialogic in nature.

In the February 1992 issue of *CCC*, editor Richard Gebhardt comments on voice from another perspective, one focused on changes in genre itself, with particular reference to voice. He explains the relationship of voice, voices, and voicing to the changes he has sought to make as editor. He has, he says, deliberately sought out different voices as well as ways to configure those voices. In spite of the "conservative influences on him as editor," Gebhardt has published, he says, two "new" kinds of voices: (1) strong individual personal voices and (2) collections of voices "defin[ing] a sort of genre, the collaborative study, different sections of which are written in different voices" (Gebhardt 1992, 8). Gebhardt's point seems well taken, given that the "collected voice" essay does seem a relatively recent genre. Moreover, from an Elbowean perspective, multiple voicing can be viewed as appropriating older, "single-voiced" constructs. Put differently, a quick look at the likes of Connors, Gebhardt, and the pages of *CCC* suggests that we are appropriating "discourse academic" and making it our own.

But it's not an either/or proposition, for Bartholomae's argument regarding authority, discourse, and voice is likewise valid. The writers represented here and in the pages of *CCC*, particularly those cited by Gebhardt, are the voices of authority within the discipline, those who are already sanctioned, the writers with sufficient authority to push the conventions, appropriate the discourses of others, and make such discourse their own. In other words, these are not writers seeking to approximate the discourse of others; they are writing the discourse others will approximate and appropriate. What's interesting here, however, even given the seeming disagreement between Bartholomae's and Elbow's views of voice (and the relationship between voice and discourse and ways of developing it) is something else as well: (1) an agreement that there is such a thing as voice; (2) what's important isn't just voice and the individual, but voice and discourse, which here seem almost synonymous; and (3) voice enables and confers authority.

Non-Western Views of Voice

The voices represented so far have all agreed that there can be voice, and that there may be some variety of one-to-one correspondence between voice and the individual. This view of voice, however, is not exactly that of non-Westerners. Gwendolyn Gong and John Powers, for instance, talk about how in Asian cultures voice isn't related so much to the individual as to that writer's "ethos"—composed of character and culture—from which "voices are evoked." Thus, for instance, it is common for the Asian writer to rely on indirect communication: "instead of the 'self' telling the audience what he or she wants, the speaker uses indirect communication and leaves it to others to determine the interpretation of the audience." Ethos demands that the self be screened from the communication, that the authority of voice derive from other and more than a self.

Native Americans, according to Tom Carr, have a similar view of voice. Writers work from a larger sense of context: voice belongs to the individual, but also to the choral, formed by the human and by the natural community. No writing can thus be only expression of the self; it inherently expresses others and nature, of whom the writer is a part. Moreover, for both Asian and Native Americans, the product, the display, is not a primary consideration; the process is. Clearly, given these cultural perspectives, voice cannot be defined in universal terms, except, again, for its suggestion of authority, of ability to enable the writer to exist. What Andrew Wiget (1984) claims for Native American writers seems true for all: "to be is to be heard, to speak into the silence of ignorance or oblivion, or to anticipate, even interrupt the utterance of falsehood with a statement of personal truth that substitutes an act of self-naming for an act of other-labeling" (604).

A Common Ground

On the other hand, it may be that voice is a myth, as deconstructionists like Pam Gilbert would claim. But this collection of essays, like this introduction, argues otherwise, argues that voice does exist—somehow literally, also metaphorically. The pertinent arguments thus aren't about whether voice exists, but about how—about how it is developed, about how it is re-created. On these topics, there is considerable contention; within the landscape of voice are various conceptions: voice

> as infusing the process of writing;
>
> as a reference for truth, for self;
>
> as a reference for human presence in text;
>
> as a reference for multiple, often conflicting selves;
>
> as a source of resonance, for the writer, for the reader;
>
> as a way of explaining the interaction of writer, reader, and text;
>
> as the appropriations of others: writers, texts;
>
> as the approximations of others;
>
> as a synecdoche for discourse;
>
> as points of critique;
>
> as myth.

To look at these differences is also to look at ourselves within composition studies, because what we find in voice is ourselves, first focusing on the writer per se, then moving to reader, and finally to discourse and to language and to self and to their interrelationships. Voice is thus paradigmatic of composition studies itself, of its recent history and its current concerns.

As suggested throughout, among these writers, whether they be nineteenth-century poets or twentieth-century writing teachers, there are, however, also significant points of agreement, points of intersection in the landscape of voice, points that provide a common ground:

- Voice is not an independent variable, isolated within itself, or within only its immediate context. It is a means of expression, creation, and communication that lives according to the interaction of several variables:

  a writer, his or her language and knowledge of language and writers;

  a reader with similar knowledge, with different knowledge, able to bring both to the reading, able to hear it in some way, on some level; and

  the language itself, the culture it embodies.

- As a metaphor, voice also suggests an ability to define oneself and to locate oneself relative to other discourses, to write ourselves by appropriating and rewriting others. As suggested in writers as diverse as Bate and Wiget, voice is thus inherently choral, too—sometimes mythically, always functionally, given language itself. Writing in a voice that seeks some correspondence to the writer and that yet functions off of and within a certain discourse is tantamount to conducting a discussion, and just as complex; it is an authoritative act.

Voice, it must be conceded, however, is also fictional: to the extent that it captures and/or expresses merely a part of us, and to the extent it is iterative, given the choral nature of language itself. Moreover, it is fictional in another way. Each time we write, it is possible to wrest from the language and from ourselves a new voice that may or may not be truthful or authentic, for what is the source for such an evaluation? Authentic to who we used to be? To who we are now? To which of the current conflicting selves? Perhaps, then, voice isn't so much authentic or nonfictional, but faithful—to the current voices composing the writer.

In the short story "In the Garden of the North American Martyrs," Tobias Wolff (1981) writes of Mary, an untenured English professor who slowly, very slowly, loses whatever voice she might have had. She learns to write her lectures out in advance,

> using the arguments and often the words of other, approved writers, so that she would not by chance say something scandalous. Her own thoughts she kept to herself, and the words for them grew faint as time went on; without quite disappearing they shrank to remote, nervous points, like birds flying away. (123)

Without the courage to speak, Mary loses her voice; she loses herself. For Wolff, as for the writers in this collection, voice and self are related, at least to the extent that voice endows the right to speak and thus to exist. For Wolff and other writers, voice provides a means to the self and to selves and to discourse and to the culture within which the writer always composes. These writers remind us as well that if Wolff and Wiget are correct, and to be is to speak, then an inquiry into voice is about more than writing, and about more than epistemology, ideology, and politics. It is, ultimately, about ourselves, about what it means to be human, and about why and how that matters.

This Text

From helping students to find a voice, to authorizing those voices, to teaching the written voice, to empowering others through voice as agency or discourse, we in composition studies seem to be about voice; to use voice, almost unconsciously, as a metaphor that informs who and what we do. So: Why this text? To inquire into voice, into the ways we use the term, into what we enable and what we constrain: theoretically, personally, conventionally, pedagogically, culturally, ideologically, technologically.

The chapters themselves move according to an inside-outside, ever-widening spiral kind of logic:

- from this introduction providing a summary background to the history of voice;

- to a theoretical reconsideration of voice, with particular reference to the role of resonance in voice, by Peter Elbow;

- to personal reflections on voice and what they reveal: by Toby Fulwiler, articulating both private and public voices; Gail Cummins, speculating as to sources of authority in voicing; and Doug Minnerly, teasing out the affective component in voice;

- to considerations of voice in common discourse communities: that of technical writing, by Nancy Allen and Deborah Bosley, and that of the print media, by Meg Morgan;

- to connections between ways that voices are situated within the conventions of the personal essay, a genre working within a specific discourse community, and highlighting the expectations readers bring to those essays, by Carl Klaus reading E. B. White and Laura Julier reading Joan Didion;

- to what voice means from and within a pedagogical perspective, as Margaret Woodworth describes a course in voice and shares some of its results; as Paula Gillespie explores the differing conceptions of voice that teachers reward; and as John Albertini, David Harris, and Bonnie Meath-Lang define voice with their hearing-impaired and deaf students;

- to resituating voice, in non-Western as well as Western worlds, with Tom Carr focusing on the otherization of Native Americans and its impact on voice in that context; with Gwen Gong and John Powers locating Asian American voice within a context of ethos; with Susan Carlton tracking various feminisms and their concept of voice; with Randy Freisinger seeking to connect liberal humanism to voice; and with Mark Zamierowski situating voice within electronic discourse, hierarchy, and networks;

- to the final chapter, written collaboratively and on e-mail by the editor and Michael Spooner, a chapter which takes as its point of departure the relationship between and among voice, self, text, and context.

Introducing the chapters this way is, however, to define them too narrowly. Each chapter discusses personal voice, each is reflective in character, and each addresses pedagogical concerns, at least implicitly, usually quite explicitly. Suggesting that they fit neatly, like puzzle pieces, into the slots outlined above is therefore misleading. We might do as well by trying an alternative, if imaginary schema: (1) Voice and the Self; (2) Voice and the Specific Discourse Community; (3) Voice and Pedagogy; and (4) Voice and Culture.

1. *Voice and the Self.* In this imaginary section would be included those who most directly seek to make the connection between the self—or selves—and voice (or voices): Peter Elbow, Toby Fulwiler, Gail Cummins, and Doug Minnerly, and the editor, with Michael Spooner's assistance. Other writers, however, include personal reflections in substantive ways: Laura Julier, Carl Klaus, Randy Freisinger, and Mark Zamierowski.

2. *Voice and the Specific Discourse Community.* In this imaginary section would be writers who consider voice quite specifically in its rhetorical situation, whether that situation be a particular kind of discourse community, or a larger, less stable one. It includes chapters composed by Deborah Bosley and Nancy Allen, Meg Morgan, Laura Julier, Carl Klaus, Paula Gillespie, and Mark Zamierowski.

3. *Voice and Pedagogy.* In this imaginary section would be writers
who consider what using the metaphor of voice has contributed
to teaching and what it might contribute. Margaret Woodworth
and Paula Gillespie speak to this issue directly, and Carl Klaus;
John Albertini, David Harris, and Bonnie Meath-Lang; Peter Elbow; Mark Zamierowski; and Michael Spooner consider it as
well.

4. *Voice and Culture.* In this imaginary section would be the writers
who relativize voice culturally, in a specific site and in ways that
remind us of the metaphor's situatedness. They include Toby
Fulwiler, Gail Cummins, Randy Freisinger, John Albertini and
David Harris and Bonnie Meath-Lang, Tom Carr, Gwen Gong
and John Powers, Susan Carlton, and Mark Zamierowski.

And we could try a third alternative. Ultimately, though, how to
read this text or any other is a decision made by the reader. Some of us
progress in the order suggested by the book. Some of us like to move
around at will. Some of us want to read the conclusion before reading
what "leads" to it. How the reader comes to any text—and to this
text—will depend in part on how much authority he or she will permit
the voice of the text, and how much "voicing" of the text he or she
seeks to do, in the sense of directing the reading, of moving around
within the text, of talking back to the text. For ultimately, as is clear
from the voices within, voice relies on a transaction among writer, text,
and reader.

Perhaps that is the best place for the reader of this text to start
hearing its voice.

Works Cited

Abrams, M. H. 1971. *Natural Supernaturalism: Tradition and Revolution in Romantic Literature.* New York: W. W. Norton.

Bakhtin, M. M. 1981. "Discourse in the Novel." In *The Dialogic Imagination:
Four Essays,* edited by Michael Holquist and translated by Caryl Emerson
and Michael Holquist, 259–423. Austin: University of Texas Press.

———. 1986. Excerpts from "The Problem of Speech Genres." In *Bakhtin:
Essays and Dialogues on His Work,* edited by Gary Saul Morson. Chicago:
University of Chicago Press.

Bartholomae, David. 1985. "Inventing the University." In *When a Writer Can't
Write: Studies in Writer's Block and Other Composing-Process Problems,* edited
by Mike Rose, 134–65. New York: Guilford.

Bate, Walter Jackson. 1970. *The Burden of the Past and the English Poet*. Cambridge, MA: Belnap.

Connors, Robert J. 1990. "Foreword." In *Dialogue, Dialectic, and Conversation: A Social Perspective on the Function of Writing*, by Gregory Clark. Carbondale: Southern Illinois University Press.

Crowley, Sharon. 1989. *A Teacher's Introduction to Deconstruction*. Urbana: National Council of Teachers of English.

Didion, Joan. 1990 [1966]. "On Keeping a Notebook." Rpt. in *In Depth: Essayists for Our Time,* edited by Carl H. Klaus, Chris Anderson, and Rebecca Blevins Faery, 165–72. San Diego: Harcourt Brace Jovanovich.

Elbow, Peter. 1981. *Writing with Power: Techniques for Mastering the Writing Process*. New York: Oxford University Press.

———. 1986. *Embracing Contraries: Explorations in Learning and Teaching*. New York: Oxford University Press.

———. 1989. "The Pleasures of Voice in the Literary Essay: Explorations in the Prose of Gretel Ehrlich and Richard Selzer." In *Literary Nonfiction: Theory, Criticism, Pedagogy,* edited by Chris Anderson, 211–34. Carbondale: Southern Illinois University Press.

———. 1991. "Reflections on Academic Discourse: How It Relates to Freshmen and Colleagues." *College English* 53.2 (February): 135–55.

Gebhardt, Richard. 1992. "Editor's Column." *College Composition and Communication* 43.1 (February): 7–10.

Gilbert, Pam. 1991. "From Voice to Text: Reconsidering Writing and Reading in the English Classroom." *English Education* 23.4 (December): 195–211.

Graves, Donald H. 1983. *Writing: Teachers and Children at Work*. Exeter, NH: Heinemann Educational Books.

Harris, Joseph. 1987. "The Plural Text/The Plural Self: Roland Barthes and William Coles." *College English* 49.2 (February): 158–70.

Hashimoto, Irving. 1987. "Voice as Juice: Some Reservations about Evangelic Composition." *College Composition and Communication* 38.1 (February): 70–80.

Kosinski, Jerzy. 1971. *Being There*. New York: Harcourt Brace Jovanovich.

Macrorie, Ken. 1970. *Uptaught*. New York: Hayden.

Miyoshi, Masao. 1969. *The Divided Self: A Perspective on the Literature of the Victorians*. New York: New York University Press.

Murray, Donald M. 1991. *The Craft of Revision*. Fort Worth: Holt, Rinehart, and Winston.

Rich, Adrienne. 1979a. *On Lies, Secrets, and Silence: Selected Prose 1966–78*. New York: Norton.

———. 1979b. "When We Dead Awaken: Writing as Re-Vision." In *On Lies*, 185–94.

Rider, Janine. 1990. "Must Imitation Be the Mother of Invention?" *Journal of Teaching Writing* 9.2 (Fall/Winter): 175–85.

Schuster, Charles. 1985. "Mikhail Bakhtin as Rhetorical Theorist." *College English* 47.6 (October): 594–607.

Stewart, Donald C. 1972. *The Authentic Voice: A Pre-Writing Approach to Student Writing.* Dubuque, IA: Wm. C. Brown.

Tompkins, Jane. 1987. "Me and My Shadow." *New Literary History* 19: 169–78; Cited in Olivia Frey. 1990. "Beyond Literary Darwinism." *College English* 52.5 (September): 507–26.

Walker, Alice. 1990. "The Black Writer and the Southern Experience." Rpt. in *In Depth: Essayists for Our Time,* edited by Carl H. Klaus, Chris Anderson, and Rebecca Blevins Faery, 690–94. San Diego: Harcourt Brace Jovanovich.

Wiget, Andrew. 1984. "Sending a Voice: The Emergence of Contemporary Native American Poetry." *College English* 46.6 (October): 598–609.

Wolff, Tobias. 1981. "In the Garden of the North American Martyrs." In *In the Garden of the North American Martyrs,* 123–35. New York: Eco Press.

1 What Do We Mean When We Talk about Voice in Texts?

Peter Elbow
University of Massachusetts at Amherst

> ... instead of considering it our task to "dispose of" any ambiguity ... we rather consider it our task to study and clarify the resources of ambiguity.
>
> —Kenneth Burke (1969, xix)

It's hard to stop people from using the word *voice* when they talk about writing, but serious objections come from three points:

- Many traditional writing teachers have long been saying, in effect, "Don't let students confuse writing and speaking. They are very different media. One of the big problems with student writing is too much speech or orality in it."

- Derrida calls voice a major problem in our understanding of discourse—the idea that voice underlies writing and that writing always implies the "real presence" of a person or a voice. This objection has spread beyond people who identify themselves as deconstructionists or poststructuralists.

- People committed to the social construction of knowledge, of language, and of the self tend to object to the concept of voice because it so often seems to imply a naíve model of the self as unique, single, and unchanging.

The rise of semiotics and sign theory in linguistics and literary criticism represents the emergence of a visual metaphor for discourse. "Text" has become the preferred word not just for discourse in general but in fact for anything that carries meaning (e.g., the textuality of clothing or the semiotics of driving). Derrida was angry that linguists like Saussure considered speech to be the paradigm form of language. Therefore if one wants to emphasize voice or to use the example of voice to represent discourse, one must swim against the tide of the dominant visual metaphor and emphasize a sound metaphor.

Yet the biggest problem for voice as a critical term may come from its fans. The term has been used in such a loose and celebratory way as to mean almost anything. It's become a kind of warm fuzzy word: people say that writing has voice if they like it or think it is good or has some virtue that is hard to pin down. We're in trouble if we don't know what we mean by the term.

So my effort in this essay is to be as precise as I can in distinguishing between different senses of voice ("clarifying the resources of ambiguity"). In the first section I will treat the literal, physical voice. Then I will describe five senses of voice as it applies to writing: (1) audible voice (the sounds in a text); (2) dramatic voice (the character or implied author in a text); (3) recognizable or distinctive voice; (4) voice with authority; (5) resonant voice or presence. By making these distinctions I think I can confine most of the dispute to that fifth meaning—the only meaning that requires a link between the known text and the unknown actual author. That is, I think I can show that the first four senses of voice in writing are sturdy, useful, and relatively noncontroversial.

Literal Voice: Observations about the Human Voice

When people speak of voice in writing or of someone "achieving voice" in general or in their life (e.g., in Belenky et al. 1986), they are using a metaphor. This metaphor is so common that perhaps it will one day become literal—as "leg of the table" has become a literal phrase. Once you start listening for the word voice, it's amazing how often you find it in books and articles and reviews—especially in titles. Sometimes the writer is consciously using the term to make some point about writing or psychology, but more often the term is just used in a loosely honorific poetic way. When there is so much metaphorical talk about voice, I find it intellectually cleansing to remind myself that it *is* a metaphor and to acquaint myself better with the literal term—and even try to immerse myself better in the experience of the literal thing itself, the human voice. If this were a workshop, it would be good to do some talking, reciting, singing, and other exercises in orality—and stop and see what we notice.

Let me put down here, then, some literal facts about the human voice. These are not quite "innocent facts" since I want them to show why voice has become such a suggestive and resonant term. But I hope you will agree that they are "true facts."

- Voice is produced by the body. To talk about voice in writing is to import connotations of the body into the discussion—and by implication, to be interested in the role of the body in writing.

- Almost always, people learn to speak before they learn to write. Normally we learn speech at such an early age that we are not aware of the learning process. Speech habits are laid down at a deep level. Also, speaking comes before writing in the development of cultures.

- We can distinguish two dimensions to someone's "voice": the *sound* of their voice and the *manner* or style with which they speak. The first is the quality of noise they make based as it were on the physical "instrument" they are "playing"; and the second is the kind of "tunes, rhythms, and styles" they play on their instrument.

- We identify and recognize people by their voices—usually even when they have a cold or over a bad phone connection. We usually recognize people by voice even after a number of years. Something constant persists despite the change. Of course there are exceptions—such as when some boys go through adolescence.

- People have demonstrably unique voices: "voiceprints" are evidently as certain as fingerprints for identification. This might suggest the analogy of our bodies being genetically unique, but our voiceprints are less dependent upon genes than our bodies.

- Despite the unique and recognizable quality of an individual's voice, we all display enormous variation in how we speak from occasion to occasion. Sometimes we speak in monotone, sometimes with lots of intonation. And we use different "tones" of voice at different times, e.g., excited, scared, angry, sad. Furthermore, we sometimes speak self-consciously or "artificially," but more often we speak with no attention or even awareness of how we are speaking. The distinction between a "natural" and "artificial" way of talking is theoretically vexed, but in fact listeners and speakers often agree in judgments as to whether someone was speaking naturally or artificially on a given occasion.

- Our speech often gives a naked or candid picture of how we're feeling—as when our voice quavers with fear or unhappiness or lilts with elation or goes flat with depression. People sometimes detect our mood after hearing nothing but our "hello" on the telephone. Our moods often show through in our writing too—at least to very sensitive readers; but it's easier to hide how we're feeling in our writing. We can ponder and revise the words we put on paper. Speaking is harder to control, usually less self-conscious, closer to "autonomic" behavior. Cicero says the voice is a picture of the mind. People commonly identify someone's voice with *who* he or she is—with their character—just as it is common to identify one's self with one's body. (The word "person" means both body and self—and it suggests a link between the person and the sound of the voice. "Persona" was the word for the mask that Greek actors wore to amplify their voices [per + sona].)

- Audience has a big effect on voice. (a) Partly it's a matter of *imitating* those around us: just as we pick up words and phrases from those we spend time with, or pick up a regional accent, so we often unconsciously imitate the ways of talking that we constantly hear. (b) Partly it's a matter of *responding* to those around us. That is, our voice tends to change as we speak to different people—often without awareness. We tend to speak differently to a child, to a buddy, to someone we are afraid of. My wife says she can hear when I'm speaking to a woman on the telephone. Some listeners seem to bring out more intonation in our speech (see Bakhtin 1976 on "choral support").

- There are good actors, on and off the stage, who can convincingly make their voices seem to show whatever feeling or character they want.

- People can become just as comfortable in writing as in speaking, indeed we are sometimes deeply awkward, tangled, and even blocked in our speaking.

- Though voice is produced by the body, it is produced out of *breath:* something that is not the body and which is shared or common to us all—but which always issues from inside us and is a sign of life. This may partly explain why so many people have been so tempted to invest voice with "deep" or even "spiritual" connotations.

- Voice involves sound, hearing, and time; writing or text involves sight and space. The differences between these modalities are profound and interesting. (To try to characterize these modalities, however, as Ong has done at length, is speculative, so I must resort briefly to parentheses here. Sight seems to tell us more about the outsides of things, sound more about the insides of things. In evolution, sight is the most recent sense modality to become dominant in humans—and is dealt with in the largest and most recent parts of the human brain. Sight seems to be most linked to rationality—in our brain and our metaphors—e.g., "Do you see?" But there are crucial dangers in going along with Ong and others in making such firm and neat associations between certain *mentalities* and orality and literacy—especially for the teaching of writing [see Elbow 1985].)

- Spoken language has more semiotic channels than writing. That is, speech contains more channels for carrying meaning, more room for the play of difference. The list of channels is impressive. For example, there is volume (loud and soft), pitch (high and low), speed (fast and slow), accent (yes or no), intensity (relaxed and tense). And note that these are not just binary items, for in each case there is a huge range of subtle *degrees* all the way between extremes. In addition, in each case there are patterned sequences: for example tune is a pattern of pitches; rhythm is a pattern of slow and fast and accent. Furthermore, there is a wide spectrum of timbres (breathy, shrill, nasal, and so forth); there are glides and jumps; there are pauses of varying lengths. Combinations of *all* of these factors make the possibilities dizzying. And *all* these factors carry meaning. Consider the example of the subtle or not so subtle pause as we are speaking, the little intensity or lengthening of a syllable—and all the other ways we complicate the messages we speak. We can't do those things in writing. (See Bolinger 1986 for a masterful and scholarly treatment of all dimensions of intonation in speech.)

It's not that writing is poverty stricken as a semiotic system. But writing has to achieve its subtleties with fewer resources. A harpsichord cannot make gradations of volume the way a piano can, but harpsichordists use subtle cues of timing to communicate the *kind* of thing that pianos communicate with volume. Mozart had fewer harmonic resources to play with than Brahms. He had to do a lot with less. To write well is also to do a lot with less. If we are angry, we sometimes press harder with the pen or break the pencil lead or *hit* the keys harder—or write the words all in a rush. In such a mood our speech would probably sound very angry, but none of these physical behaviors shows in our writing.

Consider the many ways we can say the sentence, "Listen to me"— from angry to fond—or in fact with a whole range of modes of anger.

With writing, our options are comparatively small. We can underline or use all caps; we can end with a comma, a period, a question mark, an exclamation mark. We can create pauses by using the ellipsis sign. There are other textual resources of course—such as varying the spacing, sizing, or color of letters and words, playing with the shaping of letters and words, and so forth—but these are considered "informal" and inappropriate to "literate" writing. (If we are writing by hand, we can let our anger or serenity show through quite "graphically." For some reason, we seem to have loosened the conventions for writing on computers—and allowed in more graphical play.) Perhaps the main resource in writing is word choice: choose different words, put them in different orders, set a context by what comes before or afterwards to affect how readers will experience any given sentence. These are the ways we convey significations in writing that we convey effortlessly in speech. In writing, we must do more with fewer channels. (See Brower 1962, 58–74, for an exploration of how poets add to the resources of written language by the use of meter, line, and stanza.)

Voice in Writing: A Family of Related Meanings

People have voices; radios, telephones, TV sets, and tape recorders emit voices. Texts have no voices; they are silent. We can only talk about voice in writing by resorting to metaphor. It's my argument that this is a metaphor worth using, but we can't use it well unless we untangle the differences within a family of five related meanings that people imply when they talk about voice in writing: audible voice; dramatic voice; recognizable or distinctive voice; voice with authority; and resonant voice or presence.

(1) Audible Voice in Writing

All texts are literally silent, but most readers experience some texts as giving off more sense of sound—more of the illusion as we read that we are *hearing* the words. Robert Frost (1917) insists that this is not just a virtue but a necessity: "A dramatic necessity goes deep into the nature of the sentence. . . . All that can save them is the speaking tone of voice somehow entangled in the words and fastened to the page for the ear of the imagination" ("Introduction").

How is it, then, that some texts have this audible voice? We have to sneak up on the answer by way of two facts I cited in the previous section: that most people have spoken longer and more comfortably than they have written, and that speaking has more channels of meaning than writing. As a result, when most people encounter a text—a set of words that just sit there silently on the page with no intonation, rhythm, accent, and so forth—they automatically *project aurally* some speech sounds onto the text. Given how conditioning and association work, most people cannot help it. Our most frequent and formative experiences with language have involved hearing speech.

In fact, people are virtually incapable of reading without nerve activity in the throat as though to speak—usually even *muscular* activity. We joke about people who move their lips as they read, but this movement is common even among the sophisticated and educated—and many poets insist that it is a travesty to read otherwise. (Have researchers checked out the *hearing* nerves while people read? I'll bet the circuits are busy.) Silent reading must be learned and is relatively recent. St. Augustine tells in his *Confessions* how amazed he was to see Ambrose reading without saying the words out loud.

In short, hearing a text is the norm. We are conditioned to hear words, and the conditioning continues through life. Thus the fruitful question is not, "Why do we hear *some* texts," but rather, "Why *don't* we hear *all* texts?"

There are two main things that prevent us from hearing written words. The most obvious barriers come from the text itself: certain texts resist our conditioned habit to hear. The writer has chosen or arranged words so that it is hard or impossible to say them, and as a result we seem to experience them as hard to hear. This further illustrates the mediation of voice in hearing: for of course, strictly speaking, we can *hear* any word at all. But when written words are easy to say, especially if they are characteristic of idiomatic speech, we tend to hear them more; when written words are awkward or unidiomatic for speech, we tend to hear them less.

People produce unsayable writing in many ways. Some poets, for example, want to block sound and exploit vision (as in concrete poetry, some poems by e. e. cummings, and some L=A=N=G=U=A=G=E poetry). Much legal and bureaucratic writing is unidiomatic and unsayable and thus tends to be unheard because the writers so often create syntax by a process of "constructing" or roping together units (often jargon or even boilerplate units) in a way that has nothing to do with speech. Some scholarly writing is unsayable for various reasons. (A certain amount of technical and difficult terminology may be unavoidable; and consciously or not scholars may want to sound learned or even keep out the uninitiated.) And of course many unskilled writers also lose all contact with the process of speech or utterance as they write: they stop so often in the middle of a phrase to wonder or worry about a word, to look up its spelling, or to change it to one that sounds more impressive, that they lose their syntactic thread and thereby produce many sentences that are wrong or completely unidiomatic.

But we can't blame inaudible writing only on awkward language or ungainly writers. There is a larger reason—culturally produced—why we often don't hear a voice in writing. Our culture of literacy has inculcated in most of us a habit of working actively to keep the human voice out of our texts when we write.

Notice, for example, the informal writing of adolescents or of people who are just learning the conventions of writing. Notice how often they use the language of speech. In addition they often use striking textual devices that are explicitly designed to convey some vividly audible features of speech—some of the music and drama of the voice: pervasive underlining—sometimes double or triple; three or four exclamation marks or question marks at once; pervasive all-caps; oversized letters, colors, parenthetical slang asides "(NOT!!)". (I'm sure I'm not alone in using too many underlinings in my rough drafts—as I'm trying to speak my emphases onto the page—and so I'm always having to get rid of them as I revise and try to find other means to give the emphasis I want.)

What interests me is how unthinkingly we all go along with the assumption that these textual practices are wrong for writing. That is, most of us are unconscious of how deeply our culture's version of literacy has involved a decision to keep voice out of writing, to maximize the difference between speech and writing—to prevent writers from using even those few crude markers that could capture more of the subtle and not so subtle semiotics of speech. Our version of literacy requires people to distance their writing behavior further from their speaking behavior than the actual modalities require. So when Derrida tries to remove connotations of voice from writing (though he's not saying, "Stop all that informal language and that underlining and putting things in all caps!"), he is nevertheless giving an unnecessary fillip to a steamroller long at work in our version of literacy.

Thus it is *not* lack of skill or knowledge that keeps an audible voice out of the writing of so many poor writers. It's their worry about conforming to our particular conventions of writing and their fear of mistakes. Unskilled writers who are *not* worried—usually unschooled writers—tend to write prose that is very audible and speech-like. Here is a first grader writing a large story:

> One day, well if there was a day. There was sand and dust and rocks and stones and some other things. And it was a thunder-

claps! And a planet began to rise. And they called it Earth. And do you know what? It rained and rained and rained for thirty days in the big holes. And see we began to grow. And the first animal was a little dinosaur. . . . Don't listen to the newspaperman, all that about the sun. Don't be afraid because the sun will last for ever. That's all there is. (Calkins 1986, 49. Of course this is a transcription of what the child wrote in "invented spelling," i.e., "1 day wel if thar was a day. . . ." And the text was only half the story: it went along with a series of vivid drawings.)

The very term "illiterate writing," as it is commonly used, tends in fact to imply that the writing suffers from being too much like speech. The culture of school and literacy seems to work *against* our tendency to write as we speak or to hear sounds in a text. (An important exception: our culture sanctions more audible writing in poetry and fiction and literary nonfiction—perhaps because of the stronger or more recent links to orality in these forms.)

So far I have been focusing on the question of how speech intonation gets into writing. But we mustn't forget the important prior question: how does intonation get into speech in the first place? For of course sometimes our speech *lacks* intonation. Sometimes we speak in a monotone; some people put more "expression" into their speech than others. Bakhtin (1976) focuses on intonation. He argues that intonation often carries the most important meaning in any discourse—meaning that may not be carried by the lexical, semantic meaning. As he puts it, intonation is the point where language intersects with life. And he points out that we often lose intonation in our speaking if we lack "choral support" from listeners—that is, if we have an audience that doesn't share our values. (He doesn't point out that sometimes we get our dander up in the face of an alien or oppositional audience and actually *raise* our voice and thus our intonation.)

I sense even a gender issue here. Do not women in our culture tend to use more "expression" or intonation in their speech than men—more variation in pitch, accent, rhythm and so forth?—men tending on average to be a bit more tight lipped and monotone? A recent extensive study shows that women even in writing use more exclamation marks than men (Rubin and Greene 1992, 22). Perhaps the culture of literate writing is more inhospitable to women than to men.

Indeed, perhaps Derrida attacks voice so vehemently *because* he is living at a cultural moment when the old antipathy to voice in writing is beginning to fade and writing is more and more invaded by voice. (I know this is not his point.) What McLuhan and Ong call "secondary orality" is surely taking a toll in writing. Even academic writing is much more open to informal oral features.

Despite the two formidable barriers to audibility in writing (frequently unsayable writing and a culture that wants it different from speech), most humans come at writing with echoes of speech in their ears. We hear a text if it gives us half a chance. The onus is on people who object to the idea of voice in writing to show that hearing the words *isn't* a pervasive fact of reading.

Thus, "audible voice" is a necessary critical term because it points to one of the main textual features that affects how we respond to writing. Other things being equal, most readers prefer texts that they hear—that have audible voice. After all, when we *hear* the text, we can benefit from all those nuances and channels of communication that speech has and that writing lacks. Of course I don't mean to deny that sometimes people find it useful to produce a voiceless, faceless text—to give a sense that these words were never uttered but just ineluctably exist with authority from everywhere and nowhere ("All students will . . . ")—and thus try to suppress any sense that there might be a voice or person behind them.

Naturally, not all readers *agree* about whether a text is audible. But there is at least as much agreement about the audibility of a text or passage as there is about the "structure" or "organization" of it—and we assume the usefulness of those critical concepts. A fruitful area for research lies here: What are the features of texts that many readers find audible? How much agreement do we get about audibility of texts—and among what kind of readers?[1]

(2) Dramatic Voice in Writing

Let me start again from a fact about literal voice. We identify people by their spoken voices—often even when we haven't talked to them in years. In fact we often identify someone's voice with what they are like. I don't mean to claim too much here—I'm not yet touching on voice and identity. I don't mean that we always believe that someone's voice fits their character. After all, we sometimes say of someone we know: "He always sounds more confident than he really is." My point is simply that we do tend to read a human quality or characteristic into a voice. Even in that example, we are reading *confidence* into a voice in the very act of deciding that the person is *not* confident.

The same process occurs even with people we've never met before. If we hear someone talk for more than a few minutes, we tend to hear character in his or her way of speaking. Again, the negative case clinches my point: we are struck when we *cannot* hear character: "She spoke so guardedly that you couldn't tell anything about what she was like" or even, "She sounded like a guarded kind of person."

Therefore it would be peculiar—habit or conditioning being what it is—if people *didn't* hear character or dramatic voice in written texts since they so habitually hear it in speech. And in fact I've simply been trying in the last two paragraphs to sneak up by a pathway of everyday empiricism on what has become a commonplace of literary criticism— at least since the New Critics and Wayne Booth: that there is always an implied author or dramatic voice in *any* written text. New Critics like to describe any piece of prose in terms of the "speaker" (Brower 1962). Where there is language, insist the New Critics, there is drama. Of course the speaker or implied author may not be the real author; in fact the New Critics brought in this terminology in order to heighten the *distinction* between the character implied by the text and the actual writer.

My point is this: when we acknowledge that every text has an implied author, we are acknowledging that every text has a character or dramatic voice. Indeed, students usually do better at finding and describing the implied author in a text when we use the critical term *dramatic voice* and invite them to use their ears by asking them, "What kind of voice or voices do you hear in this essay or story or poem?" (or to ask them about their own writing with the classic question that William Coles and others use so well: "Is that the kind of person you want to sound like?").

Of course the voice may be hard to hear. For example we may read certain wooden or tangled texts and say, "There's *no one* in there." But the New Critics have trained us to look again—listen again—and always find a speaker. It may just be "the bureaucratic speaker" hiding behind conventional forms, but it is a speaker. And Bakhtin continues this training—helping us hear *multiple voices* even when it looks at first like monologue.

Let me illustrate dramatic voice with a passage where D. H. Lawrence (1951) is talking about Melville in *Moby Dick:*

> The artist was so *much* greater than the man. The man is rather a tiresome New Englander of the ethical mystical-transcendentalist sort: Emerson, Longfellow, Hawthorne, etc. So unrelieved, the solemn ass even in humour. So hopelessly *au grand serieux* you feel like saying: Good God, what does it matter? If life is a tragedy, or a farce, or a disaster, or anything else, what do I care! Let life be what it likes. Give me a drink, that's what I want just now.

> For my part, life is so many things I don't care what it is. It's
> not my affair to sum it up. Just now it's a cup of tea. This morning
> it was wormwood and gall. Hand me the sugar.
> One wearies of the *grand serieux*. There's something false about
> it. And that's Melville. Oh, dear, when the solemn ass brays! brays!
> brays! (157–58)

Lawrence's dramatic voice here is vivid: the sound of a brash, opin-
ionated person who likes to show off and even shock. If we are critically
naïve we might say (echoing Lawrence himself), "And that's Lawrence." If we are more critically prudent we will say, "Notice the ways
Lawrence constructs his dramatic voice and creates a role or persona.
We sense him taking pleasure in striking this pose. It's a vivid role but
let's not assume this is the 'real' Lawrence—or even that there is such a
thing as a 'real' Lawrence." (Of course in saying this we would also be
echoing Lawrence—in his dictum, "Never trust the teller, trust the
tale.")

Compare the following passage by the Chicago critic, R. S. Crane
(1951):

> . . . a poet does not write poetry but individual poems. And these
> are inevitably, as finished wholes, instances of one or another
> poetic kind, differentiated not by any necessities of the linguistic
> instrument of poetry but primarily by the nature of the poet's
> conception, as finally embodied in his poem, of a particular form
> to be achieved through the representation, in speech used dra-
> matically or otherwise, of some distinctive state of feeling, of
> moral choice, or action, complete in itself and productive of a
> certain emotion or complex of emotions in the reader. (96)

Crane has a less *vivid* dramatic voice here than Lawrence, but anyone
who is following and entering into this admittedly more difficult prose
(and such a short snippet makes it hard to do that) can sense a character
here too. I hear a learned builder of distinctions, careful and deliberate
and precise—and someone who takes pleasure in building up syntactic
architecture. But because his prose sounds less like a person talking—
it's more "constructed" than "uttered" in syntax—readers may disagree
more about the character of the speaker than in the case of Lawrence.
Such disagreements do not, however, undermine the well-ensconced
critical notion of an implied author in any text.

Let me try to sharpen *dramatic voice* and *audible voice* as critical terms
by comparing them in these two samples. For most readers, Lawrence's
words probably have more audible voice than Crane's. Notice in
fact how Lawrence heightens the audible or spoken effect by embedding bits of tacit dialogue and minidrama. He says, "You feel like

saying:..." so that what follows, "Good God, what does it matter?" and so forth is really a little speech in a different voice, and thus in implied quotation marks. Similarly, when he writes "Hand me the sugar," he's setting up a mini *scene*-on-stage that dramatizes the mood he's evoking.

But Crane's prose is not without audible voice: he starts out with a crisply balanced pronouncement—something pronounced ("a poet does not write poetry but individual poems"). And the second sentence begins with a strikingly audible interrupted phrase or "parenthetical" ("And these are inevitably, as finished wholes..."). But as he drifts from syntactic utterance to architectural construction, I find his words increasingly unidiomatic of anything ever spoken and difficult to say and hear.

So, whereas a text can have more or less audible voice, shall we say the same of dramatic voice? Yes and no. On the one hand, the critical world agrees that every text is 100 percent chock full of implied author. Even if the dramatic voice is subtle or hard to hear, even if there are multiple and inconsistent dramatic voices in a text, the word from Booth to Bakhtin is that the text is nothing but dramatic voices. But common sense argues the other way too, and this view shows itself most clearly in the everyday writerly or teacherly advice: "Why do you keep your voice or character so hidden here? Why not allow it into your writing."[2]

So I would assert the same conclusion here as I did about audible voice. Just as it is natural and inevitable to hear *audible* voice in a text unless something stops us, so too with *dramatic* voice: we hear character in discourse unless something stops us.

(3) Recognizable or Distinctive Voice in Writing

Writers, like composers or painters, often develop styles that are recognizable and distinctive. And it is common for both popular and academic critics and writers themselves to go one step further and not just talk about a writer finding "a" distinctive voice but "finding *her* voice."

There is nothing to quarrel with here. After all, writing is behavior, and it's hard for humans to engage in *any* behavior repeatedly without developing a habitual way of doing it—a style—that becomes recognizable. Perhaps the most striking example is the physical act of writing: handwriting itself (thus the force of the concept of "signature"). And we see the same thing in walking, tooth brushing, whatever. We can often recognize someone by how they walk—even how they stand—when we are too far away to recognize them by any other visual feature. If our walking and handwriting tend to be distinctive and recognizable and usually stable over time, why shouldn't that also be true of the kind of voice we use in our writing?

Of course if we seldom walk, and always with conscious effort, we probably don't develop a recognizable, distinctive walking style. Early toddlers haven't yet "found their own walk." So it is natural that inexperienced writers often have no characteristic style or "signature" to their writing. Helen Vendler (1982) says of Sylvia Plath that she "had early mastered certain course sound effects," but in her later poetry, "she has given up on a bald imitation of Thomas and has found her own voice" (131).

But it's worth questioning the *mystique* that sometimes surrounds the idea of "finding one's voice"—questioning the assumption that it is necessarily better to have a recognizable, distinctive voice in one's writing. Surely it doesn't make a writer *better* to have a distinctive style. It is just as admirable to achieve Keats's ideal of "negative capability": the ability to be a protean, chameleon-like writer. If we have become so practiced that our skills are automatic and habitual—and thus characteristic—we are probably pretty good, whether as walker or writer. But a really skilled or professional walker or writer will be able to bring in craft, art, and play so as to deploy different styles at will, and thus not have a recognizable, distinctive voice. Don't we tend to see Yeats as more impressive than Frost (not necessarily better)—Brahms than Elgar—for the ability to use a greater variety of voices?

Notice how I am still not broaching any of the sticky theoretical problems of self or identity that haunt arguments about voice in writing. If I have a "distinctive and recognizable voice," that voice doesn't necessarily *resemble* me or feel to me like "mine" or imply that there is a "real me." Recognizable or distinctive voice is not about "real identity." We may *recognize* someone from their handwriting or their walk, but those behaviors are not necessarily pictures of what they are like. For example, we might find ourselves saying, "He has such a distinctively casual, 'laid-back' way of walking, yet his personality or character is very uptight."

So if we strip away any unwarranted mystique from the term "recognizable, distinctive voice in writing," it has a simple and practical use. We can ask about any author whether he or she tends to have a characteristic style or recognizable voice; and if so, whether a particular text displays that style or voice—whether it is characteristic or different from how that author usually writes. And we can ask our students to develop comfortable fluency and to notice if and where they seem to develop a distinctive style—and whether that style seems to be helpful for them. I tend to discourage students from lusting after a "distinctive voice," since that so often leads to pretension and overwriting.

So look again at our example from D. H. Lawrence: it may not be a picture of the "real" Lawrence (if there is such a thing) but it *is* vintage Lawrence criticism—not just a nonce style or voice he used in this essay.

(4) Voice with Authority—"Having a Voice"

This is the sense of voice that is current in much feminist work (see, for example, Julier and Carlton in this volume and *Women's Ways of Knowing* by Belenky, Clinchy, Goldberger, and Tarule). But the sense is venerable too. Indeed the phrase "having a voice" has traditionally meant having the authority to speak or wield influence or to vote in a group. ("Does she have a voice in the faculty senate?" or "in the President's kitchen cabinet?")

As readers we often have no trouble agreeing about whether a text shows a writer having or taking the authority to speak out: whether the writer displays the conviction or the self-trust or gumption to make her voice heard. As teachers, we frequently notice and applaud the difference when we see a student who is a timid writer finally speak out with some conviction and give her words some authority. We often notice the same issue in our own writing or that of our colleagues when we are asked to give feedback. One of the traditional problems when we revise dissertations for publication is getting rid of the deferential, questioning, permission-asking tone—getting more authority into the voice. It would be an interesting research project to understand better what textual features give readers a sense of authority.

Notice that this sense of voice, like all the previous ones, does not entail any theory of identity or self, nor does it require making any inferences about the actual writer from the words on the page. When we see this kind of authority in writing, or the lack of it, we are not necessarily getting a good picture of the actual writer. It's not unusual, for example, for someone to develop a voice with strong authority that doesn't match their sense or our sense of who they are. Indeed, one of the best ways to find authority or achieve assertiveness of voice is to role-play and write in the voice of some "invented character" who is strikingly different from ourselves. We see this in simple role-playing exercises where the timid person "gets into" strong speech. And we see it in the complex case of Swift. He exerted enormous authority in the person of Gulliver and all his other ironic personae, and never published anything under his own name. (Ironically, he wielded excoriating judgmental authority through personae that were nonjudgmental and self-effacing.)

Let's look at our examples again. Clearly D. H. Lawrence had no trouble using a voice with authority and making it heard in print. Some feel he overdid it. R. S. Crane uses a quieter voice but achieves a magisterial authority nevertheless. An authoritative voice in writing need not be loud; it often has a quality of quiet, centered calm. We see this in speech too: schoolchildren often talk about "shouters"—teachers who shout a lot because they lack authority.

As teachers, most of us say we want our students to develop some authority of voice, and we applaud when the timid student speaks out. However, many of our practices as teachers have the effect of making students more timid and hesitant in their writing. In the following passage Virginia Woolf (see Payne 1983) writes about voice as authority—that is, about the struggle to take on authority in a situation where she was expected to be deferential:

> Directly . . . I took my pen in my hand to review that novel by a famous young man, she slipped behind me and whispered, "My dear, you are a young woman. You are writing about a book that has been written by a man. Be sympathetic; be tender; flatter; deceive; use all the arts and wiles of our sex. Never let anybody guess that you have a mind of your own. . . ." And she made as if to guide my pen. . . . [But in doing so] she would have plucked the heart out of my writing. (Payne 1983, 83)

We may write elegantly and successfully, she implies, but if we don't write with authority, with a mind of our own that is willing to offend, what we produce scarcely counts as real writing (*the heart is plucked out of it*).

(5) Resonant Voice or Presence

Here at last is trouble—the swamp. This is the angle of meaning that has made voice such a disputed term—the arena of "authenticity," "presence," sincerity, identity, self, and what I called "real voice" in *Writing with Power* (1981). Before wading in, let me pause to emphasize what I have gained by holding back so long—carefully separating what is solid from what is swampy. For my main argument in this essay is that there is little ground to dispute voice as a solid critical term—a term that points to certain definite and important qualities in texts that cannot easily be gainsaid: audible voice, dramatic voice, recognizable or distinctive voice, and voice with authority. That is, even if we are completely at odds about the nature of selves or the ideology of identity, about whether people even have such things as selves, and about the relation of a text to the person who wrote it, we have a good chance of reaching agreement about whether any given text has audible voice, what kind of dramatic voice it has, whether it has a recognizable or distinctive voice, and whether the writer was able to achieve authority of voice. Similarly, even if teachers disagree completely about the nature of self and identity and about the value of sincerity in writing, they can probably agree that students would benefit from exploring and attending to these four dimensions of voice in their writing. With these meanings secure, *I* feel more authority to enter the arena of difficulty and conflict.

Indeed, I can begin my account of resonant voice by showing that the ground is not as swampy as we might fear. That is, the concept of resonant voice or presence is certainly arguable, and it involves making inferences about the relation between the present text and the absent actual writer; it does *not* assume any particular model of the self or theory of identity—and in particular it does not require a model of the self as simple, single, unique, or unchanging. I can make this point by describing resonant voice in contrast to *sincere voice* (something that enthusiasts of voice have sometimes mistakenly celebrated).

We hear sincere voices all around us. Lovers say, "I only have eyes for you"; parents say, "Trust me"; teachers say, "I am on your side." Even salesmen and politicians are sometimes perfectly sincere. Surely Reagan was sincere much of the time. But sometimes those sincere words, *even in their very sincerity,* ring hollow. Genuine sincerity can itself feel cloyingly false. Yet we mustn't flip all the way over to the cynical position of people who have been burned too often and say that sincerity itself is false ("never trust a guy who really thinks he loves you"), or to the sophisticated position of some literary folk ("sincere art is bad art"). *Sometimes* we can trust sincere words. Sincere discourse is not always tinny.

What is a sincere voice? When we say that someone speaks or writes sincerely, we mean that they "really really believe" what they are saying. This means that they experience no gap at all between utterance and intention. In short, sincerity tells us about the fit between intention and conscious thought and feeling. But only that; only about what the relation between what people intend to say and what they are consciously thinking and feeling. What about gaps between utterance and *unconscious* intentions and feelings?

Resonant voice is a useful concept because it points to the relationship between discourse and the unconscious. When we hear sincerity that is obviously tinny, we are hearing a *gap* between utterance and unconscious intention or feeling. Self-deception. Sensitive listeners can hear very small gaps. Thus they are also likely to be sensitive to the resonance that occurs when discourse *does* fit larger portions of the speaker—those precious moments in life and writing when a person actually does harness words to fit more of a person than conscious intention—those words which seem (in Adrienne Rich's words) to "have the heft of our living behind them."

Such words are of course rare. For a discourse can never *fully* express or articulate a whole person. A person is usually too complex and has too many facets, parts, roles, voices, identities. But at certain lucky or achieved moments, writers or speakers *do* manage to find words which seem to capture the rich complexity of the unconscious; or words which, though they don't *express* or *articulate* everything that is in the unconscious, nevertheless somehow seem to *resonate with* or *have behind them* the unconscious as well as the conscious (or at least much larger portions than usual). It is words of this sort that we experience as resonant—and through them we have a sense of presence with the writer.

Notice now how the concept of resonant voice opens the door to irony, fiction, lying, and games; indeed it positively *calls for* these and other polyvocal or multivalent kinds of discourse. If we value the sound of resonance—the sound of more of a person behind the words— and if we get pleasure from a sense of the writer's presence in a text, we are often going to be drawn to what is ambivalent and complex and ironic, not just to earnest attempts to tell the sincere truth. Can two million New Critics be completely wrong in their obsessive praise of irony? The most resonant language is often lying and gamey. Writing with resonant voice needn't be unified or coherent; it can be ironic, unaware, disjointed.

Any notion of resonant voice would have to include Swift's strongest works; even Pope's "Rape of the Lock" where he makes fun of the silliness and vanity he also loves. When Lawrence says of Melville, "The artist was so much greater than the man," he is talking about the difference between Melville's sincere sentiments and those parts of his writing that express his larger darker vision—writing that resonates with more parts of himself or his vision or his feelings than he was consciously aware of. In effect, Lawrence is saying that Melville "the man" has plenty of audible, dramatic, distinctive, and authoritative voice ("And that's Melville. Oh dear when the solemn ass brays! brays! brays!"). But he lacks resonant voice ("But there's something false")— except where he functions "as artist" and renders more of his unconscious knowledge and awareness. It's no accident that the resonance shows up most in his discourse "as artist": that is, we tend to get more of our unconscious into our discourse when we use metaphors and tell stories and exploit the sounds and rhythms of language.

Once we see that resonance comes from getting more of ourselves behind the words, we realize that unity or singleness is not the goal. Of course we don't have simple, neatly coherent or unchanging selves. To remember the role of the unconscious is to remember what Bakhtin and social constructionists and others say in different terms: we are made of different roles, voices. Indeed, Barbara Johnson sees a link between voice and *splitness* or *doubleness* itself—words which render multiplicity of self: "The sign of an authentic voice is thus not self-identity but self-difference."

Keith Hjortshoj (exploring relations between writing and physical movement) insists that cohesion is not always the goal—with writing or with selves:

> Cohesion, then, isn't always a cardinal virtue, in [physical] movement or writing. . . . To appreciate fully the freedom, flexibility, and speed with which young children adapt to their surroundings, we have to remember that they continually come unglued and reassemble themselves—usually several times a day. They have wild, irrational expectations of themselves and others. They take uncalculated risks that lead them to frustration, anger, and fear. In the space of a few minutes they pass from utter despair to unmitigated joy, and sometimes back again, like your average manic-depressive. (12)

Selves tend to evolve, change, take on new voices and assimilate them. The concept of resonant voice explains the intriguing power of so much speech and writing by children: they wear their unconscious more on their sleeve; their defenses are often less elaborate. Thus they often get more of themselves into or behind their discourse.

One reason writing is particularly important (as opposed to speech)—and why writing provides a site for resonant voice or presence—is that writing, particularly with its possibilities for privacy, has always served as a crucial place for trying out parts of the self or unconscious that have been hidden or neglected or undeveloped—to experiment and try out "new subject positions." (See Jonsberg 1993.)

When we have gotten to know a student somewhat through her writing, or when we are reading a sufficiently long manuscript, we can sometimes notice particular places where the writer seems to get in a bit more of what we sense is her self or sensibility. Often these are little changes of tone or eruptions or asides or digressions—even lapses of a sort: but they are places where suddenly we feel an added infusion of weight, richness, presence. Some important dimension of perception or thinking or feeling formerly kept out of the writing is now allowed in—and when we hear this element, we hear a kind of added correlation with the complex entity we infer as writer. I experience these passages as pieces of added resonance or presence. Often they complicate things; they may even be places where the writing breaks down. That is—except for exceptional writing—resonant voice often correlates with places where a text has a hole or crack or disjuncture. When I notice bits of resonance in others' writing—or when others notice it in mine—it is often a cue that the piece is going to have to get worse before it gets better—be reshaped or restanced or revoiced in some way—or at least before it can realize the potential resonance that is trying to get in.

When we see that the central question then for this kind of power in writing is not "How sincere are you?" but "How much of yourself did you manage to get *behind* the words?" we see why voice has been such a tempting metaphor. That is, the physical voice is more resonant when it can get more of the body resonating behind it or underneath it. "Resonant" seems a more helpful word than "authentic," and it is more to the point than "sincerity," because it connotes the "resounding" or "sounding-again" that is involved when distinct parts can echo each other (thus Coleridge's figure of the aeolian lyre). Just as a resonant physical voice is not in any way a *picture* of the body, but it has the body's resources behind or underneath it, so too resonant voice in writing is not a picture of the self, but it has the self's resources behind or underneath it. The metaphor of "voice" inevitably suggests a link with the body and "weight," and this is a link that many writers call attention to. After all, the body often shows more of ourselves than the conscious mind does: our movements, our stance, our facial expressions often reveal our dividedness, complexity, and splitness.

Here is a striking passage where William Carlos Williams (1936) sounds this theme of a link between writing, voice, and the body:

> So poets . . . are in touch with "voices," but this is the very essence of their power, the voices are the past, the depths of our very beings. It is the deeper . . . portions of the personality speaking, the middle brain, the nerves, the glands, the very muscles and bones of the body itself speaking.

Roland Barthes (1977) is particularly intriguing in this vein. Notice how he celebrates "the grain of the voice" by distinguishing it from the "dramatic expressivity" of opera—in effect, from sincerity:

> Listen to a Russian bass (a church bass—opera [in contrast] is a genre in which the voice has gone over in its entirety to dramatic

expressivity . . .): something is there, manifest and stubborn, (one hears only *that*), beyond (or before) the meaning of the words, their form . . . the melisma, and even the style of execution: something which is directly in the cantor's body, brought to your ears in one and the same movement from deep down in the cavities, the muscles, the membranes, the cartilages, and from deep down in the Slavonic language, as though a single skin lined the inner flesh of the performer and the music he sings. The voice is not *personal*: it *expresses nothing of the cantor and his soul* [emphasis added]; it is not original . . . and at the same time it is individual: it has us hear a body which has no civil identity, no "personality," but which is nevertheless a separate body. . . . The "grain" is that: the materiality of the body speaking its mother tongue. (181)

See Adrienne Rich's figure of language with "the sheer heft" or weight "of our living behind it."[3]

Of course I'm not saying that writing with resonant voice *must* be ironic, gamey, split—cannot be sincere or personal. The Rich poem is surely sincere and personal. Nor that the self does not characteristically have a kind of coherence and even persistence of identity over time. I'm just insisting that the notion of resonant voice or presence in writing does not require these things.

Examples of resonant voice? I would venture to call the Adrienne Rich poem an example (see end note 3). But examples are not easy to cite because we cannot point to identifiable features of language that are "resonant"—as we can point to features that are audible, dramatic, distinctive, or authoritative. Rather, we are in the dicey business of pointing to the *relation* of textual features to an inferred person present behind the text. Of course this inferred presence can only come from other features of the text. It's as though—putting it bluntly or schematically—any sentence, paragraph, or page can be resonant or not, depending on the context of a longer work or oeuvre.

Look, for example, at our passages from Lawrence and Crane. I hear so *much* voice in the Lawrence: audible, dramatic, distinctive, authoritative. With that much vividness and noise, I can't decide whether I hear resonance. The passage is gamey, tricky, show-offy—a pose. But of course that doesn't disqualify it either. I'm not sure; I'd have to read more.

Crane? Again we cannot decide from such a short passage. Certainly it is not rich in the kind of audible and dramatic voice that Robert Frost asked for (the "speaking tone of voice somehow entangled in the words and fastened to the page for the ear of the imagination"). But that's not the point with resonant voice. If we read more we might indeed hear behind this somewhat forbidding prose the "sheer heft of his living," and experience a powerful resonance or presence in the passage.

For of course assertions about resonant voice will always be more arguable than about other kinds of voice. Not only because we are dealing with subtle inferences rather than pointing to particular linguistic features, but also because our main organ for listening to resonance is our own self. That is, we are most likely to hear resonance when the words resonate with *us*, fit *us*. This is an obvious problem, and it is enough to make some people insist that the only resonance we can talk about is between the text and the reader, not the text and the writer. (Bakhtin uses a metaphor of *literal* resonance between speaker and listener when he says we lose intonation in our speech unless we have "choral support" from sympathetic or like-minded listeners [1976, 102–6].)

I agree that when we hear resonance, we are *most often* hearing a resonance of the words with our own predilections, tastes, obsessions. But something more than this is happening, surely, when readers of many different temperaments hear resonance in the same piece of writing—even a very idiosyncratic piece. And most of us have occasionally had a teacher or editor who is peculiarly good because she possesses the ability to "hear around" her own temperament and predilections—to hear resonance even when it doesn't fit her. This is the ability to love and feel great power in a piece while still being able to say, "But this is not my kind of writing—it doesn't really fit me"—and still help the writer revise her piece in a direction different from one's own predilections or taste. To put it another way, this kind of reader is more expert at listening for resonance even when it involves what is "other" or "different" from herself.

The Problem of the Relationship between Discourse and the Actual Author

The concept of resonant voice or presence may not assume any ideology of self or identity, but it does assume something else controversial: that we can make inferences about the fit between the voice in a text and the actual unknown, unseen historical writer behind the text—on the basis of the written text alone. We can have audible, dramatic, distinctive, and authoritative voice without any sense of whether the voice fits or doesn't fit the real author. Not so here with resonant voice or presence.

Although it may seem peculiar to say that we can sense the fit between the voice in a text and the unknown writer behind it (especially in the light of much poststructural literary theory), in truth people have an ingrained habit of doing just that: listening not only *to* each other's words but also listening *for* the relationship between the words and the speaker behind the words. To put this in a nonstartling way, we habitually listen to see whether we can trust the speaker. If we know the speaker, these judgments are natural and unproblematic. ("Alice, your words make a lot of sense, but they just don't sound like you.")

But we sometimes make the same judgments with the discourse of people we *don't* know. When we hear an announcer or public speaker or we begin to converse with a stranger, we sometimes conclude that they sound unbelievable or fake, even when *what they say* is sensible and believable in itself. Something is fishy about the voice and we feel we don't trust this person. Sometimes the speaker sounds evasive, halting, awkward. But as often as not, on the contrary, we are bothered because the speaker seems too glib or fluent—as in the case of certain overzealous salesmen or politicians. Sometimes the speaker sounds insincere, but sometimes something sounds "off" even when the person sounds sincere.

Perhaps we are relying on visual cues from the speaker before our eyes. Yet we go on making these judgments without visual cues—when strangers speak over the telephone or on the radio: nothing but literal voice to go on. Sometimes we still conclude that there is something untrustworthy about the voice of some politician or radio announcer or salesman. It's not that we necessarily distrust the message; sometimes we believe it. But we distrust the speaker—or at least we distrust the fit between the message and the speaker. How do we make these judgments about whether to trust someone when all we have is their language? Doubtless we go on auditory cues of intonation and rhythm: literal "tone of voice."

But tone of voice is nothing but a "way of talking," and when we only have *writing by a stranger*, we still have a "way of talking" to go on—that is, his or her way of writing. Even though we can't see or hear the writer, and even though writing provides fewer semiotic channels for nuance, we still draw inferences from the writer's syntax, diction, structure, strategies, stance, and so forth.

Obviously, these inferences are risky. But my point is that we've all had lots of training in making them. Repeatedly in our lives we face situations where our main criterion for deciding *whether* an utterance is true is whether to trust the speaker. When we take our car to a mechanic, most of us don't base our decision about whether the carburetor needs replacing on data about carburetors but rather on a decision about trustworthiness of voice. We often do the same thing when we take our body to a doctor—or decide to trust *anyone* about a matter we don't understand. We mustn't forget how practiced and skilled most of us have become at this delicate kind of judgment just because we remember so vividly the times we judged wrong. And we know that some people are strikingly good at figuring out whether someone can be trusted. They must be reading something. The practice of counseling and therapy depends on this kind of ear. Skilled listeners can sometimes even hear *through sincerity:* they can hear that even though the speaker is perfectly sincere, he cannot be trusted. There must be real cues in discourse—readable but subtle—about the relationship between discourse and speaker. Because we are listening for relationships between what is explicitly in the text and cues about the writer that are implicit in the text, we can seldom make these kinds of judgments unless we have extended texts—better yet two or three texts by the same writer.

Because our inferences about voice are so subtle, they are seldom based on conscious deliberation: we usually make these inferences with the *ear*—by means of how the discourse "sounds" or "feels" or whether it "rings true." We use the kind of tacit, nonfocal awareness that Polanyi addresses and analyzes so well, such as when we see a faint star better by not looking directly at it.

Notice that this peculiar skill—evaluating the trustworthiness or validity of utterances by *how* things are said because we cannot evaluate *what* is said—often does not correlate with "school learning." Schools naturally emphasize texts, and when we are learning skills with texts (and especially when our culture becomes more text-oriented or literate in the ways described by Olson and Ong and so many others) we are learning how to pay more attention to the relationship between words and their meanings and referents—and less attention to the relationship between words and their speakers or writers.

In a way, we've stumbled upon the very essence of schooling or literacy training: learning to attend better to the meaning and logic of words themselves and to stop relying on extratextual cues such as how impressive or authoritative the author is or how you feel about her. School and the culture of literacy advise us to this effect: "Stop listening for the tone of voice and interpreting gestures. These are the tricks of illiterates and animals—evaluating speech on the basis of what they think of the speaker because they can't read or judge the message for itself." Sometimes the successful student or scholar is the *least* adept at this kind of metatextual reading—at what we call "street smarts." Good teachers learn to integrate street smarts with literacy training, whether in first grade or college, for the sake of helping students be more sophisticated with purely silent textual language—instead of letting students feel that their skill at reading the person behind the text is a hindrance in school. (This is the message in Deborah Brandt's insightful *Literacy as Involvement* [1990].)

I'm really making a simple claim here—and it's the same claim that I made earlier about audible and dramatic voice: that our primary and formative experiences with language were with words emerging audibly from physically present bodies—and most of us continue to encounter this kind of language as much as encounter silent texts, if not more. For this reason, we can scarcely prevent ourselves from hearing the presence of human beings in language and attending to the relationship between the language and the person who speaks or writes it. Conditioning alone nudges us to do so, but more important, much of our functioning in the world depends on this skill. Many school practices blunt this skill—allegedly for the sake of literacy training, but Brandt argues intriguingly that these practices are based on a mistaken model of literacy.

If we explore Aristotle and the process of persuasion for a moment, we can find more corroboration for the nonstartling claim that humans naturally listen to discourse for cues about the actual person behind it. Aristotle (see Roberts 1954) defines *ethos* as a potent source of persuasion, but scholars argue about what he meant by the term.

Sometimes he emphasizes the author's real character, talking about "the personal character of the speaker," and saying "We believe good men more fully and more readily than others" (*Rhetoric* 1356a). But sometimes he emphasizes how speakers can fool listeners and persuade them with just dramatic voice or implied author. He talks about the ability to "make ourselves *thought to be* sensible and morally good. . . ." (1378a; my emphasis). And he notes that this is a matter of skill, not character:

> We can now see that a writer must disguise his art and give the impression of speaking naturally and not artificially. Naturalness is persuasive, artificiality is the contrary; for our hearers are prejudiced and think we have some design against them. . . . (1404b)

Scholars fight about this ambiguity in the *Rhetoric*, but the fight would disappear if they simply noticed and accepted the fact that he is affirming both positions in what is in fact the common sense view: in effect, "It's nice to *be* trustworthy; but if you're skilled you can fake it."

When Aristotle says that we can persuade people by creating a dramatic voice that is more trustworthy than we actually are—by saying, in effect, that a good rhetor can sometimes fool the audience—he is talking about the gap between implied author and real author, between dramatic voice and the writer's own voice. Because he's writing a handbook for authors, he's telling them how they can hide this gap if they are skilled. They can *seem* more trustworthy than they are, but to do so they must fool the audience into not seeing the gap. If he'd been writing a handbook for *audiences* rather than authors (writing "reception theory" instead of "transmission theory"), he would have looked at this gap from the other side. He would have emphasized how skilled *listeners* can *uncover* the gap that speakers are trying to hide. He would have talked about how skilled listeners can detect differences between the implied author and the real author—can detect, that is, dishonesty or untrustworthiness even through a sensible message or a fluent delivery. In short, by arguing in the *Rhetoric* that skilled speakers can seem better than they are, he is acknowledging that there is a gap to be detected, and implying that good listeners can make inferences about the character of the speaker from their words.

Since readers and listeners make these perceptions all the time about the trustworthiness of the speaker or writer on the basis of their words alone, any valid rhetorical theory must show that persuasiveness often comes from *resonant voice or communicated presence* as often as it comes from merely dramatic voice or implied author. Aristotle clearly implies what common sense tells us: we are not persuaded by implied author as such—that is, by the creation of a dramatic voice that sounds trustworthy; we are only persuaded if we believe that dramatic voice is the voice of the actual speaker or author. We don't buy a used car from someone just because we admire their dramatic skill in creating a fictional trustworthy voice. If *ethos* is nothing *but* implied author, it loses all power of persuasion.[4]

Identity Politics, the Nature of Self, "Is There a Real Me?" The Crunch Comes When We Have to Write or Teach Writing

So far, I have claimed that none of these senses of voice imply or require any particular theory of identity or self. We can take whatever ideological position we want and still use the term *voice* clearly and usefully. Even resonant voice accommodates the ideology of choice. Can I claim, then, that the identity issue *never* comes up? No. For I've so far emphasized the process of *reading*—the process of describing voice in texts produced by others. Once we set out to *write*, however, or to teach writing, it is hard to escape the identity issue.

For there is a momentous asymmetry between the position of reader and writer. As readers we have access only to the text, not to the writer; but as writers we have access *both* to the text and to ourselves. We hear the sound of our text and we usually hear whether it sounds like "us." (I won't define "us" because there's no need to: most of us don't define "us"—we simply have intuitive sense of when our speech or writing sounds as though it is coming from us or not. Perhaps "us" is the sound of or most comfortable or characteristic inner and outer speech. Who knows? But we don't have to understand that issue here.) So we are apt to notice it if we sense that our writing (our textual voice) doesn't seem to sound like us—feels somehow artificial or pretended or distanced or stilted. Of course most of us have more than one voice that feels like us: we may feel just as natural and like ourselves in talking tough slang talk with a sports team, intimate casual talk with family, and fairly formal talk at colloquia. But just because we have multiple voices that sound natural or like ourselves doesn't mean that we always feel that way. Most of us sometimes also experience our spoken or written voice as not quite fitting us or natural.

It's true that there are certain conditions where we don't notice whether our textual voice feels like ours: if we have been somehow trained not to pay attention to the sound of our textual voice at all; or somehow trained not to notice the sound of "us"—our characteristic ways of producing inner and outer speech; or if we have a sense of "us" that is completely fluid and without boundaries. And so I can hold off all identity issues try to write with audible voice, distinctive voice, authoritative voice; I can try to use the dramatic voice or persona that seems most appropriate for my audience; I can try to use a voice that "situates itself within the conversation" I seek to join—trying to take on the voices that make up that conversation; (this is what Don Bialostosky, drawing on Bakhtin [1981], calls "well-situated voice," and it is surely one of the main ways in which I can give my voice authority). I *can* do all those things and still never ask or experience whether the words feel like mine.

But surely this is fairly rare. Thus for many people (not just those women interviewed by Gilligan or by Belenky and her colleagues) the question is not just whether one *has* a strong or distinctive voice but whether that voice feels like "one's own." For of course it's not uncommon for people to develop a voice that is strong or lively or distinctive or authoritative, but which feels somehow alien—and to feel like using it means remaining without power or authority. Here a passage from an interview with a woman talking about this experience:

> Writing has always been so hard and I've always felt trapped inside myself in terms of having to put stuff on paper, um. So that ultimately when I did have to write stuff like reports, I managed to get somebody inside me to do them, but it wasn't like it was me doing it. And that's continued as an adult. . . .
>
> And I think I have sort of grown up and been an adult for a long time, thinking of myself as not having any voice. . . . [But I] started thinking of all my work with children and how my voice is in that work [she is a teacher] and that it's, you know, it's not a loud voice that says, but it's, you know, it's more like a voice like the wind or something [pause] that's there. . . . [About an important report:] it was still as though, you know, I had finally set a deadline and I got the person inside me who does that piece of writing when the deadline happens [to do it]. . . . [And about another paper for a course:] I wanted to write it in my own voice and not make the ghost writer in me, or whoever that is, basically [do] it. (Tavalin 1994, 53–55)

When we write, then, most of us cannot help brushing against the identity issue and noticing whether our words feel like us or ours—and ideally we have a *choice* about whether to use prose that feels as though it fits us. (Of course plenty of people—both inexperienced and even professional writers—don't feel as though it's possible to let writing actually sound like themselves. They don't feel capable of just uttering themselves on paper—as extensive freewriting shows one how to do.) In making this choice we notice that there are two extreme ideological or theoretical positions here about language and self. At one extreme, the "sentimental" position says, "Hold fast to your 'you' at all costs. Don't give in and write in the voice 'they' want. Your voice is the only powerful voice to use. Your true voice will conquer all difficulties." At the other extreme, the "sophisticated" position says, "Your sense of 'you' is just an illusion of late Romantic, bourgeois capitalism. Forget it. You have no self. There is no such thing. You are nothing but roles. Write in the role that is appropriate for this situation."

But in practice we don't have to choose *between* such extreme positions. It is far more helpful to move somewhat back and forth between some version of them—especially with regard to *practices*. (The purely theoretical fight loses interest after a while.) We can come at our writing from both sides of the identity fence.

First the "sentimental" side. Suppose my characteristic voice—the voice that feels like me or mine—tends to be insecure or hesitant (or tied in knots or enraged). And I know all too well that this voice of mine has repeatedly undermined my writing. I don't have to slap my wrists and say, "I guess I've just got a bad, ineffective voice, and so I'll have to get a better one." I *can* use whatever voices feel most comfortable and most like me—particularly for exploratory writing, private writing, and early draft writing.

Then for the *short run* it turns out that it isn't so hard to revise late drafts from a pragmatic and audience-oriented frame of reference and make a limited number of changes and get rid of most of the voice problems for readers. Get rid of the worst pieces of syntactic insecurity or hesitations (or convolutions or rages). When I do this, the underlying plasma of my prose still feels as though it is me, is my own voice. As I indicated in my account of resonant voice, I think good readers feel something lacking or some lack of resonance when people *don't* use their own plasma.

And, perhaps more important, in the *long run,* when I use the voice or voices that I experience as mine—such as they are and with all their limitations—use them a lot for exploratory and private and early draft writing and try them out on myself and others—listening to them and even appreciating them—these voices tend to get richer and develop. For example, an insecure voice tends to become more confident. Gradually I find I have more flexibility of voice—more voices that feel like me.

But I can also work from the "sophisticated" side of this identity issue. I can think of all discourse as the taking on of roles or as the use of the voices of others. I can take on the mentality that Auden celebrated in his wonderful poem, "The Truest Poetry Is the Most Feigning," and consciously practice role-playing and ventriloquism and heteroglossia. Role-playing and irony and make-believe often get at possible or temporary selves or dimensions of the protean self that are important and useful but unavailable to conscious thinking and feeling. To take a concrete example, people who are characteristically timid, quiet, self-effacing—who have a hard time getting heard or getting any force into language—often come up with a powerfully angry voice when they let themselves play that role. It's as though they have an angry voice in their unconscious. (I'm not sure whether the sophisticated position admits of an unconscious.) When this angry voice gets a hold of the pen, the resulting language is often very powerful indeed—though hard to control. At first this voice feels alien, but gradually one often comes to own or claim it more.

Notice that in both approaches, both sentimental and the sophisticated, we see the same crucial process: gradual development and enrichment of voice. In one case it is a matter of using, trusting, and "playing in" (as with an unplayed violin) a voice that feels like one's own—and seeing it become more flexible. In the other case it is a matter of trusting oneself to use unaccustomed or even alien voices in a spirit of play and non-investment—and seeing those voices become more comfortable and owned.

Bakhtin (1981) provides us with a good example of someone trying to do justice to both positions. All the while he is arguing that our words always come from the mouths and voices of others, he never stops being interested in the process by which we take these alien words and "make them our own."

> The importance of struggling with another's discourse, its influence in the history of an individual's coming to dialogical consciousness, is enormous. One's own discourse and one's own voice, although born of another or dynamically stimulated by another, will sooner or later begin to liberate themselves from the authority of the other's discourse. (348. See 343 *ff* on this issue.)[5]

Concluding

When it comes to our own writing, then, we can scarcely avoid noticing whether the words we put down on the page feel like our words—whether they sound like our voice or one of our owned voices. Yet even here, I hope I've persuaded you that we write best if we learn to move flexibly back and forth between on the one hand using and celebrating something we feel as our *own* voice, and on the other hand operating as though we are nothing but ventriloquists playfully using and adapting and working against an array of voices we find around us.

And for my larger argument, I hope I've made it clear why voice should be such a tempting metaphor for this family of related dimensions of texts that are so important and often neglected. It's also clear why voice is a lightning rod for ideological dispute, but I hope I've provided the kind of analysis needed to make voice a practical critical tool that we can *use* rather than just fight about. For it mostly doesn't even matter what we believe about the nature of self or about the relation of a text to the actual writer.

I think we need to make the kinds of distinctions I have spelled out between the family of five meanings for voice in writing. But once we have had our critical conversation about voice in writing so as to make the concept more solidly understood and widely acknowledged, I don't think we'll always have to be so fussy about distinctions. We'll be able to say to a friend or student, "I hear more voice in these passages; something rich and useful and interesting is going on there; can you get more of that?" and not necessarily have to make careful distinctions between audible, dramatic, recognizable, authoritative, and resonant voice. There are crucial differences between the various kinds of voice in writing—but more often than not they go together. And surely the richly bundled connotations of the human voice are what hold them all together.

Notes

1. Here are a couple of important points to keep in mind in such research. Idiomatic speech qualities are not the only source of audibility in a text. Certain rhythmic, rhetorical, or poetic features also increase audibility even though they are uncharacteristic of how people actually talk. Thus we are likely to hear audible voice in the following passage even though we don't hear people talk this way:

> Because these men work with animals, not machines or numbers, because they live outside in landscapes of torrential beauty, because they are confined to a place and a routine embellished with awesome variables, because calves die in the arms that pulled others into life, because they go to the mountains as if on a pilgrimage to find out what makes a herd of elk tick, their strength is also a softness, their toughness, a rare delicacy. (Ehrlich 1985, 52–53)

Also, as Crismore points out in an interesting study, passages of "metadiscourse" in writing tend to be heard as more voiced (e.g., "Let me now turn to my second point"). But I think her insight is really part of a larger point: it's not just metadiscourse that creates audibility, but rather the signaling of any *speech-act.* "I disagree" is not metadiscourse, but as with any speech act, it highlights the presence and agency of a writer. See Elbow 1989. See the work of Palacas, described in end note 2, for other important syntactic features that heighten audibility.

2. Palacas (1989) provides an extremely interesting analysis—one of the best I've seen—of syntactical or grammatical features that give readers a heightened sense of the writer's voice or presence. He's pointing to what he calls "parentheticals" such as my insertion above of "—one of the best I've seen—." These insertions or reflections bring into a text the sound of the author commenting on, reflecting on, or in a sense editing, his own assertions, and they heighten and complicate the intonational pattern of the text. They also make the text seem an enactment-of-thinking-going-on rather than a record-of-completed-thinking. (The fact that these features also increase audibility in a text shows that the different kinds of voice that I am working so hard to distinguish often blend into each other.)

3. It is worth citing the whole poem—not only as a definition of resonant voice but also, I'd say, as an instance:

Poetry: III*

Even if we knew the children were all asleep
and healthy   the ledgers balanced   the water running
clear in the pipes
                        and all the prisoners free

Even if every word we wrote by then
were honest   the sheer heft
of our living behind it
                        not these sometimes
lax indolent lines
                  these litanies

Even if we were told   not just by friends
that this was honest work

Even if each of us didn't wear
a brass locket with a picture
of a strangled woman   a girlchild sewn through the crotch

Even if someone had told us, young: *This is not a key*
nor a peacock feather
                        not a kite nor a telephone
This is the kitchen sink   *the grinding-stone*

would we give ourselves
more calmly over   feel less criminal joy
when the thing comes   as it does come
clarifying grammar
and the fixed and mutable stars—?

—Adrienne Rich (1984)

4. This is a perplexing business. We are sometimes tempted to ascribe great power to the dramatic voice alone when we see people *seeming* to be persuaded by blatantly fake or inauthentic voice—for example, in the realm of politics and advertising. "Look at all those people voting for someone who is so patently unbelievable. How can they be taken in?" But when people seem to be persuaded by glib dramatic voice, I think there are often dynamics of alienation, powerlessness, and cynicism at play. Those same people who vote for the speaker with glib dramatic voice often say things like, "Yeah, I can tell he is a crook. But what can you do?" It's not that they don't hear the gap between language and person. We need good research about what people actually hear and understand when they hear glib, untrustworthy dramatic voice.

---

*"Poetry III" is reprinted from *Your Native Land, Your Life*, by Adrienne Rich, by permission of the author and W. W. Norton & Company, Inc. Copyright © 1986 by Adrienne Rich.

5. William Coles (1988) and Walker Gibson (1966) provide two more examples of midway positions on the issue of voice and identity. They may not have intended to take a middle position, for in fact both of them repeatedly insist that they are not interested in the real writer at all, only in the textual voice; they insist that we create ourselves anew every time we speak or write. Yet the test they often use for language is not whether it is strong in itself or well suited to the audience but rather a certain sense of authenticity. Here is Coles writing about the textual voice in a letter by Nicola Sacco (of Sacco and Vanzetti) that Coles uses in his teaching: ". . . for me there's no 'facade' here, not any more than Sacco is 'behind' anything. That language of his, so far as I'm concerned, he's in. He's it. And it's him" (179). When they criticize a textual voice, they often call it "fake"; Coles sometimes even calls it "bullshit." (If we create ourselves anew every time we speak or write, how can our creation ever be anything but real?) Here is Coles working both sides of the voice/identity street in two adjacent sentences where he is describing his process of "rewriting" himself in the process of revising his own book. In one sentence he says he is doing "no more than trying to solve a writing problem"; but in the next sentence he says his revising is "a way of seeing what it could mean to belong to one's self . . ." (276). (Coles and Gibson have some the best ears around for the subtleties and nuances of voice in a text—and this clearly derives from their work in Theodore Baird's famous English 1-2 course at Amherst College—in which Robert Frost also seemed to play a lurking role [see Varnum's forthcoming book and Harris's forthcoming article entitled "Voice"]. In the culture of that course we can see the same ambivalence about voice and identity: an insistence that voice is nothing but a phenomenon of text—yet a continual, intuitive listening for how textual voice reverberates in relation to a person behind the page. Gibson's *Tough, Sweet and Stuffy* seems to me one of the best books around about voice and writing.)

Works Cited

Bakhtin, Mikhail. 1976. "Discourse in Life and Discourse in Art (Concerning Sociological Poetics)." Appendix to *Freudianism: A Marxist Critique*, by V. N. Volosinov. Translated by I. R. Titunik and edited by Neal H. Bruss. New York: Academic Press. [Holquist's attribution of this work to Bakhtin is generally accepted.]

———. 1981. "Discourse in the Novel." In *The Dialogic Imagination: Four Essays*, edited by Michael Holquist and translated by Caryl Emerson and Michael Holquist, 259–422. Austin: University of Texas Press.

Barthes, Roland. 1977. *Image, Music, Text*. Essays selected and translated by Stephen Heath. New York: Hill and Wang.

Belenky, Mary Field, Blythe McVicker Clinchy, Nancy Rule Goldberger, and Jill Mattuck Tarule. 1986. *Women's Ways of Knowing: The Development of Self, Voice, and Mind*. New York: Basic Books.

Bolinger, Dwight. 1986. *Intonation and Its Parts: Melody in Spoken English*. Stanford, CA: Stanford University Press.

Brandt, Deborah. 1990. *Literacy as Involvement: The Acts of Writers, Readers, and Texts*. Carbondale: Southern Illinois University Press.

Brower, Reuben Arthur. 1962. *The Fields of Light: An Experiment in Critical Reading*. New York: Oxford University Press.

Burke, Kenneth. 1969. *A Grammar of Motives*. Berkeley: University of California Press.

Calkins, Lucy McCormick. 1986. *The Art of Teaching Writing*. Portsmouth, NH: Heinemann Educational Books.

Coles, William E., Jr. 1988. *The Plural I—And After*. Portsmouth, NH: Boynton/Cook-Heinemann.

Crane. R. S., ed. 1951. "The Critical Monism of Cleanth Brooks." In *Critics and Criticism: Ancient and Modern, 83–107*. Chicago: University of Chicago Press.

Crismore, Avon. 1989. *Talking with Readers: Metadiscourse as Rhetorical Act*. New York: P. Lang.

Ehrlich, Gretel. 1985. *The Solace of Open Spaces*. New York: Viking.

Elbow, Peter. 1981. *Writing with Power: Techniques for Mastering the Writing Process*. New York: Oxford University Press.

———. 1985. "The Shifting Relationships between Speech and Writing." *College Composition and Communication* 36.2 (October): 283–303.

———. 1989. "The Pleasures of Voices in the Literary Essay: Explorations in the Prose of Gretel Ehrlich and Richard Selzer." In *Literary Nonfiction: Theory, Criticism, Pedagogy*, edited by Chris Anderson, 211–34. Carbondale: Southern Illinois University Press.

Frost, Robert. 1917. *A Way Out*. [One-Act Play.] *Seven Arts* 1.4 (February): 347–62.

Gibson, Walker. 1966. *Tough, Sweet, and Stuffy: An Essay on Modern American Prose Styles*. Bloomington: Indiana University Press.

Harris, Joseph. Forthcoming. "Voice." In *Contested Terms*.

Hjortshoj, Keith. [n.d.] "Language and Movement." Unpublished ms.

Johnson, Barbara. 1986. "Metaphor, Metonymy, and Voice in Zora Neale Hurston's *Their Eyes Were Watching God*." In *Textual Analysis: Some Readers Reading*, edited by Mary Ann Caws, 232–44. New York: Modern Language Association of America.

Jonsberg, Sara. 1993. "Rehearsing New Subject Positions: A Poststructuralist View of Expressive Writing." Paper presented at the Annual Convention of the Conference on College Composition and Communication. San Diego. April.

Lawrence, D. H. 1951. *Studies in Classic American Literature*. Garden City, NY: Doubleday.

Olson, David R. 1977. "The Languages of Instruction: The Literate Bias of Schooling." In *Schooling and the Acquisition of Knowledge*, edited by R. C. Anderson, R. J. Sior, and W. E. Montague. Hillsdale, NJ: Lawrence Erlbaum.

———. 1981. "Writing: The Divorce of the Author from the Text." In *Exploring Speaking-Writing Relationships: Connections and Contrasts*, edited by B. M. Kroll and R. J. Vann, 99–110. Urbana: National Council of Teachers of English.

Ong, Walter J. 1982. *Orality and Literacy: The Technologizing of the Word.* New York: Methuen.

Palacas, Arthur L. 1989. "Parentheticals and Personal Voice." *Written Communication* 6.4 (October): 506–27.

Payne, Karen, ed. 1983. *Between Ourselves: Letters, Mothers, Daughters.* New York: Houghton-Mifflin.

Polanyi, Michael. 1964 [1958]. *Personal Knowledge: Towards a Post-Critical Philosophy.* New York: Harper and Row.

Rich, Adrienne. 1986. "Poetry III." In *Your Native Land, Your Life,* 68. New York: W. W. Norton.

Roberts, W. Rhys, trans. 1954. *Rhetoric,* by Aristotle. In *"Rhetoric" and "On Poetics,"* translated by W. Rhys Roberts (*Rhetoric*) and Ingram Bywater (*Poetics*). New York: Modern Library.

Rubin, Donald L., and Kathryn Greene. 1992. "Gender-Typical Style in Written Language." *Research in the Teaching of English* 26.2 (February): 7–40.

Tavalin, Fern. 1994. *Voice.* Unpublished Doct. Diss. University of Mass.

Varnum, Robin. Forthcoming. *English 1-2 at Amherst College, 1938–66.* Urbana: National Council of Teachers of English.

Vendler, Helen. 1982. "An Intractable Metal." *The New Yorker* (15 February): 131.

Williams, William Carlos. 1986 [1936]. "How to Write." In *New Directions in Prose and Poetry, 50th Anniversary Issue,* edited by J. Laughlin with Peter Glassgold and Griselda Ohannessian. New York: New Directions.

2 Claiming My Voice

Toby Fulwiler
University of Vermont

Lately, because of loud and unruly debates within our profession, I've begun to wonder about the nature and origin of the voice in which I write. In fact, spurred on by friends on both sides of this debate, I've begun a methodical quest to track down my own voice—to identify it, describe it, and explain where it comes from and why.

The debate goes something like this: One side emphasizes the uniqueness or naturalness (nature) of each writer's voice, arguing that readers can know "authenticity" when they see or hear it. This primarily *constructivist* view is influenced by Jean Piaget, who views the self as emerging primarily from within. Composition scholars loosely identified with this constructivist position include Peter Elbow (1981), who describes our "real" voices as having "power and resonance" (292), and Don Murray (1984), who explains, "Our voice tells the reader how we think, how we feel, how we live, who we are" (145). According to Peter and Don, when we write honestly, each of our voices will be unique and recognizable.

The other side of the origin-of-voice debate emphasizes social rather than individual development, arguing that everything we write or speak takes place within social contexts which make (nurture) our voices what they are. This *social constructionist* position is influenced by, among others, Lev Vygotsky (1978), who believes the self emerges primarily from without. Composition scholars associated with this social constructionist position include Ken Bruffee (1984): "language and its products, such as thought and the self, are social artifacts constituted by social communities" (641); and David Bartholomae (1985): writers "write in a history that is not of the writer's own invention" (143). According to Ken and David, when we write honestly, our voices will reveal less of us and more of our discourse community.

I would like to thank my Vermont writing group for suggesting thoughful revisions of the present version: Glenda Bissex, Laura Fulwiler, Corrine Glesne, Charles Rathbone, and Joan Smith.—T.F. A previous version of this chapter appeared in *College Composition and Communication* 41.2 (May 1990): 214–20. Used with permission.

Quite frankly, I vacillate between these seemingly dialectic positions with remarkable ease, depending upon what I'm reading, writing, teaching, or to whom I'm listening or talking—one day feeling my thoughts are rather uniquely mine; the next, that I have stolen virtually everything I utter. In truth, however, I'm not uncomfortable believing both positions, remembering now that, as an undergraduate, I finally decided to major in English rather than philosophy because I could live with contradictions while philosophers could not.

Actually, if truth really be told, I seldom worry about the matter at all, raising it here only because these philosopher-friends of mine insist on having it one way or the other. Who, I wonder in my saner moments, could possibly have enough information to identify all the determiners of self that are reflected in an author's voice? Sure, biographers and critics attempt such definitive answers about authors with great regularity, but soon after, their successors, and sometimes their subjects, call their answers into question.

Who, in the end, could know the forces that really shaped the writer's writing? What would the critics know that the author could not? What would the author know that the critics could not? If I bet on the critics, I take sides with the social constructionists. If I bet on the author, I side with the constructivists. But I've got to start somewhere.

For the balance of this chapter, let me try to answer these essentially unanswerable questions, believing, as I do, that losing battles can be good learning experiences. As the nominal author of my own compositions, I will examine myself as an author, try to describe and locate the verbal constructions associated with *my own name* that apparently presents me—re-presents me—for good or ill, to the rest of the world. What, for example, do people mean when they tell me—as quite often they do—that they hear *me* in my published writing: "That really sounds like you" or "I really heard *you* in that piece." I infer these to be statements about my "voice" ("Yes, that really sounds like Toby's voice"). Are they saying something about my voice—hence my values and beliefs—or are they saying something more superficial about style? ("Yes, that really looks like the style in which Toby writes"—formal, informal, blunt, pretentious, whatever.)

If people hear my voice as somehow unique within my own discourse community (the National Council of Teachers of English?), what does that mean? Where, how, and why does my voice distinguish itself from others who also dwell in this same community, presumably reading the same books, attending the same conferences, teaching at similar institutions? If I look closely at samples of my own writing, will I be able to identify the uniqueness that others say they find? And will that uniqueness be a telling or a trivial difference?

In the past, I have not pressed these friendly voice-finders on the source of their knowledge about my voice, but now I wish that I had. (If they knew, it would certainly make my struggle easier, this chapter shorter.) Is my voice to be found, for instance, in the particular use of skillful verbal constructions—say noun clusters, prepositional phrases, or appositives? Or in the frequency of more dubious constructions such as split infinitives, dangling modifiers, or mixed metaphors? Is my voice characterized, definitively, by a truly unholy number of frag- ments, dashes, and contractions? Or by the absence of active verbs, coordinating conjunctions, and semicolons? Am I identified by even more elusive stylistic features of texture, rhythm, balance, scale, or symmetry? Or in more structural features—say in airtight logic, clever transitions, or cogent conclusions? Or is it my choice of topics—like this one about authorial voice—that inescapably marks me? Or in a predict- able attitude toward these topics—as in "A personal voice, along with truth, justice, and beauty, is a good thing to have."

While I am having some fun picking at the particular features of what some of us would call "voice" and others call "style," I am, at the same time, genuinely curious about whether or not one can answer any of these slippery questions: If I have a voice, is it single or several? Which one(s) is (are) authentic? Where can I locate it (them) most definitively? What does it (do they) actually look (sound) like? How much does it (do they) vary according to audience, purpose, and cir- cumstance? And how much conscious control do I (or anybody else) exert over it (them)?

My Private Self

I began looking for evidence of my own voice where I expected most unequivocally to find it, in the pages of my personal journals in which I write privately to myself. I have kept personal journals on and off since 1962, when I was a sophomore at the University of Wisconsin and Professor Herb Smith required his creative writing class to keep what he called "writer's notebooks." Wouldn't my voice, I reasoned, be most identifiable in these long-kept notebooks, my most candid and un- guarded writings? So I flipped through a several-year-old journal to a random page dated 2/29/88, and here is what I found:

Laura's out with Carol at her book group; Meg's out after work w/friends; Anna's upstairs with Allison, mad because I banned the telephone tonight. I have spent all afternoon on catch-up writing tasks—until I really am caught up! (Even got the CCC review done in a record two days!) The reason for a lot of this blocking out of small stuff is to allow me to concentrate tomorrow on the VOICE piece for CCCC—as yet just in the discovery stages. Too, I'd like to get the piece with Hank up and off the computer & sent to the Chronicle . . . why have I been so slow here?

Is this my authentic voice, I asked? ("Sure," I answered, "it looks like dozens of similar entries on surrounding pages and in current journals.") And if it is, what are the elements that reveal it to be mine and not somebody else's? ("Good luck!") So with as much objectivity as I could muster, I began to analyze the language of this voice as if the author were anonymous, to see what could be said from the outside (at the same time, I'll let you know what I know from the inside). Here is what I found:

1. *Topic:* You see the writer (me) reflecting on the current state of his professional life, apparently taking stock of where he is, checking on what projects are finished, what still needs to be done. (As the author, I also know that I write this way as a warmup exercise to prepare for more rigorous, demanding, formal writing later on. I also strongly suspect I do it to procrastinate and put off the more demanding writing for yet a while longer.)

2. *Context-bound references:* Since the writer writes to himself, he refers to people that strangers cannot be expected to know unless he explains who they are. (As the author I can tell you that Laura is my wife; Carol, a teacher friend of hers; Megan, my older daughter; Anna, her younger sister; Allison, her friend; Hank, a colleague in history at the University of Vermont.) Since the author knows, why bother to amplify to himself?

3. *Informal language:* Many features here suggest language in an informal or colloquial mode: frequent contractions and abbreviations (& and w/), a parenthetical construction, a variety of marks denoting special emphasis (underlining, capitalization, exclamation marks), vague words ("stuff", "a lot"), and something that's either a fragment or a run-on sentence (or both) at the very end. The language suggests a writing that is not self-conscious, as if the writer were talking to himself, not intending it to go very far away from himself. (As the author, I can assure you that I am

talking to myself, taking shortcuts, not thinking much about what the language looks like, being neither clever nor careful, certainly never intending to show it to anyone or even to reread it myself later.)

4. *Punctuation:* Here, in addition to commas and periods, are a whole range of marks, from informal (dashes) to formal (semicolons). Some imply emphasis (exclamation marks, underlining), digression (parentheses), and questioning (?), while others are used unconventionally (an ellipsis for a dash, capitalization to italicize). (As the author, I will tell you that, when writing to myself, I punctuate fast, using marks that are approximately correct and quick to come to mind.)

But, in making these observations, I begin to feel frustrated, if not somewhat silly. As a writing teacher, I've read enough rhetorical theorists, including James Britton and Janet Emig, to know that my journal-entry voice has all the characteristics that typify most people's private voices: personal ruminations, tentative planning, abbreviations, contractions, digressions, fragments, casual punctuation, and imprecise diction. In other words, my so-called most personal and private language is more typical than unique, more like others' journal writing than not.

My mistake becomes clear. Why would a public voice be heard in private writing? Since I share my journals with nobody else, no one has ever claimed to hear my voice in that medium. If I really want to identify the *me* people say they hear when I write, I, too, have to look at my public writing.

My Public Self

When I turn to my public writing for evidence of the voice that is myself, I look at the same sources in which people claim to have heard *me* speaking. To examine my public voice, I selected a short passage from an article in the *ADE Bulletin* (Fulwiler 1987) that argues for more in-class writing to promote more active learning—the kind of argument I made then and continue to make now:

> *The Monologue in the Classroom.* The dominant mode of instruction in American colleges and universities—especially the larger ones—is top down and one way. Walk down the halls and look in the classrooms and what you most commonly see is an instructor standing in front of a class talking and rows of students sitting, listening, and copying. Sometimes these classes number in the

hundreds, making other modes of instruction difficult—but not impossible—to conceive. Even in smaller classes of twenty-five and thirty, the lecture/copy mode often prevails. In such classrooms it is the teacher, not the students, who practices and explores her language skills. This is the mode of education which Brazilian educator Paulo Freire aptly describes as "banking"—depositing knowledge in people as you do in savings accounts. (36)

This writing is clearly different from that in my journal. There are no context-bound references—at least, I don't think there are—for the English teacher audience whom I'm addressing, the broad discourse community to which I obviously belong. Even so, simple concepts are carefully explained in case the reader does not know them. The only possibly obscure reference, the name of Paulo Freire, is identified as "Brazilian educator" just in case. Though dashes are used three times (which seems like a lot in one paragraph of professional writing) each is used conventionally—as is all the other punctuation. There is little of the variety or imprecision found in the journal entry. The diction, too, is more formal, with no contractions, abbreviations, first-person pronouns, or colloquial words (all of which, by the way, might appear in other selected samples of my published writing, such as this one).

In other words, the features in this single sample of published writing are less varied and more conventional, suggesting language aimed at readers who do not know me personally—readers to whom I apparently want to appear conventional and respectable.

At this point, however, the enormity of the task dawns on me: obviously, the only convincing way to locate "me" in my own prose will be to locate, at the same time and on similar topics, a significant number or "not me's" in other people's prose—or for that matter in my own. To locate, in other words, voices against which my voice might be tested for distinction. In order to hear the authenticity of my voice I will also need to hear in-authenticity as well, won't I? So, what do I do now—look for a bogus sample of my own published voice? (In truth, I can't think of anything I've published in which I don't—or didn't then—believe.) Should I look at dozens, nay hundreds, of samples of other authors' writing? (I wouldn't know where to start nor stop.) Should I type all of my samples into a computer for voiceprint identification? If so, who else's samples do I add for comparison? (Maybe I should do all of these, but, this is not, I suspect, what others do when they claim to hear me.) Help!

In the face of other possible, more sophisticated, more time-consuming—but no more certain—approaches to identifying the features that distinguish my voice from others, I agree to settle for less. It is already apparent to me that many writers, in addition to me, have written about active learning (John Dewey, Paulo Freire, James Britton) informally (Don Murray, Peter Elbow, Nancie Atwell). To distinguish my voice absolutely from all others would be very difficult, if not ultimately impossible.

Yes, I think this published passage from the *ADE Bulletin* sounds like me: the tone, the rhythm, the balance, the passion, and maybe the politics. At least I could still imagine myself writing it—though perhaps I'd temper some of the rhetorical stridency ("top down and one way"). But it's certainly possible, even probable, that others have written similar prose that could be mistaken for mine.

As I continue looking at this sample of my published voice, as well as this current writing about my published voice, however, I am aware of a noticeable lack of sophistication in the language. Instead of being aimed directly at my professional discourse community—the NCTE audience I had (have) in mind for both pieces—the aim is lower, as much toward educational novices as experts. My writing, I imagine, would make sense not only to English teachers, but to first-year college students as well. Its style and sense may be labeled, if not simple-minded, perhaps simplistic—at the very least, simple. And this simplicity suggests an answer that biographers could only guess at and no critics know.

My Eighteen-Year-Old Self

When I examine the characteristics of my public writing voice, I see language that seems a composite, at once original and indebted. Until I undertook this light-hearted (but I hope not half-hearted) investigation, I had not been fully aware of its creation. At the same time, I know that as I write and revise I am continually reading back to myself my sentences to see if they "sound right." Until now, I have not examined what I mean by "sound right," but now I ask "to whom?" and "like what?" Simple enough, it seems: I want my written language to be clear *to me*, and to sound *like me*—the me I would like to sound like. Before I risk sending out for publication this or any other piece, I make sure it is intelligible, reasonable, and readable to this editor (me) first. My first audience remains the one in my own head—an argument made several decades ago by Walter Ong and more recently by both Don Murray and Peter Elbow (1987).

But it is not that simple. Not, at least, if the "me" on whom I test my writing is multiple, dynamic, complicated, or shifty—and it is, I suspect, all of these. I could actually locate many selves to whom I try to get my writing right, selves, created at key social, emotional, and intellectual life markers, for whom I write: the self shaped by protesting the war in Vietnam, graduate school poverty, teaching assistant strikes, first-year teaching, marriage, children, and so on. All selves shaped by life-changing experiences, selves which coexist quietly (and not so quietly) along with my present fifty-year-old self, which emerge at this or that prompt to remind me of who I have been in the past and to whom I still speak in the present.

So, to *which* of these innumerable self-audiences do I most commonly write (right)? I don't think that I can prove this, but I have a good hunch: I write primarily to my approximately eighteen-year-old self. The me to whom I read aloud my prose is less my current full-English-professor self than my first-year college-student self.

In fact, it was in reading David Bartholomae's "Inventing the University" (1985) that I recalled just how much I had in common with his portrayal of the first-year student struggling to join a university community—a community whose governing rules seemed arcane and mysterious. Bartholomae explains that in order to write successfully for him, his students must figure out "what I know and how I know what I know . . . they have to learn how I write and offer some approximation of that discourse" (140). Or, as I many years ago must have asked a hundred times, "What do you want?"

Of course. And that was exactly my problem as a semi-serious college student of eighteen at the University of Wisconsin–Milwaukee in 1961. Unlike many of my classmates who intended to become scientists, engineers, businessmen, doctors, and lawyers, I was not sure why I was attending college. I struggled mightily to locate myself in the university community, situate myself to speak and write coherently in all my subjects, but I still ended the year on probation—a 3-credit B in English not quite offsetting a 4-credit D in French. (I also totaled my 1953 Studebaker, lost my girlfriend, attended too many parties, and let down my parents.) In other words, hindsight tells me, I was forced to make decisions that year about changing my habits of both mind and body, or dropping out of the academic community altogether.

So I changed my habits. I began to look deliberately for points of entry into a world whose values and habits I did not well understand. In truth, I don't remember the particular insights or moves I made to get off probation, to satisfy academic requirements, and to find a major or plan a career. But, looking back, I can almost hear my eighteen-year-old self knocking at the door, ready to invent or reinvent that university and get on with my life. I knew so little, wanted to know so much, and began the long apprenticeship of trial and error, replicating the discourse of the masters that eventually gets English majors into graduate school, graduate students into teaching jobs, and teachers tenured.

My eighteen-year-old self belonged to discourse communities whose values were shaped largely by local midwestern, white, suburban, middle-class conditions and which resulted in values that were generally materialistic, conservative, apolitical, anti-academic, and so on. The community that I currently inhabit is still primarily white, suburban, and middle class, but also liberal, political, and academic. My former community may be described best as virtually "pre-academic" and "predisciplinary" and, at the same time, essential, elemental, and formative.

That eighteen-year-old self for whom the world of intellectual ideas, historical contexts, and multisyllabic words were puzzles of enormous proportions is still with me. Consequently, I have always tried hard to make my own writing intelligible to that confused kid who wanted *in* thirtysome years ago. If I can speak clearly so that earlier self understands me, maybe I can be understood by other equally confused, lost, or alienated people as well. In fact, I credit that eighteen-year-old self— for whom nothing could be assumed, for whom everything had to be explained—with my ability to conduct writing workshops for faculty members outside of English for whom nothing—about current rhetorical theory—can be assumed, for whom everything needs to be explained in clear jargon-free prose that cuts across disciplinary boundaries.

Observations

By now, I have approached, grappled with, or answered as many of these questions as I'm able to within the scope of this chapter. I still do not know whether the distinguishing traits of my voice are telling or trivial, whether that voice was shaped more from inside than out, or even how many voices (pitches? registers?) I possess. However, I think the attempted answers have taught me a few things:

1. My private voice is less distinctive than my public voice. In that sense, it represents the public me less well to others than my published voice—which is why it stays private and undeveloped in my journal. Its linguistic features resemble other private voices at least as well as it resembles my own public voice. Most often

my private voice sounds/reads as fast and loose, fragmentary, uncertain, digressive, and egocentric. However, the concerns, attitudes, and beliefs represented in my private voice are consistent with my public voice. It is authentic in the sense of being the voice in which I *really*, often, and rapidly write when I am thinking out loud to myself, without conscious artifice. While my private voice is "authentic," it is not distinctive.

2. My public, published voice is carefully constructed—composed, revised, and edited—to present a certain and perhaps collective self to the world. I fuss over words, ideas, and especially rhythms in my writing to portray a writer who is at once liberal yet committed; informal yet scholarly; ironic yet serious. It is protean, multiple, and shifty, having more than one manifestation, depending upon whom it is addressing and why. I cannot remember writing words that I do not believe—though in documents such as grant proposals and letters of recommendation I may be less candid than elsewhere. The writing that most sounds like "me" is writing I have crafted to do so, which is why so much of my writing is rewriting rather than fresh composing. If it is "authentic," it is self-consciously so.

3. The style of my public voice is largely determined by a discourse community from long ago and far away, one long thought left behind, my first-year college self. It is that earlier audience that I credit with keeping my voice loosely conversational, relatively jargon free, vaguely egalitarian, and perhaps overly simplistic. In fact, I believe that in person I am more interesting, lively, and socially aware than my rather dull private voice suggests. But also more conventional, self-centered, and dull than my livelier published voice reveals.

4. The topics of my writing are posed by the discourse community I currently inhabit. I write about matters of concern within my profession, entering these conversations where I think I have something to contribute. These topics about which I write, along with my attitudes toward them, may prove to be stronger determiners of what I would call "voice" than any specific linguistic trait. In other words, I think voice-finders characterize me as much by a certain kind of argument as by an argument made in a certain kind of language. (Most of my published writing is about writing—in favor of more and certain kinds of it, for instance—so it is unlikely you would find *my* voice in a piece about computer chips, monetary reform, or grizzly bears.)

5. The tone of my public voice, which is both earnest and self-consciously ironic (this latter, more evident in this piece than in the
   sample I examined), is created, I think, by the juxtaposition of the
   full professor to the first-year student, both of whom vie for
   attention when I write. Some of the stylistic and tonal features of
   my voice are actually at odds within my own professional community—which like all academic communities, has adopted a
   specialized discourse that makes it difficult for eighteen year olds
   to enter in and participate. As much as I can, I construct my
   public voice to resist the exclusionary language of my profession,
   in the process simplifying, explaining, clarifying, and preferring
   always the rhythms of informal speech.

Given the way I began my academic career—awkwardly and in great
ignorance—my voice could have developed in one of two rather different directions: the first, viewing the academic enterprise as a privileged
ritual into which one is admitted after a careful screening and thorough
initiation; the second, viewing it as a parlor game, full of rules and
nonrules, cues and miscues, and, in the end, not all that serious. You can
see in which direction I traveled.

As a result of this small private study, in which I approached my
voice from both inside and out, I have come to believe that my own
historical development—and the trials and errors contained therein—
has made me forever uncomfortable within the more theoretical realms
of the discourse community to which I otherwise belong. It is my own
paradoxical need to be inside, yet write outside, that most determines
the total shape of my voice. If you think about it, which I don't recommend, where in the world does your voice come from?

Works Cited

Bartholomae, David. 1985. "Inventing the University." In *When a Writer Can't
Write*, edited by Mike Rose, 134–65. New York: Guilford.
Bruffee, Kenneth. 1984. "Collaborative Learning and the Conversation of
Mankind." *College Composition and Communication* 46.7 (November): 635–52.
Elbow, Peter. 1981. *Writing with Power: Techniques for Mastering the Writing
Process.* New York: Oxford University Press.
———. 1987. "Closing My Eyes as I Speak: An Argument for Ignoring Audi-
ence." *College English* 49.1 (January): 50–69.
Emig, Janet. 1970. *The Composing Process of Twelfth Graders.* Urbana: The Na-
tional Council of Teachers of English.

Fulwiler, Toby. 1987. "Writing Across the Curriculum: Implications for Teaching Literature." *ADE Bulletin* 88 (Winter): 36.

Murray, Donald. 1984. *Write to Learn.* New York: Holt, Rinehart & Winston.

Ong, Walter. 1975. "The Writer's Audience Is Always a Fiction." *PMLA* 90 (January): 9–21.

Vygotsky, Lev. 1978. *Mind and Society.* Cambridge, MA: Harvard University Press.

3 Coming to Voice

Gail Summerskill Cummins
University of Kentucky

The masks, *las mascaras,* we are compelled to wear, drive a wedge between our intersubjective personhood and the persona we present to the world . . . These masking roles exact a toll.

> —Gloria Anzaldúa
> (1990, xv)

My mask is control / concealment / endurance / my mask is escape from myself . . . over my mask / is your mask / of me.

> —Mitsuye Yamada
> (1990, ll. 6–14)

"We are all bleeding, rubbed raw behind our masks."

> —Chrytos (1990, xv)

After years of wearing masks we may become just a series of roles, the constellated self limping along with its broken limbs.

> —Gloria Anzaldúa
> (1990, xv)

In 1969, Walker Gibson defined voice in writing as an "author's created persona, his mask or voice" (xi). As a metaphor for voice in writing, mask works well: it identifies, disguises, protects. But it lends itself to a nominalization of the concept; the written voice is seen as something a writer has or finds, or as capable of having fixed attributes, as for example, a false voice, an authentic voice, or a resonant voice. Left out of these characterizations are the verbs, the actions or processes that help the writer come to her voices—know her identities and/or disguises and protect her acts of voicing as a writer.

The voice of the writer works more like the mask of classical antiquity than Gibson suggests. In classical antiquity, the mask both identified a character and helped project that character's voice. Although portraying a "false" identity, the mask served also as a projection device to aid the wearer in the process of voicing, and the audience "knew" the character because the mask conveyed instant attribute. In short, the mask worked both internally as an amplifier for the wearer and externally as an identifier for the audience.

Like the classical mask, but a more complex one, the writer's voice projects internal attributes, qualities, and selves of the writer, while at the same time protecting the writer's identities. Most definitions of voice do not include this protective aspect, nor do they explain how writers come to know their identities when voicing in writing, nor how those identities might change through the process of voicing. That is why defining voice in writing as "something" a writer has or as a quality found in text is incomplete and inaccurate. Such definitions fail to answer several questions, among them: How does the writer come to have a particular voice? Does the voice change over time? How is the authority to voice granted? Does a writer have more than one voice? How are these voices nurtured? Is it necessary to know these voices in order to write?

Voicing in writing is a process of continually creating, changing, and understanding the internal and external identities that cast us as writers, within the confines of language, discourse, and culture. Although some writers may not require an understanding of this process in order to voice effectively, others require "some dramatic role-playing, some assumption of a persona" (Gibson 1969, 11), in order to voice as writers. To understand how these personae, masks, are made is to comprehend the constitution of our voiced selves. From where, whom, and what authority do they come?

If we see voice in writing as more than nominal, as instead being the process of "coming to voice," the metaphor that bell hooks (1989) uses for self-transformation, we will allow for both identity and disguise:

> Moving from silence into speech is for the oppressed, the colonized, the exploited, and those who stand and struggle side by side a gesture of defiance that heals, that makes new life and new growth possible. It is that act of speech, of "talking back," that is no mere gesture of empty words, that is the expression of our movement from object to subject—the liberated voice. (9)

For hooks, coming to voice is a movement from "object to subject," which requires an initial awareness of who does and does not silence us.

I contend that coming to voice in writing is a similar process, a self-transformation of the writer as a writing object to a writing subject. This is a much different concept than seeing voice in writing as merely nominal. It is a process of seeing, reseeing, and redefining our selves and the role-relationships we, our selves and others, play as we create written voices within the constraints of our language, our discourses, and our culture. It is a comprehension of how our written voices develop through the roles and relationships that cast us variously, now as subjects, now as objects.

Coming to voice is a reconciliation between what Gloria Anzaldúa calls our "intersubjective personhood and the persona we present to the world" (xv), a reconciliation between what and who we are with what we project. Understanding this process of coming to voice in writing is a way to reconcile our voicing selves. Through this understanding, we may begin to identify the authorities which empower us to voice or to keep us silent.

Story Number One

I am struggling to lift off masks as I write this text. The voices in the room deafen. I hear the voices in my editor's comments and suggestions; I hear the voices of my "research"—articles by Toby Fulwiler and Nancy Sommers, books by Gloria Anzaldúa and Melanie Sarra Hanson, poems by Sharon Olds. I feel like a giant channel, trying not to drown in the streams of ideas, trying not to succumb to others' authority, trying to allow myself, somehow, to author.

The scene here is familiar. Like other writers, I engage in it every time I write. It is a scene of action, of tension, of potential for agency, as described by Nancy Sommers (1992):

> It *is* in the thrill of the pull between someone else's authority and our own, between submission and independence that we must discover how to define ourselves. (31)

The pull between submitting to an other's voice or depending on our own is defining. To author, it is necessary to have authority and the courage to author, as well as the will to challenge authority.

This complicated juggling of relationships—between author and text, author and language, author and other authors—forces us into roles we may not be prepared to take, roles we may not be able to make conscious. In writing, we may not know, or even sense, that we are battling between submission and independence, in part because we don't see identity at the core of the task, and we don't see identity as a function of—and dependent upon—our various role-relationships. In thinking about the nature of communication and its connection to identity, Catherine Belsey (1987) puts it this way:

In order to formulate its needs the child learns to identify with the first person singular pronoun, and this identification constitutes the basis of subjectivity. Subsequently it learns to recognize itself in a series of subject-positions ("he" or "she," "boy" or "girl," and so on) which are the positions from which discourse is intelligible to itself and others. "Identity", subjectivity, is thus a matrix of subject-positions, which may be inconsistent or even in contradiction with one another ... Subjectivity, then, is linguistically and discursively constructed and displaced across the range of discourses in which the concrete individual participates. (61)

According to Belsey, then, first there is an "I" which is in relation to a "you." There has to be language in order to speak the "I"; therefore, the self is always in relation to an other constructed in language. Or as Bakhtin (1981) puts it, "Language for the individual consciousness lies on the borderline between oneself and the other. The word in language is half someone else's" (2).

I know this firsthand, as I write this text. I panic when I place myself in relation to the others, the Published Writers. When I think in the mode of "Why-bother-writing-I-will-never-be-able-to-place-my-text-next-to-Yancey's- Fulwiler's-Sommers's-etc," I stop writing. I stop writing because the pull of someone else's authority, in this case the authority of the Published Writers, makes me doubt my ability to voice, to have anything to say at all.

In order to still those voices of panic and self-doubt, I pause; I remind myself that I have the faculty to think and write. I remember that all good writers make multiple, multiple drafts of any given text and get helpful feedback from editors. I tell myself that the worst thing that can happen is that this text will not be used in *Voices on Voice*. Brainstorming ideas and drafting a text, I also relax, and then, rewrite—still in my role as Unpublished Writer. But now, I write as aspiring writer in relation with other writers and myself.

It is not until I am able to make conscious the voices that are directing my writing, and the context of my writing, that my own voices come. Making conscious my subject-position with my editor and the other contributors to this book, I decide not to "identify with the position of object to someone else's subject" (Anzaldúa 1990, xiii).

This role-relationship can have a facilitating effect, if I allow it. The relationship with my editor, our dialogue, helps me move my written voice from thing to process, me from object to subject, particularly after she responds favorably to my second revision of this chapter. I begin to cast myself in the possibility of another role, that of Published Author; I have the confidence to voice. At the same time, I make my subjectivity to the Published Others conscious, as conscious as the constraints of language, discourse, and culture will allow, and thank them for their good ideas—without letting those ideas silence me, without my giving up my own voices.

All written voices are relational and in role; the task of the writer is to come to know these role-relationships through and in the act of writing. This coming to know, this deciphering of, role-relationships is what makes the process of coming to written voices so difficult. The deciphering requires an awareness of self as writer—and as writer in relation to a community of other writers, as George Dillon (1986) suggests:

> It remains extremely one-sided to view writing as the self-defini-tion of the writer, since the self that is defined is a Self-on-a-foot-ing-with-an-Other. One could as well describe writing as an imagination of a relationship. (41)

The imagination of the relationship of myself with the voices of the others to whom I write can silence me, or it can enable me to act—to write—and accordingly, make possible agency. Composing this text, I imagine my editor's pleasure in seeing my drafts become clearer as I try to enact her editorial remarks. Knowing I have only a week to make my revision, I imagine she will like the new draft; I do not have time to allow the voice of doubt to come close to my computer. The voice I do allow to enter this room appears on the last paragraph of her cover letter to me: "I look forward to hearing from you soon. And I am counting on using this text for the book." This role-relationship—in part fact, in part fictional—empowers me to voice. It allows agency; it does not subjugate me.

Balancing subjectivity and agency is the delicate part of voicing when writing. It is like the description John Donne gives of the relation-ship between two people who are apart. He likens their relationship to the diaphanous, invisible line that goes from one peopled compass point to the other: "Like gold to ayery thinnesse beate" ("Valediction," l. 24, in Hayward 1950), which, in the case of voicing, means that to be unaware of subjectivity is to give up agency. Not knowing what voices guide our writing undermines the potential to write our own voices.

Writing our voices is thus, in part, an act of imagination. The imagi-nation works as both ally and adversary for voicing—capable of both motivating and undermining—depending upon the role-relationships the writer creates and/or uses in the voicing process. When I was not certain I had anything to write for *Voices,* I imagined I wasn't capable. My imagination undermined my efforts. Later, after a positive response from another reader, my imagination helped me see myself successfully sharing my perceptions. It became productive.

Story Number Two

In 1986, Melanie Sarra Hanson completed her dissertation, *Developmental Concepts of Voice in Case Studies of College Students: The Owned Voice and Authoring*, for the Doctor of Education degree at Harvard University. Since that time, she has gone on "to other data, other languages" (844): she has become a Novice at the Holy Community of the Annunciation in Greece. Before leaving the academic world, however, Hanson completed a study of voice in writing that is interesting on two counts: (1) She gives us a developmental conceptualization of written voice; and (2) she argues that voice in writing hinges on the question, "Which voices govern?"

Her dissertation first describes a developmental conception of voice in writing, based on an "underlying structure of naïve epistemology and ontology as conceived by William Perry (1970) and Robert Kegan (1982)" (iv). The dissertation's second half is an ethnographic study of the development of the written voice in the work of several college students.

Hanson concludes that looking at voice developmentally "offers ways of naming and tracing the interactions of various influences, experiences, and personal histories within the students' developmental transformations of making sense" (288). Her developmental scale gives us a way to interpret the "transformations of the students' inner 'governments'" (288), a function of the interactions of influences, experiences, and personal histories mentioned above.

On Hanson's scale there are five stages of voicing:

1. My Voice (an unconscious, experientially grounded voice);
2. My Voice and the Foreign Voice (telling or showing what is learned, usually in the third person, and written in passive-voice exposition);
3. The Learned Voice (a voice beginning to take in and use that which is heard);
4. The Inherited Voice (the familial, internal voice);
5. The Owned Voice (a voiced self as owner and authority).

The writer alters her or his voice through each of the five stages, with each stage subsuming the next. Part of the writer's developmental process is to know which of these five voices governs; however, this knowing doesn't occur until stage four, when the writer begins to distinguish between his or her experientially grounded voice and the voice of others. It is this ability to explain the different voices that brings the writer to create her or his Owned Voice.

Hanson's model dovetails with the insights of others. For example, in Hanson's model, what Peter Elbow might call the resonance in voice derives from the raising to consciousness of the various voices that make up her Owned Voice (see chapter 1, this volume). A writer does not come to this voice until she or he works through the other four stages. In order to have a mature voice, Hanson believes, a writer has to "hear" from all her or his voices. These voices include the first and third persons, the voices of authorities, and the internal and/or familial.

Likewise, some of Hanson's stages correspond to sources for voice as identified by Toby Fulwiler. Fulwiler (see chapter 2, this volume) looks at his private voice, his public voice, and his eighteen-year-old-self voice. But the process of listening to these voices is perhaps more recursive for Fulwiler, while more linear for Hanson, because he still writes to his earlier self:

> That eighteen-year-old self for whom the world of intellectual ideas, historical contexts, and multisyllabic words were puzzles of enormous proportions is still with me. Consequently, I have always tried hard to make my own writing intelligible to that confused kid who wanted *in* thirtysome years ago. If I can speak clearly so that earlier self understands me, maybe I can be understood by other equally confused, lost, or alienated people as well. In fact, I credit that eighteen-year-old self—for whom nothing could be assumed, for whom everything had to be explained— with my ability to conduct writing workshops for faculty members outside of English for whom nothing—about current theoretical theory—can be assumed, for whom everything needs to be explained in clear jargon-free prose that cuts across disciplinary boundaries.

For both Hanson and Fulwiler, voices change; they are in process. According to Fulwiler, "If there is such a thing as an authentic voice, it is protean and shifty." However, in Fulwiler's conceptualization, it is possible to return to and evoke an earlier voice, and this may be helpful to a writer trying to understand his or her voiced selves.

Hanson and Fulwiler concur on another quality of voicing: that raising to consciousness the voices inside us helps guide our writing. Our written voices change as a result of our awareness of the constitution of our voiced selves, be they our own, others', authorities', or our families'. Moreover, without understanding the subject-object relations of our written voices, it is difficult to evoke those that may help us voice and rid ourselves of the voices that silence our own.

Story Number Three

In 1979, I took an independent study in poetry with a scholar at Columbia University. After I submitted my work to him at the semester's end, I waited patiently for his response. Months later, the poetry was returned, framed at the top by a single sentence: "This *might* be O.K. if you were *only* an undergraduate." His other comments were inside the envelope, specific references to places in the poetry that seemed "vague" to him, but little advice on how to make the poems clearer.

Since I was no longer an undergraduate, I concluded the obvious: I was already "behind" in my poetry writing and should stop writing poetry altogether. I did. Accepting my professor's authority over my voice, I allowed it to silence me.

It was not until ten years later that I had the courage to write a poem again—and then only because I was teaching middle schoolers about poetry. Writing poetry with them, I began to understand my previous silence. I worked through my self-doubt as a poet who was already "behind" by sharing my poetry, at first with my students, and then with my colleagues.

Eventually, through writing, revising, sharing, and trusting my voices as a poet, I felt able to submit a poem for publication:

> The Step Mother*
>
> You were appalled
> at the rips
> in my underwear,
> but the price
> of a new bra
> was too high.
> I could feel
> your eyes through
> the dressing room
> sizing me up,
> chortling at my
> cellulite thighs.

---

*"The Step Mother," by Gail Summerskill Cummins, from *Womanwarp* II: 6. Used by permission of the author.

> You placed me next
> to your daughters—
> they at the
> Miss America Pageant,
> me in a jail
> house line-up.
>
> The morning
> you leaned over
> your coffee and said,
> "Do you have
> any idea how
> ugly you are?"
> I merely turned
> and stared at
> my father.
> He swayed toward you—
> a silent, silenced stone.

Although publishing a poem in a literary journal was validating, it wasn't until several more years passed that I was able to shed another layer of feeling inadequate as a poet. A friend of mine was in charge of the drug and alcohol program for crash victims at the Center for Living of the Montebello Rehabilitation Center in Baltimore. She invited me to the Center to do some "right-brain work" with the crash victims, some poetry therapy. During one session, I read "The Step Mother" to four young people in wheelchairs.

When I finished reading the poem, one wheelchaired man looked up at me. Silent for the previous two days, he said, "Oh . . . what a Cinderella story." Painstakingly moving his almost paralyzed hand, he scrawled onto his paper, "Once I was strong/Now I am not." Through another's story and another's voice, he found the safety that would permit him to share his voice. Identifying with "Cinderella's" pain, he was able to release his own.

It was at that moment that I felt a different voice dislodge the voice of my professor's of so long ago. The criteria by which I validated my poetry—and my voices as a poet—shifted. If through my voice I could establish a linguistic site of safety where another writer could create his voice, I too could move in and out of various linguistic sites of my own. Finally, I could silence the professor's voice from twenty years ago.

It may be that if writers are properly "situated" in rhetorical places where they have the psychological safety that permits risk, they will not confront authority that debilitates. They may choose instead to write themselves. My six-year-old daughter Kathryn, for example, seems to exemplify this. Writing her own text, *The Ballerina Book* (1992), she wonders if she can both illustrate and write her story—she, of course, wants to do everything. I read her excerpts from *Talking with Artists* (Cummings 1992):

> My stories always begin with something real from my life. My first story, *Begin at the Beginning,* is a combination of autobiography and fiction. I had enrolled in a children's book writing and illustration class and was making my first attempts at writing a story. I sat down to work, and sat there, and sat there. I sharpened all my pencils.I got up and drank a glass of water. Then I went and looked in the mirror for a while, and so forth. (68)

Along with reading from Pat Cummings's book, I read her the names of the illustrators and/or writers of books, so she knows that some people both write and illustrate while others do not.

Kathryn never assumes that she cannot write or illustrate her own book. In fact, she can't even "write." But she can dictate her words to me and copy them above her drawings. She is an excellent *periquita,* the "parrot copier" referred to by Gloria Anzaldúa (1990, xxiii); she wonders if Katharine Holabird, the writer of *Angelina Ballerina* (1983), will mind her changing, "One night Angelina even danced in her dreams, and when she woke up in the morning, she knew that she was going to be a real ballerina some day" to "Little Kathryn loved to dance even in her dreams and when she woke up she knew she was going to be a real ballerina some day." Kathryn tries on the voices of authority as if she were dressing up, experimenting with rather than being subjugated by them. She sees these voices as synthetic, fluid, and herself as creator, able to work with the writing of others.

As I write this, it is my hope that Kathryn will not stop writing because she has given up her voice to authority. Certainly, she will have times when she doesn't know which of her voices is being heard, and she may hit pockets of silence. But it is my hope that she will continue to write for and with others who acknowledge and encourage her continuous coming to voice.

Story Number Four

In the book *Making Face, Making Soul = Haciendo Caras,* Gloria Anzaldúa (1990), the editor, connects the metaphor "making face" to constructing identity:

> [U]sted es el modeador de su carne tanto como el de su alma. You are the shaper of your flesh as well as of your soul. According to the ancient Nahuas, one was put on earth to create one's "face" (body) and "heart" (soul). To them, the soul was a speaker of words and

> the body a doer of deeds. Soul and body, words and actions, are
> embodied in Moyocoyani, one of the names of the Creator in the
> Aztec framework, "the one who invents himself/herself . . . the
> Builder Kachina himself/herself." (vi)

As expressed in this Aztec concept, construction of self, "making face,"
occurs on two fronts: through words and actions, or, as Anzaldúa says,
through "self-reflectivity and active participation" (xvi).

Anzaldúa discusses how women of color "make face." This is a
process with stages, not unlike the stages in Hanson's conception of
change to the Owned Voice, and it provides a way to conceptualize
coming to voice for all writers. First, women of color raise their subjectivities to consciousness and learn, within the confines of discourse,
how they are constructed. Doing this, they work through the denial and
betrayal of their "(de)colonized selves: finding hope through horror"
(149). Next, they name the horrors that surround them and, finally,
break out of silence:

> We cross or fall or are shoved into abysses whether we speak or
> remain silent. And when we do speak from the cracked spaces, it
> is *con voz del fondo del abismo,* a voice drowned out by white noise,
> distance and the distancing by others who don't want to hear. We
> are besieged by a "silence that hollows us." (xxii)

Anzaldúa discusses the process out of this horrendous silence, a process that seems to describe writers generally. First, as writers, we are
periquitas, "parrots," imitators. Then we untie our tongues, and our
writing runs away with us. Finally,

> we come into possession of a voice, we sometimes have to choose
> with which voice (the voice of the dyke, the Chicana, the profes-
> sor, the master), in which voice (first person, third, vernacular,
> formal) or in which language (Black English, Tex-Mex, Spanish,
> academese) to speak and write in. (xxiii)

Voices construct writers: we do not write alone but in the company
of, and with, voices from different discourse communities. Anzaldúa,
Hanson, and Fulwiler all acknowledge this movement in and out of
discourse communities as a process that places us in a variety of subject-positions, and role-relationships, when we write. To ask which
voices are controlling and/or manipulating whom, we need to understand the potential for subjugation, for it is this understanding which
empowers us to come to our written voices.

An End to the Story

Provided linguistic sites of safety and risk for voicing, writers come to voice with the dignity and self-respect to "make face," acquire the "agency of making 'caras'" (Anzaldúa 1990, xvi). In the case of this text, I initially felt safe writing it because I had "nothing to lose." I heard about the *Voices* text at the Penn State Conference on Rhetoric in 1992, where in a discussion the editor encouraged me to send her a draft. In response, I tried to write a piece keyed to our mutual interests.

I tried to create a place of safety in which to write the essay by telling myself that these ideas were new to me, that if the piece were not accepted, I would not read it as a personal rejection, a rejection of my personae, voices. I would accept it as a dismissal of newly conceived ideas, immature voicing. The risk was sending someone I barely knew something I had just drafted.

The stakes changed after I received Yancey's (1991) response:

> In sum, it is *possible* that I'll be able to use it in the collection. I don't know if you want to revise with no more of a commitment than that, but I read it as though it would find a place in the volume. ("Letter")

My voices as a writer, in relation to this piece and the personae who would read it, changed at that point. From then on, I let go of the voices inside of me that were objectifying myself as a writer with merely "untested" ideas, which was what had originally freed me. I began to take my voices for this text seriously.

In making this leap, I found safety in new sites. I could come to my voices within this piece because I was in role-relationship with my editor and with a community of writers who would also be included in the collection. This enabled me to see my voice in this context, in role-relation to them.

The process of voicing in writing is just that: the ability to know, claim, and change our dialectical entwinings of subjectivity and agency within the constraints of language, discourse, and culture, working in role-relationship with others. Coming to voices is not a new concept. bell hooks (1989) mentions the concept of coming to voice in feminist circles:

> [A] metaphor for self-transformation, it has been especially relevant for groups of women who have previously never had a public voice, women who are speaking and writing for the first time, including many women of color. (12)

Coming to voices is the movement from object to subject, particularly for the oppressed, those who have been silenced. It is the beginning of self-transformation, if we believe with Paulo Freire that to know our constructions is to begin to construct differently.

Works Cited

Anzaldúa, Gloria, ed. 1990. *Making Face, Making Soul = Haciendo Caras*. San Francisco: Aunt Lute.

Bakhtin, M. M. 1981. *The Dialogic Imagination: Four Essays*. Edited by Michael Holquist and translated by Caryl Emerson and Michael Holquist. Austin: University of Texas Press.

Bartholomae, David. 1985. "Inventing the University." In *When a Writer Can't Write*, edited by Mike Rose, 134–65. New York: Guilford.

Belsey, Catherine. 1987. *Critical Practice*. London: Routledge.

Chrytos. 1993. From a letter to Gloria Anzaldúa. In Anzaldúa, xv.

Cummings, Patricia, comp. and ed. 1992. *Talking with Artists*. New York: Bradbury.

Cummins, Gail Summerskill. 1989. "The Step Mother." *Womanwarp* II: 26.

Cummins, Kathryn. 1992. *The Ballerina Book*. Baltimore, MD.

Dillon, George. 1986. *Rhetoric as Social Imagination*. Bloomington: Indiana University Press.

Gibson, Walker. 1969. *Persona: A Style Study for Readers and Writers*. New York: Random House.

Hanson, Melanie Sarra. 1986. *Developmental Concepts of Voice in Case Studies of College Students: The Owned Voice and Authoring*. Doct. Diss. Harvard University.

Hayward, John, ed. 1950. "Valediction: Forbidding Mourning" by John Donne. In *Complete Poetry and Selected Prose of John Donne*, 54–55. New York: Random House.

Holabird, Katharine, and Helen Craig. 1983. *Angelina Ballerina*. New York: C. N. Potter.

hooks, bell. 1989. *Talking Back: Thinking Feminist, Thinking Black*. Boston: South End Press.

Sommers, Nancy. 1992. "Between the Drafts." *College Composition and Communication* 43.1 (February): 3–31.

Yamada, Mitsuye. 1990. "Masks of Women." In Anzaldúa, 114–15.

Yancey, Kathleen. 1991. Letter written to Gail Summerskill Cummins. September.

4 Affect and Effect in Voice

Doug Minnerly
Queens College

I am a writer, although I have only recently come to know that. Before I started to think of myself as a "writer," I suppose I would have thought of myself as "someone who writes," in particular as someone who writes out of necessity to accomplish certain goals. Through the recent development of my career, however, those two states of being have meshed, leaving me to wonder what my "writer's voice" sounds like.

Maybe I should start by talking/writing about my physical voice. I hate it, always have. My speaking voice has, in my opinion, a whiny, nasal quality which is tortuous for me to hear. It is something about which I am always self-conscious. Aside from my repulsion at the sound of my voice, I often feel that I am not good at persuading others through oral argument. Not surprisingly, to persuade, I usually turn to words on a page.

Perhaps there is an issue of avoidance here as well: I have always found written communication, especially when of a confrontational nature, to be much less stressful than face-to-face communication. When I had my own business, I found it nearly impossible to talk about money to my clients (which is one big reason why I got out of business and back into academe). It was always more comfortable for me to write to them about money. Unlike the spoken word, which, once uttered, hovers forever and cannot be changed, the written word can be crafted, tooled to just the right shape to do what I want it to do. Thus, when submitting a bid in writing, for example, I could preface the objective of the letter with lots of smaller invitations that in theory made the numbers worth reading.

I have even experienced moderate success in writing, dealing with both the IRS and the North Carolina Department of Revenue. Being reasonably inept at business, I have had several occasions to write to the tax people, usually with good results. Two of those letters are, in fact, included later in this text.

Because of the circumstances in which I have been most likely to use writing in the past, my writing has almost always been transactional, often in the form of direct correspondence addressed to a specific and limited readership with the intent of convincing those readers to take some course of action (Britton et al. 1977). Until I decided to examine the question of my own writer's voice, I would have assumed that I had written these correspondences without conscious consideration of the voice I used in the writing. If asked, I might have said that, at least in my clearly transactional writing, one thing I write sounds pretty much like another. But does it?

Purposely thinking about voice has caused me to look at writing, particularly my own, in a new light. I have always been an "aural" reader, clearly "hearing" every word on the page. My recent and deliberate examination of the whole idea of voice as an aspect of writing has made me realize that I am equally "aural" as a writer. I am now more aware of the ways in which I express myself, how my words "sound," and how these vary depending on the purpose of my writing. Are these various "ways of expressing myself," these different "sounds," in fact, various "voices" that I have as a writer? Various aspects of one "voice"? The same "voice" which varies in pitch and timbre, as the spoken voice does, according to mood and circumstance? Or are they, like the different "selves" that might be found in a writer's notebooks, manifestations of how I "sounded" at various points in my life? (Didion 1966). It seems that what may actually be voice, or different aspects of it, should really be called something else: style, tone, attitude, demeanor, approach, anything but "voice."

One result of these *vocal* musings is that I have come to believe that all writing and, by extension, all "voice," seeks in some way to be effective—to achieve some end result, to cause the reader—who may also be the writer—to consider or inquire, to act or react. Regardless of the reasons why they started writing a given piece in the first place, at some point in the process writers invariably will discover that their writing is going somewhere; that it wants to accomplish something; that it has some end. The point at which this discovery takes place may be very early or even precede the actual writing, or it may come very late, even after the writing is done. Joan Didion doesn't discover the "why" of her notebook entries until well after they are made, when she realizes that she was, in fact, recording who *she* was at the time the entries were written. That she was both writer and reader is inconsequential—her notebook writing, originally thought to be random bits of data, had a clear and profound effect on her as the reader.

In trying to achieve an end, to accomplish a goal, to write with an "effective" voice, the writer composes in a voice that will almost certainly contain some degree of emotion. It may be heavily laden with emotion, acknowledging the writer's feelings out loud, or it may be almost devoid of emotion, presenting only the writer's ideas without (intentionally) presenting the writer as *person*. The level of emotion that the writer uses is what I will term here as the affective content of the writer's voice.

Affectiveness doesn't belong only to the writer. Writing is, after all, a transaction between writer and reader. The writer may hope or even try intentionally to evoke an emotional reaction in the reader. In some cases, the emotional reaction/affective response of the reader may be, at least, a part of the desired effect of the writing. And although the reader, like the writer, is a human being with the same range of emotions, these two partners in the transaction most likely manifest their emotions differently. The writer can only *try* to second guess what affective reaction the reader will have and how that reaction will translate into the writing being effective as intended—i.e., whether or not the reader will do/behave/react in the way the writer intended.

If, then, I am claiming that affective content, or even the lack of it, is a feature of all writing and that all writing seeks to be effective, then it would follow that the degree to which voice is *affective*—the degrees and kinds of emotion that the writer uses—can be directly related to the *way* in which the voice attempts to be *effective*—i.e., what the writer is asking or expects the reader to do.

To test this hypothesis, I will examine samples of my own writing. I use my own work only because, having intimate knowledge of the circumstances surrounding the writing, I can most readily address the motivations behind what I have written, whereas I would only be able to guess at the motives of someone else's writing. I think that, by extension, the thesis presented here may be applicable to a wider universe of writing.

Throughout the following discussion, I will attempt to show that I have, probably unwittingly, always altered my voice by adjusting affective content to make it appropriate to the specific goal I was trying to achieve. Four of the five samples to be discussed here are classically transactional pieces of writing. I wrote each in response to specific rhetorical situations and circumstances; each seeks to achieve a specific end result. The remaining sample is something of a "wild card" in that it is not what might generally be considered transactional writing, but would fall more toward the expressive corner of Britton's scale. I chose to include this piece precisely *because* it is of a very different nature from the others; yet I think it too seeks to achieve something, to be "effective," to conclude a transaction, just as surely as my much less affect-laden correspondences do.

Bureaucratic Banter: Two Letters to the Tax Collectors

As I've already mentioned, I once had my own business, though I had no business background whatsoever. I was constantly overwhelmed with and baffled by the principles of accounting and corporate taxation. Most often, I got things right, but the occasional glitch happened, and it was one of these that prompted the writing of the first two pieces I will discuss: a letter to the IRS and a similar letter to the North Carolina Department of Revenue.

Aside from receiving income paid to the corporation DMS, Inc., my wife (and partner) and I occasionally received income paid to us personally. Such income generally was paid to us as "independent contractors"—much as consultants are paid—and no tax was deducted from the payments. We would dutifully record all such income in the corporate books and report it on the corporate tax returns; our clients would, just as dutifully, report their payments to the IRS. After a lag time of about three years, the IRS eventually discovered that the income our clients had reported as having paid to us personally had not been reported on our personal income tax return. The IRS felt we owed them quite a bit more money than we had already paid. We disagreed, as the letter in figure 1 attests.

Like most, if not all, American taxpayers, I react quite strongly to the three letters *IRS*. The strongest of my reactions is fear. I am firmly convinced that at the very moment I, no matter how unwittingly, might write down an incorrect number on my form 1040, armed IRS agents will appear at my door ready to cart me away to tax prison for the rest of my life. Put another way, I have no more desire to tangle with the IRS than I do to wrestle with an alligator. Unfortunately for me, in this instance the alligator snuck up on me and got me in a headlock, leaving me no choice but to defend myself.

The main purpose of the letter to the IRS was to have what I knew to be an incorrect tax assessment removed. Prompting such action by the IRS was, then, the way in which this piece of writing sought to be effective. In reading over this letter now, I judge that I tried to keep my voice as neutral as possible, so as not to anger the IRS. I probably thought that having direct communication with this agency was a lot like coming upon a large, mean-looking, unleashed dog: the calmer you

---

DMS INC.
a design company
2000C West Morehead Street/PO Box 9084
Charlotte, North Carolina 28299
(704) 376-3758

February 15, 1988

To: Internal Revenue Service
    Memphis, TN 37501

From: Susan R. & Douglas Minnerly

Re: Proposed Changes to 1985 Income Tax Return.

The first listed payment from Encyclopaedia Britannica (36-1042995), Account #0010, is an error. This payment was never made and apparently was reported to IRS by mistake. We thought this had been cleared up by Encyclopaedia Britannica. Therefore this is money which was never received, nor was it due, which is why it was not declared.

We are the owners and officers of our own business, DMS, Inc. (Fed. ID #56-1431909). All of the other payments listed in this notice were received by us. However, these payments were deposited into the account of DMS, Inc., and later declared as corporate income on the corporate tax return for 1985. We in turn drew salaries from the business.

This situation will also exist for 1986 & 1987.

Therefore, our income is as reported on the 1985 return. I am hopeful this explanation will clear up this matter. I will be happy to meet with a representative of the IRS, if necessary, to further clarify this matter.

I hope to hear soon about this matter.

Thank you,

Doug Minnerly

Fig. 1. Letter to the IRS.

sound and act, the better your chances for survival. Essentially, the voice of this letter eschews affect in an effort not to produce affect, or at least negative affect (i.e., anger), in the reader. Even the format of the letter—written in memo style with no personal salutation—suggests that I view the letter's recipient not as an individual person, but as some sort of sentient entity.

My voice is therefore likewise impersonal. There is no embellishment in the syntax of this letter. Sentences and paragraphs are short, specific, and unequivocally stated. I attempt to show simple cause and effect—if "X," then "Y." I make almost no attempt to strike a "human" chord, with the possible exception of some tenuous feelers put out near the end of the letter.

In the last lines, I switch from the previously consistent use of "we" to the use of "I." The initial use of "we" is a way to hide behind the corporation—like the IRS, a nonpersonal entity. If I can make it look like I, the individual with a name and personal identity, was not personally responsible for the problem, then the reader of the letter, whom I imagine to be a nonpersonal entity, might react more positively.

Switching to "I" at the end is an attempt to close by finally putting a real person behind the letter. I hope I can show that, regardless of who actually made the original blunder ("we"), it is now one individual person ("I") asking for understanding. I even go so far as to say, "I will be happy to meet with a representative of the IRS, if necessary, to further clarify this matter." That I would really be "happy" to do such a thing is, of course, a complete lie. I know it, the IRS knows it, and I know that the IRS knows it, and so on, ad nauseam.

At no time do I ever allude to the possibility that an actual individual with a distinct identity and personality might read and respond to this letter. I assume that the entity called IRS will deal with it; that the process will be mechanical; and that the machine will not appreciate emotion or embellishment. Ironically, with the noted exception of the prevaricative use of the word "happy," and although I seek to eliminate affect entirely from the voice used in this letter, the conditions surrounding its writing are, of course, heavily affect-laden. I am operating out of fear of the power of the IRS, though I try not to let that fear, or any other emotion, creep into the voice of the letter.

This letter, with its impersonal, nonaffective voice, was effective in the way in which I had intended it to be. Six or so weeks later, a letter arrived from the IRS informing me that my explanation had been accepted, and the (incorrect) tax assessment removed. I was delighted by this result, my faith in the ultimate triumph of justice restored. Unfortunately, other bureaucrats in another part of the country had different ideas.

When the IRS conducts something like a tax audit and an assessment of additional tax, it also informs state tax departments of such actions. It does not, however, inform the states when such matters have been resolved. Some time after my successful encounter with the IRS, the North Carolina Department of Revenue caught up on its backlog of cases, and again I received a similar tax assessment from the state. A written response again seemed appropriate (see figure 2).

Doug Minnerly
2008 Chatham Avenue
Charlotte, North Carolina 28205
704/332/4720 [Home]
704/337/2259 [Office]

May 5, 1990

Michael H_____
North Carolina Department of Revenue
P.O. Box 25000
Raleigh, North Carolina 27640

Dear Mr. H_____:

This letter is in response to the just received, and enclosed, "Notice of Income Tax Assessment."

As you will see by the enclosed copies of correspondence, this matter came up to me from the IRS over two years ago. I had thought it had been settled then. I did indeed receive from the IRS a final letter indicating that the matter had been settled. Unfortunately, I am unable to locate that particular letter, and am therefore unable to enclose it in this correspondence to you. To that end, I am also writing to the IRS Service Center in Memphis, TN, to obtain a copy of that letter. I have been informed by the IRS that normal response time for such a request is 45 days. I am sending this to you now so that I may be in compliance with the 30 day limit stated in the Notice of Assessment.

I ask that you read the copy of my letter to the IRS dated February 15, 1988. In essence, it states that all income received by myself or my wife, whether paid to us individually or paid to our business, DMS, Inc. (since dissolved), was deposited into our business account and subsequently declared as income on DMS, Inc.'s Corporate Tax Returns. My wife and I, in turn, drew salaries from the business. The letter also states that one of the reported payments, from Encyclopaedia Britannica, was reported to the IRS in error. This matter was, I believe, cleared up by Encyclopaedia Britannica.

DMS, Inc. was a very small scale operation, comprised at that time of only my wife and myself. The method of accounting described above was the only way we knew to handle that particular income. The income was indeed reported—only it was reported on the corporate rather than individual returns.

I also enclose copies of DMS, Inc.'s monthly journals with each of the entries in question notated.

As soon as I either locate the letter from the IRS which, I thought, resolved this matter two years ago, or receive a new copy of that letter, I will forward a copy of it to you.

I am not formally requesting a "hearing" as I hope that the matter may be cleared up through correspondence. However, I will gladly meet with a representative of your department, if that is necessary.

Sincerely,

Doug Minnerly

Encl.

Fig. 2. Letter to the North Carolina Department of Revenue.

This letter to the state tax department essentially sought the same result as the letter to the IRS. One might think, therefore, that the voice used in this letter would be the same as the voice used in the IRS letter. It's not, and for three very important reasons.

First, this letter to the state was written following a telephone call during which I was rather rudely informed that it was up to me to inform the state of changes made by the Feds. I thought that this was unreasonable since I had not even been aware that the Feds had told the state anything in the first place. As can be imagined, I was somewhat annoyed after this telephone call. This annoyance influences the affective content of this letter since it sets up an affective context which is wholly different from the context of the IRS letter.

Second, the North Carolina letter is written not just to a bureaucratic entity, but to Mr. Michael H_____—a real person! When dealing with the IRS, I had no individual's name on which to focus. In this letter, I do. Here, I know that someone, perhaps someone who might have similar problems, will read and deal with this letter. The approach is immediately more *personal*, though not necessarily more *personable*. I certainly do not consider Mr. H_____ a friend.

Third, by this point in the process, I was quite fed up with the whole matter. The corporation had been dead, and I thought buried, for nearly two years. I may even have been feeling a bit cocky, having taken on the IRS two years earlier and having won. I might have felt that if I could beat the machine of the IRS, I could certainly handle the rubes in Raleigh.

On review of the letters, I detect major differences in them. The formats differ. Whereas I used a "memo" format for the IRS letter— which is, coincidentally, the format the IRS uses in the letters it sends— in writing to Mr. H_____ , I wrote an actual business letter. As important, I wrote this letter as a private citizen—not as the owner and president of a corporation, as the letterheads demonstrate. I have used different sentence and paragraph structures in the two pieces. In the state letter, they are lengthier and more complex. This could mean a number of things: that I think Mr. H_____ is more sophisticated than the faceless IRS, or that I am trying to impress Mr. H_____ , or that I am trying to exhibit a degree of intellectual superiority over Mr. H_____.

Comparing these two letters, I see a real difference in the affective content, and accordingly a difference in the voice of each. Whereas the IRS letter, as discussed earlier, seeks to exhibit little or no affective content, the state tax letter demonstrates the presence of affect, specifically of annoyance.

After a cursory introductory sentence/paragraph, I say, "As you will see by the enclosed copies of correspondence, this matter came up to me from the IRS over two years ago. I had thought it had been settled then." Though on the surface this seems like a simple and straightforward statement, I can read between the lines of the text to find a richly insulting subtext, at least in intent.

The following is an *annotated* version of the same letter. The actual text of the lines is in plain print. Contained in the bracketed italics is what I can hear as a possible subtext for these lines:

> As you will see [*will see—this is a command. I'm not asking you to see, I'm telling you!*] by the enclosed copies of correspondence [*I've already dealt with this once*] this matter came up to me from the IRS [*the big boys, you schmuck*] over two years ago. [*Listen, the federal bureaucracy is bigger than the whole state of North Carolina, and they managed to discover this years before you did, and they even did all the detective work for you. Sheesh!*] I had thought it had been settled then. [*Why are you bothering me with this? Isn't what's good enough for the IRS good enough for you? By the way, did you catch the use of the past perfect tense, pal? If you had ever even learned that in whatever school you attended, then you would know that I'm saying that this matter was settled not only in the past, but in the distant past. All reasonable and civilized people had been satisfied by the outcome at that time!*]

I will not attempt to make the claim here that I ever expected, or wanted, the reader of this letter to perceive this degree of insult. I only claim that, reading this letter now, several years after its writing, and remembering how I was feeling at the time, the annotated subtext depicts those feelings fairly well. The voice I hear in this letter, unlike the voice of the IRS letter, has definite overtones of annoyance, perhaps even sarcasm.

My attitude toward the state tax department remains consistent throughout the letter. In the third paragraph, I refer to a letter (which is, in fact, the earlier IRS letter) for explanation of the situation. Nevertheless, I don't believe that Mr. H____ is really capable of making this leap of logic on his own, so I restate everything from that letter in this one.

In the final paragraph, I make the cursory offer to "gladly" meet with someone. However, in this case, I demonstrate some disdain at the prospect. I begin with, "I am not formally requesting a 'hearing . . .'," a hearing being the course of action suggested in the letter from the state tax department. Putting the word hearing in quotes indicates a lack of respect for this particular part of the process. Here I am only willing to "gladly meet" with someone. I certainly do not even make the attempt to let the reader think that I would be at all "happy" about it, as I did with the IRS.

Both letters sought, and achieved, the same result—the removal of the unjust tax assessment—and were therefore "effective" in the ways in which I intended. However, while the reasons for writing them were essentially the same, the motivating emotions were quite different: fear, worry, concern on the one hand; annoyance and anger on the other. Each voice, then, has its own affective content, or seeming lack thereof. Despite the obvious differences between the two letters, I think that what really distinguishes the voices is the degree of "humanity" each contains. The voice in the state tax letter is, in fact, a much more human voice than that used in the IRS letter. The "humanity" of the voice is shown by its greater affective content—emotions being uniquely human qualities.

A Report to "The Powers That Be"

Another job I once had in my checkered career was the responsibility of managing and caring for a college auditorium. Thinking that part of this job was to attempt to persuade the administration to spend some real money on upfitting this facility, I spent months investigating current conditions and researching solutions. I wrote an eight-page report on what I had discovered, including in it some specific proposals.

While I was preparing to write this report, certain of my colleagues urged me to stress any potentially dangerous conditions that I could find. This approach of concentrating on potential danger caused the voice I used to have considerably more affective content than it might have had otherwise. I had already learned, having done a stint years earlier selling encyclopedias, that a direct appeal to the intellect rarely works when trying to convince people to spend money they really don't want to spend. To be effective at this requires at least some appeal to the emotions—pride, guilt, and fear being among the best to target in such situations:

INTRODUCTION

The purpose of this document is to express my concerns about the present and future condition of the fine arts building. I will endeavor to point out the needs of the facility as I see them.

I see this facility as having the potential to become the premiere facility of its type in the area. There is no other facility of this size available. The current civic auditorium is @ 2 1/2 times as big in seating capacity, and we've all heard the horror stories of the acoustics there. Other facilities in the area do not have the seating capacity, the rentals are rather high, and they are very heavily booked. The new performing arts center will be a wonderful addition to the cultural life of our region, but it has some built-in problems—it will probably be extraordinarily expensive and difficult to rent, and it will be located downtown. This location is still a drawback for a large segment of the potential audience.

Here we sit, in what is probably the safest part of town. Of course our location is extremely desirable to potential users of such a facility. We should take full advantage of these conditions.

However, it will come as no surprise to anyone that our facility is in less than top condition. Virtually every piece of equipment is original to the building, and, to be honest, was not state-of-the-art when the building was new. While it may have been functional then, much of it has long since gone past that point. Mechanical or electrical equipment, like most other things, has a finite lifespan. It is time we recognize that the equipment has outlived its usefulness, and do whatever we can to rectify that situation.

In the very first line of the introduction of this piece, I pitch my voice affectively by saying, "The purpose *(showing that the voice seeks to be effective)* of this document is to express my concerns *(attempting to show that I really care)* about the present and future conditions *(saying that things are not good now and, unless something is done, will only get worse)* of the Fine Arts Center." This opening statement is actually an attempt to relax the readers by demonstrating that I will not be whiny or complaining, but that I am truly concerned about the situation, as I know they are.

The second and third paragraphs are clear and direct appeals to "civic pride." I hope that by pointing out the benefits to the college of improving the facility, I can better convince the reader to take appropriate action. I also, very mildly, cast aspersions on other, comparable facilities in an attempt to establish our own potential superiority. The third paragraph is also something of an appeal to snobbery—sometimes an important aspect of pride.

The fourth and final paragraph of the introduction begins to explore the guilt that I want the readers to feel. This paragraph says that our predecessors are guilty for not planning better, and we, perhaps, should feel guilty for not rectifying their mistakes before now.

My voice in this introduction is at once personal and professional. I want to present myself as a competent and caring member of the community, making an appeal to other competent and caring members of the same community. My voice is not dry or officious, nor is it overly emotional. This voice does clearly utilize affective content, though mildly and in a nonaccusing way, as a device to aid its hoped-for and intended effectiveness.

Stage Rigging. This is the scariest thing I have found here. Our rigging is composed of steel cable which runs on ancient winches. These winches operate with screw type gears which are run with a large electric drill. Aside from the obvious inefficiency of such a system, there are a great many potential dangers connected with this system. The winch gears show visible signs of severe wear and deterioration. The main cables which wrap around the winches have in almost all cases gotten off track and are doubling back on themselves, creating stress and friction which is certainly weakening them. By virtue of their age and use over the years, the cables are very likely weakened far from their original test strength. The configuration of the system is such that none of the pipes come to the floor (or at least within 3' of the floor) as they should. What this means is that in order to get to any of them, one still must climb a ladder, even after the pipes have been lowered as far as they will go. Lowering them as far as they go is risky business as well. A simple examination of the method by which the cables are connected to the winch drums would make anyone nervous about getting too close to the end of the cable. In addition, the way things (particularly the acoustic "clouds") have been hung on the pipes has done little to keep the rigging in good shape.

The above paragraph, from within the body of the document, shows how I tried to use emotional appeal, specifically an appeal to fear, to make my points. This excerpt is the beginning of a discussion of the stage rigging system. It starts out appealing to fear by saying, "This is the scariest thing I have found here." I am saying that I am scared by it and you should be too. I go on to speak of "ancient winches," "a great many potential dangers" and "severe wear and deterioration." Certainly I could have described the same conditions in much more neutral terms. For instance, I might have said, "the original winches," "some potential problems," or "wear and metal fatigue." These alternate phrases would present the same information, but in a less affective way. Such neutral phrases would not, however, produce quite the same effect on a reader who had not done the same sort of investigation I had done, or one who might equate "metal fatigue" with "iron-poor blood." Here is a clear case of my using an affective voice in a deliberate attempt to be more effective. I feel that the more descriptive phrases will be more likely to cause the readers to want to *act*—to do what I am asking them to do.

This paragraph goes on to support, with detailed description, the direct emotional appeal made at the beginning. It builds the image of the dangers of the entire system, placing bad situation on top of bad situation to present a final construction that will be viewed by the reader as unacceptable.

Orchestra Shell. Then there is the orchestra shell. It currently takes two men several hours to move the pieces. They are extraordinarily heavy and tenuous in nature. There apparently have been disasters with them already. One of our maintenance workers described to me a case where one of the pieces fell over. Fortunately, no one was under it, but it did fall on some chairs and, in his words, "mashed 'em like crackers." One can imagine what it would have done to a person.

The second excerpt from the report, the discussion of the orchestra shell, uses much the same approach. However, for this discussion I have some anecdotal, empirical evidence to support my claims. At the time of writing of this report, the college maintenance personnel had been directly involved in the operation of the equipment in this facility. One of these workers had used the wonderful phrase "mashed 'em like crackers" to describe the effect on some chairs of a large, heavy, and extremely unstable structure falling out of control. This illustration allowed me to use not only my own voice, but the voice of another who has been intimately involved with the particular item being discussed. The use of the phrase "mashed 'em like crackers" adds a degree of authenticity to the discussion of my case.

By using this quote from the maintenance worker, I included the colorful words of another person who was able to see the same problems I saw. Additionally, using this quote brought home the point that it does not take years of higher education to see the situation clearly. If this "uneducated" individual could assess the situation so accurately and vividly, the readers of this report should certainly be able to do so. In this instance, I am using a "compatible" voice, different from my own, yet no less affective. Coupling this other voice with mine creates a sort of "voice within voice," and adds some authority to my argument.

My report did not, alas, achieve the intended effect—to upgrade the facility right away. It did, however, have a definite and immediate effect on the then-head of maintenance, whose job it had been to oversee the care of the college's facilities. He apparently read this report as an attack on the quality of his work (which it probably was, to an extent). He responded with a three- or four-page counterattack in which he attempted to refute all of my contentions. His position was basically one of "it's never happened before, so it probably won't happen at all."

So, while this report did not really achieve the result I had intended, I nevertheless wrote it with a specific result in mind. In the process of doing that, I calculated the amount of affective content that would be most useful for my purposes and most effective for my readers. That this attempt was not entirely successful is not really important—I claim only a direct relationship between affective content and desired effect. It's more a question of the intent of the writer rather than actual results.

I hear the voice of this report as seeking to sound rational and professional in trying to persuade the readers to a certain course of action. At the same time, the voice is openly, though not overly, affective in that it freely appeals to the emotions of the reader. By seeking to provoke an affective reaction in the reader, this voice also seeks to do the opposite of the "impersonal" voice I used in my letter to the IRS. Unlike the voice I used with the IRS, the voice in this report does not try to mask its affective content. By openly demonstrating my feelings about the situation, I attempt to demonstrate my concern and fear for the safety of those who use the facility in question, and I invite others to share those concerns with me.

A Question of Confidence

I have examined in the preceding discussion how I seem to have changed the affective content or emotional pitch of my written voice to suit—in my mind at least—the specific circumstances surrounding the writing of each piece. As I stated early on, I most likely did so somewhat unconsciously. I must have felt at the time that each of these pieces "sounded" right for its stated purpose. Why did I feel that way and how did I know to do it?

At least part of the answer to these questions might be what I will call my "confidence level." The particular conditions which prompted the writing of each of these pieces placed me, as it were, in differing and unique rhetorical situations. In making my appeal to the IRS, I started out firmly convinced that they had the power; I did not. Here, my confidence level was quite low. In terms of the letter, I need to establish *ethos* with the IRS starting at ground zero, so I write with a voice that is timid and nonprovoking (I hope!). The voice is not confrontational, is impersonal, has a low affective content, and should not produce affect in the reader.

By the time I got to dealing with the state tax department, I felt that I had the upper hand. Though I knew that they might not actually accept my explanations, I also knew that eventually I would be able to prove the IRS had accepted them. In this situation, my confidence level was a bit higher, and, I think, it shows in the writing. In writing to the state, I have already established some *ethos* because of my previous encounter with the IRS, so I write in a voice that is calm, rational, but not quite as timid as the other. The affective content is higher, but still not overly evident.

The third example, my report on the college auditorium, is written from a very different position. Here I am appealing to the reader to do something, as I was in the two tax letters, but the appeal is based on my *professional* judgment. These are the sorts of things I have been trained to discuss. While dealing with matters of accounting and taxation, I can only pretend to know what I am talking about. While analyzing the condition of a theatrical facility, I *know* what I am talking about. This is my field—this is where I grew up. In this piece, my confidence level is at its highest; my *ethos* is pre-established. I am already acknowledged as the "expert" on the premises, so I can write in a voice that, while being professional and rational, can also be somewhat more "relaxed" than the other two. Also, in this situation, I not only know *who* my readers are, but I know them *personally*. This knowledge allows my voice to have a still higher affective content, to be more conversational, more personal, and even more personable.

The Personal Essay: A Nontransactional Transaction

I have always wanted to write "just for myself." About a year previous to the time of this writing, I finally worked up whatever it takes to do it, and began work on some personal essays. The funny thing about them is that when I began work on the first one, I started out to write a reflective essay/article on the nonlinear development of my career. The result, as I reflected on the influences in my life, was something very different, something much more personal, and, I think, much more valuable. This was indeed a case where I was "writing to learn" though I didn't know it when I started.

My Mother's Hands
by
Doug Minnerly

My mother's hands are grotesque.

Arthritic years have ravaged joints, nerves, and tendons, and surgeries have not helped. Rather than healing wounds, time works in partnership with the disease to increase the wounds and create new ones. My mother's hands are only the most visible manifestations of the degenerative horror that is rheumatoid arthritis. They give witness to years of constant, relentless, and ever-increasing pain. I cannot know and hope to God I never will

know what it is like to live every moment of one's life in such pain
and frustration.

My mother's hand are grotesque and yet in the grotesqueness,
hidden within the deformity are the hands which first held me.
Locked away beneath their alien mask of gnarled knuckles and
shrivelled digits are the mother's hands which pulled me, tiny
and trying to swim, from the coral sea bottom through clear Bermuda waters to the surface where life is possible. Pulled me up
through the blue-green waters of my childhood, through the
warm currents of the gulf stream, sputtering and crying, "I
drowned! I drownded!" Pulled me up into the warm and pure
Bermuda air, like birth. My mother's hands pulled me from the
water to plant me more securely in the child-size floating device
to continue my toddler paddling around Hungry Bay.

On a tree just above the beach of Hungry Bay was a wooden
box which held a bottle of alcohol. It was there in the event of
jellyfish stings. A people who exist in the midst of the sea know
there's no use trying to avoid it, just be prepared for the possible
consequences of enjoying it. So my mother would watch for tides
and jellyfish and my security in my innertube. My mother's hands
would be ready to pluck me from the crystal deep or bathe a
jellyfish wound with the alcohol in the box on the tree. My
mother's hands, which are now grotesque.

This excerpt is the opening of an essay which grew out of a discussion with a poet friend and colleague. Unlike the previous examples in
this discussion, it does not attempt to resolve any situation or persuade
the reader to take any course of action. It does, though, force me to look
at my mother in a certain way and to examine the emotions I have when
dealing with her physical condition, her age, her mortality—and the
implications those have for me. By no means is it classically transactional, though, as in all writing, a transaction takes place. In the following discussion, I will examine the transaction that takes place not
between me as writer and someone outside as reader, but what takes
place internally—within myself as writer *and* reader.

When I decided to write this essay, I had the title, "My Mother's
Hands," the opening line, "My mother's hands are grotesque," and, as
a result of a recent trip back to Bermuda, the phrase, "the blue-green
waters of my childhood." As I wrote, I found that the opening line, "my
mother's hands are grotesque" seemed to keep wanting to appear, so I
let it. As the reader, I see now how it serves as a unifying device which
allows me, the writer, to jump around through time and look briefly at
different periods in my life with my mother, as well as to look ahead to
a time without her.

My voice in this piece is unashamedly loaded with affective content,
both positive and negative, though I hope mostly the former. This is

nowhere near the dispassionate voice of the IRS letter, and may be only vaguely related to the quasi-affective voices of the state tax letter and my auditorium report. My voice in this personal essay is, I think, loving and honest. My voice says to the reader that I not only care deeply about the subject but am indeed a major part of the subject. Here is my most personal voice. I, the writer, cannot be separated from the material, for I am the material. This voice is my voice—the voice of the writer as a living, breathing human being; not of the writer serving some function or merely doing a job. It is the voice of the writer *being*. I, the reader, recognize my voice and, unlike my reaction to hearing my spoken voice on tape, I like what I hear.

The other voices discussed in this essay are, by the nature of their attempts at effectiveness, to varying degrees removed from the writer, as if I create "characters" to say the lines I am writing. The voice in this essay is the writer. There is no mediator, no created character. Here, voice is not a place to hide, but rather a place to expose. This is *my* voice as it is, not as I think it should be. Of the four voices or voice-variations already discussed, this one is the least *manipulated*.

And yet, there are goals I hope to accomplish with this piece of writing. As I contended early in this discussion, all writing seeks, in some way, to be effective. "My Mother's Hands" is no exception—only the *way* in which it seeks to be effective is different from the others. It seeks to have an effect as much, or more, on me, the writer/reader, as on the outside reader. It seeks to give me insights into how I feel about certain aspects of my life, about my mother, and about my relationship with her. Considering this goal, I am using my voice in this essay, in large part, to talk to myself. But in giving me a way to talk to myself, my voice—heavy-laden as it is with affect—might have an effect on the reader by providing the reader with a sense of the emotions I have invested in the writing of this piece, like those I experienced reading Faye Moscowitz's (1985) account of her mother's illness and death.

Why should I, the writer, think that the reader should even care? Perhaps I feel that all readers, regardless of the specifics, can use the emotions I present in this piece in thinking about their own relationships with their parents. All of the people I know who are close to my age are in one way or another having to deal with aging parents. Perhaps I feel, in writing this piece, that my examination of my feelings might in some way help others examine their feelings about their own situations.

Therefore, my thesis remains. The degree to which the voice is affective in this essay *is* directly related to the way in which the voice seeks to be effective. We only have to look at the concepts of effectiveness and transaction in writing in less literal ways.

Where does confidence fit in here? In the writing of the personal, autobiographical essay, I should have full confidence in the subject matter. While I may, and do, struggle mightily over the crafting of the words, I know what I want to say. At least I will know, as soon as I say it. What makes this writing different is that its goal, its desired effectiveness, is completely open-ended. So I have no need to establish *ethos* in this arena. Because I am writing about me, my *ethos* is unassailable. Having full confidence and no need to establish *ethos*, I am left free to let my voice be what it will be.

Given the freedom of voice allowed by such full confidence as just described, and the severe restrictions of voice I experienced with the IRS letter, it would appear that "confidence level" somehow fits with "degree of affective content." Perhaps I should rearrange and restate my thesis to include this confidence idea: the *way* in which writing seeks to be *effective*—the intended goal of the writer—coupled with the writer's *level of confidence* in a given rhetorical situation directly informs and even dictates the *degree of affective content* found in the writer's *voice*.

A Final Example

I end this discussion with a brief look at one other sample of my writing. This sample is, like the first three, a truly transactional piece of writing, setting out to accomplish a specific goal and having a definable purpose. Its purpose is to contribute to a collection of writings about voice, and its goal is to explore the affective/effective nature of my writer's voice through the examination of several samples of my own writing. I am talking, of course, about this essay.

The voice I am using now is probably made up of all the other voices already discussed. It is most certainly *my* voice, though not nearly so uninhibited as it is in "My Mother's Hands." It is something of a professional/literate voice since I am, after all, writing for a literate and professional readership. However, it differs from either of the voices used in the two tax letters. My voice here and now does not ask the reader to take any action, as the voices to the tax people did, unless asking the reader to consider and think about my ideas can be called action. My voice in this essay is neither "affect-less" as in the IRS letter, nor composed of "negative" affect as in the state tax letter. The voice I am using now may be most closely related to the voice of my auditorium report—the voice of one member of the community speaking to other members of the same community, hoping to make common cause with them.

As I write this, I think I am not trying to convey much emotion. At the same time, I am definitely not trying to be mechanical or "stuffy," though some occasionally stuffy phrases might find their way into the writing. This is, perhaps, an "academic" voice, if for no other reason than the context in which it operates. At the same time, the omnipresence of the "I" in the voice makes it quite personal. The voice may be trying to be personable, as well—*I* would like the reader to like *me*.

To an extent, the voice is trying—and maybe I shouldn't admit this, though I believe my readers are clever enough to know it already—to manipulate the reader into seeing my point of view and accepting my thesis. This manipulation, however, is not of the same emotional type found in any of the other samples where affective content is present. It is, rather, intended more as a gentle manipulation of perception. Here I am trying to talk *with* my readers, rather than *at* or *to* them.

I want my readers to understand what I am saying, so I try to be "clear." I want them to see my point, so I present a number of samples and a fair amount of analysis. I want them to agree with me, so I re-present my thesis toward the end of the paper to show that is does indeed apply to divergent types of writing.

If I have calculated correctly, knowing the desired effect of this piece and having a reasonable level of confidence, I will have imbued my voice with just the right amount of affective content to get the agreement I want. If I can't get that full agreement, I wish my readers to accept what I have said as plausible. At the very least, I wish my readers to conclude that I have written something worth reading.

Works Cited

Britton, James, Tony Burgess, Nancy Martin, Alex McLeod, and Harold Rosen. 1977. *The Development of Writing Abilities (11–18)*. Rpt. ed. London: McMillan Education Ltd.

Didion, Joan. 1990 [1966]. "On Keeping a Notebook." Rpt. in *In Depth: Essayists for Our Time*, edited by Carl H. Klaus, Chris Anderson, and Rebecca Blevins Faery, 171–77. San Diego: Harcourt, Brace, Jovanovich.

Moskowitz, Faye. 1988 [1985]. "From *A Leak in the Heart*." Rpt. in *The Borzoi College Reader*, 6th ed., edited by Charles Muscatine and Marlene Griffith, 905–7. New York: Knopf.

5 Technical Texts/Personal Voice: Intersections and Crossed Purposes

Nancy Allen
Eastern Michigan University

Deborah S. Bosley
University of North Carolina at Charlotte

> You come in with a personal voice, but you submerge it before you even know that it's happening.
> —Computer Industry Writer

> Most people don't argue with my use of personal voice because it *works*.
> —Scientist

The comments above are taken from interviews with two writers talking about their use of voice in technical writing. One was trained in computer programming, the other in geology, but both now spend much or all of their professional time writing technical documents. How could they hold such different views about personal voice? Is one of them simply misled?

The issue of personal voice in technical writing, as the King says in *The King and I,* "is a puzzlement." Peter Elbow (1981), for instance, speaks for many in contending that technical writing has no voice (288). Technical writing focuses on the world of things, they say, and tries to present it objectively. Moreover, in order to objectify documentation and improve efficiency, corporate writing often uses "boilerplates"; that is, technical writers frequently reuse standard sections in more than one document. How can the voice in a document be personal if entire sections are copied from previous documents?

The perception that technical writing has no personal voice is a common one, but is it accurate? To answer this question, we talked to writers (see "Interviews," 1992) who represent a range of backgrounds and experience from inside the technical writing worlds: (1) a *Scientist:* the principal geologist at an environmental consulting firm, who spends approximately 50 percent of his time writing; (2) a *Manager:* the director of a technical communication department at a major insurance company, who was trained in technical communications; (3) a *Contract Writer:* a publications services company writer, who was trained in philosophy, literary studies, and education and has thirteen years of technical writing experience; (4) a *Computer Industries Writer:* a technical writer with two years of experience writing for a major computer services company, who has a degree in computer programming; and (5) a *Freelance Writer:* a technical writer for a variety of companies, who was trained in French and business administration. What we found was a more complex view of voice in technical writing than is frequently assumed. Although these writers agree that constraints work to eliminate personal voice in technical texts, they also believe that writers often find ways to counter these forces and interject a personal quality into the documents they create.

In this chapter we will explore the various elements that work to suppress voice in technical writing, and the ways that writers have found to subvert those forces and integrate their own voices into their writing. The constraints operating against voice that we will describe come principally from three areas: (1) the traditions of technical writing; (2) the control exerted by corporations within which so much technical writing occurs; and (3) the power of particular communities within the technical writing world. As we will illustrate, these forces overlap in the expectations and constraints of the technical discourse community. Using excerpts from the interviews described above, we will consider how writers work within the constraints and freedoms of the technical communications world—sometimes submerging their own voices, and sometimes subverting conventions in order to express a personal voice.

Traditions of Objective Technical Communication

One major influence on the use of voice in technical writing has been the field's dominant epistemology. Technical writing developed from the epistemology of scientific objectivity; that is, technical writing operates within an ideology that holds that facts speak for themselves. Technical writing is part of the scientific tradition that focuses attention on objects and what happens to them, and away from the people who operate on objects. It is the "what" that matters in traditional technical writing, not the "who." Because of this ideology, technical writers are often charged with producing "objective" documents devoid of personal or emotional elements (Bazerman 1988; Olsen and Huckin 1991); because they are asked to "deliver the information," there's "no room for a personal voice" ("Contract Writer").

Adherence to an "objective" perspective is based on the presumption that technical writing is "fair-minded, rational, and uninvolved" (Dobrin 1989, 77) and, therefore, more likely to present "the truth." The technical world's insistence on producing documents devoid of subjective judgment results from an epistemology that posits reality as a fixed, knowable entity and holds that language devoid of human involvement will allow us to perceive and understand that reality. (For a broader discussion of relationships between language, epistemology, and ideology, see Berlin 1987; Miller 1979.) Arguments presented in technical documents ought to be rational; any intrusion of ethos or emotion clouds the issues.

An epistemology of objectivity maintains that we can make judgments that are repeatable, justifiable, interchangeable, and reliable—as opposed to subjective judgments that are "biased, emotional, or involved" (Dobrin 1989, 77). In other words, technical communication often is based on the assumption that we can know the world in only one way, that we can render the world knowable through the language we use, and that the documents we produce will be knowable *in the same way* by all readers. The writer's primary task is to represent the world *as it is* by becoming invisible (Miller 1979, 612). In fact, Anne Eisenberg (1989) refers to the "negative stereotype of the engineer, scientist, or technical professional as a person who cannot write, who comes from a tradition that is essentially mute" (4). In this tradition, writers should attempt to make their language transparent so that readers might better "see" the truth without subjective interference. Voiceless texts are "clearer" and, therefore, better able to present true reality.

Many theorists and analysts of technical writing, however, question even the possibility of objectivity in writing. Dobrin (1989), for instance, says that "the objectivity expressed in technical writing is the objectivity of the group of people who make technological judgments" (81). John Coletta (1992) relates this position to Foucault's analysis of reality as mediated by language. Scientific writing that appears to describe a thing objectively is, in fact, offering propositions about the thing that are both the result of interpretation and must, in turn, be interpreted. In this process, description becomes assertion. As Coletta says, "Every description of a 'thing' or 'object' is an assertion or 'proposition' about that thing; there is no purely objective description" (60). Yet, in spite of these theoretical assertions about relationships between reality and language, belief that the technical world participates in an objective reality persists. The consensus of the corporate, technical community still appears to be that technical documents should represent a nonhuman, object perspective.

There are reasons, then, deriving from objective epistemology and scientific traditions for ascribing a lack of voice to technical texts. Technical writing, however, is not monolithic. Technical writers produce a wide variety of documents that serve many purposes. Accordingly, a technical writer might create a computer manual or a series of instructions for microwave ovens for consumers, describe the design of a new product to a potential client, or recommend action to solve a technical problem for corporate managers. In addition to working on a range of documents, technical writers also work in a variety of situations. They may be members of a large technical communications department within a corporation or the only on-site writer in a company. They may produce documents related to one specific service or product, or they may function in a freelance capacity, contracting their services to many different companies. Within this variety, technical documents do tend to have one feature in common: they attempt to render technical information usable and understandable to a reader. Despite these differences in environments or documents, writers who deal with technical information are constrained by the conventions of technical writing and its traditions. Writers commonly learn to create documents which project an impersonal, object-oriented technical voice.

Corporate Silencing of Personal Voice

A second major influence on voice in technical writing is corporate control. To gain a clearer understanding of how voice operates within the corporate setting, we need to look more closely at the different ways in which voice exists there. We know, for example, that corporations can themselves have voices that can be quite distinct from one another in several of the ways they speak to their customers and to the public in general. We recognize corporations' voices through public relations materials and ads, in which voice is one component of the image corporations strive to project. Marion Merrell Dow, Inc., does not speak to us about pharmaceuticals in the same way that Nabisco tells us about cookies, nor would they want us to imagine (image to ourselves) the same persona behind the ads.

Two good examples of differing corporate voices within the technical field are IBM and Apple. IBM's advertising voice is a "buttoned-down collar" image that emphasizes the traditional, established reliability of a large corporation with long experience involving business installations. Note, for instance, the institutional character of their corporate logo, which appears as narrow, architectural blocks whose stripes suggest the venetian blinds of a corporate office. Apple, on the other hand, developed as a company focused on personal computers. Their voice is informal and playful, reflecting a casual image, as we see in their symbol (an apple with a "byte"). A company's ability to control the image the public has of it is, in part, a function of the corporation's ability to control the voices with which individual employees speak. Despite the fact that advertising is created for the purposes of selling products, services, and image, and technical documents are created for the purposes of providing information and description, corporations control the company's image by controlling both. The writers who produce such images and such documents learn to create them in the corresponding voice that "speaks for the company."

In both internal and external technical documents, corporations control the corporate voice through the mandated use of corporate style guidelines. These guidelines are sometimes developed through research and usability testing and sometimes through established custom. In both cases, guidelines are quite prescriptive in terms of content to be included and style to be followed for any particular writing task. For example, most corporations' style guidelines prescribe matters of punctuation, diction, and format particular to that company's idea of appropriateness. Guidelines can be as specific as requiring writers to use no more than five items in any list of information, to omit the comma before "and" in a series of three items, or to use only one particular acronym when referring to a company product.

While such conventions and guidelines are confining, they also can be liberating. The Manager that we interviewed said that conventional requirements placed upon her by editorial guidelines actually facilitated her own voice. Because the conventions were clear, they could ensure that she met her corporate responsibilities. This assurance then granted her the freedom to move around within conventions and focus on issues, such as audience needs, that were important to her. Her feeling of freedom developed because she knew the guidelines well and believed that they had been well researched and tested. Consequently, she could operate within them comfortably.

One intention behind the use of such guidelines, of course, is for technical writers to produce a series of documents which appear to have been written by the same author: to develop a unified corporate voice that is not undermined by issues of personal style and preference.

The underlying assumption is that if a corporation controls style, textual variations of style or terminology that could result from personal voice and lead to confusion for readers will disappear. In addition, close adherence to guidelines also makes chunks of text interchangeable from one document to another. Corporations assume that by controlling style, writers will produce documents that have the same voice. This emphasis on the documents, not on the writer, means the documents are more efficient to produce.

The goal of furthering corporate efficiency contributes to a more indirect control of voice, one that textbooks on writing and on technical communication do not prepare writers to meet. In introducing technical writing to students, for example, Anderson (1989) tells them, "Most of your communications will be designed to help your employer achieve practical, business objectives, such as improving a product, increasing efficiency, and the like" (7). Ornatowski (1992) sees this functional focus in organizational writing as further eroding possibilities for personal voice, leaving writers with "no provision, at least in theory, for action that does not 'efficiently' further the goals of the institution or interests she serves" (93). Though textbooks promise that "writing well enables you to make a personal impact" (Anderson, 6), Ornatowski says, "Not much scope is left in the end of the 'personal impact' Anderson promises students" (93). When writers are concealed behind corporate identities and bylines, a sense of personal responsibility may be more difficult to muster and may even appear to be inappropriate.

Finally, corporate legal concerns act to silence writers' voices. The litigious nature of our society demands that the corporation's legal department sign off on most corporate documents. Consequently, documents and the voices within them are filtered through the company's legal department, making them subject to yet another set of criteria for silencing. These criteria are primarily based on the company's need to avoid litigation; thus, the lawyers' responsibilities are to peruse the document and rid it of any language which could place the corporation in legal jeopardy.

However, another set of criteria may result in personal silencing. The Scientist told us that he recently wrote a series of "stinging" comments on a report to a state regulation board because of the board's insistence that his client might have violated legal limits for toxicity. The Scientist indicated in several places within the report that such violations were *not* upheld by his findings and that the board was overzealous in its attempts to obstruct his client. He states:

> I was basically confrontational with the state (I was working with a facility that didn't need regulations because it had been cleaned up), so I was writing "stinging comments" about these require-ments—appropriate comments for the situation, but the lawyer exorcised the tone, and the report became a strictly factual techni-cal report. He exorcised the emotions, not because of *any legality* but because of *his* notion of what is professional. My choice of language was very specific to a frustrating situation, and if the comments were gotten rid of, then the report could sound like it applied to many different situations. ("Scientist")

The lawyers silenced this writer's personal voice, not for legal or corporate reasons, but because his voice interfered with *their* perception of what technical writing should be. The Scientist later complained that the lawyers' actions rendered his report interchangeable with any num-ber of reports written by others. The lawyers' changes made the report more generic, hence more likely to be useful to the lawyers in other situations. Thus the lawyers' perceptions of good technical writing (not the company's legal vulnerability) and their interests in efficiency com-bined, in this instance, to silence the Scientist's personal voice.

Discourse Community's Constraints on Voice

In technical discourse communities, we find overlapping influences and constraints on the use of voice emanating both from the writing conventions for technical documents and from social and economic pressures within the corporate community. In requiring objectivity and a single corporate voice within corporate technical writing, not only individual but also entire subcommunities existing within a corpora-tion may be rendered silent. Organizations may thus reflect worlds in which many voices may speak but not be heard.

The now classic example of a silenced community is found in the memos exchanged between Morton Thiokol, Inc. (MTI) and NASA concerning the decision on the ill-fated Challenger launch. Carl Herndl, Barbara Fennell, and Carolyn Miller (1991) describe the ways in which MTI engineers and NASA managers were unable to communicate with one another adequately because of differences in the kinds of issues each group considered important and the accepted ways of talking about them, particularly ways that included no emotion. The "commu-nication failure" (295), they say, was caused by differences in conceptual frameworks and ways of arguing held by each group rather than by incompetence in writing. Because the management group controlled decision making, the voices of the engineers were, in effect, silenced.

In his report on the president's commission that investigated the Challenger accident, Richard Feynman (1988), a California Institute of Technology physicist who was a member of that commission, similarly describes what he calls a "lack of communication," attributing the problem between engineers at MTI and managers at NASA to differences in understanding and style: "We saw that NASA had no system for fixing the problem, even though engineers were writing letters like, 'HELP!' and 'This is a RED ALERT!' Nothing was happening" (34). Because the managers devalued missives with emotional content (indeed, they considered an absence of emotion to be one of the characteristics of effective technical writing), management dismissed the engineers as being overly emotive and, therefore, alarmist. Feynman checked further and concluded that such differences in the expectations of how messages were written and received, and the concomitant miscommunications, were widespread. In another study of the Challenger accident, Arnold and Malley indicate that "[t]he technicians knew of the impending danger but that their warnings were ignored by decision makers. *They* [the decision makers] *chose not to listen*" (qtd. in Winsor 1990, 12). As the Challenger example shows, the assumption that technical communication should have no personal voice because it may weaken "objectivity" can have dangerous results.

This phenomenon of silencing particular communities of voices that use unconventional styles or support values different from those of the dominant community appears in other areas as well. Beverly Sauer's research on coal mining disasters, from the late 1970s to the early 1980s, indicates that accident reports authored by mine inspectors were written to obscure the responsibility for miners' safety. This was achieved by failing to link reported safety hazards to accidents, even when a causal relationship seemed obvious. The official voice of the mines was the mining inspectors themselves. However, in the 1982 congressional hearings on mining disasters, the miners' widows, in direct contrast to the accident reports issued by mining companies, reported stories their husbands told them of dangers in the mines. Because these women lacked the authority of "the expert," the credibility of the mining regulators, and the power to challenge accepted "factual" knowledge, their voices were silenced outside the hearings. Changes in mining regulations did not occur as a result of these widows' voices (Sauer 1992). Thus, not only were the miners' wives silenced by corporate control over writers, but so too were the miners themselves through inaccurate (and intentionally misleading) accident reports.

Divergent Voices within Technical Communication

Because of the constraints on personal voice in technical writing imposed by traditional epistemology, corporations, discourse conventions, and the value structures of powerful corporate communities, we might ask whether an individual can, within a technical context, write with a personal voice. Can writers who deal with technical information achieve and maintain a sense of personal voice without being submerged by and within traditional objectivity or corporate identity? Evidence would indicate that they can. Just as we are able to distinguish particular writers within our own discourse communities, those familiar with technical discourse can hear individual differences between writers dealing with highly technical subjects.

One example of distinctive, even contrastive, voices in technical writing emerged from Gay Gragson and Jack Selzer's (1990) analysis of two articles written on similar topics by different biologists. Though both articles were addressed to other professional biologists, one was written in an authoritative voice, as though from a teacher to pupils. It kept to a narrowly focused topic and used constructions such as passive verbs, nominalization, and conventional qualifiers often found in traditional scientific writing. The writer of this article spoke with authority, assuming a stance of neutral, scientific detachment. The voice found in the second article was more informal, as though addressed to colleagues and collaborators. It drew on knowledge from a wide range of areas, such as references to cathedral architecture, and used emotional terms, active verbs, metaphors, and analogies, all features not typically found in scientific writing. The writer's voice in this case was not objective and distant, but instead personal, involved, and enthusiastic. Instead of using the more conventional "describe" and "discuss," the writers of the second article "confront" and "contend." Since both articles were accepted for publication in professional journals, both could be considered successful representatives of scientific writing, yet the voices reflect the particular authors.

Different disciplines also hold varied attitudes toward the use of personal voice in technical writing as well as varied degrees of allegiance to traditional scientific discourse conventions. Geologists, for example, develop their technical reporting skills by nullifying the traditional technical or scientific stance of striving toward "objectivity." As the Scientist we interviewed stated, "Geology is a more interpretive discipline: we are interested in beauty and wonder as well as information. . . . It is within the tradition of geology to create subjective prose.

Subjective matter lends itself to interpretive, qualitative responses" ("Scientist"). Thus the traditions of some scientific (and/or technical) disciplines carry with them a sense of technical communication as having an interpretive function, one which allows for a personal voice.

Because technical explanations are embedded within the author's personal story, the book *The Cuckoo's Egg* (Stoll 1990) illustrates interesting interactions between personal voice and a more technological one. *The Cuckoo's Egg*, a nonfictional account of tracking a computer spy, is not a typical technical document, but in it author Cliff Stoll performs the sort of writing task that is often required of technical writers as he attempts to explain the intricacies of a highly technical subject, computer networks, to nonspecialist readers. We include this book in our discussion of personal voice in technical writing because it deals with a technical subject and illustrates an author's voice shifting between personal and objective technical styles to support different purposes within a single text.

The overriding voice in the book is personal. Indeed, the book begins with a personal pronoun: "Me, a wizard?" (1), and includes several personal descriptions: "By 12:29, most of my clothes had dried off, though my sneakers still squished. I was part way into a soggy bagel, and most of the way though an astronomy article . . ." (47). In addition to developing a personal relationship with his readers, however, Stoll also needs to explain complex computer components and provide historical background. When he does so, his voice becomes objective: "Named after the Muppet hero, Kermit is the universal language for connecting computers together. In 1980, Frank da Cruz of Columbia University needed to send data to a number of different computers. Instead of writing five different, incompatible programs, he created a single standard . . ." (47). Yet while Stoll provides facts, he also keeps personal contact with his readers. For example, he describes the complexities of changing passwords so that his readers can imagine sitting at a terminal keyboard, "If you chose the password 'cradle'. . ." (39), making this mechanical process more friendly.

Even when Stoll speaks in his objective voice, his writing includes distinguishing characteristics. For instance, his use of analogies, an effective method for technical explanations, is not only frequent but also humorous and accessible. In explaining why the process for encrypting passwords to computer accounts can't simply be reversed, Stoll says, "If you turn the crank of a sausage machine backwards, pigs won't come out the other end" (148). Because Stoll juxtaposes varied voices within a single document, we become aware of the writer behind the text both through the features that characterize his voice and through the shifts in voice themselves.

These examples from Gragson and Selzer, Stoll, and the Scientist illustrate variations among voices even when these writers deal with highly technical subjects. Gragson and Selzer describe individual authors who speak about the same topic in different ways; Stoll shows how a single author speaks in varied voices; and the Scientist describes a technical discipline that invites personal interpretation. These differences show us individual technical authors manipulating language to meet their purposes in speaking to readers. Particular writers tend to favor particular manipulations, giving distinguishing characteristics to each writer's voice even within a technical context. These examples, in combination with those of constraints on personal voice described earlier, provide a complex view of technical writing and the place of personal voice within it. We might even think of technical writing as a conversation of many voices: objective, corporate, community, and personal.

Personal Voice, Experience, and Power

As we've seen, personal voice can exist in technical writing along or integrated with other voices found there. Within certain contexts, however, some writers feel their voices do not diverge from the objective or corporate voice, but instead are lost. This loss of voice may be a function not only of traditional, corporate, and community control, but also of the writer's degree of experience. In joining a new discourse community, we may feel that we lack a voice because we are novices within that community. A writer cannot manipulate language structures to achieve a feeling of individuality within a discourse community until he or she becomes familiar with the ways language conventions within that community operate. David Bartholomae (1985) refers to this process as "trying on the discourse," since at this point in the novice's learning, he or she "doesn't have the knowledge that would make the discourse more than a routine, a set of conventional rituals and gestures" (136). Novices in such communities, however, may be required to speak and write within these conventions well before the skills are actually "learned" (135).

What sorts of topics do community members expect to find discussed in particular technical documents? What style variations are acceptable? What technical expertise is needed to write a particular document? Writers need answers to these questions and others concerning what counts as knowledge and what is accepted as conventional before they can exert control over creating effects, as writers use voice to do. In describing research on student technical writers entering corporate settings, Anson and Forsberg (1990) report:

> Our research shows that becoming a successful writer is much more a matter of developing strategies for social and intellectual adaptations to different professional communities than acquiring a set of generic skills, such as learning the difference between the passive and the active voice. (201)

For writers new to a discourse community, personal voice becomes difficult to achieve. Personal voice may involve taking a stance on a subject (see Fulwiler's definition in chapter 2, this volume). Novices are unsure of what sort of stance is expected; consequently, they may feel that they can exert no personal voice in this context. As one technical communication manager at a major insurance company explained,

> The issue of voice is more an issue for the inexperienced writers. We get many new writers who just came from school or work where they are still pumped up with cerebralizing and writing to be creative. . . . Most of the time they have to submerge their own personal voice. . . . The neophyte technical writer finds it difficult to fit into the mold, although, for some, it is comforting to discover there is a specific way to create documents. ("Manager")

The Computer Industries Writer, the least experienced of the writers we interviewed, would concur, as we see from his statement quoted at the beginning of this chapter. Inexperienced writers find that they must submerge their personal voices as they become initiated into the corporate culture.

Once writers become active members of a discourse community, however, they may regain a sense of voice by creating their own variations within community conventions. One of the experienced writers we interviewed suggested that after such initiation is over, a writer may begin to look for ways to overcome conventions, infusing the writing with a personal voice:

> You begin to start making technical judgments and become focused on audience. You begin thinking of the user because the structure of the document has become second nature. That's where you find your ability to express personal style. When you are new, you're so busy learning the rules of the road, so then you probably have to *suppress* your personal voice. . . . It takes about six months to a year to be absorbed into the structure. That's when you realize that the standards are merely guidelines and that we do appreciate innovative approaches. ("Manager")

The Freelance Writer, who has had several years of experience and worked in a variety of companies, also reported that greater experience gives her more power and freedom. "By having such a varied experience base, I can go to a higher level [of respect and salary] because I have more skills. . . . Sometimes I can persuade a company to design a document differently." She also sometimes creates her own style guidelines if the company has none.

Experienced writers, those who have mastered the technical and stylistic demands of the corporation, may choose to integrate their own voices within the corporation's voice. The Contract Writer, who is an experienced technical writer of thirteen years and currently works for a publications service company that contracts its writers to corporations, indicated that her writing voice has become so recognizable (and effective) that other members of her company have adopted her style: "Now others [in her department] have adopted my style so now I say to myself 'Did I write that?' . . . My way of phrasing or formatting is now integrated into others" ("Contract Writer"). Because of her experience, her authority, and her comfort in using her personal voice, hers is becoming the corporation's voice. Other writers may emulate her way of saying things because they see it as effective or because they believe her voice exemplifies the corporation's standard. Whatever their reasons, she believes her style was not dictated by the corporation and that others recognize it as distinctive.

Conversely, when the topic or situation warrants it, writers may in fact attempt to subvert conventions and the corporation voice to emphasize a point or achieve an effect. For example, within the insurance company where this Manager works, one of the writers had to create instructional information for computer screens. She took a humorous, Laurel and Hardy approach. As the Manager reported, "The humor was subtle and it got readers to read the material so her personal voice created for this task worked" ("Manager"). The Computer Industries Writer reported another instance of a writer working successfully against corporate conventions and demands. Describing work he did on a set of training manuals for a client, he said:

> Basically, I subverted what the client wanted because what the client wanted was not the best way to handle the writing—doing so would have left too much ambiguity. They wanted a "nameless document." ("Computer Industries Writer")

In this case the writer reported that the client "eventually was pleased." Though the writers we interviewed agreed that clients have the last word on document content and design, occasionally writers convince them to accept changes and variations.

Examples of some of the methods writers use to subvert convention to assert personal voice were reported by the Scientist. He defies his engineering company's insistence on an "objective" style by inserting subjective judgment words like "insignificant" for small and "mammoth" for large because these words "have value judgments, and since I am always interpreting, never just giving all the facts, more subjective adjectives are appropriate" ("Scientist"). In a carefully constructed proposal, he used the personal pronoun "I" throughout because "since you are often including, in a proposal, comments to change someone's mind, you must obviously be personal to create an understanding from your perspective. The personal point of view is a call to action." This writer believed that because the function of a proposal is to convince the reader that the company or the writer is capable of carrying out a job, the writer's projection of ethos is critical to the recipient's decision to accept one proposal over another.

The experience these writers reported show that once they have gained experience, writers often find ways to employ personal voice within technical documents, sometimes circumventing corporate guidelines, sometimes integrating personal and corporate voices. The sort of voice that is found and the freedom a writer feels to use a personal voice rather than or concomitant with a corporate voice also depends, however, upon the power or status a writer has within a particular discourse community. In reporting on students' interviews with professionals in one legal, court community, instructor Jim McDonald (1992) says that lawyers reported wanting to use less legal terminology in documents they wrote for judges and court officials in order to increase clarity. Parole officers who wrote for the same readers reported wanting to learn and use more legal terminology in their writing because they felt the shorthand of this terminology improved their clarity and because such terminology situated them within that discourse as knowledgeable language users. Since the parole officers were trying to ascertain a secure place in such a community, they felt the necessity of using the community's jargon. The lawyers, on the other hand, had no such feelings of insecurity (their places in the community were already assured) and, thus, were able to dispense with such jargon without jeopardizing their own ethos. Either the absence or the inclusion of legal terminology in court documents could constitute part of a writer's voice; the differences in the voices reported here may reflect differences these writers perceived about their positions within the hierarchy of the court discourse community. Those in the lower end of the hierarchy have to "invent" their environment and, as Bartholomae (1985) suggests, "must learn to try on a variety of voices and interpretive schemes . . ." (135).

Use of personal voice, then, is related to both experience and power within a discourse community. Novices to a discourse community, both in terms of longevity and recognized skill level within it, and community members low in the power hierarchy seldom have the freedom or ability to manipulate discourse features equal to that of longer-term, more skillful or powerful members. Lack of experience and power may bring the concomitant feeling of voicelessness some technical writers experience. Members who have greater potential to achieve experience and power in a community also may be more likely to develop an individual voice within it.

Evaluating Voice in Technical Communication

The representation of the self in discourse, of which voice is a part, and the degree of autonomy or cultural influence that this self and its voice express, have been problematic concepts throughout the history of writing. While composition researchers and teachers have not wholeheartedly accepted the elimination of the self and the author that some philosophers have proclaimed, compositionists do feel that the self and its voice reflect the experience and situation of the speaker. In technical writing we find no unified, noncontextualized self whose voice speaks either for the individual or for the corporation. Instead we find, as we do in other kinds of writing, a tension of voices and influences in which the individual both supports and subverts the constraints of traditional technical discourse, and sometimes finds a comfortable integration of individual and corporate voices.

The voice that speaks in technical writing is one that has been socially formed and is situationally framed. Any piece of technical discourse is likely to include multiple voices, those of various individuals as well as those of a corporation. Such multiple voicing, which we find in technical writing, is normal for discourse, according to Bakhtin. Indeed the tensions between individual and conventional or corporate voices can be seen as one sort of dialogic interaction that Bakhtin tells us is the natural sphere for language. "Discourse," he says, "is by its very nature dialogic" (1984, 183). The examples and interviews included in this chapter show such a dialogue occurring within these texts.

The voices we have been describing function within particular discourse communities. The features that combine to distinguish one individual's voice from another's vary, depend upon the conventions of the particular discourse community within which each voice speaks. Features used to describe a writer's voice in technical writing are not necessarily the same as those that describe the writer's voice in other contexts.

Our evaluations of a writer's voice are dependent upon our knowledge of the language conventions within any writer's discourse community. Writing within the corporate and technical worlds involves many constraints and requires adherence to many conventions, as does writing in any situation. These constraints and requirements show up to us as outsiders in a very obvious way, making the corporate voice appear to us to be dominant, monolithic, and fixed. Yet within the constraints of corporate and technical writing, individual voices can and do emerge. By looking at this discourse from within its community, we are better able to see the individual characteristics and to hear the multiplicity of voices speaking to us.

Works Cited

Anderson, Paul V. 1989. *Technical Writing: A Reader-Centered Approach.* 2nd ed. New York: Harcourt, Brace, Jovanovich.

Anson, Chris M., and L. Lee Forsberg. 1990. "Moving Beyond the Academic Community." *Written Communication* 7.2 (April): 200–31.

Bakhtin, M. M. 1984. *Problems of Dostoevsky's Poetics.* Edited and translated by Caryl Emerson. Minneapolis: University of Minnesota Press.

Bartholomae, David. 1985. "Inventing the University." In *When a Writer Can't Write: Studies in Writer's Block and Other Composing-Process Problems,* edited by Mike Rose, 134–65. New York: Guilford.

Bazerman, Charles. 1988. *Shaping Written Knowledge: The Genre and Activity of the Experimental Article in Science.* Madison: University of Wisconsin Press.

Berlin, James A. 1987. *Rhetoric and Reality: Writing Instruction in American Colleges, 1990–1985.* Carbondale: Southern Illinois University Press.

Coletta, W. John. 1992. "The Ideologically Biased Use of Language in Scientific and Technical Writing." *Technical Communication Quarterly* 1.1 (Winter): 59–70.

Dobrin, David N. 1989. *Writing and Technique.* Urbana: National Council of Teachers of English.

Eisenberg, Anne. 1989. *Writing Well for the Technical Professions.* New York: Harper & Row.

Elbow, Peter. 1981. *Writing with Power: Techniques for Mastering the Writing Process.* New York: Oxford University Press.

Feynman, Richard P. 1988. "An Outsider's Inside View of the Challenger Inquiry." *Physics Today* (February): 26–37.

Gragson, Gay, and Jack Selzer. 1990. "Fictionalizing the Readers of Scholarly Articles in Biology." *Written Communication* 7.1 (January): 25–58.

Herndl, Carl G., Barbara A. Fennell, and Carolyn R. Miller. 1991. "Understanding Failures in Organizational Discourse." In *Textual Dynamics of the Professions: Historical and Contemporary Studies of Writing in Professional Communities,* edited by Charles Bazerman and James Paradis. Madison: University of Wisconsin Press.

Interviews with corporate writers. 1992 (June). Interviewees are identified in this discussion as "Scientist," "Manager," "Contract Writer," "Computer Industry Writer," and "Freelance Writer."

McDonald, Jim. 1992. "Stretching Imbrication." Electronic Mail Message to Megabyte University Mail List (MBU). 26 April.

Miller, Carolyn R. 1979. "A Humanistic Rationale for Technical Writing." *College English* 40.6: 610–17.

Olsen, Leslie A., and Thomas N. Huckin. 1991. *Technical Writing and Professional Communication.* 2nd ed. New York: McGraw-Hill.

Ornatowski, Cezar M. 1992. "Between Efficiency and Politics: Rhetoric and Ethics in Technical Writing." *Technical Communication Quarterly* 1.1 (Winter): 91–103.

Sauer, Beverly. 1992. "Sense and Sensibility in Technical Documentation and Accident Reports: How Feminist Interpretation Strategies Can Save Lives in the Nation's Mines." Paper delivered at the Annual Convention of the Conference on College Composition and Communication. Cincinnati, Ohio. 23 March.

Stoll, Cliff. 1990. *The Cuckoo's Egg: Tracking a Spy through the Maze of Computer Espionage.* New York: Pocket Books.

Winsor, Dorothy A. 1990. "The Construction of Knowledge in Organizations: Asking the Right Questions about the Challenger." *Journal of Business and Technical Communication* 4.2 (September): 7–20.

6 Voices in the News

Meg Morgan
University of North Carolina at Charlotte

Teachers often refer to student writing as "voiceless." What we usually mean by such a description is that the writing seems highly denotative, emotionless, objective, and straightforward, expressing no point of view and appearing indistinguishable from the writing of most other students. And yet what we as teachers often look for is the opposite: writing that is highly suggestive of the person who wrote it, that somehow reflects the life and the personal worldview of the writer. We are looking for a little "style," a little "flavor," even perhaps something that we can hear in the student's writing that makes it sound like the student who wrote it. When we find it, we rejoice; as often, we despair of ever finding it.

Ironically, perhaps, as readers we read the same type of writing every day in our daily newspaper, without despair. If asked, we might even say that a "good" news story has certain very observable characteristics: it is highly denotative, emotionless, objective, straightforward, expressing no point of view and appearing indistinguishable from stories written by other news writers. We might say, too, that hard news has no "voice," and that such "voicelessness" is good because many of us who read the news do not want a distinguishable voice in our news. We prefer the seeming objectivity of the reporting that informs us of the local, state, national, and international events crowding our complicated world. We are happy—or satisfied, at any rate—with that seeming objectivity because we believe it allows us to form our own opinions, to make choices based on our own beliefs and values.

In this article, however, I argue that news writing does indeed have a voice, the news that is thought of as "hard": the daily *recording* of hurricanes, fires, new legislation, presidential elections, murders, birth announcements, obituaries, and other such events. Hard news creates a public record of that event. *Timeliness* is a second defining feature of hard news—nothing is as old as yesterday's news, so they say. This distinguishes it from "soft" news or features, stories which often report non-events—the thrill of playing adult soccer, Aunt Mamie's 104th birthday, articles which clearly have a "voice."

This "hard news" voice is a historical voice; it is not individualistic, nor is it institutional. Because of its historical nature, the voice resists change. In accepting such a voice, readers buy into a static picture of the world emphasizing continuity and concreteness; they give up change and ambiguity. Moreover, as I will argue here, this historical voice is the BIG VOICE, the background voice for all news writing. I often think of it terms of a scrim curtain in the theater; it is there, but it is so inconspicuous and so much a part of the scene that we often forget about it until a particular scene calls for its effect. In other words, the historical voice is the backdrop to our reading. Because it is both a part of the way we read and what we read, this voice is one we as readers expect to hear, as well as the voice against which we measure standards of news reporting.

Of course, the historical voice is not the only voice in news writing. Hard news has, in fact, many voices that support the historical voice, a veritable chorus of voices, many of them speaking *sotto voce,* so *sotto voce* that we do not realize that they are speaking at all. These voices disperse themselves around the stage: some speak front and center, some from stage left, some from backstage. Some play the role of actors, some producers, some are props and some scenery. Although these voices may not always be obvious, their presence also makes a difference to us as readers of news. These many voices (despite their seeming objectivity) not only create but also *shape* a reality for us as readers, a reality so tacit that in many cases we do not even realize we are being formed as we are being informed.

The BIG VOICE: History and Objectivity

The BIG VOICE in journalism is the voice of objectivity, although it is not a voice that has undergone much scrutiny. One possible reason for the absence of discussions on voice has to do with the location of voice within the individual. Journalism researchers (like English teachers) associate voice with individuals; if the voice is not unique, it does not exist. Reporters cannot be individuals; they cannot write about an event in a way that expresses their feelings about that event or attempts to convince readers about the value of the event or its place in their lives.

Rather, the voice reporting a news event is the voice of an observer, a recorder, one who brings nothing to the event but a skill for seeing events and retelling them as they occurred. Thus, only the most denotative language is acceptable—only verbs, nouns, and denotative adjectives like "red", "square", "bloody", and" bipartisan."

Within this paradigm, the only way voice in a journalistic context can be examined is within the concept of objectivity, a concept at the very center of news reporting. And the best way objectivity can be understood is historically, a perspective that seems to explain the denial of voice in journalistic research. Because objectivity is so central to news reporting, the history of objectivity in news writing has been the subject of several important investigations in recent years. Michael Schudson (1978), for instance, looks at objectivity "in its relationship to the democratization of politics, the expansion of a market economy, and the growing authority of an entrepreneurial, urban, middle class" (4). He notes that objectivity was not always the core and goal of news writing. Before the 1830s, most newspapers were arms of either a political party or a commercial venture. They were clearly partisan with no pretense of objectivity.

The penny press, which arose in the 1830s in direct competition with the commercial and political presses, marked the beginning of the move toward "objective" reporting. It offered cheap (about a penny an issue), convenient (it could be bought on the street corner instead of by subscription only), relevant reading for the middle class. It offered ads designed to attract the middle-class consumer, the reader who now needed or desired to purchase things not available within the home. It avoided political bias and printed local, national, and international news: "[F]or the first time, the newspaper reflected not just commerce or politics, but social life" (Schudson 1978, 18–22). Later, the Civil War expanded the readership of the middle class and "intensif[ied] the direction in which journalism had been turning since the 1830s" by increasing circulation and stimulating technical innovation and change (66–67). Technical innovation—the invention of the telegraph—is also seen by some to enable a move toward valuing objectivity. Using the telegraph necessitated the shortest and barest of transmissions—a style that was denotative, and fact-centered.

Just because epistemelogical and technological changes moved readers toward an appreciation of objectivity does not mean, however, that such change would be embraced by the public as their mode of receiving information. Why and how was such an objective stance accepted into the mass media? At or about the same time as the rise of the penny press arose the popularization of the scientific method. Science claimed to arrive at truth by carefully observing phenomena, by recording those observations, and then by drawing certain conclusions—or truths—from those observations. At the midcentury mark, other fields adopted their own versions of the scientific method, so much so that this method became the reigning methodology for many disciplines. Historians, a group perhaps more accessible to the public than scientists, were making the same kind of claims for truth (Schiller 1981, 85–87).[1] In addition, realism in literature and the popularization of photography created a serendipitous climate for objectivity as the goal of the press. Journalists, too, embarked upon the scientific method. They observed, recorded, and reported their observations, and did so in the name of the public good.

But we all know—now—that such objectivity is a myth. Perhaps even the newspaper professionals—reporters, editors, publishers—know that objectivity is something they strive for but never achieve. Given this history, however, what's interesting is that certain newspaper practices pretty much not only guarantee subjectivity, but also ensure a degree of bias. Take, for example, the case of the reporter with a bias. Although "good" reporters attempt to compensate for bias by reporting all sides of an issue, thus achieving balance and objectivity, some biases are part of a reporter's worldview to which she may be blind. A conservative Republican reporter covering George Bush will write an election story quite differently from a liberal Democrat, no matter how vigorously she tries to overcome her bias. A pro-environmentalist will write a quite different article on business development of watersheds from the one written by the business reporter. Often the reporter is unsuccessful (sometimes even deliberately unsuccessful), and the public does detect the bias in the news article. As a recent letter to the editor of the *Charlotte Observer* puts it, "Why can't you just print the facts given by the [presidential] candidates without your constant liberal slant?" ("Letter," 1992, 2C).

There are other kinds of bias, however, which are not so easy to detect. First is the editor's or publisher's bias. Gaye Tuchman (1978) uses the metaphor of a net to describe this type of bias (21). Publishers and editors throw out the net and report what gets caught, but the net is not wide enough to include everything that happens; moreover, the net can be thrown in one direction rather than in another. A local newspaper has a pro-business bias: it covers a lot of stories with positive business implications. Because that bias fits into the current feeling of the majority of the public toward the community, the bias is often seen as simply the way things are. The bias states (as in the case of

Charlotte): this is a growing, vigorous southern city; the growth of business in this city is good for the city; new business ventures in the city will promote the quality of life for residents by providing jobs and infusing the city with additional capital. Readers seldom see articles that report the cost of new business to the city in additional required services, strains on the environment and infrastructure, and loss of old, perhaps smaller, business. The business voice, even in apparently objective news articles, makes content choices only within the parameters of the newspaper's pro-growth bias.

This pro-growth bias is part of a general bias in favor of capitalism and corporate big business, according to Michael Parenti in *Inventing Reality: The Politics of the Mass Media* (1986). Parenti points out that newspapers as well as other types of media are in business "to make money for their owners," and "[a]lthough declining in numbers ... continue to be a major profit-making business in the United States ... " (28). Because powerful corporate interests sit on the boards of the media organizations and because heads of media organizations are "partners, directors of banks, insurance companies, big law firms, universities, and foundations," the bias in newspapers favors these interests (29).

Although Parenti does not push the historical connection between corporate influence and capitalistic expansion, it seems reasonable to note the historical context: the current corporate bias toward big business may reflect not only the corporate status on current newspaper business but also the nineteenth-century bias toward capitalistic expansion that the newspapers assumed during their own period of growth. The sympathy toward growth is deeply ingrained in the newspaper industry, so ingrained that it may suggest an ideological stance rather than a conscious bias. This ideological stance is a third kind of bias that makes objectivity impossible to achieve. This ideology is tacit—for example, the citizens of this country hold a reverence for the rights of the individual which is taught at mothers' knees, reinforced through schooling, and further reinforced in the workplace. Citizens, before they become journalists, consume that ideology, which later becomes reinforced in journalism schools when they are taught what kinds of stories to cover and how to write them. Consequently, it's hardly surprising that newspapers privilege stories about individuals: individuals who commit murder, who rape other individuals, who commit crimes against the country, who embezzle, who achieve great things. Group crimes (or achievements) and crimes against groups are less reported, and less often.

Deliberate bias aside, the mission of objectivity espoused by most newspaper people is one rejected by most other disciplines, at least to one degree or another. Many of the disciplines mentioned above—science, history, literature, and art—have all modified the belief in observation leading to truth. They and we recognize the interpretative nature of all observation, no matter how objective, controlled, and systematized that observation may appear. Yet objectivity is still espoused by newspapers, in part because they believe that we, the readers, want to believe in the voice of objectivity. Newspaper people take seriously their history and the voice that evolved historically. Readers take that voice seriously because the hundred-year-old traditions are closely tied in to the growth of this county and its culture. In addition, the belief in objectivity in the news is reinforced daily millions of times over as people read news. The news reporter's voice is a legacy of our past, a legacy most readers, writers, and newspaper publishers value.

To sum up: the voice of hard news reporters is historically based; it came out of a widely held epistemology in which truth could be uncovered and told if certain rigorous procedures were followed—objective and careful observation and recording of data. Even today, the reporter's voice upholds that epistemology—the belief that truth is possible if events are objectively observed, recorded, and reported. The reporter speaks the truth because she is trained to observe and record.[2]

Understanding that BIG VOICE—the historical, objective voice—helps us understand other characteristics of journalistic voice. First, the hard news voice that we read every day doesn't vary very much. There may be some differences between the voice of the *Los Angeles Times* reporters and the *New York Times* reporters, and some of these variations may be tracked, but the changes are still relatively minor and not noticeable to most newspaper readers.

Second, the voice has not changed over time. If you were to read the *New York Times* in 1960 and the *New York Times* today, you might see some minor changes in voice, but the major impetus of the voice, the stretch toward objectivity, is fundamentally the same. (*The New York Times,* known for its lack of descriptors, is in fact loosening up, according to the May 6, 1992 issue of *Time*). One motivation working against such changes is reader expectation. The public, steeped in the history of public reading, reads with certain expectations (objectivity). If newspapers were to give up their historical voices and move toward individual voices—which might be perceived as less objective—our expectations would be violated. For the voice to change, we would have to have changed; for us to change, it would have to have changed.

The symbiotic relationship between reader and writer in hard news writing exists because of the high level of trust between the writer and the reader. Objectivity precludes lying, cheating, obfuscation, conceal-ment, and other forms of deception. As readers, we buy into objectivity because that way we can believe what gets reported. And even if we don't believe everything, we believe certain things. For example, we believe that the reading matter reflects an event which has occurred. We never doubt that an event did occur, although we may doubt—depend-ing on certain factors such as perceived bias of the newspaper and our own level of cynicism—whether it occurred in exactly the way the reporter said it did. Educated readers know that if the event was not observed by the reporter, or cannot be recalled or discussed by an eyewitness, the event cannot be reported. The suggestion, in fact, is that without these objective assurances, the event did not occur. We trust that the reporter is an observer, not a participant; a recorder, not a creator. The reporter's voice is not that of a fiction writer, no matter how realistically that fiction writing might be represented. (In fact, many journalists became fiction writers: Jack London, Mark Twain, and Er-nest Hemingway.)

Of course, there have been violations of this trust in the past. Several years ago, for example, Janet Cooke, a young reporter with the *Wash-ington Post*, wrote a story about a street kid named Jimmy, a heroin addict. In effect, this story was a fiction. Jimmy did not exist, but was rather a composite of several children the reporter met in the process of investigating illegal drug use in the capital. Such a violation of trust gets punished: the Pulitzer Prize awarded to Cooke was withdrawn. The *Post* also suffered a loss of credibility, and Cooke the loss of her position at the paper. The fabrication of an event—the use of the voice of a fiction writer, the assumption of a voice of a story creator rather than of a story recorder—violates the public trust in news reporters who record events that actually happen.

Of course, we can doubt the objectivity of the reporter and withdraw our trust from the relationship. We could, for instance, create an objec-tivity scale: stories at the lowest end mean an outright lie, and those at the highest mean the absolute truth. The question we ask is: What is the probability of the recounting of this event being objective? For each story that we read, we could conduct an analysis like this: "OK, this reporter always covers public education so he knows something about the subject; however, he enrolled his two kids in the local Christian school, so this means that either he is a devout Christian, or he knows something I don't know." High or low on the objective scale? Alterna-tively, this newspaper always supports Democrats; this year it is ap-parently supporting another Democrat and just reported that the

Republican candidate has been involved in an illegal land-grabbing scheme. How probable is the truth of that reportage? Such a daily exercise on each and every story in the newspaper would consume incredible time and energy, even if we had the knowledge to perform such an exercise. So . . . we trust the relationship; we trust the voice to be "objective" even as we know that objectivity is impossible.

There have been other notable breaches of the trust between news-paper people and their readers. Violations of the trust between readers and writers can be, in the words of the *Baltimore Catechism*, either sins of omission or commission. Sins of omission are obvious only in retro-spect: we understand that something should have been covered and it was not. I suppose, given my analogy, that we could also consider these sins as mortal or venial. A mortal sin is a serious sin of omission. We all have our favorites: the press conspiracy to cover up the sexual exploits of John F. Kennedy and possible links to the mob seems a likely candi-date for a mortal sin of omission. A widespread media conspiracy to withhold information about the Bay of Pigs invasion likewise (Parenti 1986, 188). Venial sins of omission generally go unnoticed because of the Catch-22 that is newspaper reporting: if (such) events are not covered, (for many of us) they don't exist. Let's take as an example women's sports. Noncoverage exists at every level—professional, college, high school—and in every sport. Women's sports are fillers. Now, perhaps some might say that this is mortal sin because the practice reinforces the privilege given to males in all aspects of the news. How might it rate, we can ask, compared to the mortal sins listed above?

Sins of commission—also of the mortal and venial varieties—are more obvious because there is usually a correction subsequent to a printing. The previously mentioned Janet Cooke story that appeared as "soft" news in the *Washington Post* is a good example of a mortal sin of commission. The *Post* publicly disclaimed the story after giving it ex-tensive coverage and publicly retrieved the Pulitzer Prize from Cooke. Although we might explain Cooke's temptation to write such a story as the desire to enhance her authority, the same case cannot be made for the editors and reporters involved in the libel suit between William West-moreland and CBS News and "60 Minutes" where experienced journal-ist Mike Wallace was a major player (Klaidman and Beauchamp 1982, 75–89). Newspapers try to avoid such sins because they are embarrass-ing—the voice that readers have come to trust has "lied" to them, and newspapers often have to work to regain that trust. Venial sins, on the other hand, happen and are forgiven almost daily—a name misspelled or a picture mislabeled—and corrections appear to adjust the error.

Multiple Voices in the News

I have been discussing voice in the news as if news voice were a single entity. This, as I suggested early in this article, is not true. I suggested that the BIG VOICE is a scrim curtain; multiple voices are actors on the stage. This metaphor can be extended a bit more: the curtain remains from performance to performance, from season to season. Removing it is a major undertaking: it is expensive and actually may entail a significant philosophical and theoretical shift. The actors change, sometimes from performance to performance. Many of their voices are not heard, although we in the audience are aware of their presence. The reporter is the lead actor in news writing; however, just as the star needs other actors for support, to carry out the mission of the play, so the reporter needs the muted, multiple voices in the shadows or off stage to carry out the mission of the newspaper.

I have changed what I mean by voice here. The BIG VOICE, the scrim, influences the conventions of the writing: a direct style, a reportorial stance. It's the big brother of news reporting. The multiple voices are less entrenched, more volatile, less stable. Changing a multiple voice is easy—and the change may make some substantial changes in such things as how the reporter angles a story, where the story appears in the newspaper, which facts are covered and which are not.

There are at least four "hard" news multiple-voice situations:

- reporter and editor(s)
- reporter and her source(s)
- several reporters working on the same story
- reporter(s) working on the same story over time

The list moves from simple to complex, and the categories are not mutually exclusive. For example, several reporters working on a single issue over time must submit their stories to one or more editors and consult the same but also different sources as the story changes. Listing these situations, then, fails to account for the dynamic nature of breaking news where situations change from day to day as well as for the dynamism that these voices can bring to hard news.

Reporter and Editor

Much of what appears in the local section of a daily paper is a story written by a lone reporter and checked by an editor for accuracy and correctness (Brooks et al. 1992, 26–27). The editor reinforces credibility.

Sometimes the editor makes changes, shortens the story, or reorganizes it in some way. Many readers understand this relationship and see the editor as a backup, another authority, a further hedge against bias, a voice of authority added to the reporter's expert voice. However, while this editorial voice is seldom heard, we do feel its effects. Editors determine what stories appear in the paper, where they are placed on the page, and what, if any, changes must be made to the story, including changes in focus and content.

Reporter and Sources

Because reporters cannot report their own experiences—their personal voices are not supposed to be heard—they use sources to create and authenticate stories. Some source voices are pretty static and uninteresting: telephone and city directories, encyclopedia, almanacs, and, more recently, electronic databases, such as Vutext, Dialog, and CompuServe (Brooks et al. 1992, 43). Live sources tend to be much more lively and quotable. For example, a recent article on prison life in North Carolina came "to life" through including the voice of a prison official: "I've been hit by soap. I've been hit by batteries. The inmates are thinking of things to do 24 hours a day. . . . It can get very scary. If a couple of them get fighting, you hope there's another officer within the sound of your whistle" (*Charlotte Observer.* 1992. June 7: 1A). The voice of the prison official re-created for the reader the environment in which he worked every day. The reporter could not do that, nor could that reporter inject too much of his own opinion into the article: that prisons are violent places to live and work. So, the prison official spoke for himself, but he also spoke for the reporter writing the story. Indeed, in this story, there are several voices in addition to the BIG VOICE of the news reporter, all of them prison officials concerned about their safety.

Interviewing multiple sources with varying perspectives on a single issue will allow the reporter to achieve a balanced perspective in a story (and thus further the myth of objectivity). Interviewing several people with the same perspectives may give the reporter an opportunity to express an opinion "by getting others to say" what the reporter may think (Tuchman 1978, 95). Sources also allow the reporter to get into the "how" and "why" of reporting, which are by nature problematic because they hint at motives and causes and significance (Carey 1986, 167). The "why" and "how" questions ask for opinion and judgment, and the reporter's voice talking about motives, causes, and significance is no longer seemingly objective but is explicitly subjective. In short, the source's voice allows the reporter to seem to maintain balance and objectivity within a subjective framework.

But the "seem" here is important because it goes to the illusion of objectivity. "Seem" is really all it is because the sources themselves are not neutral, not objective, are in fact highly political: "The higher the status of sources and the greater the scope of their positions, the higher the status of the reporters" (Tuchman 1978, 69). Thus, it behooves reporters to cultivate voices in high places, a practice that tends to constitute a position toward an issue and continue to reconstitute that position by referencing the same sources over and over. Sources also bring credibility to the story: if two or more voices say the same or similar things, then that is closer to truth than if only one source says it, as we saw in the Watergate investigations. Tuchman recalls the Watergate investigation in 1974 in which reporters Woodward and Bernstein were required to substantiate each fact using "two independent sources" (85).

Live sources used in a story also tend to fold back to previous stories, to reiterate the history of the story itself and to thus validate the "truthfulness" of the reporting of it. For many readers, Richard Nixon, no matter what position he may have taken on a contemporary issue, will always be the president who declared himself "not a crook" before resigning from the presidency before full-blown impeachment proceedings could get under way. Thus, the voice of contemporary Richard Nixon, a man trying to reestablish himself in the public eye, merges with the voice of the only president forced to leave office.

Several Reporters Working on the Same Story

Increasingly, more than one reporter will work on a single story. Often a story begins on the wire, but becomes regionalized when a local reporter captures/creates a hometown angle. Sometimes two reporters will divide interviews and write the story together. Sometimes two beat reporters will combine beats to broaden the scope of a story. Obviously, many permutations are possible. Because of the influence of the BIG VOICE, readers seldom hear the multiple voices, but they make possible a story that may not have been able to be covered by a single reporter.

Single Reporter or Several Reporters
Working on the Same Story Over Time

A single reporter, a beat reporter, for example, may cover an issue over days, weeks, or months. Over that period of time, the voice of the reporter becomes more authoritative—she knows her story, her sources, her angles. Her readers may trust her reporting beyond the ordinary trust attributed to any reporter. TV news coverage is a good example here. The war in Kuwait was covered by news reporters who appeared nightly in our living rooms. We got used to and comfortable with CNN. But longitudinal coverage may backfire: the reporter covering the same story may become more knowledgeable, but she may also become more biased, inclined to favor one position over another or consult one source more than another.

Increasingly, more than one reporter will work on a single issue over time. Woodward and Bernstein provide a good case in point. For months during 1972 and 1973, they chronicled the events surrounding the Watergate break-in and the subsequent cover up. Many readers learned to trust them and their voices, especially as the roll call of participants revealed names that shocked and alarmed us.

Stories written over time may create another effect: myths, larger-than-life figures or concepts that help us define our culture. Schudson (1986) shows how such a process evolves (89–91) as he describes the reporting of an initially relatively simple event. The process began with the arrest of several individuals for spying in May of 1985. According to Schudson, the "news began unspectacularly," appearing on page 19 of the *New York Times*. Two days later, a follow-up appeared on page 22, but a week later, Schudson writes that the *New York Times* called the case "one of the most serious spy cases in the Navy's history."

With those words, the myth began, and subsequent stories, both hard news and news analysis, which appeared on the front pages of that paper, and of the *Los Angeles Times* and the *Chicago Tribune,* created and recreated the myth. Schudson notes that the story moved from a single arrest story to "a specific tragedy of American security endangered and then . . . into an exemplar of a growing incidence of a new kind of espionage" (90). An extended analysis might see this story as playing into the then-still-alive American myth of the "great Red menace," and a recounting of the even deeper myth of the good guys against the bad guys, played out not against the backdrop of the American West or 007, but in the national media.

Conclusion

The BIG VOICE in hard news writing is historically situated and continues the convention of objectivity that the readers have come to expect and demand from the press. Basically, it is a voice that creates order out of chaos: by assuring us that reality does exist (even when we know it does not), because the questions "who," "what," "when," "where," "how," and "why" are answerable. Other individual voices work within, enact, and reinforce the BIG VOICE. These voices create hierarchies of what is to be known and what is not to be known, they authenticate events, and they create and perpetuate myths. The voice(s) of the news are not voiceless; rather they speak quietly and unobtrusively in ways that shape what we know and accept.

Notes

1. I was in college before I realized that my northern perspective on the Civil War was not "the truth." I read a textbook written by a southerner who alluded to the "War of Northern Aggression." I figured something was amiss here.

2. Allen and Bosley in this volume make the case that technical communication assumes the same stance. This is true, but few practitioners of technical communication describe what they do in epistemological terms. The vigor with which newspapers defend their objectivity and the need for journalistic objectivity is not matched by an equally vigorous defense of and need for objectivity by technical communicators.

Works Cited

Brooks, Brian S. et al. 1992. *News Reporting and Writing.* 4th ed. New York: St. Martin's.

Carey, James W. 1986. "The Dark Continent of American Journalism." In *Reading the News: A Pantheon Guide to Popular Culture,* edited by Robert Karl Manoff and Michael Schudson, 146–96. New York: Pantheon.

Klaidman, Stephen, and Tom L. Beauchamp. 1987. *The Virtuous Journalist.* New York: Oxford University Press.

"Letter to the Editor." 1992. *The Charlotte Observer* (June 7): 2C.

Newman, Jay. 1989. *The Journalist in Plato's Cave.* Rutherford, NJ: Fairleigh Dickinson University Press.

Parenti, Michael. 1986. *Inventing Reality: The Politics of the Mass Media.* New York: St. Martin's.

Schiller, Dan. 1981. *Objectivity and the News: The Public and the Rise of Commercial Journalism.* Philadelphia: University of Pennsylvania Press.

Schudson, Michael. 1978. *Discovering the News: A Social History of American Newspapers*. New York: Basic Books.

———. 1986. "Deadlines, Datelines, and History." In *Reading the News: A Pantheon Guide to Popular Culture*, edited by Robert Karl Manoff and Michael Schudson, 79–108. New York: Pantheon.

Tuchman, Gaye. 1978. *Making News: A Study in the Construction of Reality*. New York: The Free Press.

7 The Chameleon "I": On Voice and Personality in the Personal Essay

Carl H. Klaus
University of Iowa

Voice. The word itself immediately leads me to think of a familiar phrase—"the sound of a person's voice." That phrase moves me, in turn, to remember the singular combination of pitch, tone, timbre, and inflection that I hear whenever I'm listening to someone talk. And the distinctive sound in each case leads me to think of the equally distinctive person I associate with that voice. So, whenever I hear the word "voice" applied to a personal essay or essayist, or whenever I use it that way myself, I'm naturally inclined to imagine a particular person, the author of the piece, talking or conversing, musing or reflecting—giving voice to recollection and perception, thought and feeling, in an audibly distinctive way. I realize, of course, that the voice I hear is not spoken; it's written. And therefore it's not really audible, except in my mind's ear, unless I happen to be reading it aloud or hear it read aloud by someone else, such as its author, in which case it's mediated by a distinctly different kind of voice from its own—spoken rather than written. I also realize that voice literally refers to a vocal sound so distinctive to each person that it could never actually be reproduced or even approximated in writing. One's voiceprint is as unique as one's fingerprint. Still, personal essayists have perenially been so adept at creating the illusion of a spoken voice, a conversational manner, a "familiar style" (viii, 242), as Hazlitt calls it, that even when I'm silently reading an essay, I often find myself resonating with something hauntingly akin to the sound of a person's voice, the sense of a human presence, as if there were another person inside my head or in the same room, carrying on a conversation with me.

The desire to create such an illusion in the personal essay can be traced to Montaigne's espousal of a spontaneous conversational voice—"I speak to my paper as I speak to the first man I meet" (599). Although Montaigne's self-conscious announcement suggests that his professedly "simple, natural, ordinary fashion" (2) might have been as studied as the "artifice" (2) he sought to avoid, his commitment to "speak" in such a way constitutes so powerful a precedent that echoes of it can repeatedly be heard in the commentary of other personal essayists on the essay. Hazlitt, for example, looks back upon Montaigne as "the first person who in his Essays . . . had the courage to say as an author what he felt as a man. . . . He does not converse with us like a pedagogue to his pupil . . . but like a philosopher and friend . . ." (vi, 92). Lamb, in turn, pays special attention to the "uniformly conversational" quality of Hazlitt's essays, which "resemble occasionally the *talk* of a very clever person, when he begins to be animated in a convivial party" (302). Virginia Woolf bears witness to such an audible sense of connection that she claims to "look back upon essay after essay by Mr. Beerbohm, knowing that, come September or May, we shall sit down with them and talk" (223), as if to imply that Beerbohm's essays are so animated by a distinctive voice that she could virtually carry on a conversation with them. Edward Hoagland (1982) does not go quite so far as to imagine himself capable of sitting down and talking with the essays he reads, but he does believe that "A personal essay is like the human voice talking, its order the mind's natural flow" (25); that its "emphasis" is "upon mind speaking to mind" (25); and that "through its tone and tumbling progression, it conveys the quality of the author's mind" (27).

As these passages and my own experience suggest, the voice in a personal essay often seems so spontaneous and immediate that it leads one to feel in touch with something animate and sentient beyond the essay—a human presence, or some aspect of human existence, that for lack of a better word one may refer to as the essayist, or the voice of the essayist, or the mind of the essayist, or the personality of the essayist, or the persona of the essayist. Even essayists who are not professedly spontaneous or conversational evidently have voices distinctive enough or dramatic enough to create an illusion of personal presence. Joyce Carol Oates (1991), for example, remembers the childhood experience of being "utterly captivated by another's voice sounding in my ears" (xiv), so much so that she not only considered such essayists as Emerson and Thoreau to be "voices of adult authenticity" (xiv), but also came to believe that "the writing attributed to them *was* them" (xv). In some sense, of course, the voice in a personal essay does put one in connection with its author, more directly and closely perhaps than any other form of writing, except perhaps a personal letter. But the nature of that connection is inherently so tangled and indefinite, as well as so variable from one essay or essayist to the next, that despite the strong inclination of some commentators to talk about "authentic voice," one cannot reliably define or describe the connection beyond asserting that it exists. To determine the authenticity of an essayist's voice in any particular essay, one would, after all, have to know as much about that essayist's inner life, public behavior, and personal experience as the essayist herself.

Essayists, in fact, rarely claim to achieve an authentic match between their voice and themselves. Instead, they tend to acknowledge some kind of difference and to speak of their essayistic voice or personality as involving an element of imposture. Montaigne, for example, despite his professed commitment to a "simple, natural, ordinary fashion" (2) gradually comes to acknowledge the artifice in his seemingly natural voice—"I am quite conscious that sometimes I let myself go too far, and that in the effort to avoid art and affectation, I fall back into them in another direction" (484). E. B. White does not make any pretense about the authenticity of his voice, but claims instead that "The essayist . . . can pull on any sort of shirt, be any sort of person, according to his mood or his subject matter" (1977, vii), and admits that "I have worn many shirts, and not all them have been a good fit" (viii). In a similar vein, Nancy Mairs (1990), whose intensely personal essays might seem to be unrehearsed confessions, openly acknowledges that "I am not the woman whose voice animates my essays. She's made up. . . . But I am more the woman of my essays than I am the woman of my fiction" (7). Even Scott Sanders (1991), who proclaims that "In the essay, you had better speak from a region pretty close to the heart or the reader will detect the wind of phoniness whistling through your hollow phrases" (191), also acknowledges that "What we meet on the page is not the flesh and blood author, but a simulacrum, a character who wears the label *I*" (201).

Essayistic voice, according to these essayists, is evidently both an authentic and a fictionalized projection of personality, a resonance that is indisputably related to its author's sense of self but that is also a complex illusion of self. To some extent, this paradoxical combination of qualities is a consequence of the fact that an essayist's voice or written presence, though created by its author, is, as Sanders indicates, "a simulacrum, a character" (201) made of words rather than of flesh and blood and thus cannot possibly be a fully authentic reflection of the self even though it is an expression of self. But as Sanders's consciousness of role-playing suggests, the paradoxical quality of an essayist's voice also arises out of the natural desire to put on a mask, to impersonate "a character," even (or perhaps, especially) in a personal essay. The irresistible appeal of role-playing is suggested by E. B. White's exuberant listing of the parts an essayist can perform—"philosopher, scold, jester, raconteur, confidant, pundit, devil's advocate, enthusiast" (vii). Edward Hoagland bears witness to a similar enthusiasm for role-playing in his assertion that "the artful 'I' of an essay can be as chameleon as any narrator in fiction" (26). Essayistic role-playing has its historical roots, of course, in the practices of the periodical essayists, whom Hazlitt properly describes as having "assumed some fictitious and humorous disguise, which, however, in a great degree corresponded to their own peculiar habits and character" (VI, 95). But the ultimate roots of such impersonation probably should be traced to the paradox that exists at the heart of any personal essay, which by virtue of being an act of self-dramatization is at once a masking and an unveiling, a creation and evocation of self. Or as Montaigne says, "I have no more made my book than my book has made me" (504).

In a very real sense, then, one might go so far as to say that voice in the personal essay is an enigma, as Virginia Woolf implies in her paradoxical remarks about Beerbohm:

> He has brought personality into literature, not unconsciously and impurely, but so consciously and purely that we do not know whether there is any relation between Max the essayist and Mr. Beerbohm the man. We only know that the spirit of personality permeates every word that he writes. The triumph is the triumph of style. For it is only by knowing how to write that you can make use in literature of yourself; that self which, while it is essential to literature, is also its most dangerous antagonist. Never to be yourself and yet always—that is the problem. (222)

The insistently paradoxical mode of Woolf's comments not only about Beerbohm but also about the place of personality in an essay, as well as about the relation of it to the self of an essayist, eloquently reflects the enigmatic nature of the connection between an essayist's voice and self.

Though the connection between voice and self is evidently so problematic that Woolf does not even know if it exists at all, the familiar expressions that figure in discussions of voice tend to suggest otherwise. Such expressions as "having one's own voice," or "having an authentic voice," or "having a distinctive personal voice," or "having the immediacy of a real voice" predicate so intimate a connection as to imply that voice is a fully authentic expression and reflection of self. The grammatically singular form of such expressions also tends to suggest that voice is singular not only in the sense of being distinctive or unique, but also in the sense of being a single, unified entity in and of itself. The singular grammatical form of those expressions is, in fact, so deeply ingrained in the idiom that it would be strange, indeed, even in a postmodern age, to hear someone speak of an essayist as "having authentic voices," or "having his own voices," or "having distinctive personal voices," though E. B. White's remark about having "worn many shirts" (viii) or Edward Hoagland's about "the chameleon" (26) nature of essayists might invite one to think of them as having created such multivoiced selves in their essays. Such remarks might at least suggest that an essayist's voice is likely to change from time to time, as Nancy Mairs acknowledges in her declaration that "I have indeed always had *a* voice, but it wasn't *this* voice" (92), and as Geoffrey Wolff (1989) displays in a vividly detailed chronicle of his protean voice, which he describes as having turned from "puffed-up gravitas" (xvi) to being "increasingly intimate" (xxvi) to being "willing to lighten up, to giggle, to play the fool" (xxvi) to being inspired by the "high-voltage, high-pitched, bully great ruckus" (xxvii) of the sixties to being "less cocksure, I think, more sociable (on the page)" (xxxv).

Despite such confessions, the inclination remains quite strong to perceive every personal essayist as having a single, unchanging voice. Even so thoughtful a contemporary essayist as Scott Sanders cannot resist the temptation:

> It is the *singularity* of the first person—its warts and crotchets and turn of voice—that lures many of us into reading essays, and that lingers with us after we finish. Consider the lonely, melancholy persona of Loren Eiseley, forever wandering, forever brooding on our dim and bestial past, his lips frosty with the chill of the Ice Age. Consider the volatile, Dionysian persona of D. H. Lawrence, with his incandescent gaze, his habit of turning peasants into gods and trees into flames, his quick hatred and quicker love. Consider that philosophical farmer, Wendell Berry, who speaks with a countryman's knowledge and a deacon's severity. Consider E. B. White, with his cheery affection for brown eggs and dachshunds, his unflappable way of herding geese while the radio warns of an approaching hurricane. (1991, 196–97)

It would be all too easy to mock such tidy, one-dimensional characterizations—one might even call them caricatures—were I not conscious of having been long inclined to focus on such singular, distinctive, and persistent qualities in my own reading of personal essayists. I'm still beguiled, for example, by my own tidy impression of White, as he of the disarmingly modest, engagingly candid, and wryly humorous voice—the plain style, saltwater farmer, sharing the experience and insight born out of his pastoral retreat from the city. I still take pleasure in that voice, still feel its special resonances whenever I turn to his essays, still hear it linger in my ears long after I've finished one of his pieces, even though I've come to realize that the resonance arises from a highly selective perception of White's essays. I hear what I want to hear.

To some extent, of course, we all hear selectively, picking up some frequencies and tuning out others, particularly given the natural tendency to look for continuities in the several works of any author with whom one is familiar. Selective perception, however, is so pronounced in the way we listen to personal essayists that it seems to be the result of a compulsion to dwell on the recurring aspects of an author's voice and thereby invest them with special weight and significance, as Sanders does in his characterizations of Eiseley, Lawrence, Berry, and White. If Sanders is correct, if "the *singularity* of the first person" (196) is, indeed, what "lures many of us into reading essays" (196) and what "lingers with us after we finish" (196), then it would seem to be the case that our attachment to the personal essay is occasioned in large part by a hunger not just for what he refers to as "an idiosyncratic voice in an era of anonymous babble" (190), but also for a stable personality in an unstable time, someone who like Eiseley is "forever brooding" (196), or like Lawrence is forever "volatile" (196), or like Berry is forever "philosophical" (196), or like White is forever "cheery" (197). Even (or perhaps, especially) in a postmodern age, many readers, it would seem, still hunger for the assurance of being able to find a strong sense of continuity—to hear a distinctively stable voice—throughout the work of any individual author. And personal essayists can clearly be used to satisfy that hunger, as I and many others have discovered to our satisfaction and self-delusion.

But I have a hunch that such a selective perception of personal essayists may arise not only from an innate hunger to hear continuities of voice but also from so strong an identification with a particular essayist as to obscure the perception of any changes or modulations in that essayist's voice. When I first made the acquaintance of E. B. White's essays, for example, they talked to me, it seemed, in so direct and genial a voice about experiences so akin to my own that I could easily have imagined they were addressed to me and me alone. I too was living near the Maine coast and was learning my way around a sailboat and in turn around the coves, the channels, the inlets, and the islands of its rocky shoreline, as White had some twenty years before. And before my years in Maine, I had lived on a small acreage in upstate New York, where I tended a little flock of hens and a few ducks, as White had been doing from the time he started living in Maine. So I felt a special kinship with his farming adventures, as well as with his saltwater perspective. I too lamented "the shape of television" as well as the end of passenger service on the Maine railroads. And I too had a young son, then only a few years old, who I imagined I might take fishing someday on a lake in Maine. So for these and a host of other coincidences, the voice of White's essays resonated for me like a haunting echo of my own experience—an echo that became even more arresting when I discovered that my interest in the craft of prose had its counterpart in his devotion to "the elements of style." Now, some thirty-five years later, I'm living in Iowa rather than Maine, and I've only been back there for a couple of brief visits. I haven't done any sailing since I left Maine, I don't keep hens anymore, I don't worry much about the state of television, and I never did take my boy to that lake in Maine, though we did get to a reasonable facsimile in Wisconsin. Except for tending a vegetable garden and worrying about the land as well as about the niceties of prose style, my experience nowadays has so little in common with White's that I can see him, I think, more dispassionately and more clearly than I once did.

Sometimes, however, it takes more than a change in one's personal circumstances to open one's ears to the changes or modulations or variations in an essayist's voice. In my own case, for example, I'd been living in Iowa for some fifteen years before White publicly acknowledged that he had "worn many shirts" (viii), and it was another ten years before I took that remark seriously enough to sense that it might be a significant bit of information about the voice and personality in his essays. In fact, I didn't begin to notice the variations in White's voice until just a few years ago, when I was rereading "Once More to the Lake," "The Ring of Time," and "The Geese," for an article I planned to write about White's preoccupation with time, change, and mortality. Though I'd read those essays many times before, I didn't remember any significant differences in his voice from one piece to the next, except of course for tonal differences occasioned by differences in his mood or subject matter, such as the reverie in his early memories of the lake, the admiration in his description of the young circus rider, the sorrow in his account of the defeated old gander. But this time, perhaps because I was reading the essays in close conjunction with each other, I found myself noticing substantial differences in his voice and his implied personality from the very beginning of each essay—differences that dramatically outweighed any similarities in the well-known plainness of his language, wryness of his humor, modesty of his self-depiction, or nostalgia of his general outlook. The differences were so clearcut that I could hear them right off at the beginning of each piece. But I didn't at the time have a satisfactory way of defining or describing, much less of interpreting, those differences, nor could I find any help in scholarly or textbook commentaries on the essay. Most discussions of the essay, even of the personal essay, invariably focus so heavily on matters other than voice, such as the story, or the structure, or the imagery, or the style, or the ideas, that they deal with the essayist's voice, personality or persona only in passing. And even the few that do touch upon such matters tend to offer quite broad descriptions of voice and personality with little reference to specific passages and virtually no guidance in methods of analysis.

It's difficult, of course, to get a quick or sure grasp of an essayist's voice, because it's not directly stated, like an idea or a feeling, nor is it directly reported, like a story or a scene, and therefore it doesn't make a direct or immediate claim upon one's attention, unless it is dramatically heightened in one way or another, as in the stripped-down style of Hemingway's essays or in the hyped-up style of Tom Wolfe's essays. Indeed, an essayist's voice is often so deeply embedded in the more prominent aspects of an essay that it is quite easy to ignore. Given so implicit and elusive a phenomenon, I've come to believe that one can only get a clear, precise, and exacting perception of it by examining specific passages from essays as closely and as painstakingly as if one were reading the lines of a lyric poem or a dramatic monologue, with an ear to the nuances of the speaker's voice. Such a method of analysis, of course, is so time-consuming, given the length of most essays, that common sense forbids the wholesale use of it. But some personal essays are so complexly and richly voiced as to warrant a detailed analysis of this kind, and most personal essays will benefit from being read at least with the heightened awareness of voice, that one can develop by doing some close analysis of a few specific passages. So, in the following section of this piece I propose to look closely at a few passages from "Once More to the Lake," "The Ring of Time," and "The Geese," not only to illustrate the method of analysis that I suggest, but also to hear White's changing voice in these essays, and thereby, I hope, get some further insight into the workings of voice and personality in the personal essay.

The best place to begin listening closely to voice in a personal essay is at the beginning of the essay. As with any human encounter, of course, the first impression one gets of an essayist's personality is likely to be modified, complicated, possibly even reversed, by later passages, but as in any human encounter one's enjoyment and understanding of an essayist's presence are most likely to arise from the sense of a deepening relationship that can only be attained by paying close attention to someone from the very start. I've also found that one's initial impression of voice in an essay is likely to be sharpened and clarified by hearing it side by side with the opening voice in another essay or two by the same author. So, I've reproduced below the first two sentences from "Once More to the Lake," "The Ring of Time," and "The Geese." Here is how White sounds at the opening of "Once More to the Lake":

> One summer, along about 1904, my father rented a camp on a lake in Maine and took us all there for the month of August. We all got ringworm from some kittens and had to rub Pond's Extract on our arms and legs night and morning, and my father rolled over in a canoe with all his clothes on; but outside of that the vacation was a success and from then on none of us ever thought there was any place in the world like that lake in Maine. (197)

Here he is at the beginning of "The Ring of Time":

> After the lions had returned to their cages, creeping angrily through the chutes, a little bunch of us drifted away and into an open doorway nearby, where we stood for a while in semidarkness, watching a big brown circus horse go harumphing around the practice ring. His trainer was a woman of about forty, and the two of them, horse and woman, seemed caught up in one of those desultory treadmills of afternoon from which there is no apparent escape. (142)

And here he is at the opening of "The Geese":

> To give a clear account of what took place in the barnyard early in the morning on that last Sunday in June, I will have to go back more than a year in time, but a year is nothing to me these days. Besides, I intend to be quick about it, and not dawdle. (62)

In looking over these three narrative passages, I'm struck right off by how different a storyteller and how different a person White appears to be just in the first sentence of each. In "Once More to the Lake," for example, he's careful to begin by giving a clearly stated and relatively full set of information about the time and place of his memory, but he's not so fussy as to bother about identifying the exact location of the lake or the exact year of the experience he's remembering. It's enough to know that the experience took place at "a camp on a lake in Maine," during "the month of August," "along about 1904." His willingness to be openly uncertain about the year and to register his uncertainty in that old-fashioned colloquial expression, "along about," tends to create the impression of someone who's relaxed and at ease with himself. His uncertainty about the exact year, together with the indefiniteness of the opening phrase, "one summer," which seems faintly reminiscent of "once upon a time," also suggests that he looks upon that summer experience as being in a distant past, as far removed but as affectionately remembered as a childhood fairy tale. And as if to suggest that he's somewhat in the mood and voice of a remembering child, he uses the idiom of a child in saying that "my father . . . took us all there. . . ."

In the first sentence of "The Ring of Time," by contrast, White doesn't offer any expository information whatsoever, but jumps right into the middle of things, giving me no time to catch my breath or locate myself until the end of his complex opening sentence, when I discover that he's evidently remembering an experience in which he and a group of others were watching some circus animals going through their paces. He comes across, therefore, as being so immersed in his recollection of the lions and the horse that he's forgotten the usual obligation of a storyteller to reveal the time and place of his story as clearly and as quickly as possible. And yet in describing the lions, "creeping angrily through the chutes," and the "big brown circus horse . . . harumphing around the practice ring," he seems to be much more concerned with conveying details precisely and expressively than he did in the first sentence of "Once More to the Lake." So, by contrast with "Once More to the Lake," he speaks in the voice of a careful observer rather than a wistful rememberer.

In the opening sentence of "The Geese," by contrast with the other two pieces, White pays less attention to the details of his story than he does to himself and to his task as a storyteller. In the course of his first sentence, for example, the only information he divulges about his story is that it concerns something that "took place in the barnyard early in the morning on that last Sunday in June." But the structure of his opening sentence subordinates even that tantalizingly little bit of information to his announcement that "in order to give a clear account of what took place . . . I will have to go back more than a year in time, but a year in time is nothing to me these days." In the first part of that unusually formal announcement White speaks in a voice suggestive of a detective or some other kind of public official, huffing and puffing himself up with a declaration of his official responsibilities. But in the last clause of the sentence, "a year is nothing to me these days," which sounds quite relaxed and colloquial by comparison with the opening, he seems more concerned with letting us know that though he's on in years and conscious of his age, he's also proud of his ability to move nimbly back and forth across the events of a single year. Overall, then, the opening sentence of "The Geese" displays White in a somewhat self-conscious and humorously discordant voice, posturing as the official barnyard detective or chronicler, whose age has enhanced rather than diminished his memory of events.

Having noted how differently White comes across in the first sentence of each piece, let me step back for a moment to make clear how I've been reading these passages in order to get so distinct a sense of his differing voices and stances. In each case, I've been trying to make myself acutely aware of what every utterance, every nuance in wording and phrasing, suggests about White's voice and personality, as if he were the character in a dramatic monologue or the speaker in a lyric poem. Given the narrative mode of these passages, I've also been reading them as if they were the opening passages from short stories, especially short stories with first-person narrators, whose temperament and personality are usually as important as the stories they have to tell. Though the essay is often considered to be a distinctly different kind of writing from poetry, drama, and fiction, the personal essay does, after all, combine elements of poetic, dramatic, and narrative utterance, so it seems only fitting that it be read in similar ways. Indeed, if one reads successive statements in an essay as one might the utterances of the speaker in a dramatic monologue or the character in a play or the narrator in a short story, then it is possible to perceive them as gradually creating the impression of a quite complexly voiced personality.

To see how White's voice develops in these passages, I'd like to look closely at the second sentence of each. In "Once More to the Lake," I'm immediately struck by how fully and dramatically the second sentence resonates with the childlike voice that seemed faintly present at the end of the first. The pervasively childlike quality of this sentence emerges not only from the verb "got" and the indefinite adjective "some" in the opening clause, "We all got ringworm from some kittens," but also from the very simple, heavily monosyllabic diction that prevails throughout the second sentence. Above all, the childlike voice emerges from the simplistic grammar of the syntax, from the exuberant and excessive compounding of nouns, verb phrases, and clauses that pile up throughout that sentence, much as they might in the eager talk of a youngster carried away by the heady rush of remembering—"We all got ringworm from some kittens and had to rub Pond's Extract on our arms and legs night and morning, and my father rolled over in a canoe with all his clothes on, but outside of that the vacation was a success and from then on none of us ever thought there was any place in the world like that lake in Maine."

The second sentence of "The Ring of Time," far from sounding childlike, conveys the air of someone who's not only old enough and discerning enough to feel confident about identifying the age of others—"His trainer was a woman of about forty"—but is also experienced enough and jaded enough to know something himself about "those desultory treadmills of afternoon from which there is no apparent escape." The knowing outlook, the sophisticated diction, and the complex syntax of that noun clause also project White in a more worldly wise posture than he appears to have adopted in the first sentence of this piece, where he comes off as being an expressive observer and detailed reporter, but not much more, attuned as he is primarily to the "harumphing" sound that the horse makes as it goes "around the practice ring."

In the second sentence of "The Geese," by contrast, White continues to speak in the no-nonsense, self-important style and voice that he has assumed from the start of that piece. And as if to authenticate his fitness for the role of official barnyard detective or chronicler, he speaks in an idiom that suggests a plain-talking country farmer rather than a city sophisticate—"Besides, I intend to be quick about it, and not dawdle." If he really intended to be "quick about it," of course, he would have gotten right into his story, rather than dawdling around as he does in this sentence and the one before. So, at the end of this passage, I find myself wondering what to make of this humorously contradictory old-timer and wondering, too, whether he will continue to be so in the story that follows.

In each of these essays and any other essay, for that matter, I find myself wondering what to make of the voice and personality that come across at the beginning and whether they will persist throughout the piece, be modified in some way, or be superseded by a distinctly different resonance and presence. These questions can only be answered by continuing to read with as persistent and detailed an attention to voice as I have tried to give these opening passages. Such a full-scale analysis cannot, of course, be provided here for even one of these essays, much less three, but as an indication of what might be learned from this kind of analysis I'd like to consider a few additional passages from "Once More to the Lake," with an ear to hearing and understanding the range of White's voice in the remainder of that essay.

Just a couple of sentences after the opening passage, White's child-like voice suddenly gives way to the intonations of a much more mature presence:

> I have since become a salt-water man, but sometimes in summer there are days when the restlessness of the tides and the fearful cold of the sea water and the incessant wind that blows across the

> afternoon and into the evening make me wish for the placidity of
> a lake in the woods. (197)

The maturity of that voice is signalled not only by the explicit assertion that "I have since become a salt-water man," but also by the elevation of the language, the evocation of the images, and the sophistication of the syntax in the second clause, containing as it does an elaborate suspension produced by the serial accumulation of three parallel noun phrases. Above all, the maturity of that voice is embodied in the intense sense of adult yearning the sentence expresses for "the placidity" and simplicity of a world that even at this early point in the essay seems to be irretrievably far removed, given the thirty-seven momentous years intervening between the date of White's first visit to the lake, August 1904, which he refers to in the opening of his first sentence, and the dateline of the essay, August 1941, which he notes just above the opening of that sentence.

Faced with two such different voices and persons—childlike and mature—one might well ask which of the two, or what combination of the two, will hold forth during the remainder of the essay, and whether White will speak in any other voices. During most of the essay, White maintains the style and voice of a mature consciousness, as is appropriate, given that the remainder of the piece focuses on the experiences he went through during his week-long return to the lake as a middle-aged man. But occasionally during the essay, he does slip into a somewhat boyish style and idiom, because during his return visit he occasionally found himself totally absorbed by his childhood memories and thus by his boyhood consciousness of things:

> I kept remembering everything, lying in bed in the mornings—the
> small steamboat that had a long rounded stern like the lip of a
> Ubangi, and how quietly she ran on the moonlight sails, when the
> older boys played their mandolins and girls sang and we ate
> doughnuts dipped in sugar, and how sweet the music was on the
> water in the shining night, and what it had felt like to think about
> girls then. (201)

In the course of this passage from the last page or so of the essay, one can distinctly hear White slipping out of a mature perspective and back into the wistfully boyish way of looking at things and piling up recollections that he had exhibited in the second sentence of the essay. Here, as elsewhere in the essay, the childlike grammar and style of repeatedly compounding clauses seems especially evocative, and not just because it enables White to accumulate poignant images of a gentler era long since past, but because it bears witness to the continuing presence in him of two distinctly different selves—both the boyish son who first visited the lake with his father thirty-seven years before, and the middle-aged father who has recently come back with his son to visit the lake again. Indeed, it is the very coexistence within him of these two different selves that gives rise to the confusing sensations that White reports himself as having experienced throughout his return to the lake. So, it is altogether fitting that in the course of this essay White occasionally wavers back and forth between two distinctly different voices, which embody two different ways of thinking and feeling about the lake, about summertime, about the passage of time, and about mortality.

Were I to continue this sort of analysis, I would trace the interplay of these two voices, noting the specific points at which the boyish presence appears, as it does somewhat briefly right before the most unusual moment in the essay, when a decidedly different voice momentarily takes over the piece:

> Summertime, oh, summertime, pattern of life indelible, the fade-proof lake, the woods unshatterable, the pasture with the sweet-fern, forever and ever, summer without end. (200)

This paean to summer, with its opening apostrophe to "summertime" and its celebration of "the fadeproof lake, the woods unshatterable, the pasture with the sweetfern," resonates with the style of neither the boy nor the man but with the voice of a nineteenth-century romantic nature poet. The exultant voice of that paean, however, constitutes the virtual embodiment of the wish animating both man and boy—the wish for "summer without end"—a wish the inflated wording of which ironically suggests its illusoriness, as does the echo of advertising talk in "the *fadeproof* lake." Still, the language of Christian prayer is so resonant in the last two phrases, "forever and ever, summer without end," that the utterance as a whole poignantly implies the terror of mortality and the desire to escape it which is actually at the heart of the essay, though the terror does not make itself explicitly known until the very end of the piece when White suddenly feels "the chill of death" (202).

That final phrase, I've discovered, comes as a surprise to most readers during their first encounter with the essay, and even sometimes on subsequent readings, in part, of course, because the essay doesn't ever seem to be literally or explicitly concerned with mortality until the very end. I've often forgotten the phrase myself in the course of rereading the essay. But I also believe that the evocative tones of White's different voices lull many readers into such a pleasant reverie—a reverie so akin to White's own—that they are completely unprepared for the "chill of death" with which the essay suddenly ends, as unprepared for the chilly recognition of mortality as White himself evidently must have been. So, the essay ends abruptly in a mature voice resonant with the shock of a recognition that creates an audible distance between White and his boyhood self—"As he buckled the belt, suddenly my groin felt the chill of death" (202). "Once More to the Lake," then, is not only a multivoiced essay, but its multiple voices seem to be complexly attuned to the nature and significance of the experience with which the essay is concerned. Indeed, it would not be too much to say that White's multiple voices seem to be a way of enacting or reenacting the experience in the processing of narrating it.

———

If the multivoiced quality of "Once More to the Lake" were unique or unusual among White's essays, I'd have been less inclined to discuss it here in such detail. But the prevalence of this quality is unmistakable in many of his pieces and thus has implications for an understanding of voice and personality in the personal essay. In the two parts of "The Ring of Time," for example, White sustains an even more complex array of voices and postures. In the first part, which is centered on the enchanting spectacle of a young circus girl riding her horse around the practice ring, White gradually emerges from the somewhat jaded, sophisticated voice he had assumed at the beginning of the piece and becomes a role-playing acrobat himself, first stepping forward in a playfully self-regarding comment on his status as "recording secretary for one of the oldest societies—the society of those who, at one time or another, have surrendered, without even a show of resistance to the bedazzlement of a circus rider" (143). Then just a bit later, he turns from being the playfully confessional enthusiast of the circus to speaking in the voice of a much more thoughtful, even philosophical observer, when the young circus rider makes him "painfully conscious" (144), as he puts it, "of the element of time" (144). Then just a few paragraphs later, he reclaims the voice of a playfully self-regarding commentator, this time on his supposedly failed acrobatics as a writer (145). So, in just this brief segment, White appears in at least three distinctly different voices and guises, each occasioned, it seems, by his shifting perceptions, thoughts, and feelings about the circus rider's performance, about his own performance, and about the ring of time.

In yet another display of his chameleon-like behavior, White speaks in a somewhat different set of voices during the second segment of "The Ring of Time," as he tries not only to evoke the rhythm of life and the movement of time in the South, but also to reflect upon racial problems in the unintegrated South of the 1950s. At the beginning of the second segment, for example, he appears in the guise of a verbal musician, playing a riff upon the letter "s": "Everywhere, for the appreciative visitor, the letter 's' insinuates itself in the scene: in the sound of sea and sand, in the singing shell, in the heat of sun and sky, in the sultriness of the gentle hours, in the siesta, in the stir of birds and insects" (145–46). A couple of pages later, however, reflecting on the Southern resistance to racial integration, he assumes the voice of a very deft social critic: "Probably the first slave ship, with Negroes lying in chains on its decks, seemed commonsensical to the owners who operated it and to the planters who patronized it. But such a vessel would not be in the realm of common sense today" (148). And then just a couple of paragraphs later, the voice of the social critic gives way to the stance of the vacationer: "Lying in the warm comfort by the sea, you receive gratefully the gift of the sun, the gift of the South" (148).

Confronted by such a dazzling array of voices and poses as one finds both in "The Ring of Time" and in "The Geese"—where White speaks not only in the voice of the crusty barnyard detective, but also in the voices of an overly fretful farmer (64), a witty raconteur (65), and a compassionate old man (67–68)—one might be moved to wonder if there is any element of consistency in White's essayistic self, or if he assumes so many different voices and postures as to have no abiding and distinctive voice at all. One might also wonder just how typical White's multivoiced behavior is of other personal essayists, and what such behavior suggests about the nature of voice and personality in the personal essay.

At first thought, it's tempting to answer the questions about White's voice by noting that, despite the wide range of distinctly different voices resonating in many of his essays, there's also a recurrent voice that tends to prevail or predominate or have the last word in many of those essays, such as the voice of the mature man who holds forth in "Once More to the Lake," or the discerning social critic who emerges in the second segment of "The Ring of Time," or the compassionate barnyard observer who laments the fate of the old gander at the end of "The Geese." But in each case, these serious voices often alternate with playful or wryly humorous sides of White's essayistic personality that it would be misleading to slight or ignore. In fact, White traverses a wide tonal or attitudinal range in many of his essays, and not just from one essay to the next, but often from one segment or paragraph of an essay to the next. Given his tendency to move quickly and deftly from the nostalgic to the buoyant, the reflective to the playful, the sardonic to the comic, and back again, it seems difficult to pin him down, especially when one recognizes that he tends to dramatize those different states of mind and feeling by embodying them in distinctly different voices. His voice encompasses such a wide range of voices that perhaps it would be most accurate to talk about the voice(s), or the multivoiced personality, of E. B. White.

Against such a view, it might be argued, I realize, that White's voice is ultimately determined by the plain wording, the careful phrasing, the meticulously and vividly detailed description to be found in most of his essays. His style, one might say, is completely in keeping with the rules laid down in Strunk and White—rules that have the effect of producing a candid and unpretentious voice, the voice of someone whose statements can be taken at face value. But those stylistic traits, no matter how distinctive they seem to be, do not constitute the sole source of White's voice, as one can see by looking at the following piece of description:

> Before the swallow, before the daffodil, and not much later than the snowdrop, the common toad salutes the coming of spring after his own fashion, which is to emerge from a hole in the ground, where he has lain buried since the previous autumn, and crawl as rapidly as possible toward the nearest suitable patch of water. (383)

This piece of natural observation has all the characteristic marks of White's prose style: the plain and simple words, almost all just one or two syllables long as in the opening of "Once More to the Lake"; the parallel phrasing of coordinate ideas as stipulated in Strunk and White; the vividly detailed and well-informed description of the toad's behavior; and the witty, but understated personification of the toad who "salutes the coming of spring after his own fashion." But as it happens, this sentence and others exactly like it come from the opening of an essay by George Orwell, "Some Thoughts on the Common Toad" (1956). Though style is a significant determinant of voice, it's evidently not the sole determinant. Equally important is the character of the human presence that one creates out of any particular style, and in this particular passage Orwell is typically self-effacing, rather than "congenitally self-centered" (vii), as White exuberantly professes to be. So, the passage lacks the self-conscious presence of White observing the toad that I would expect to find in one of his essays.

Though White's chameleon-like behavior may seem unusual or extreme, it represents, I think, a quality that is evident, though perhaps to a somewhat lesser degree, in many personal essayists. Lamb and Hazlitt come immediately to mind, as do Beerbohm and Forster, and more recently James Baldwin, Tom Wolfe, Norman Mailer, Joan Didion, Annie Dillard, Richard Selzer, and Alice Walker. Most human beings, in fact, perform a variety of roles during just a single day in their lives, as they move back and forth between a variety of public and private situations, so it's hardly surprising that an essayist, as White says, "can pull on any sort of shirt, be any sort of person, according to his mood or subject matter" (vii). Indeed, one might even claim that the capacity and willingness to do so are essential to the creation of authentically personal essays—essays, that is, in which a personality comes to life in something like the rich variety of its actual being. The drama of one's personality depends, after all, on the *dramatis personae* one is capable of performing. I don't, of course, mean to imply that every personal essay and essayist is, or need be, multivoiced. But I do believe that the myth of a singular and unchanging voice has tended to distort the perception and understanding of personal essays and essayists. And it may also have subverted instruction in the writing of personal essays. How many teachers of writing, I wonder, invite their students to produce essays in which they play a variety of roles, put on a variety of shirts, speak in a variety of voices? How many even invite their students to try out different voices in different essays? How many invite them to write personal essays that are true to the range and richness of their actual voices?

The myth of "finding one's voice" strongly implies that once having found it, one will never lose it, never change it. But the nature of experience suggests otherwise, as Montaigne makes clear in his Heraclitean assertion that "I may presently change, not only by chance, but also by intention" (611), and as Didion (1968) bears witness to when she declares that "keeping a notebook" is a way "to keep in touch with the people we used to be, whether we find them attractive company or not" (139). So, it's not surprising that Didion's voice seems to have changed quite drastically in *After Henry* (1992), her most recent collection of personal essays, which no longer resonate with the emotionally evocative echoes of her earlier fondness for anaphora, but instead broodingly work their way through suspended sentences, the grammar of which is complicated by extended listings of information and detail. So, too, the changing voices I've noted in White's three essays may be the result of his having written them fifteen years apart—"Once More to the Lake" in 1940, when he was 41, "The Ring of Time" in 1955, when he was 56, and "The Geese" in 1970, when he was 71. So, after all, the voices of personal essayists may be more deeply expressive of themselves than anything they could say to us in person.

Works Cited

Didion, Joan. 1968. *Slouching towards Bethlehem.* New York: Dell.

———. 1992. *After Henry.* New York: Simon and Schuster.

Hazlitt, William. 1931. *The Complete Works of William Hazlitt.* London: Dent.

Hoagland, Edward. 1982. *The Tugman's Passage.* New York: Random House.

Lamb, Charles. 1980. *Lamb as Critic.* Edited by Roy Park. Lincoln: University of Nebraska Press.

Mairs, Nancy. 1990. *Carnal Acts: Essays.* New York: HarperCollins.

Montaigne, Michel de. 1957. *The Complete Works.* Translated by Donald M. Frame. Stanford, CA: Stanford University Press.

Oates, Joyce Carol. 1991. *The Best American Essays 1991.* New York: Ticknor & Fields.

Orwell, George. 1956. *The Orwell Reader.* New York: Harcourt, Brace and Company.

Sanders, Scott Russell. 1991. *Secrets of the Universe.* Boston: Beacon.

White, E. B. 1977. *Essays of E. B. White.* New York: Harper & Row.

Wolff, Geoffrey. 1989. *The Best American Essays 1989.* New York: Ticknor & Fields.

Woolf, Virginia. 1953. *The Common Reader.* New York: Harcourt, Brace, Jovanovich.

8 The Difference It Makes to Speak: The Voice of Authority in Joan Didion

Laura Julier
Michigan State University

I want to tell you a story about my reading of Joan Didion. It is a story in which finally I have come to see her essays—her literary nonfiction—as attempts to tackle the dilemma described by Virginia Woolf in "Professions for Women" (1942): what it is like to try to go against the grain of internalized dominant cultural voices, or in Woolf's terms, to try to write while the Angel in the House hovers over our shoulders, whispering all those cultural messages about what women are supposed to be and do. Woolf's Angel, an embodiment of Victorian ideals, told her to "flatter, deceive . . . never let anybody guess that you have a mind of your own" (237). "Had I not killed her," Woolf writes, "she would have killed me" (238). The room of one's own and the annual income may be secured, Woolf says, but what does one do about the more subtle, more invisible warping of thought that occurs in the imaginations of women? How to silence the voice of the Angel, the internalized and powerful voices which define women's experience and identity, and prescribe even what it is possible to talk about? How, she might have asked, to have a voice of one's own?

My own voice has always been problematic. When I was in the third and fourth and fifth grades, I could not be heard by the teacher, even from the front row. I was told all through those years in school (and all through the university, and even now) to speak up. At home, my mother told me I had a loud voice and a big mouth, a voice like my father's side of the family, not a "nice" voice, which was of course a coded way of telling me that it was not the right voice for a girl. I also spoke about unspeakable things, things my family did not want named. To my mother, what I said and how I sounded were indistinguishable. In university classes in which the males outnumbered the females, I can remember sitting day after day, counting down as each of my classmates raised their voices in discussion or to ask a question, keeping track of the dwindling number left who, like me, had not yet spoken,

130

marking down the time until there was only me, and I would not speak at all, imagining how everyone would at that point turn to see who it was who had suddenly raised her voice. I spent the entire term silent and accepted whatever grade resulted.

Much later, when I had moved from the East Coast to the Midwest, and friends there told me that my voice was abrasive, they did not mean that it was gravelly or shrill or loud. They were referring rather to the way in which I addressed myself and spoke up or held forth. My regional upbringing had trained this loud voice, my socialization as a female urged a soft and conciliatory one, and my family background had imposed unpalatable consequences for speaking out. The quality of voice that is pitch had always been meshed for me with one's right to speak, to name one's experience, to voice oneself into being. What, I have always wondered, sometimes with shame, am I to do with my voice? What does it mean to have a voice?

It was by noticing the responses to my own voice that I learned to think better about Didion's. I was captivated by Didion's essays long ago because of something that seemed powerful to me, something I believed I recognized. I was caught by some part in the rhythm, the turns, the patterns that I reflexively called her voice, long before I thought ideologically about what it meant to be a woman, or a woman writing, and certainly long before I was aware that what I had struggled with about my own voice was not so much a personal problem as a set of distinctly gendered cultural messages with which many women struggled. Back then, all I knew was that in some way Didion spoke from the page in ways I heard myself speaking, and in some strange sense, I felt this voice coming from inside my own head, as if her voice were my voice. As I continued reading, I came to realize that I was drawn by a powerful sense of identity with what has been called the intense, often incantatory voice in her essays. And as I became more aware of myself as a woman reading, I found myself deeply moved to find someone writing powerfully about what it is like to feel marginalized or dysfunctional, trying to live and breathe and be in a culture from which one feels profoundly distanced. For me, it was a culture in which oppressions of all kinds were being protested but which continued silent on the particular oppression—so much of it internalized—that I saw and felt in the women around me.

There followed a period of years when my reactions to this voice were strongly negative, because I was becoming inclined to hear it as artificial, masked, safely clothed in appropriately gendered patterns. As a woman reader who was discovering the explicit naming of women's victimization and the sins of patriarchy, I became wary of Didion's essays. Instead of raising her voice, instead of speaking out strongly, Didion seemed to settle for the role of a frail, pained woman, refused to identify that alienation as having anything to do with being a woman or to take an explicit stance against women's victimization, and indeed scoffed in "The Women's Movement" at the idea that women were victimized, though she called herself a victim in one interview (Kakutani 1984, 31). We were, some of us, learning strength, learning to say no, learning what to say no to. It was threatening to be reminded of the pervasive power of patriarchal culture to undermine us, of all the ways it has always hit below the belt, so to speak. So, at an earlier period in my reading of Didion, I wanted, with Woolf, to slay every Angel in her House, especially the ones which seemed to whisper that it was all a personal problem of adjustment. These Angels hovering over Didion's shoulder seemed to urge a requisite whine, highly self-conscious and all, but helpless in the end. I wanted to kill her.

This response of mine was extreme, of course, precisely because I found Didion's voice simultaneously so compelling and so disturbing. And so I reasoned that it might be useful to see what other readers have had to say about the voice in her essays, to see how they speak about it and what they say, and what they attend to as distinctively recognizable, and so perhaps also to see what it is we mean by the very concept of voice in the essay.

Of the scholarly and critical writing about Didion's work, most focuses on her fiction, while the writing on her literary nonfiction has been limited: either it is read as simple autobiography, or in order to provide clues about her fiction.[1] While reviewers and critics have praised her "spare, elegant prose" (Duffy 1979, 43) and called her essays "obsessive" (43), "elegant and passionate" (Braudy 1977, 65), and "brilliant and inert" (Kazin 1971, 114), none of these refer very clearly or specifically to voice. Only two refer to voice, and they do so metaphorically: one calls the writing lyrical (Schow 1986, 43), and the other says it is "subtly musical in . . . phrasing" (Towers 1979, 30).

Some critics refer to vision, not voice. The "striking characteristic of Didion's work," writes one, is an "excellence of eye" (Stimpson 1973, 37), while to another it is her "clear, cold eye" (Kazin 1971, 122), or her "caustic eye" (Schow 1986, 37), or her "eye for the telling detail" (Kakutani 1984, 31). Another speaks of "the focusing lens through which she searches" (Schow 1986, 45) and refers to her "preternaturally sharp focus" (Towers 1979, 30), while yet another says that she focuses our attention in "a series of verbal snapshots, like a Diane Arbus of prose" (Harrison 1979, 280).

More interesting still are those who speak of Didion's essays in terms of psychology: *The White Album* (1979) is called "journalism-as-nervous-breakdown," "its effectiveness" attributed to the "use to which personal neurosis has been put" (Towers 1979, 1). She is called "self-indulgent" (Hulbert 1979, 36), her voice alive with "nerve-frayed awareness" (Towers 1979, 30).

But most interesting—or disturbing—is the pervasive, almost obligatory confusion between voice and body, as though her physical appearance were a map to her prose style. Describing the jacket photo of Didion, one writes: she has "enormous, haunted eyes . . . [like] a wounded bird, menaced and fragile. . . . [T]his alarming vulnerability is an affectation and a part of her strategy as a writer" (Morrow 1979, 69). Another writes:

> At five feet two and ninety-one pounds, Joan Didion does appear slight and delicate and she has been plagued by more than her share of ill health. *Accordingly,* her writing is informed by an exquisite sensibility, forged at least in part by a feeling of personal vulnerability. (Winchell 1980, 25; emphasis mine)

The subtitle of an interview in *Ms* announces, "Frail chronicler of emotional paralysis reveals her toughness" (Braudy 1977, 65). Even Alfred Kazin (1971) writes:

> The thinness, the smallness, the inescapably alarmed fragility of the woman is probably the most important physical element surrounding her and *perhaps explains* the impending sense of catastrophe that informs so much of her work. (114, 116; emphasis mine)

Didion's spare and "elegantly chiseled" (Snyder 1986), precise and cool and "beautifully evocative" (Chace 1987, 3) voice is read in physical appearance: one speaks, it seems, with one's body. And if one is a woman, as Susan Brownmiller (1984) has pointed out, one speaks with one's body in very particular ways.

In these readings by reviewers and academics, then, voice is something variously attended to in musical metaphors, or metaphors for vision, or in terms of psychology, or—most insidious of all—in terms of physical appearance. These last two—especially in their neat congruences between body and voice—seemed to reiterate the kinds of responses I had received and internalized about my own voice: they seem, that is, to read voice unself-consciously in light of gendered behavior and qualities. So while these readings may indeed be descriptive, none of them seemed to adequately deal with my complex response to Didion's voice.

Now the very notion of voice, particularly in the essay, is a slippery thing. Though we talk about it all the time, it is not always clear that we mean the same thing each time. Not only are we listening to some very different things to mark the quality and tenor of voice, but it is also the case that we are referring to different things when we speak of "voice." As Peter Elbow (1989) points out in writing about the literary essay, what we call voice may mean that which we recognize on the telephone as belonging to someone we know, or it may mean what we recognize as a certain kind of person. We may alternately respond to resonance of voice, or the integrity in one's voice, but we also refer to having a voice, as in having the authority to speak, speaking up, and speaking out. It is this last—having the authority to speak—which those sometimes glib, sometimes glittery little quips from the critics and academics evade in their readings of Didion. Indeed what I want to suggest in this essay is that in the progress of my own reading of Didion I was, like these critics, mistaking one thing for another. I had wanted the women to whom I turned to be raising their voices, overpowering those domi-nant cultural voices. I had hoped Didion would claim her authority and her voice by taking her place among them, at the center of things. But because I heard her speaking from the margins, or as she herself said, from the periphery (Didion 1984), I assumed she was giving in to the power of socially legitimated authority to exclude and marginalize her. I did not yet see that one could transform authority. It was only through a careful reading of some of Didion's essays that I came to see that one could transform authority.

On what does one ground one's authority to speak? In "The White Album" (an essay in her collection of the same name), Didion suggests that cultural narratives provide an often unquestioned authority be-cause they are shared, corroborated, and thus a source of comfort. Many times these opening lines of "The White Album"—excerpted as follows—are read as an existentialist statement about the randomness of experience and the essentially arbitrary nature of things:

> We tell ourselves stories in order to live. . . . We live entirely, espe-cially if we are writers, by the imposition of a narrative line upon disparate images, by the "ideas" with which we have learned to freeze the shifting phantasmagoria which is our actual experience. (1979, 11)

Read in the context of the entire essay, however, I would contend that Didion's point is not merely the arbitrariness of the narratives in which we invest ourselves, but rather that the narratives we impose are often inherited, infused with an external authority, and may thus achieve a certain tyranny over us. As in most of the other pieces in *The White Album*, this essay asserts the inadequacy of such cultural narratives: they don't hold up. Furthermore, it's not only that they're inadequate—they lead us astray. If we listen only to them, or borrow their authority, we cannot find or create or come to recognize our own voice, our own authority.

Although in the essay "Georgia O'Keeffe" (also in *The White Album*) Didion praises O'Keeffe's canvasses because they are "clean of received wisdom" (127), ironically what you find in Didion's essays and nonfiction are canvasses filled with received wisdom, filled with culturally sanctioned narratives and meanings—filled, that is, with other voices. But rather than borrowing them to bolster her own authority, Didion is highly conscious of them *as* other voices, of their power to impose, freeze, distort, and silence. I am speaking here of the voices of doctors and psychiatrists, the Army and the diplomatic corps, the media and the studios and the L. A. *Times,* movie stars and bishops and planners of suburban communities, self-serving generals in El Salvador and more than one president of the U.S., the monied, the powerful, the elite. Each implicitly claims authority from its right to speak on behalf of a group or organization, or its status as a representative of a certain field of expertise such as mental health or national security. Each derives its authority, in part, from the cultural status accorded it by means of money or position, elected or appointed, or because of its proximity to power, conferred or acquired. Ironically, the cultural agreement that these voices will be regarded as expert and authoritative is unspoken: we agree to believe them, to hold their meanings and their interpretations to be the most valid, the most informed. Indeed, the cultural collusion is so automatic that often we do not even hear them as "other," so much do they seem to be coming from inside one's own head. And as teachers who design their courses and pedagogical practices to develop critical thinking well know, separating the seemingly univocal into distinct and often conflicting parts is difficult, and problematic. Students are not always thankful. As an acquaintance of mine has pointed out,

> Many people cannot free themselves of other people's voices precisely because they cannot recognize them as other people's voices. . . . And for many people that recognition would be hell: they would fall mute. . . . [T]he "tyranny of other voices" may well be the benevolent despotism many people crave. (Rubinstein 1991)

In Didion's essays is a relentless effort to negotiate a space clear of those received meanings and overly loud voices. She creates this cleared space by reproducing those other voices and texts, inviting them onto her canvas, into dialogue, not—as it may be said that I have done in this essay with those previously cited critics—merely in order to displace them, but so that she can come round to forging a position of her own. Through examining and working against these other voices, encountering and countering them, she develops a trustworthy inner authority, a "different voice." I have come to understand voice, then, not in the sense that my earlier reading suggests, as something merely distinct and personal, a romantic creation of the individual, but also in the Bakhtinian sense of a position constructed and earned dialogically.

Thus the double meaning of my title. On the one hand, I refer to voices of authority—those voices we recognize as carrying socially legitimated, externally validated authority. On the other, I refer to the authority in one's own voice, the authority which one claims for oneself, mindful of but not subject to official social legitimation. Much of Didion's nonfiction maps a complex negotiation in this web of competing voices—or as she calls them in "The White Album," competing narrative lines—using them to work out from under their authority to the authority of her own voice.

In order to more clearly demonstrate what I mean, I would like to talk about another of the essays from *The White Album.* "In Bed" is an essay about migraine headaches, a subject which, except to those who suffer from them, may seem to be rather insignificant, hardly suggestive or poetic, merely a personal problem. The essay, however, also tracks Didion's struggle from deep inside the cultural "wisdom," through inherited meanings, to a final transformative understanding of migraine which is achieved only once she negotiates her way through those voices. It is an essay which tracks a movement from the experience of authority to the authority of experience. She begins with the personal particulars:

> Three, four, sometimes five times a month, I spend the day in bed with a migraine headache, insensible to the world around me. Almost every day of every month, between these attacks, I feel the sudden irrational irritation and the flush of blood into the cerebral arteries which tell me that migraine is on its way, and I take certain drugs to avert its arrival. If I did not take the drugs, I would be able to function perhaps one day in four. The physiological error called migraine is, in brief, central to the given of my life. (168)

The first three sentences prepare the ground for the fourth, an unequivocal and powerful assertion: "The physiological error called migraine is . . . central to the given of my life." She is talking about something she knows quite well; her experience is a ground for authority. It is an assertion she has arrived at, not one she always held. And indeed, the very next sentence moves us back to the point in time when she did not accept it at all, when, as she puts it,

> I used to think that I could rid myself of this error by simply denying it, character over chemistry. "Do you have headaches *sometimes? frequently? never?*" the application forms would demand. "Check one." Wary of the trap, wanting whatever it was that the successful circumnavigation of that particular form could bring (a job, a scholarship, the respect of mankind and the grace of God), I would check one. "*Sometimes,*" I would lie. That in fact I spent one or two days a week almost unconscious with pain seemed a shameful secret, evidence not merely of some chemical inferiority but of all my bad attitudes, unpleasant tempers, wrongthink. (168)

Filling out the form represents a kind of gatekeeping: having the right answer will net rewards, but her "actual experience" does not seem to her to match the expected "narrative line." How does she know this? She is surrounded by voices which tell her that her migraines are unreal:

> For I had no brain tumor, no eyestrain, no high blood pressure, nothing wrong with me at all: I simply had migraine headaches, and migraine headaches were, as everyone who did not have them knew, imaginary. (168–69)

In other words, as the saying goes, they're all in her head—or in another part of her anatomy: in response to her first migraine, she tells us, "the Air Corps doctor prescribed an enema" (169). At first, she absorbs these voices and denies the migraines:

> I fought migraine then, ignored the warnings it sent, went to school and later to work in spite of it, sat through lectures in Middle English and presentations to advertisers with involuntary tears running down the right side of my face, threw up in washrooms, stumbled home by instinct, emptied ice trays onto my bed and tried to freeze the pain in my right temple, wished only for a neurosurgeon who would do a lobotomy on house call, and cursed my imagination. (169)

Her first move away from submission to this sort of "wisdom" about migraines is to intellectualize and study, to become a good scholar. She writes, "It was a long time before I began thinking mechanistically enough to accept migraine for what it was: something . . . more than the fancy of a neurotic imagination" (169). She begins to give recognition to her experience by gathering facts: who suffers from them, that they are hereditary, what can trigger an attack. Through possession of such information, she gives up the debilitating notion that migraines are indicators of moral failure, and accepts that they represent, simply, genetic identity:

> In other words I spent yesterday in bed with a headache not merely because of my bad attitudes, unpleasant tempers and wrongthink, but because both my grandmothers had migraine, my father has migraine and my mother has migraine. (169–70)

But as Didion says, this is mechanistic thinking. In the contrast and tension between knowledge and knowing, she is still deferring to other voices of authority: "No one knows," she goes on, "precisely what it is that is inherited" (170), and follows in the rest of the paragraph with factual information about chemicals and drugs. This sort of knowledge does help: it enables her to function, as she has told us in the first paragraph of the essay, far more than if she did not take the drugs, and it relieves her of the guilt and shame. Despite all the mechanistic study and scientific data, she writes, "Once an attack is under way, however, no drug touches it" (170). Medical authority seems to promise relief but only partially delivers it: in fact, it enables her to have only a measure of control, and only within the parameters, the "given," of migraine. It does not change what is essential to migraines, for Didion who lives with them. This knowledge reveals—not by what it points to but by what it does not say—that there is still much about migraines that cannot be pinned down.

At this point in the essay, Didion counters her earlier denial and gives further substance to the experience of migraines by listing a series of things that happen for and to migraine sufferers. Presented as more information, this is a different sort of knowledge, detailing what it is like to live with—not to research or lie about—migraine.

> Migraine gives some people mild hallucinations, temporarily blinds others, shows up not only as a headache but as a gastrointestinal disturbance, a painful sensitivity to all sensory stimuli, an abrupt overpowering fatigue, a strokelike aphasia, and a crippling inability to make even the most routine connections. When I am in a migraine aura . . . I will drive through red lights, lose the house keys, spill whatever I am holding, lose the ability to focus my eyes or frame coherent sentences, and generally give the appearance of being on drugs, or drunk. The actual headache, when

it comes, brings with it chills, sweating, nausea, a debility that seems to stretch the very limits of endurance. That no one dies of migraine seems, to someone deep into an attack, an ambiguous blessing. (171)

These are not disembodied symptoms, but things which happen to people, and happen differently to different people: "migraine gives *some* people mild hallucinations, temporarily blinds *others*." She names behaviors she herself exhibits. All of these are features of migraine an attentive observer could learn, but as the list progresses they move closer and closer to her, until in the last sentence she names what it is like from deep inside the experience, a sentence poignant in its twists, its turning back on itself: "That no one dies of migraine seems, to someone deep into an attack, an ambiguous blessing." This is something no medical form asks, no scientific data address, no observer perceives. The authority can only be Didion's.

Then she shifts, bringing in the other voices again, now not the threatening and falsely promising, but the admonishing, pitying, patronizing ones:

"Why not take a couple of aspirin," the unafflicted will say from the doorway, or "I'd have a headache, too, spending a beautiful day like this inside with all the shades drawn." All of us who have migraine suffer not only from the attacks themselves but from this common conviction that we are perversely refusing to cure ourselves by taking a couple of aspirin, that we are making ourselves sick, that we "bring it on ourselves." (171)

This is cultural baggage: migraines are headaches, they're all in your head, your imagination, you can do things about them, you can control them and yourself—take drugs or change your attitudes, or pull up the shade at the very least. At this point in her essay, what is significant is not the cause or substance of migraine, not the headaches in and of themselves. The significance of migraines at this point in the essay is that they bring into sharp relief the tyranny of those voices of authority, and our submission to the meanings they make out of our experience. Didion has told us she has believed, at a cost to her own psychic health, that she—by her bad attitudes or by something over which she might have control—is the cause of her blinding headaches, and that belief is learned, echoed, and reinforced by the voices all around her: "'You don't look like a migraine personality,' a doctor once said to me. 'Your hair's messy. But I suppose you're a compulsive housekeeper'" (171). None of the information available from various cultural authorities— from popular psychology to medicine and chemistry—can satisfactorily make sense of nor do justice to her lived experience, and there seem to be no available, audible voices which do so.

This essay traces the transition from an internalized acquiescence to available cultural voices, to a reliance on the particular voice of her own experience: that is, from received wisdom, which has authority because it is inherited, to interior knowing, the authority of experience. Only by first listening and then resisting all other voices—by finally, that is, pushing them out of the frame—can she author her own meanings and speak with the authority we hear in these last two paragraphs of the essay:

> I have learned now to live with it, learned when to expect it, how to outwit it, even how to regard it, when it does come, as more friend than lodger. We have reached a certain understanding, my migraine and I. It never comes when I am in real trouble. . . . It comes instead when I am fighting not an open but a guerrilla war with my own life, during weeks of small household confusions, lost laundry, unhappy help, canceled appointments, on days when the telephone rings too much and I get no work done and the wind is coming up. On days like that my friend comes uninvited. (172)

When she writes about the migraine "as more friend than lodger," and having "reached a certain understanding with it," she has transformed the migraine into something with which she has a relationship. Her experience of migraine is reconceived and rewritten in such a way that she can metaphorically and literally listen to *its* voice, and so signals a shift in her attention from the authoritative external voices to this inner one. The voice of the migraine is the voice of her experience. By paying attention to it, she learns to displace the voices of cultural authority with the authority of her own experience, her own voice:

> And once it comes, now that I am wise in its ways, I no longer fight it. I lie down and let it happen. At first every small apprehension is magnified, every anxiety a pounding terror. Then the pain comes, and I concentrate only on that. Right there is the usefulness of migraine, there in that imposed yoga, the concentration on the pain. For when the pain recedes, ten or twelve hours later, everything goes with it, all the hidden resentments, all the vain anxieties. The migraine has acted as a circuit breaker, and the fuses have emerged intact. There is a pleasant convalescent euphoria. I open the windows and feel the air, eat gratefully, sleep well. I notice the particular nature of a flower in a glass on the stair landing. I count my blessings. (172)

The old voices of authority urge a denial of the fact of pain: that it is neurosis, not pain, can be cured with a drug or an enema or a change of attitude. She has chosen instead to listen to her experience, on its own terms. Didion is *wise* in its ways, she says, not knowledgeable, nor omniscient, nor expert. It is a different kind of knowledge, and a different sort of authority.

A commitment to demonstrating the tyranny of received wisdom is evident throughout much of Didion's nonfiction, regardless of subject. I have examined closely this one brief essay in order to show that Didion's essaying her use of other voices represents a highly self-aware resistance to this tyranny. This resistance takes the form of a dialectic, two differing narratives she positions oppositionally: the voices of cultural authorities and the voice of her own experience, struggling to assert its own authority. Her resistance is made evident by her awareness of how deeply entangled she is by those culturally sanctioned narratives, heard variously in human voices, official documents, and cultural images and icons. Cultural voices are authoritative because they are to some degree internalized, as she makes clear in "John Wayne: A Love Story" when she writes that

> when John Wayne rode through my childhood, and perhaps through yours, he determined forever the shape of certain of our dreams. (1979, 30)

Didion recognizes that while we may talk about internalized cultural voices collectively, we nonetheless deal with them personally and individually. In this essay, as in "The White Album" and "In Bed," Didion's resistance to those hegemonic voices—and the assertion of her different voice—is understood through examining its consequences on the individual: that is, Didion is herself the subject and ground upon which the distance between them is explored. The inability of the expert voices to adequately account for the experience of migraine, for instance, is demonstrated through Didion's individual struggle to come to terms with migraine; the failure of the old cultural narratives to adequately account for public and private upheavals in the 1960s is traced in Didion's inability during those years to make appropriate connections, in her sense that her "basic affective controls were no longer intact" (1979, 46), and in the diagnoses of her physical and psychological health. But by calling attention in this way to the power of cultural voices to shape the individual imagination and silence alternative voices, Didion opens herself to those previously cited comments about personal neurosis, responses which dismiss social problems as *merely* a personal and individual problem, or worse, marginalize the individual as maladjusted, ill, or dangerous.

As Didion's nonfiction has progressed, she has not lessened her focus on the power of cultural voices (or what she has in later work more consistently called "preferred narratives") to silence other voices, but her work has demonstrated a different use of the personal, a different kind of subjectivity. Whereas in "In Bed" and "The White Album," Didion begins by exploring the ways in which she was led to doubt herself, her experience, her own voice, and her right to counter cultural voices with her own, in later works she does not doubt these things. The works call attention to the tyrannies of dominance without making Didion herself the template upon which we come to recognize those tyrannies.[2]

My own essay here about the meaning of "voice" arose from my reading of "In Bed" as Didion's working out from underneath persistent, authoritative, nagging voices. Those voices with which I began are authoritative in part because, being published, they have been stamped with the mark of social legitimation; in part because they claim (in the politics of textual reproduction) an authority over the text and its producer, the right to speak about it and thus reshape it. And of course in part, their authority is a result of the history of my own negotiation for space and voice. I have found myself wanting to push aside these other voices about Joan Didion and her essays because in what I hear as a repeated dismissal of Didion's voice and personality, I recognize the same sort of dismissal and condescension which the Didion of "In Bed" experiences and represents about migraine. It is, that is to say, precisely when the essay represents her as submitting herself to the tyranny of these other voices that *she* is read as neurotic, self-indulgent, vulnerable, victimized. The text disappears and becomes seen as the writer herself.

What these readers steadfastly refuse to recognize—and I began by telling you that I once read the essays this way too—is that by placing herself at the center of her essays, whether as the subject of "In Bed" or the observer in *Salvador* (1983), Didion demonstrates the struggle to extricate oneself from, and to resist, dominant cultural narratives. By thus representing herself as vulnerable to these tyrannies, she also becomes subject to the kind of mistaken reading which blames the victim rather than the oppressive agent, its gaze fixed upon the individual rather than the sociocultural context. Such a reading ignores the fact that the vulnerability in the essay is represented, not actual: she is not writing from a position of vulnerability but from having already seen it through to its resolution. It is also a romantic and gendered reading, rendering her illness, fragility, and vulnerability the source of attraction in the voice of her essays.

And so I have come, as a consequence of attending closely to the voices writing about Joan Didion, and the kinds and uses of voice in the essays themselves, to a different and more complex sense of what may be referred to as voice in Didion's work: as not merely something located in sentence structure or choice of detail, nor a matter of failing to project the sort of tough resonance culturally equated with authority. Didion's essays demonstrate that it may be necessary to invent for oneself the right to speak and be heard, to make one's own meanings and not merely to repeat others'—to invent, that is, one's own authority, the right to author one's own meaning, and in this way to find one's voice. Despite what she writes at the end of "The White Album"—that "writing has not yet helped me to see what it means"—and her oft-noted refusal to hold out this kind of hope, Didion's essays do bear witness in the repeated triumph finally of the authority of her own voice and experience, that it does make a difference to speak, to claim the authority of one's own voice.

Notes

1. The most notable exception is Chris Anderson's *Style as Argument* (1989).

2. *Salvador*, for instance, is filled with officially sanctioned voices. But in a culture not one's own, it is harder to mistake the disjunction between cultural narratives and one's own experience—or one's resistance to them—for something purely personal: the voices are not already internalized, not so long ago lodged and carefully couched that one cannot even recognize them as "other." *Salvador* is not enactment of Didion's own doubts about the authority of her experience and the veracity of her meanings. This is not to say, however, that her voice overpowers the others, or replaces them, for the book bears witness to the self-perpetuating nature of these hegemonic voices. The central issue in *Salvador* is their persistence and the ways in which they collude to distort and obscure what she sees, what is known, and what can be spoken. But here Didion herself is not the ground upon which this array of voices compete.

Works Cited

Anderson, Chris. 1989. *Style as Argument: Contemporary American Nonfiction.* Carbondale: Southern Illinois University Press.

Braudy, Susan. 1977. "A Day in the Life of Joan Didion." *Ms* (February): 65+.

Brownmiller, Susan. 1984. *Femininity.* New York: Fawcett Columbine/Ballantine.

Chace, James. 1987. "Betrayals and Obsessions." *New York Times Book Review* (25 October): 3.

Didion, Joan. 1968. *Slouching towards Bethlehem*. New York: Delta/Dell.

———. 1979. *The White Album*. New York: Simon and Schuster.

———. 1983. *Salvador*. New York: Washington Square Press.

———. 1984. "Why I Write." *Joan Didion: Essays and Conversations*, edited by Ellen G. Friedman, 5–10. Princeton, NJ: Ontario Review.

Duffy, Martha. 1979. "Pictures from an Exhibition." *New York Review of Books* (16 August): 43–44.

Elbow, Peter. 1989. "The Pleasures of Voice in the Literary Essay: Explorations in the Prose of Gretel Ehrlich and Richard Selzer." In *Literary Nonfiction: Theory, Criticism, Pedagogy*, edited by Chris Anderson, 211–34. Carbondale: Southern Illinois University.

Harrison, Barbara Grizzuti. 1979. "Joan Didion: The Courage of Her Afflictions." *The Nation* (29 September): 277–86.

Hulbert, Ann. 1979. Review of *The White Album* by Joan Didion. *The New Republic* (23 June): 35–36.

Kakutani, Michiko. 1984. "Joan Didion: Staking Out California." In *Joan Didion: Essays and Conversations*, edited by Ellen G. Friedman, 29–40. Princeton, NJ: Ontario Review.

Kazin, Alfred. 1971. "Joan Didion: Portrait of a Professional." *Harper's Magazine* (December): 112–22.

Morrow, Lance. 1979. "American Death Trips." *Time* (20 August): 69.

Rubinstein, S. Leonard. 1991. Letter to Laura Julier. 16 May.

Schow, H. Wayne. 1986. "*Out of Africa, The White Album*, and the Possibility of Tragic Affirmation." *English Studies* (February): 35–50.

Snyder, Lela Fern Kropf. 1986. "A 'State of Rather Eerie Serenity'." *DAI* 46 (January): 1943A. University of Oregon.

Stimpson, Catharine. 1973. "The Case of Miss Joan Didion." *Ms* (January): 36–42.

Towers, Robert. 1979. "The Decline and Fall of the 60's." *New York Times Book Review* 17 (June): 1+.

Winchell, Mark Royden. 1980. *Joan Didion*. Boston: Twayne.

Woolf, Virginia. 1942. "Professions for Women." In *The Death of the Moth and Other Essays*, 235–42. San Diego: Harcourt, Brace and Company.

9 Teaching Voice

Margaret K. Woodworth
Hollins College

Anyone who studies or teaches English knows and perhaps uses the term "voice": an authentic voice, a strained voice, an omnipotent voice, a consistent voice, a stiff voice, a formal voice, an informal voice, a Southern voice, an unbiased voice, a strong voice, a feminine voice. The term appears in book titles, tables of contents, professional journal articles; teachers and students alike use the word as if a single, specific meaning for it exists somewhere.

In spite of the confusion about what voice is and what it is not, I teach through voice. And unlike those who believe "voice" cannot be taught explicitly, I argue that indeed it can. Furthermore, student engagement in the activities of learning about voice releases them from the paralyzing belief that they already possess "a voice," one voice, one *authentic* voice, and that anything else belies their personhood.

The following practicum presents one possible approach to "teaching voice," i.e., leading students to a fuller awareness of the repertoire of voices they already own; to an understanding and control over the stylistic techniques that allow a broadening of that repertoire; and to a level of self-confidence, beyond what even experienced student writers usually possess, and a willingness to take risks and experiment with word choices, sentence structures, and hypothetical audiences.

The series of activities and assignments presented here, based largely on the works of Gibson, Hayakawa, and Kenyon, accelerate the natural development of language acquisition, both rhetorically and stylistically, through imitation, practice, performance, and revision. I have found that the plan succeeds with beginning writers as well as with more advanced students, primarily because the discovery of what they already know intrinsically motivates more learning.

In practice, I postpone defining "voice" until the students feel confident enough to participate in creating a definition; but for present purposes, a brief definition is in order. "Voice," as I am using the term, is a composite of all the rhetorical and stylistic techniques a writer chooses, consciously or unconsciously, to use to present his or her self to an audience. Related but not identical terms might include "persona," "ethos," "tone," "attitude."

The following exercises can be used in virtually any course where writing constitutes part of the coursework. Whether students write about history or literature, physics or art, approaching the subject from a variety of viewpoints can only strengthen their understanding of an individual's relationship to the subject/idea at hand: "Dear Grandfather, In my physics class today I learned that . . ." vs. "Dear Pats, Whatever else you take, be sure to get in Prof. X's Physics class next semester. Today we talked about. . . ." In my own experience, I have used some or all of the exercises in the following courses: first-year expository writing, advanced nonfiction prose writing, introductory creative writing, advanced fiction writing, and a wide variety of literature courses.

Procedures

The first day of any class, I ask students to write a brief autobiographical paragraph or page for the purpose of introducing each other to the rest of the class. This writing, while serving the stated purpose, serves also as a blind exercise in voice. Later in the term, it is retrieved for a voice analysis exercise to be described below. Because I use a portfolio system in my courses, students save everything they write and the originals rarely get lost. They are asked to label the piece "Writing #1," date it, and store it in their portfolios.

The next exercise, "Hit and Run," starts with a hypothetical situation where the student has found a neighbor's dog lying dead on the curb in the neighborhood. For hypothetical reasons, the student must inform three people, in writing, of the dog's demise: the neighbor; the neighbor's young child; and the student's best friend. Students automatically make good rhetorical choices for this exercise, from "I'm really sorry there was nothing either I or the veterinarian could do for Spot" to "That yippy little mutt next door got creamed and I've got to take it to the vet—so I'll be about an hour late. Really sorry—don't start without me!"

For the faint of heart, a variation on this exercise might also be called "Hit and Run": the student has recently wrecked the family automobile in a minor accident and the car is in the repair shop. The student needs to borrow a car for the Sadie Hawkins Day Dance. Her choices are her grandmother, who owns a new Cadillac; an older co-worker at the Computer Center, who owns a fairly new Acura; and her best friend, who owns an RX-7. The students' wording again reveals a highly developed rhetorical ability: the event is variously called "an important school event," "a dry party just across campus," or "a hot date." The "logic" in each case varies, and reading these requests aloud both entertains and inspires the students. At the same time, they see how much they already know about the rhetorical choices that partially constitute "voice."

With evidence fresh in their minds that they are already quite capable of varying their prose to meet a variety of occasions, students accept an otherwise dry lecture on the classical rhetorical triangle with some degree of enthusiasm. Identifying themselves as rhetors, they understand the terms "ethos," "audience," "topic + claim" ("thesis"), "purpose," "occasion," "emerging text," etc., in terms of the "Hit and Run" exercise. This discussion can lead to an explanation of genres, oral and written, and how they overlap and how they differ, which is especially relevant in a literature course. In writing courses, a model and overview of John Kenyon's (1969 [1947]) "Cultural Levels and Functional Varieties of English," still germane after nearly half a century, can reinforce in students' minds the notion that as sophisticated language users, they can—and perhaps should—change voices for different occasions. Kenyon's article also dispels the attitude that changing voice is in some way hypocritical, one of the arguments that has been leveled against teaching voice.

As a follow-up to "Hit and Run," students list the particular words they used and/or remembered from others' writings that establish the relationship with the audience, portray a particular "ethos," and/or serve the purpose of the discourse particularly well. These lists, discussed and analyzed in class, set up the next class activity: practicing levels of abstraction, as presented by S. I. Hayakawa in his book, *Language in Thought and Action* (1978). The words students still remember after a day or two are usually the most concrete, imagistic nouns and verbs. So we have a foundation for a discussion of the "Ladder of Abstraction," which begins with an example of a cow standing in a field. From a distance, we see four legs, an udder, stubby horns, a tail. Up close, we see the color of the eyes, feel the coarseness of the hair, smell the cud and dung, hear mooing. Under a microscope, we see the cells that make the horns porous, the eyes brown, the hair coarse. These millions of sense impressions, or "dots," instantly form a picture in our minds, and, for convenience, we call what we see "cow," which serves many purposes. But if we want to specify a particular cow standing in a particular field, we need concrete language to capture as many dots as necessary to the purpose.

For practice, I draw a straight line across the middle of the blackboard, with the words "abstract," "general," "specific," and "concrete"
listed vertically along the side. Placing "cow" at the horizontal center, I
ask students how to make this picture more or less clear, then move to
other simple words like "dog," "plant," or "light" for further practice
in working up and down the ladder until they grasp the concept fully.
Dog (is a kind of) mammal (is a kind of) animal (is a kind of) living
organism. . . . The further up we go, the more "things" the word might
refer to, and thus the more "gaps" might exist between the mind of the
writer and the mind of the reader. To make a clearer picture, to fill in
the "gaps," we move down the ladder: e.g., "Collie" limits the number
of possible referents without changing the number of words. To limit
further, we add a variety of modifiers: single words, phrases, and
clauses, specifying color, size, location, etc. Rewriting their "Hit and
Run" exercises to add more dots gives the students an opportunity to
experience the various effects of a range of levels of abstraction.

With this foundation, students are asked to develop the general
sentence, "A person walked by a building," first by simply changing the
three meaning-bearing words (e.g., a nurse strolled by a restaurant),
and then filling the picture: How was she dressed, what cafe, where?
"An aged nurse, in a crisply starched white uniform, white hose, and
white orthopedic shoes, strolled by Joe's First-Rate Barbecue and Grill
at the corner of Tenth and Main." Students are then asked to give
the person a companion, describe the way the companion is dressed,
indicate the relationship between the two, and finally add "on the way
to . . . for the purpose of. . . ." As they read their mini-novels to the class,
they learn that "dots" can have a comic effect, a poignant effect, a
ludicrous effect—but they always begin to close the gaps between
writer and reader, and they are both more interesting and memorable
than generalities. At this point in the term, students rewrite one of their
earlier papers for more development, i.e., adding more dots. In peer-
editing groups, they respond to the two versions, the original and
revised, usually with deep appreciation for the level of interest created
by the new dots.

The next step relies heavily on Walker Gibson's book, *Persona: A Style
Study for Readers and Writers* (1969). In Part II, "Writing: The Voices We
Pitch," Gibson presents a comparative analysis of the opening paragraphs of Dickens's *David Copperfield* and Salinger's *A Catcher in the Rye.*
Hearing the two paragraphs read aloud, students readily *sense* a difference in the two voices. As they attempt to articulate the differences they
hear, we begin to list the textual particulars on the blackboard. Specific
words (dots) usually emerge first: "all that . . . crap," "two hemorrhages

apiece," "Madman stuff", "that station," "sage women," "acquainted," "inevitably attaching." In most classes, students will also notice a difference in the use of pronouns, and contractions, and present specifics in that category.

Sentence structure differences, although clearly sensed, are more difficult to define. With the written texts in front of them, however, students do begin to notice sentence lengths, unusual punctuation, placement of modifying phrases and clauses, and parallel structures. While the students' interest is high, I present a brief explanation on the differences between grammatical and stylistic categories of sentence structures. With this new terminology, students write their first stylistic analysis of prose, actually identifying and counting the number of certain types of sentences for comparison.

Gibson's exercise with birthdays (58–59) provides a numbered scale by which the students can begin to analyze the prose styles of writers—including themselves. Beginning with the Copperfield and Caulfield texts, students compare the two, concentrating first on sentences. They work in groups to establish the average number of words per sentence, extremes of sentence length, numbers of simple/compound/complex sentences, numbers of loose/periodic sentences, numbers of stylistically marked sentences, habitual placement of modifiers, numbers of phrasal/clausal modifiers, numbers of sentences, etc. From these numbers, they place the two writers on Gibson's scale for levels of formality.

Following practice with sentence analysis, students study the two authors' words. Expanding the list of words noticed on first reading, the groups hypothesize about numbers of syllables per word, numbers of Latinate/Anglo-Saxon words, numbers of abstract/concrete words, numbers and types of pronouns, contractions, and other marked words (swear words, slang, etc.); they then count the numbers in each of these categories to test their hypotheses. Using countable stylistic features, they can compare Copperfield's and Caulfield's voices with an intellectual understanding that enhances the *sensed* differences. In doing so, they also learn how to create at least two extreme varieties of voice for their own writing.

The assignment that follows the Gibson exercise and the analysis asks the students to choose a writer whose work we've read and discussed and to analyze it stylistically. A first-year biology major at a major midwestern university, who had dreaded taking English and who had plodded through the course without distinction, wrote the following analysis of her favorite essay, "The Potato," by John Stewart Collis (1981):

Loni's Analysis of "The Potato"

In his essay "The Potato," John Stewart Collis exemplifies most of the characteristics of adult prose, through his use of words (especially figurative language), sentences, paragraphs, and punctuation. Collis also illustrates the foremost requirement of adult prose, a discernable purpose, which he states in the very last sentence of the essay, "But it doesn't matter; in spite of them, faith is reborn whenever anyone chooses to take a good look at anything—even a potato." His method of supporting this thesis is to describe a potato to faith in God. The audience actually "sees" the potato as it grows, blossoms, and withers away.

Through his employment of words, Collis makes the essay interesting and full of life. He uses a variety of words of different lengths, 70% of which were monosyllabic for easy understanding of the essay and 7% of which were trisyllabic or more in order to avoid insulting the intelligence of the adult audience. "I took one in my hand and offered it my attention." This is a good example of the syllabic distribution of the words in Collis's sentences. The words Collis uses are not often concrete such as in this sentence, "It is not a root, the botanists say, because roots do not bear buds and do not bear leaves, while this, the potato, does have buds and does have leaves (in the shape of scales)." Such a sentence is also an example of the accuracy of Collis's writing. Although he uses sound repetition, it is Collis's use of figurative language that makes "The Potato" interesting and alive. "They had curly heads like purplish knots, and some of these knots had half opened into a series of green ears." This is one example of a sentence rich in figurative language, in this case, simile and personification is illustrated. There are also metaphors, such as "I found that the protuberances had become much longer and had curled round at their ends—now white snakes coming out of the humble solid." Collis uses allusion in his sentence, "True, William Cobbett abused it, and Lord Byron made it interesting by rhyming it with Plato; but for the most part it enters politics more easily and has done more to divide England from Ireland than Cromwell himself."

In the construction of his sentences, Collis demonstrates the characteristics of adult prose sentences, although he falls short of the adult prose average of 20–40 words per sentence. Collis only averages 17.3 words per sentence but his sentences vary in length from 2 words per sentence to 82 words per sentence. His sentences are consistent in tone and vary in structure. "What is an infidel? One who lacks faith." This is a good example of the variety of sentence types Collis uses, in this case, a question and an elliptical sentence as the answer. Collis also uses sentences that begin with a conjunction, such as "But it had nothing in the middle, no seed-box, no seeds."

"We sing the flower, we sing the leaf: We seldom sing the seed, the root, the tuber." This is an example of an asyndeton in Collis's essay. There are also many common sentence types, such as "During my first year in the agricultural world I decided to have a good look at the potato and carefully watch its operations." Such is a main clause preceded by an introductory adverb clause.

"The Potato" contains nine paragraphs which average 9.5 sentences totalling 163 words. This number, which far exceeds the adult paragraphs in the essay, varies in length from 5 sentences per paragraph to 30 sentences per paragraph. Each paragraph makes a statement that is supported, although sometimes the topic sentence is not always clearly stated.

Although there is no specific adult prose style of punctuation, Collis shows his expertise in writing by his uncommon use of punctuation. The thesis of "The Potato" uses a dash rather than a comma. Another example of the emphasis Collis creates by this is "As all flowers have fruit, so had these—potato fruits, of course." Collis also commonly uses semi-colons where commas would be sufficient such as in the sentence, "Some people even imagine that the grape is today just like that from which Noah obtained the juice that made him drunk; that the cauliflower, merely with the idea of being pleasant, has of its own accord evolved its creamy-white head; that turnips and carrots, being keenly interested in human affairs, have always of their own motion done their best for man; and that the potato, since the world was young, wishing to please us, has gone through its curious performance." This sentence also happens to be the longest one in the essay, with the second longest only half as long. Without this sentence, the average sentence length would have been only 16 words!

Loni's paper, even with its imperfections, reveals an engaged and intellectually restless mind at work. It also makes clear that Loni, by midterm, had learned to apply many of the techniques she had studied to the prose she didn't like as well as to the prose she loved. She also learned that she could write, and write well.

Following this assignment, about three-fourths of the way through the term, I ask the students to retrieve "Writing #1," the blind autobiography, and to rewrite it twice, once in the Copperfield extreme and once in the Caulfield extreme, and then to rank the three pieces using Gibson's scale. The first draft for virtually all the students fell in the 3–4 range; they reacted with dismay when they revisited the "natural voice" they had started the course with, but borrowing another voice wholesale was uncomfortable for them, too. The final assignment in this series was therefore much freer: write at least two versions of the same event, using the rhetorical and stylistic techniques you've learned.

As often as I can, I myself do the assignments I give my students, partly to experience the difficulty level and the potential problems with the assignment, and partly to exercise my own writing. I found this assignment stimulating and highly productive. After the semester was over, I turned this "exercise" into a ten-page short story:

Voiceplay

I.

I might say:

I was born in West Lafayette, Indiana, on July 1, 1942. My father, impressed by my mother's timing, called me his fiscal year baby. He was a lawyer, county prosecuting attorney at the time, which kept him out of the war; as the third child, I was added insurance—in case he didn't get re-elected. Although my mother didn't have a job then, she was rarely home. My real mother for the first twenty years of my life was a black woman from West Virginia named Hattie.

No no, no. Wait.

II.

Neither my father nor my mother anticipated my arrival on the first day of the fiscal year 1943. With a birthday on Independence Day, my father, an attorney, rather hoped I'd wait till July 4th. But my mother, who had been "graciously confined" since the middle of April, got tired of me long before I was born. When the day finally came, she handed me over to Hattie, who then and for the next twenty years devoted her life to my welfare.

That's not it either. Maybe:

III.

You'd never believe this, but I was born in the same hospital room, the very same room, that my dad was born in 26 years before me. He was one of the first kids born in the hospital my grandfather built, his first big job after graduating in the first class of the Engineering School at Purdue. My grandmother said if she had her baby in the hospital, it would set a good example.

Our birthdays were almost the same, too. Mine is July 1st, Daddy's is the 4th. Obviously, my family tends to hang around the same town, generation after generation, which is kind of cool when you're little. Every April, my grandfather would take me and my big sister and brother to the first Lafayette Generals baseball game at Columbian Park, and everyone there knew Grandpa and would say, "Hiya, Cap. These Charlie's kids?" He'd always nod and introduce us and say something about us like "Pegs found a fourleaf clover this morning. Can you beat that?" Then on July 4th, he and my dad and Hattie, my mother's maid, would take us out to the park for fireworks. Until I was ten, I thought the fireworks were for my dad's birthday. I was pretty disappointed when I found out it was a national holiday. "Hiya, Cap. Hiya, Charlie. These your kids?" Daddy would nod and add, "and this is Mrs. Swanson." That's what he called Hattie in public. Daddy was quiet, but everyone knew him, too. From the time I started school, everyone called me "Little Kemmer." I couldn't get by with anything.

Nope.

IV.

The humiliation of being sent to remedial reading in first grade cannot easily be described, nor even recalled. What I do remember, and this is my earliest recollection, is my mother's fingernails digging deep into my skin as she stomped down the marble hall without even pausing to look at my finger-painting of "Fall in the Woods," artfully centered on the first grade bulletin board, only stopping to catch her breath before we entered the principal's office where undoubtedly he had penned the grievous news: Mary Margaret cannot read. Highly incensed at the mere suggestion that one of her children was less than precocious, she appeared to be rehearsing her counter-attack as we sat, waiting, on the hard oak chairs.

What do they mean, I can't read? Of course I can read. I've been reading for years. I always get stars for reading and I'm always a reading group leader. My brother and sister taught me. They'd bring their readers home from school and read to me on rainy days and every single night when they tucked me in, 'till at some point, I knew the books so well that I could take them into the kitchen and read to Hattie while she padded back and forth across the white tile floor between the stove and the sink, cleaning up from breakfast. I even taught Hattie to read. I told her what to say with each picture, and she'd say it. "See Spot run. Funny, funny Spot." She would laugh and seem pretty proud. "Am I really readin', honey?" she'd ask. Which made me wonder myself what reading really is.

What had happened, the principal was explaining, was I'd just memorized the books, right down to when to turn the pages, and that worked till we got the new reading series and the teacher asked me to read the first story to the class. As she handed me the book, open to page 1, the strange smell and the stiff way it creaked made it seem not a book at all. I simply handed it back to her and told her I didn't know that story. The look on her face was something I had never seen before. I stood sort of frightened for a minute and then walked back to my desk. The other kids sat stiff as the new book. I couldn't think what was wrong. Later, after the letter and everything, I discovered that all the books in remedial reading smelled like that.

Although my mother never fully recovered from this devastating experience, I did. Six months later, as a result of my mother's insistence that there was no brain dysfunction and my father's unending patience, I had regained my reputation as ace reader and my first accolades as a writer. My teacher displayed October's prize-winning essay on the bulletin board:

My Future
by Mary Margaret, gr. 2

When I grow up I want to be a bran sargeant.
I am defintely seven years old.
My name is Mary Margaret.

My dad drove to the school the evening the prizes were announced to see my essay. When we got home, my mother asked me where I ever got such an idea, but she told all her friends about the prize. She told them I must be following in the footsteps of my brother and sister. It was her favorite thing to say. Hattie said, of course I could be a brain surgeon, I could be anything I wanted to be. My father had the essay framed in May. I still have it.

In the process of learning how to read all over again, I taught Hattie all the sounds and words I learned, I showed her how to make letters, I made her practice, and just before my birthday, together, we managed to sound out BREAD. She left her first note for my mother: Mz K get braid.

That's it.

IV.

The four rows in the front of the church were reserved for family. My aunts and uncles, all seated in order of age, filled the second row; the cousins filled the rest. The first was for us. We entered as my mother had arranged us: first, my sister, who had to leave an empty space for my brother. Next was my mother, then me, then Hattie. The sons-in-law and grandchildren entered last, in order of age.

I was no longer able to cry about my father's death. It had been a long time coming; my grief had become a part of me. I was struck, simply, by the number of people who had come to honor him. Hattie sat silently beside me, but I could feel her grief. We had shared death before, when I was too pregnant to come home for my brother's funeral, and she rode the Greyhound to South Carolina so I wouldn't be alone.

Like hunger gnawing
the autumnal equinox bares my raw edge
rattles the marrow of my rage
rips blank pages from my book
as the moon drools its wax
on my art. . . .

Sharing these attempts with my students created a bond of trust and a sense of adventure. The writing that was produced by the class, finally, included the two pieces below by Amy Guthrie, a junior at Hollins College last fall. From the bland "Writing #1," Amy produced the following two pieces, which by themselves answer the question we started with: Can "voice" be taught?

Brothers in Two Voices

Once upon a time and all that medieval gobbly gook, on a big farm in Pennsylvania, covered in fields, woods, a reservoir, and barns filled with farm animals, lived a girl (me) and two boys (my brothers).

The grass in the fields would irritate the skin on your legs, you know, like if some jerk was running a brush over them, and the woods, well, let me tell you that crushing nuts between two stones is no way to fill an empty belly, and the reservoir, damned if I wasn't fool enough to believe that the Loch Ness Monster got tired of Scotland and flew over to this body of water. And if this wasn't enough to try Thoreau's soul, James Herriot's menagerie established residency there as well—you know, stupid cows, dirty pigs, hairy ponies and noisy geese. So much for a nap in the sun, your hands behind your head, a piece of grass in your mouth, your eyes closed—it was impossible in Doctor Doolittle's world of daily activity.

Well, three scrawny kids decided to conquer this kingdom—as noted earlier it was me and my brothers, "Amy and the Boys."

One day, it was probably 100 degrees, the 3 of us decided to build a dam, stopping the flow of water into the reservoir, maybe we were going to beach the Loch Ness Monster, who knows. If you believe for a second that a man built the pyramids without extraterrestrial intervention, you're crazy, because if you carried rocks all day you'd never believe they are anything but gifts from heaven. And God only knows what kind of microorganisms lived in the mud that we called cement.

All summer long, on the dark side of the lake, digging around snakes and other such creatures of Hell, we had to displace ferns and present them to Mother with a big "to do" as peace-offerings for our latest misdeed. If I remember right it cost us about ten such ferns for the time my brothers redecorated our parents bedroom with a rainbow assortment of oil paints, and you know, no matter how careful we were those damn ferns usually died.

It's a wonder today, with all the racing around as the Three Musketeers and other such mounted characters, that our brains aren't mush, but then, maybe that's our excuse. And the thought of pony hair, pony dirt, and pony sweat on my bare thighs gives me the heebie jeebies. No wonder the Indians lost to the white man.

As if this piece of God's green earth wasn't enough to deal with, three of God's greatest creations (me and my brothers) were thrown into one of the devil's greatest creations, school. Suddenly tempted with a new sins, new sinners in a sinfilled world, I was lured away from Eden, and with one last lunge to return I was rejected by those who had once shared it with me.

But all is not to be suffered alone, my brothers too must have felt the pulls of growing up, after all, my teenage years are remembered as me against two of God's greatest pains in the ass.

Imagine a 160 acre playground. A playground consisting of fields, woods, and water, and barns filled with animals—a playground made for adventure.

The uncut field grass, like so many fine brush bristles, ran green under our fingertips and against our legs, and hid many tales of lions, tigers, and bears. Bordering the field, its edges a blanket of purple violets, were the woods, whose interior often became a banquet hall with nuts as staples of imaginary feasts. Although the vast sea was actually the town's reservoir, its shores held the Loch Ness Monster and other such adventuresome creatures.

Animals added heartbeats to this backdrop. Ponies, solid and two-toned hues, grazed in the tall grass, adding splotches of color to the summer landscape. Stoically, their mouths forever chewing, the cows stood, indifferent to one's fingers occasionally run through the curly hair between their eyes, while the pigs would grunt their appreciation to the one holding the stick for their backscratch. Coaxing a game of chase out of the geese was easy then.

Into this fairyland entered three children, one sister, the elder, two brothers, the younger—forever known as Amy and the Boys.

Through the field ran a creek and one day we deemed it necessary to build an elaborate dam in order to stop the water flow into the reservoir. No matter that this trickle of water was known to dry up in a dry summer. Rocks were gathered for hours, sorted into appropriate piles, big rocks for main construction, smaller rocks for filling in the holes. The cement was created from mud. As with many projects begun that summer though, interest soon died, and we were onto something else.

Along one side of the lake, where the sun rarely shone, ferns grew abundantly. The ground was damper here, smelling somewhat moldy. Against this dark background, the lime-colored plants grew in all sizes and shapes. Throughout the summer, numerous plants were dug up by the newly appointed "plant experts" and presented as gifts to Mother. Taking turns with the shovel, digging often with our fingers, we were careful of the fragile roots. Since we had moved a few times ourselves, we knew firsthand the relocating scares, and were always careful to include some of the plant's home dirt.

If anything draws three children closer together than constant companionship, it's the influence of animals. The ponies particularly increased adventure possibilities, providing mounts for the Three Musketeers, cowboys and Indians, or derby racers. To this day, I can remember the scratchiness of their backs, so like the hair left in your collar after a haircut.

A sister and her brothers, young and lonely, shared a true friendship. "Back then" are peaceful and easy memories. Abruptly though it ended. School began. Suddenly dams lost their importance, ferns lost their worth, and riding lost its appeal. Since we showed so little interest, the ponies were turned out into a larger field, far from the house.

One day though, I went in search of my friends, down through the yard, into the woods. I was hurrying; it had been awhile since we had been together. I entered into the field, now a beige sea, and I saw them. They weren't alone; other boys were with them.

Like a shove to the ground, I felt rejection, a forced change in my lifestyle—and I didn't like how it felt.

They never knew I was there. I turned and walked back to the house, and that evening they never asked where I had been.

Conclusion

Amy Guthrie's performance on this assignment was typical of the class's work; some students did more with the project, and some did less. All students, however, were proud of what they had accomplished, all voluntarily signed up for the campus reading arranged by the English department for our class to perform, and all submitted this project to the class anthology. In the course evaluations, every student mentioned this assignment as one that really made them feel the control that they had lacked before; that had made them understand why some writing was "better," or more appropriate and/or effective, than other writing. Subsequently, most of the students have reported that they have used the techniques they had learned on other writing projects, both academic and professional.

Specifically, one student expanded her paper into a master's thesis, which she began in a well-controlled academic voice to explain her purpose: to maintain her own Appalachian dialect in telling the history of her home town. She developed the thesis, in large part, by retelling stories she remembered from her childhood, using the voices of the storytellers. Her own voice as narrator varied according to her age at the time of the incidents reported and, with the control she had learned, she concluded the work using again the voice of the academic researcher, the observer. Other students have reported that the techniques they learned helped them in their subsequent fiction writing courses and in jobs they have held since graduation.

For me, this more structured method of teaching voice, which has seemed essential to me, for a number of years, to teaching writing, has produced consistently positive results:

1. Students learn that inside each self there resides a multitude of selves, each of which has a valid point of view, an already developed voice, and a right to speak with that voice. Two of the female students wrote alternative autobiographical stories from a male's point of view, and several tried voices from different ages, in different levels of formality, or with different audiences in mind.

2. Students learn to free themselves from the paralyzing belief that they have only one voice; in exercising their freedom to explore other possibilities, they develop confidence and competence as writers.

3. Students learn to enjoy the act of writing, with a sense that each draft is a trial, a "play," a rehearsal. As a result, their intrinsic motivation to learn more about words, to read a variety of authors and types of writing, and to analyze discourse increase. Their response to and criticism of works of literature of all types becomes less subjective and more controlled because of the specifics they have learned about writing. Furthermore, their respect and understanding of other authors increases with their understanding of the writing process as they have experienced it.

To the extent that these results are seen as positive, and seen as part of what a teacher hopes to instill in her students, we can conclude that teaching "voice" is, in fact, both important and possible. A teacher's ability to help her students develop this sort of exploratory attitude toward writing enhances whatever else may transpire between teacher and students in the writing classroom.

Works Cited

Anderson, Loni. 1981. "Analysis of 'The Potato.'" Unpublished manuscript. Purdue University.

Collis, John Stewart. 1981. "The Potato." In *Elements of the Essay: A Reader for College Writers*, 2nd ed., edited by H. Wendell Smith, 421–24. Belmont, CA: Wadsworth.

Gibson, W. Walker. 1969. *Persona: A Style Study for Readers and Writers*. New York: Random House.

Guthrie, Amy. 1991. "Brothers in Two Voices." Unpublished manuscript. Hollins College.

Hayakawa, S. I. 1978. *Language in Thought and Action*. 4th ed. New York: Harcourt, Brace, Jovanovich.

Kenyon, John S. 1969 [1947]. "Cultural Levels and Functional Varieties of English." In *Readings in Applied English Linguistics*, edited by Harold B. Allen, 294–301. New York: Appleton-Century-Crofts.

Woodworth, Margaret K. 1991. "Little Kemmer." Unpublished manuscript. Hollins College.

10 Classroom Voices

Paula Gillespie
Marquette University

My brother Fred hated to fish alone, so when I grew old enough to be able to look after myself, he used to take me on the long drive far into north central Ontario to stay in cabins on a farm and fish for small-mouth bass in the Madawaska River. In my cabin each night, I would snuggle under warm patchwork quilts, stitched together during the long Canadian winters by Olive, the owner of the farm. Each quilt was a history, made up of castoffs from anyone who would contribute; pieces from a well-worn flannel shirt from Sibley's buddied up with squares from a cherished party dress, now worn beyond respectability. For the most part, the pieces of the quilt were simple squares, the fabrics grouped together without any apparent order and no rules, except that it seemed to be taboo to put any two like squares together. In a few of the fancier quilts, Olive would create a simple pattern from pieces old and new, interspersing faded squares with the obviously store-bought, obviously new pieces.

The back of the quilt was always made of large pieces, cut from a single bolt, often of flannel. The stitching that kept the front and back together and that kept the batting from shifting was a straightforward outline of the squares. Simple as they were, these quilts were eloquent symbols of the waste-nothing economy that kept the farm prosperous, and I remember the warmth and comfort of both.

These quilts came back to me vividly at the CCCC in Cincinnati in 1992, where the cover of the program was a color photograph of an elaborate and beautiful quilt. This quilt became for me a metaphor for several things at once: teaching and learning, collaboration, and the writing process itself. But the workshop session I had participated in was on voice, so most of all, the quilt began to represent voice for me.

And it's not an unlikely association. If we think of voice in Bakhtinian terms, we can see that the concept is much like a patchwork quilt. If student texts are composed of the various discourses the writers encounter, then we can say that voice is made up, sometimes consciously and sometimes unconsciously, of pieces that come from somewhere else, from someone else, like the fabrics that give the quilt its look and feel. Like the pieces of the quilt, these pieces that are constitutive of voice are often previously used: many individual pieces have great meaning for the maker, meaning not always apparent to others; some pieces are selected exclusively for utility; others are selected, not for their usefulness, but for their beauty and for the way they will fit into the overall design. Like text and voice, the quilt is then stitched, usually consciously, into a pattern that is something quite different from and yet more significant than the fragments that comprise it.

In other ways, too, the metaphor is revealing, for in the typical quilting process, the maker begins from a pattern, sometimes merely copying a set of instructions but sometimes adding unique touches to make the pattern her own. For students in the college writing situation, there is also an element of pattern following, more in certain types of classes than in others. In some classes, students are taught to adhere strictly to a five-paragraph theme, and in this case, they must fit their available pieces into a predesigned form. However, in the ideal writing situation, the preconceived pattern is less important than the pattern which emerges as the quilt takes shape, the pattern that is revised, rethought, resketched while it is taking shape. This sort of writing situation is a little like quilting, for the pieces—the ideas—the sentences which arise from them and which give rise to new ideas, create the form of the finished paper. "Form finds form," as Ann Berthoff (1988) says. Yet while the overall pattern may give rise to itself, the pieces which make it up are still quiltlike.

This essay, too, is a bit like a patchwork quilt: it is made up of separate segments and formed into a design, a discourse on voice and on teaching voice. The segments may at first seem unrelated, but the questions about voice, and the concerns about the way we talk about and teach it, are stitched together to form a pattern revealing what we think we know, and what we need to know, about voice and its teaching.

This inquiry into voice had its beginnings in classroom challenges over the years, but it took an interesting turn on a train between Chicago and Milwaukee. I was finishing the last leg of my long trip home from the CCCC in Boston, and I was drowsy, hoping to sleep the last two hours away. Just in front of me sat two Marquette students, a young man and a young woman, coming home from separate weekends in Chicago. The young man was doing all the talking, and the young woman, probably also hoping to sleep, was listening. I heard the young man relate to her two discourses in two distinct voices. As he tried to amuse and interest his friend, his voice changed effortlessly and unselfconsciously.

His first discourse was a story about a bicycle ride he took on a trail through some woods and about his scary encounter with a large animal he couldn't identify. His story went something like this:

> So I'm riding on the trail, and all of a sudden, like this like animal is on the trail? Right in front of my bike? And it sees me and I see it, and I'm like AAAH, and it's like AAAH, and I fall off my bike, and I'm like AAAH. . . .

His narrative fit the pattern of stories teens tell one another, but do not tell their parents, if the parents are both lucky and persistent. It was full of inappropriate use of the present tense, overworked conjunctions, and the overuse of the word "like" to fill in for whatever words he couldn't quite find. The act of transcribing the story made it clear to me that it was almost impossible to punctuate. It was also blissfully free of causal connections.

His second monologue was totally different. It was an exposition about a religious reformer he had been studying for a theology or history class and about whom he was writing a paper. He was truly interested in this reformer and in the research he was doing on him, and when he spoke about him, he used academic discourse, with a carefully constructed narrative, lots of subordination, precise verbs, and even mention of sources for his research. I never did hear the name of the reformer, but I remember that his discourse took the form of a true expository essay. It began with background about the reformer, and the context for his interest in him. He went on to spell out the highlights of the accomplishments and the impact this man had on the church, and how close he was to heresy, and how close to trouble with the Spanish Inquisition. He included virtually everything a listener needed to know, and enough to get him or her interested in knowing more. He concluded by telling his friend what he still needed to look up to finish his paper. He embedded narratives, gave dates, mentioned research sources, and generally sounded very scholarly, as if he were a college professor. He took on an academic voice as he filled the role of educator.

When, during these two narratives, did I hear "his" voice, a voice some rhetoricians would call authentic or authoritative (see Sommers 1992)? Did I ever actually hear a voice that was truly his, or were these stories narrated in a sense by personae? Is the teen-style argot of the first narrative truly his? To me, an outsider who was starting to feel decidedly guilty for eavesdropping, both voices sounded like what Bakhtin (1981) refers to as "internally persuasive." Internally persuasive discourse, Bakhtin says, is

> affirmed through assimilation, tightly interwoven with 'one's own word.' In the everyday rounds of our consciousness, the internally persuasive word is half-ours and half-someone else's. Its creativity and productiveness consists precisely in the fact that such a word awakens new and independent words, that it organizes masses of our words from within, and does not remain in an isolated and static condition. (345–46)

Bakhtin goes on to say that internally persuasive discourses are always in competition with other equally persuasive discourses, so the concept is different from "authentic voice."

If this ardent young man's context (a friendly conversation) and the audience (a good listener: a silent, unresponsive young woman) remained the same, was it the formality of the second discourse that caused him to change his voice? What was the purpose of the first narrative? To break the ice and amuse his friend, perhaps? What was the purpose of the second? It sounded to me like the sort of information one shares out of a sense of excitement and enthusiasm, the way academicians go on and on when anyone asks how their research is going. Would our young man ever use the teen argot of the first narrative to relate the more expository discourse of his second? Would the first story have been as compelling in the second voice? Could he have started his conversation with the second discourse, or was it necessary for him to begin with the more "between kids" talk?

If what we want to do is encourage or enable students to find a voice, how do we know when we have heard it? Do we ever know?

My second narrative, the second design in this patchwork quilt, is set in my kitchen one morning early in March. Ann, my youngest daughter, age ten, was telling me that her friend Jenny wants to become president of the United States, and that she wants to become Jenny's speech writer. "You can tell," she said, "that George Bush *never* wrote *this*." She opened a book entitled *The Buck Stops Here* (Provensen 1990) and began to read:

> Some see leadership as high drama, and the sound of trumpets calling, and sometimes it is that, but I see history as a book with many pages—and each day we fill a page with acts of hopefulness and meaning. The new breeze blows, a page turns, the story unfolds—and so today a chapter begins: a small and stately story of unity, diversity, and generosity—shared and written together. (n.p.)

When Ann began to read this passage, she used "her own voice," the ardent voice she would use if she truly believed what she was saying, or as if she were trying to make the listener believe. But after a few clauses, her voice changed. She adopted a Dana Carveyesque/President Bush impersonation voice, along with the whining tinge of the voice of TV wimp Steve Erkel. The discourse stayed constant, but the parodying, ironic voice undercut the moving content the speech was intended to have and made it ludicrous.

Whose voice did I hear that morning? *Not* the voice of the education president, though he was invoked by it. Certainly I heard the protean voice of Ann Gillespie, and Ann's version of the voice of Dana Carvey. The well-meaning or well-paid speech writer or committee who surely, as Ann claimed, wrote the speech, was invoked as well. And in the artful metaphors and balanced rhythms of the speech, I heard the traditional rhetoric of highly formal, highly patriotic situations, so I heard echoes of other great speeches and their traditions, Lincoln's, Martin Luther King, Jr.'s, and Kennedy's moving addresses.

Ann's playful reading of a speech which is only powerful in the right context and for the right audience raised questions not only about Ann's interpretation, but about students and their use of material which is potentially powerful or potentially ironic in their hands. When our students quote from outside sources, whose voices do we hear? Whose voices do they hear when they find or when they quote potentially powerful material? How can we get them to use the power of the quoted word effectively or ironically or both, as the occasion demands, and how can we help them know the difference? When public figures unself-consciously use speech writers but call the speech their own, how can we help our students to understand the need for originality, the need to draw in their own voices, or the need to acknowledge that the powerful word rightfully belongs to someone else, especially if it has become internally persuasive and is in the process of becoming this student's own? How can we help them to see that their own voices have power as well? What is the relationship between orality and voice?

———

The three parts of the design that make up the following segment of this essay are not found scraps or used fragments, as the first two are, but the store-bought pieces I went out to get. The next three segments aren't really narratives; they come from interviews with members of our Marquette teaching staff about classroom teaching and the use of voice. In my own teaching I hoped to become more knowledgeable about voice, at CCCC I was taking part in a roundtable on voice, in my dissertation I deal explicitly with voice in Joyce's *Ulysses,* and I wanted my classroom experience and my research experience to integrate well. I asked a number of instructors about the way they talk about voice (if they do) and what they teach their students about it. The three instructors who gave me the most articulate responses taught in different sorts of classes. Two postdoctoral teaching fellows taught a combination of freshman and upper-division expository and creative writing classes, and the third, a second-year teaching assistant, taught freshman classes exclusively. I chose the three responses which follow because they are so different from one another and illustrate how, even in a university with a markedly unified program of teaching writing, instructors can understand very different things about voice and function according to different definitions.

Jim is a playwright and a poet teaching while he finishes an M.F.A., and he finds that his playwrighting experience influences his conception of voice. His metaphors for describing voice, in italic type below, were telling and very interesting, because they illustrate his bias for a singularly impressionistic interpretation of voice.

Jim feels that voice is *in there,* but that it's *deep in there,* and that students have to develop a self-critical apparatus to *get at it.* That is, Jim believes in the Romantic tradition of the authentic voice that defines and expresses our nature. The writer has to *develop* this voice and, in order to do this, develop an openness to criticism. There are, he believes, certain transcendent moments a writer experiences and that freshmen can experience these moments, too, moments when the content and the form create a blissful union. He feels that the writer often knows when this is happening, experiencing a very self-conscious moment in the writing process.

When he finds a piece of student writing which exemplifies voice for him, Jim brings it to class. Voice for Jim is, as he defines it, "a perfect union between structure and sense," a magical moment in writing when excitement is expressed by broken syntax, or where a sense of harmony is expressed by parallelism and balance. He will share these segments with the class and invite the students to share with him his excitement over these examples that work for him. Then he will ask the writers what was happening when they wrote these parts of their papers. Jim says that his students reply that it just sounds right, that it's a sensual thing. Jim wants the students to focus in on the processes that *uncovered* this voice, and he wants the rest of the class, the students who have not experienced this sense of the rightness of their work, to see what this experience is like and to try to emulate it.

Jim feels that if students can find a potent image or metaphor, sometimes it can *free the voice*. He described to me a time when he was writing a paper on Richardson's *Clarissa*, and how he found, as if by magic, the metaphor of the hyperbola to describe the way Clarissa and Lovelace interact. He saw Clarissa and Lovelace as the curves of the hyperbola, forever approaching, but never touching one another, forever bending away from one another. He saw the lines that divide these curves as the forces in their lives that keep the characters apart. Also, of course, he was enthralled with the way the geometric and the rhetorical figure of hyperbola created a playful tension. This metaphor, once he discovered it, controlled his paper, letting him write effortlessly and in his own voice, he said.

Jim feels that freewriting exercises *release* style. The first draft often has the style, while the second draft *charges toward argument*. He tries to get his students to trust the voice of the first draft and listen to it, not to dismiss their early ideas and their ways of expressing them.

He left me with three rather random thoughts: he feels that there is an essential mystery, something romantic, at the heart of language. He also feels that any interpretation is a Berthoffian journey of knowing and unknowing, of movement from the particular to the general, then back again.[1] He also feels that some students are afraid of language and need to be made more comfortable with it.

When I heard Jim describe and define voice as something imprisoned, as something essentially individualistic, as personal as the voice-print, as something repressed, waiting for the right teacher to come along on a white horse and free it, I knew that his impressionistic version of voice and my Bakhtinian one were in conflict, and yet I could understand why his students seem to worship him and try to take his classes semester after semester. To be told that they are capable of magic, to be urged to look inside to find this inherent goodness, is motivating, very similar to Toby Fulwiler's technique of telling students, "You're a good writer,"[2] and it is affirming of their essential goodness.

Jim's metaphors suggest freeing, uncovering, discovering something that is inside, while his metaphor for the second or third draft, "charging toward argument," makes argument or the movement away from the personal to the public sound military. Jim said that the examples he brings to class to share are often not the favorite examples of the other students in the class, though the writers report liking their own pieces. So it seems that in the process of "freeing" and "uncovering," Jim is teaching the students to free and to uncover what he as the powerful and well-loved teacher approves.

———————

Bronwen is a second-year teaching assistant. When I visited her class as part of the evaluation of our freshman program, I heard her give some clarification to an item on a grading criteria sheet she had handed out: "Try to write in a strong voice. You do this by avoiding vague or unclear terms." Somewhere along the line she had been influenced by the "use concrete language" school and was anxious to pass this advice along to her students. To illustrate the slippery nature of abstract words and to show how vague they could be, she had her students write a definition of "society" and compare their responses. From the difficulty they had in doing this assignment thoughtfully and from the differences in the definitions they came up with, they concluded that words such as "society," which seem so clear when you write them, can be very vague. For Bronwen, vagueness and voice do not go together.

Over a muffin in the union one day, Bronwen and I were discussing the letter I would put in her file describing the class I visited. After we discussed her two classes and the challenges they presented to her, I asked her some questions about voice. She told me that this second semester freshman class was the first in which she had mentioned voice. I asked her what she meant by voice, and she replied that her definition depended a great deal on the paper in question. Since her students were writing argument, she felt it was important to help them avoid the sort of pseudo-objective voicelessness students often adopt when they move from the personal essay to the argument. For Bronwen, writing an argument with a voice meant "being objective yet passionate, being academic with a tone of feeling."

A few days later, Joan, one of our teaching assistants who works as a tutor in our Writing Center, came to me to tell me a story that showed how the students in Bronwen's class "translated" this definition and criterion. (Joan and I had worked very closely on the topic of voice and had suffered over the vague definitions we encountered.) When one of Bronwen's students came to her for a conference and showed her the grading criteria sheet, Joan was, naturally enough, struck by Bronwen's requirement that students write with a strong voice. Joan asked the student what that meant. The student, it turned out, a good student, had understood nothing of Bronwen's explanation. He said, "Oh, that's easy. You write in the first person."

Bronwen had not gone as far as Jim had in demonstrating what she meant by voice or by a strong voice. Her exercise had showed students what specific words to avoid (and we all have a list: it usually includes "factor," "aspect," and "in today's society") but not what positive examples of strong voice might look or sound like in a student essay.

Voice for Jim was a magical moment in the writing process where the self, the idea, and the expression all came together. For Bronwen, voice is something the student achieves by *not* trying to project the sort of false objectivity we often see in the writing of naïve students. Bronwen wanted feeling or passion in these essays. Here she falls into the category of teacher described by Lester Faigley in his essay "Judging Writing, Judging Selves" (1989). In this essay, he critiques the instructors in Coles and Vopat's *What Makes Writing Good* (1985) for judging as good only those essays which were either personal or passionate. He asks, at the end, if there is something wrong, in the judgment of these instructors, with writing up the results of a research project or with projecting objectivity. He asks if those papers must necessarily be written without voice, and he issues an implicit challenge to teachers to find a way to help students find voices for such assignments.

How would a student make a transition from Jim's first-semester class to Bronwen's second-semester section of freshman writing? Jim urges students to become passionate by looking inside and uncovering what is there, while Bronwen insists that students follow a set of proscriptions *to avoid not having a voice.* "Write in the first person," the student concludes, and why shouldn't he?

My final interview was with Eleanor, a poet and postdoctoral teaching fellow at Marquette. Like Jim, Eleanor is an extremely popular teacher who regularly converts freshmen into English majors. Eleanor does not use the term voice and does not plan the teaching of voice into her classes. She believes that the great myth of voice is that there is only one; she feels—with Bakhtin—that everyone has many voices. Rather than teach voice, she discusses authorial personae, because she finds these two concepts very closely related. During conferences with her students, she will point out to them the sort of persona she finds in their papers and ask them if what she finds is what they intend her to find. She might tell them, for example, that when she reads their papers she hears the persona of a teacher, or a cheerleader, or a "jock"—occasionally in the same paper. When she can't discern a persona, she will say to them, "I can't hear your voice here," or "I can't see you here," intentionally using synesthesia to convey the sensory element of discerning the writer.

Eleanor told of an editing workshop in an upper-division writing class where two very different students worked on one another's papers. A young man who could, as Eleanor said, "go up and down the stylistic register in a single paper" had his paper edited by a young woman whose preferred style was straightforward and simple. (Perhaps she had been a student of Bronwen's!) She crossed out and crossed out as she edited, leaving only a very factual paper. The young man did not take any of her suggestions (some of them good, Eleanor said), but left the paper exactly as it was. In conference, Eleanor had him read to her just the paper the young woman left him, and had him describe the differences between this paper and the one he liked. This was Eleanor's way of helping him to become more flexible in his use of voice.

Eleanor's most interesting experiences with voice evolve from her own writing group, where her friends, familiar with one another's work, will become excited when a new voice emerges in a poem. Once again, in this context, Eleanor's emphasis is on persona, not on a sense of authentic voice, a voice which somehow conveys the self.

In all three of these interviews, it came out that, to a greater or lesser degree, and despite the best intentions, the instructor is in control of voice. He or she decides when voice is present and tells the student when it is effective. Yet in every case, there is an attempt to enable or teach students to release or manipulate voice to their advantage. Jim tries to teach them to trust the inner voice on the first draft, yet Bronwen teaches her students not to, for the inner voice might use the word "society." Eleanor teaches the students not to mistrust the inner voice, but to consciously decide what persona they want to be and to try to project that more or less fictional mask into the writing.

Yet how different from these instructors are we? What are the best ways of conveying our sense of what voice is? Having our students read Bakhtin, since our ideas might well be shot through with his theories? Is such difficult reading counterproductive or challenging? Jim's technique of using examples of voice in student writing is effective in showing them *what he likes and what he wants*. But how else could we possibly help them understand what we consider good except to show them? Is it possible to have students look at drafts of one another's work and share segments that *they* feel convey an effective voice? Is it necessary for the student to feel that a moment in the composing process had to be magical or feel just right? It seems necessary to ask these writers how they succeeded so well so that students who have not done so will be able to learn, but we should remember that what came naturally for one student might have been the labor of hours for another, and that there is no magical formula for producing writing that sounds alive. If the students choose the pieces they like, what happens when the students love the "in today's society" segment? Or perhaps we need to focus in the classroom on the "heard" element of voice. The more we can give students the opportunity to hear their own drafts, the more likely they are to become aware of the different voices they have at their disposal and to make good choices about them.

When we try to help students convey their own individual selves, in papers of whatever degree of objectivity, we show that we value and accept those selves—that we want to know more of them or that we enjoy that "voiceprint." So trying to get students to convey a self, for most writing tasks, is an affirmation of them, their ideas, and their minds. We undermine that affirmation when we take complete control of voice, and by stacking the deck we assure that we will get an entire roomful not of authentic voices but of sentimental, self-revelatory, revolutionary, or whatever other kinds of selves we tell the students we like to hear from. As Fan Shen (1989) says in an article about the way he had to learn to write for classes in an American university, he had to leave his Communist Chinese self behind and find a Western self he could be and convey in his essays. This must happen to a lesser degree in classrooms everywhere: the student must decide which self will make the teacher happy and then be that self.

I believe that many of us, with the possible exception of Bronwen, were taught by mentors like Jim who convinced us, sometimes in a magical way, that our voice is our essence, that it somehow defines and represents us. Jim still believes that this is so, and that through the mysterious process of writing, we can transform not only our voices but ourselves. Eleanor believes that we create personae to suit our audiences and purposes, and that manipulating those personae is playful fun. Bronwen tries to assign a specific voice to suit an assignment and its purposes. But all of us, I believe, still hear the powerful words of those early mentors of ours who told us that our voices are ourselves (see Faigley 1989) and that we must struggle to find a true voice for ourselves.

I believe that we can better meet the challenges that teaching presents for us if we are conscious of the dialogism set up for us by a Romantic conception of voice on one hand, so prevalent in our culture if not in our learning background, and a Bakhtinian or social construction notion of voice on the other. I also believe that the more we listen, literally, to the voices of the students we teach, the more we learn about the artifice we call writing and the more we can tap into the students' natural polyvocality.

On the wall, just outside my daughter Ann's purple and black sixties-ish room, hangs a baby quilt in shades of Wedgewood and navy blue calico. It was once the blanket we wrapped her in to take her outside on chilly days; it was once the mat she sat on, propped up by plush toys when she still toppled over while trying to sit alone; it once decorated her room when she was less worldly and less cool (purple and black, you know). Now it stands as a reminder of her infancy and as a memory of the loving hands that shaped and designed it. The front and back of this quilt are stitched together, not with the simple outline of Olive's quilts, but with sunflowers and concentric circles. On the back, a bright red with a tiny blue print, is a cross-stitched square with a tiny sunflower and embroidery which reads, "Ann Gillespie's Puzzle Quilt," the date of her birth, and the initials of the artist, E. T. B., Beth Black, who made it out of friendship and loving welcome. In a strange way, this quilt speaks in Beth's voice. It has her imprint, her name, and somehow her intentions stitched throughout, front and back.

Voice itself is like a quilt: the accents, the intonations, the very words come from others but are designed by us and express us as the quilts in my life have expressed their makers, Olive and Beth. Sometimes the voice is functional and unadorned, serving a specific purpose. Sometimes it is a crafted work of art for us to treasure. But like the quilt, it is never simple, and it is always something of a mystery.

Notes

1. See Berthoff 1988, 114. The diagram on generalizing and interpreting, was specifically what Jim was referring to, but the concept is discussed throughout the book.

2. Toby Fulwiler, at a writing-across-the-curriculum workshop, Marquette University, in fall 1990.

Works Cited

Bakhtin, M. M. 1981. *The Dialogic Imagination: Four Essays.* Edited by Michael Holquist and translated by Caryl Emerson. Austin: University of Texas Press.

Berthoff, Ann E., with James Stephens. 1988. *Forming, Thinking, Writing.* Portsmouth, NH: Boynton/Cook.

Coles, William E., Jr., and James Vopat. 1985. *What Makes Writing Good: A Multiperspective.* Lexington, MA: D. C. Heath.

Faigley, Lester. 1989. "Judging Writing, Judging Selves." *College Composition and Communication* 40.4 (December): 395–412.

Shen, Fan. 1989. "The Classroom and the Wider Culture: Identity as a Key to Learning English Composition." *College Composition and Communication* 40.4 (December): 459–78.

Sommers, Nancy. 1992. "Between the Drafts." *College Composition and Communication* 43.1 (February): 23–31.

11 Voice as Muse, Message, and Medium: The Views of Deaf College Students

John A. Albertini
National Technical Institute for the Deaf
Rochester Institute of Technology

Bonnie Meath-Lang
National Technical Institute for the Deaf
Rochester Institute of Technology

David P. Harris
Georgetown University

The catalyst for our consideration of writer's voice was a brief excerpt from a book of reminiscences by one of America's most respected writers, Eudora Welty:

> Ever since I was first read to, then started reading to myself, there has never been a line read that I didn't *hear*. As my eyes followed the sentence, a voice was saying it silently to me. It isn't my mother's voice, or the voice of any person I can identify, certainly not my own. It is human, but inward, and it is inwardly that I listen to it. It is to me the voice of the story or the poem itself. The cadence, whatever it is that asks you to believe, the feeling that resides in the printed word, reaches me through the reader-voice. I have supposed, but never found out, that this is the case with all readers—to read as listeners—and with all writers, to write as listeners. It may be part of the desire to write. The sound of what falls on the page begins the process of testing it for truth, for me. Whether I am right to trust so far I don't know. By now I don't know whether I could do either one, reading or writing, without the other. My own words, when I am at work on a story, I hear too

Earlier versions of this paper were presented at the Bergamo Conference, Dayton, Ohio, 1986, and at the conference, "Removing the Writing Barrier: A Dream?" at Lehman College, CUNY, 1987. An earlier version also appeared in the proceedings of the Lehman conference. We are grateful to the colleague and students who allowed us to use their reflections on voice.

as they go, in the same voice that I hear when I read in books. When I write and the sound of it comes back to my ears, then I act to make my changes. I have always trusted this voice. (1983, 12–13)

Welty's description of her "inward voice" struck a familiar chord for all three of us, at least in its essential features. Yet, we wondered how alien the concept might be to others who had never had the opportunity to analyze their writing habits. As an experiment, our collaborator at Georgetown University gave the Welty quotation to his newly formed graduate class in "Linguistics and Writing," asking the students to allow a little time for reflection before writing down prior to the next class meeting whatever reactions they had to the Welty statement.

Somewhat to our surprise, we found that almost every student reported experiencing some form of inward voice in the writing process, though they varied considerably in their descriptions of the precise nature and function of that voice. Particularly interesting were the accounts of two of the students who, in acquiring English as a second language, experienced a painful, "soundless period" before the gradual acquisition of an inward voice to guide their writing in the new language. On the basis of this first experience, we were encouraged to raise a question more immediate to two of us: how might the notion of writer's voice be received, constructed, and interpreted by undergraduate students at the National Technical Institute for the Deaf (NTID)?

The connection between students of English as a second language (ESL) and students who are deaf is not without precedent. Since at least 1975, ESL materials and methods have been used to teach students who are deaf (Goldberg and Bordman, 1974). Several comparisons of grammatical ability have appeared (for example, Berent 1983), and, as recent comparisons of written samples have shown (Langston and Maxwell 1988; Swisher, Butler-Wall, and Stavans 1988), the writing of deaf students is difficult to distinguish from other (hearing) learners of English, this in spite of the fact that most deaf college students have grown up in homes where only English was spoken. (Fewer than 10 percent of American deaf students grow up learning American Sign Language as a first language.)

Culturally and politically, there are parallels as well. Though defined by the Federal Government of the United States as persons with a "disability" (see, for example, the Americans with Disabilities Act of 1990), many deaf people regard themselves as members of a linguistic and cultural minority. Writers such as Padden and Humphries (1988) point out that there are community-based conventions, protocols, and courtesies, often emanating from interrelated family and school histories, and from the distinctive demands of a visual language. The political voice of the deaf community was heard in 1988 when students at Gallaudet University—a university primarily for deaf students in Washington, D.C.—protested the appointment of a hearing person as the new president of the university. Their campaign for a "Deaf President Now" was compared in the media to the civil rights demonstrations three decades before. Given our experience with the perspectives on voice of hearing students at Georgetown and our teaching of deaf students, we wondered how students at NTID, who were born deaf or deafened before the acquisition of a spoken language, would react to the voice metaphor. Would they find it relevant or appealing?

We also saw the metaphor of voice contextualized within some of our earlier work with these students. Our autobiographical and journal work with this group of students (for example, Meath-Lang, Caccamise, and Albertini 1982; Albertini and Meath-Lang 1986) has elicited personal and autobiographical perspectives from students that might be said to have been written in their own voices. A more direct examination of voice, we thought, might help to explain why some teachers use journals to help students move to more formal types of discourse. A number of writing texts for college students, for example, argue that personal writing, journals, and first-person monologues are imbued with voice. As such, they are frequently viewed as a preparation for "formal writing" (Shaughnessy 1977; Moffett 1981; Murray 1985; Burnham 1989). Likewise, with elementary students, it has been argued that dialogue journals can serve as a curricular transition between a student's well-developed oral communication strategies and more formal types of written discourse (Peyton 1988; Shuy 1988). Similarly, for ESL students (for example, Vanett and Jurich 1990) and for deaf students (for example, Peyton 1989), it has been proposed that informal and interactive writing can prepare students directly for academic writing, by giving evidence of transition and such functions as comparing or contrasting. When students write about personal topics to a known audience and are permitted to focus on function rather than form, they often write with confidence and fluency.

We should proceed cautiously, however, with wholly instrumental rationales for the use of journals and other forms of personal writing, since such rationales implicitly devalue personal writing, or writing in one's own voice. "Decentering" becomes a goal in the writing curriculum (Elbow 1985). Formal writing is termed more abstract, and writing for unknown audiences is regarded as a cognitively superior achievement. In one text for writing teachers, the ability to write impersonally on a preassigned topic is likened to the child's emergence from Piagetian or Vygotskian egocentricity (Moffett 1981, 145). Viewed from this perspective—as preparatory or as an initial step—personal writing or writing with voice may be viewed as immature. Fortunately, such assumptions are currently being reconsidered by those investigating relationships between and functions of speech and writing (for example, Elbow 1985; 1989; and others in this volume).

Having used journals with deaf college students in the past, we decided to ask the students in an NTID writing course directly about voice. Since the syllabus included a discussion of voice in writing based on a text by Macrorie (1985), we decided to elicit their perspectives at the beginning of the course. The twenty students in this course were all first- and second-year, technically oriented deaf students. The course was preparatory in that it was intended for students who had not been admitted into the regular liberal arts sequence, which begins with an English composition course. In other preparatory courses, these students had focused on reading, vocabulary, and sentence-level grammatical structures. The students all had severe to profound hearing losses as college students and, as young children, had hearing losses which prevented complete access to spoken English; most were born deaf. Differences in degree and type of hearing loss, age of onset, and personal choice all affect the extent to which these students understand speech and use their own voices. As children, most had speech training; as adults, the choice of whether or not to use one's voice may have as much to do with social identity as with ability. In other words, the students in this class were representative of the NTID student body: some were proficient users of American Sign Language or another form of signing; others were learning to sign as adults; some could speak intelligibly, while others rarely used their voices; some relied on lipreading, others on sign language. We also asked a late-deafened colleague, someone who could remember spoken voices, for his thoughts on the topic. Thus, the twenty students and colleague were asked to write a response to the following general, open-ended prompt (concerned that undergraduates might be heavily influenced by the views of a professional writer, we decided not to use the Welty quotation):

Voice

Many people talk about something called "voice" in a person's writing. They say that writing has a voice. Some writers talk about hearing a voice; others talk about finding a voice. What does voice mean to you? What do you think voice might be?

One student wrote less than a page and commented at the bottom, "This topic is bad for me to write [about]." Most of the others, however, seemed engaged by the topic and wrote two or three handwritten pages; two wrote three-page, typewritten responses. As expected, the students had generally not thought about the topic before. Only one student, Patricia Lynn Bruce, indicated a previous encounter with the metaphor; she had performed in a play entitled, "One Voice." Another had read ahead for this assignment, quoting accurately from the Macrorie text. While nine of the twenty students included "speech" in their definitions of voice, all except one went beyond the sound-based description of voice to include the metaphorical and metaphysical.

Out of the various and complex definitions of voice, we were able to identify three themes that recurred frequently across the twenty responses. Seven students referred to an inner voice or to inner speech, and we have interpreted these as being similar to the voice Welty "hears" when she reads or writes—similar in function, at least, since we cannot know the internal voices of others. The common feature of these descriptions seems to be that the internal voice is regarded as a *muse* or a guide. In addition, students wrote that voice was either feelings or knowledge which they wanted to communicate to others; for a total of fourteen students, voice was their *message*. Third, five students felt that their written voices bore the stamp of their personalities; the style of their writing, or the *medium*, was a distinctive and recognizable voice. In addition, three students mentioned sign language as a part of their voice; and one summarized the grammatical distinction between the active and passive voice. Here, we will focus on the three main themes: voice-as-muse, voice-as-message, and voice-as-medium.

Voice-as-Muse

The seven students who wrote of an inner voice described the experience as either hearing their own voice as they wrote or, in four cases, sensing a voice telling them what to do. In this analysis, we consider them as one category. For one of the students, Troy Dayton, the acoustic sense of his own voice was very strong. He calls it his "brain voice" and claims, like Eudora Welty, that he could not write without it:

> When I am writing personal letters such as writing to my mother or friends of mine, I hear my voice talking as if I was talking aloud.
>   I always depend on my voicing as I am writing. Without my voice, I would not be able to concentrate on what I want to say. If

> I didn't hear no voicing in my mind then I am writing nothing on paper. It's like I am an air-head with no voice.

His voice is a source of focus for topic or process. For another student, voice means you "talk to yourself as you write, which means you are thinking and saying what you think inside of your head. . . ." This sounds very much like Vygotskian inner speech, a merger of language and thought (see Vygotsky 1962). One woman describes this "internal dialogue" in terms of a concrete, visual metaphor:

> A voice in my clear image, reminds me of myself as talking to myself in front of a mirror. There are as well emotions in it. I feel the voice in me, [as] if it was correcting my errors, emotions and my writing.

The merger of voice and vision becomes an act of imagination for one student, who hears both his own voice and the voices of others when he writes:

> When I write I imagine my own voice in writing, something that doesn't involve any other characters; but when I write a story or an essay with different characters, then I imagine I'm hearing different voices from each character.

In essence, he seems to be describing what T. S. Eliot has called the "dramatic voices" in a poem (1957). For Eliot, a poem is, among other things, a collection of dramatic voices; and the reader's task is to discern those voices. The attitudes, qualities, and personalities projected in these voices give meaning to the poem.

Three students focus on the voice of another, a voice telling them what to do. In the first part of her response, Cheryl Gard describes a voice in her head, and she is not sure whose voice it is:

> Sometimes I feel that I have voices in my head. Sometimes I feel like the voices in my head were talking to me. It is usually about good & evil. Like when I was about to do the evil things, the good things in my head tell me not to; "It is evil if you do this." It is like thinking of what is right or wrong to do that. The voices from my head tell me something, like it is controlling my behavior. . . . It is like there is a different person which doesn't exist talking to me. I wonder if it is my soul. When I write to someone, it is like my voice is talking to another people while they were not there. And when those people get my letter, they "hear" my voice when I wasn't there.

In the last sentence of this excerpt, Ms. Gard connects the metaphysical notion of voice, the "other" voice, with the notion of voice as medium, which we shall consider below.

Tracey Wyant describes voice in wholly metaphysical terms and is the only one in this group who does not relate the concept of voice to her own writing:

> Voice means someone to inform you about something. Voice could be spoken to you in writing or in person or feel something is speaking to you thru voice. Voice could be someone to warn me or guide me to do something right. In my mind, I have thought about this before. I believe the voice is a mystery. From my own experience, I was going thru a rough time, one day, someone called my name and I looked all over my apt for someone calling me. . . . I believe it was the Lord calling me to warn me about something to be prepared [for].

Kathleen Walsh, like Cheryl Gard, mentions both notions, voice as medium first and then as muse (a muse that sounds suspiciously like an English teacher):

> Often, I think about my writing [as having] a voice when I see the word that I expressed, the personality descriptions. I used to listen to the second opinion inside the voice, like telling me, "watch out your grammar" or something to warn me. So that I can be very careful to look back when I finished the story.

Troy Dayton and his two classmates made the basic association of voice to speaking or signing, an association possibly suggested by the wording of our prompt. Nevertheless, Ms. Gard's and Ms. Wyant's are clearly metaphysical, moving beyond this basic association and beyond Welty's notion of the "trusted other" that she hears when writing. Again, the comparison we are attempting to draw here is one of function: for some of our respondents, voice is that which provides direction for life, as well as for writing.

Voice-as-Message

Voice-as-muse is an internal construct: the writer listens to and follows the voice. Voice-as-message and voice-as-medium, on the other hand, are external in that they refer to what is produced in the act of writing. Voice-as-muse has to be described by the writer; voice-as-message and voice-as-medium can be described by the reader. For our deaf writers, the construct of voice as something to be communicated (message) loomed large in their responses. All mentioned communication, whether it was communication in general, "a way of communication," or "talking to someone." Communicating one's feelings, as described below by Jeff Dillenburg, was mentioned by eleven of the writers:

I think a "voice" means a message. It is a message that we use in order to communicate with someone as in writing. We use "voice" to understand each other. "Voice" is a sound that comes from our minds from our writings to give out messages. It is hard to explain what is "voice" deeply. It is very unique and interesting to figure out what is "voice." I think "voice" is a way of reaching people's feelings, giving them a message that is important to them. People use their voices to get the other person attention. . . .

Oh yeah, I think my writing has a voice, because I am expressing how I feel and what is important to me, of course to them (the other readers) too. Everything that I say in writing is a way of giving message into one's minds as a "voice." It (voice) is a sound that we express our feelings or ideas in our writings.

Without a voice or sound how would we communicate or express our feelings. I mean sometimes it is hard to know how a person feels when he/she has a problem without a "voice." . . .

Finding a "voice" is another way when a person is reading another person's writing or letter. It is another way to get people to read books or whatever. . . . Finding a voice is like knowing whose voice it is on a note or letter. Everyone write differently which means everyone's voices are different too (I hope you understand what I mean) It is hard to explain it in deeply.

I think "voice" might be a message or sound that expresses one's feelings, thoughts, and ideas, or of course opinions. It shows how ones can communicate with another person or people. . . . And it is the sound where we say in our writings into one's minds. I guess it is a way of understanding with another person. . . .

For Jeff Dillenburg, voice is the expression of feelings but also a way of "reaching [other] people's feelings." He opens and closes his description by stating that voice is communicating with *and* understanding another. In the first two paragraphs, he asserts that the message is important for others and for himself. Should others fail to recognize its importance, voice will get their attention. Voice is a message but also a *quality* of that message which allows us to reach or to engage the mind and feelings of another. Understanding occurs when we can communicate; and communication is extremely important for this student. In the last two paragraphs of his description, he writes, as others have, of finding the distinctive voice of another in letters.

Another student, Patricia Lynn Bruce, describes a more specific message. For Ms. Bruce, voice is describing what it is like to be a deaf person in a hearing society. She recalls a high school play entitled "One Voice," the title of which stands both for the play and for a message disabled people have for those who are not:

There are so many things that people have different physical or problems. Only one thing we have is voice. We also use voice in

> writing that describe voices. Voice can tell the people who do not
> have [the] kind of thing we have such as deafness, blind, crippled,
> etc. People would be aware how selfish they have [been] but
> voices can guide to help us to be altogether in a one world as "One
> Voice."

Here, Patricia Lynn Bruce uses voice in a political sense, much like
other groups in American society—women and language minorities,
for example—have used the term. Writers such as Gilligan (1982),
Spender (1985), Belenky, Clinchy, Goldberger, and Tarule (1986) have
pointed out the dominant male voice in studies of moral development
and the biases against voices of relationship and caring in academic and
business discourse. Richard Ruiz (1989) likens voice to agency and
empowerment. He has visited classrooms where the variety of Spanish
brought to school by the child was rarely spoken, much less taught.
Here, he asserts, exclusion of a minority language has coincided with
the exclusion of that minority's voice. Ms. Bruce's contention is that
persons who are "disabled" in this society have a common message or
voice, the expression of which can inform and unify.

Mary Denise Patin is the student writer who most clearly introduces
the reflexive aspect of voice-as-expression of feelings:

> From the experience that I have learned in writing recently, I
> realize that writing is a way of expressing your feelings toward a
> topic or an issue. So, voice in writing is a way to speak out or
> express your feelings and opinions that relates to the topic and
> yourself.
>
> Voice in writing has helped me to express my feelings to the
> paper as if I was talking to someone. For example, I had to do the
> journal-writing to my English teacher and had learn how to ex-
> press my feelings or thoughts when it comes to writing. In doing
> this, this has help me get the feedback on my own personal values
> and expectations. Also, writing letters to someone I care about and
> don't see them for a long time has helped me to build up a
> confidence in me. After all, what does "voice" means to me? I
> think voice means it has to do with the idea of having an imagi-
> nation of someone to be a part of you to be friends with and
> knowing that you can know who to count on when you have
> doubts about something—like on "voice in writings" which I
> strongly believe in . . . you can always (sometimes) write a letter
> to relieve the stress or worries off on you.

In expressing one's feelings and in getting feedback, it seems, one
understands the feelings better. One shapes one's message in the actual
act of writing to another, and getting a response to one's voice (as in a
dialogue journal or a letter) helps build confidence.

Ms. Patin's allusion to letter writing is echoed by nine of our student writers, suggesting that letters are a primary genre for them. We note this for two reasons: first, the students are clearly aware of their conversational voices in letters; and second, some have developed a strong sense of the self-as-writer in relation to a reader. Linda Grot explains:

> [Voice] shows the feelings of expressions as it seems a voice in it. But when you write to someone as a letter, there is a voice in it also . . . When I wrote a letter to my family or friend, they said on this letter that they are happy to hear from me. So that means they heard my voices . . . as they are thinking about me.

This sense of the self as a writer may be rooted in childhood experiences. In her investigation of literacy in the deaf community, Maxwell found that writing for personal interaction (for example, notes about appointments and TTY/telephone conversations) was more often used in families with deaf parents than in families with hearing parents (Maxwell 1985, 216). Whether or not these students come from families with deaf parents, they have corresponded and are clearly aware of the power of their own written voices in conveying their attitudes and opinions and in eliciting response and interest.

Not all the messages were about feelings, however. For Stevee Stayer, voice has to do with telling the truth:

> In my opinion voice is the true writing from the person, but not always. It is like when someone wants to write or say without his own voice, he is more likely to cover everything that belongs to writing or conservation. If I don't want write about voice, I would for sure make up that does not make sense or doesn't fit with the topic by not telling right words. This is a fake voice. I've a perfect example below.
>   Over these years, a woman finally told the court the true about her false experience of rape. This was her voice. Before that, she didn't use her voice to prevent something she did wrong. When she used her voice, I noticed she had so much to tell, to say, to write and to express. She wrote a very long story that fascinated to readers. It means she found the right voice that made her story successful. Also it means that everything seems belong together that can't easily be denied or forgotten. She knew she could [not] deny the truth for the rest of her life. I'd love to deny everything I did wrong, but I cannot at all because they (the facts) were already existed.

Finally, related to the expression of feelings and ideas, we should note that three students extended the voice metaphor specifically to include signing. One example is Paulino Patino's view, excerpted below:

> In general, a voice means to you that people in their community use "spoken" language to communicate ideas and feelings with each other. If the people do not have the voice, how can they communicate them with each other? I think that the voice might be a sign, a speech and an English writing because these are kinds of "spoken" language.

In Patino's definition, it is difficult to distinguish between voice as message and medium. On the one hand, voice means communicating ideas and feelings; on the other hand, voice is the means of communicating with each other. Furthermore, the means is broken down into the three forms of common, everyday language (in his terms, "spoken language"): signing, speech, and writing. Voice, or the message, may be conveyed in all three modes of communication.

Voice-as-Medium

Saying you can "hear" a person in a letter implies that the print conveys something of the individuality of that person; and our third category arises from frequent references made to the individual nature of voice in personal letters. Five students wrote of being able to identify the writer of a letter from the words and expressions used, as well as from the content. This attention to form we call "voice-as-medium." One student provided the following scenario:

> The voice mean to me that when someone is writing on the papers, most of time, the paper has the voice of that person who wrote. Let suppose when we know someone very well and that person write us the letter without their name on it. When we read that letter and start think who have those feeling, expression, habit of say. All sudden we will know that person who wrote that letter. It can be connected with person's voice as feeling, expression on the paper.

This student claims to be able to identify the writer from familiar feelings expressed but also from the "expression[s]" and turns of phrase ("habit of say") themselves. The moment of recognition occurs when the reader connects the person's "voice as feeling" with the "expression on the paper."

All of the students who mentioned voice-as-medium either connected the notion to expression of a message (usually feelings) or to an internal voice-as-muse. As cited earlier, Cheryl Gard described both a metaphysical notion of voice and also writing as a medium of her personality. When people got her letters, they "heard" her voice. Jeff

Dillenburg, also quoted earlier, described both voice as message and voice as medium. Here we repeat a segment:

> Finding a voice is like knowing whose voice it is on a note or a letter. Everyone write differently which means everyone's voices are different too. (I hope you understand what I mean) It is hard to explain it in deeply.

Patricia Lynn Bruce, who wrote of the disabled person's message, touches on all three kinds of voice in the beginning of her response:

> I, Patricia Lynn, believe that VOICE in writing is using for communication and feelings. We write each other as writing journals, letters, or stories. In the feeling, we shared the experience with people who are not similar except the voice. We used voice to help us to guide in right place where we can be together . . . we use that kind of voice in writing. . . .
>
> In journals, I write many things I can think of, share the problems, or anything I want to write. I can show how much the voice is saying such as little mad or very mad. I used alot of adjectives or descriptive to make the reader understand the words by using explanations of what I am trying to say. In letter, I used my writing but I also used some voices as the way I write with punctuations.

Ms. Bruce is aware that adjectives and other forms of description give a distinctive character to her writing. Like Mr. Patino and the first student cited in this section, Ms. Bruce's definition points to an overlap of voice-as-message and voice-as-medium: a blurring, perhaps, of the distinction between content and form. Their definitions do not differentiate between the two; rather, they integrate the two aspects.

Finally, we would like to briefly discuss a colleague's response. Professor Harry Lang's definition of voice includes both message and medium. As a late-deafened adult, his voice (message) "bridges the worlds of the other, helping those who will always remain in one world understand the world of the other." As it did for Ms. Bruce, voice has a political meaning for Professor Lang: voice is the understanding of a life (or lives) in different worlds. He also treats voice as a medium by comparing written voice to the individual quality of a person's spoken voice. In a letter addressed to two of us, he writes:

> "Ouch!" in print calls up my own or my sister's or a friend's exclamation from the past. "Ouch!" seen on the lips of one of you appears in my mind with the voice it has assigned to you, each different, each mysteriously given a pitch or quality which my mind, acting very much like a computer, has assigned to your physical build and personality as I have grown to know it. . . .
>
> This is a very broad concept to me. Every writer has voice. I like to compare a writer's voice to the spoken voice. Quality is shown

> by the harmonics of the mind—intelligence, wit, style, the flow of energy in conveying the message intended. . . .
>
> Inflection, stress, intonation—all are unique to each writer as she or he voices a message to the readers. . . . The resonance of a vocal tract is where the energy peaks. Resonance in a writer's voice is found where he or she chooses to focus the energy. . . .

Professor Lang draws an analogy between the qualities of spoken voice and the features of a person's writing. The resonance of a piece of writing comes from a coalescence of a message and the way it is constructed. He also implies that just as a speaker can modify one's vocal tract, so can a writer alter the combination of features in a text, thereby conveying a different focus of energy, a different resonance, a different voice.

Conclusion

Writing about voice proved a difficult but reasonable task for the students; some clearly enjoyed it. All except one student responded to the metaphor, and their responses seem best characterized as voice-as-muse, voice-as-message, and voice-as-medium. Seven of the responses fell into more than one category; and as a group, their definitions spanned the range of definitions that we have encountered in the literature. Regarding their notions of voice, we draw three additional conclusions from this analysis. First, students associated voice with dialogue, whether they talked to themselves or to another in letters or journals. This is consistent with current thinking on the nature of voice informed by Bakhtin (Todorov 1984), where voice, the speaking personality, anticipates the answering word. Second, the students commonly associated voice with the expression of feelings or individual personalities, often merging the two. Third, students regarded voice as an effective, even necessary, component of personal writing. These writers' suggestion of dialogue and emphasis on communication of feelings (recall Jeff Dillenburg's excerpt) may reflect a prominent concern for communication at various points in their lives. Deafness may isolate a child from hearing parents and siblings, a classmate from other classmates, a person who signs from one who does not. For over 100 years, the teaching of communication (primarily the English language) has been the central preoccupation in the field of education of the deaf (Moores 1978). It should come as no surprise, then, that these writers define voice in terms of communicating with another.

As teachers of writing, we can respond to these students' concerns for dialogue and understanding. While not "process writing" per se

(Elbow 1981), writing about voice may help students to reflect on their writing. When we respond to the individuality and personality in our students' writing, or describe our impressions of a student's written voice, we may provide a mirror. In responding to students' messages, we may help them to shape ideas and opinions; possibly, we begin or sustain a dialogue. This dialogue will, at some point, involve an examination of ourselves as readers—what *we* bring to the reading as well as what students have brought to the writing. We provide the mirror which sends back, not a faithful reproduction, but an *interpreted* message or image. In this sense, too, voice is dialogical.

There is a specific pedagogical loop possible in this process which connects our three notions of voice. By focusing on voice-as-muse, we encourage students to listen to themselves and to reflect on what they have said. By addressing voice-as-message and voice-as-medium, we encourage students to consider what they have to say and how they come across to others. The connection is that focusing on all three notions may foster confidence. Being allowed to listen to our own voices, we develop a faith in those voices; we build up our confidence. This, in turn, enables us to write confidently, knowing that our message is important to others; we can focus on the medium and write with authority. For those deaf students who have experienced failure and frustration as writers, a practice that leads them to think of themselves as writers, possessing voice and messages for others, would be a unique and possibly emancipating educational experience.

Postscripts

Having presented our findings collaboratively—with one voice, so to speak—we would clearly be untrue to our topic if we did not each add a few words in our individual voices, voices that inevitably reflect, *inter alia*, differences in our professional experience.

David P. Harris

I have worked almost exclusively with hearing students, a considerable portion of them speakers of English as a second language. As suggested earlier in this essay, it appears that a number of parallels can validly be drawn between the teaching of second-language learners and the teaching of deaf learners. Thus, as I have thought about the findings of our study, I have found myself interpreting these in part from an ESL perspective. One of the most interesting topics to emerge from this exercise involves what might be called the political implications of the deaf students' responses. We in the ESL field have become increasingly sensitive to the fact that "second-language learning in some respects involves the acquisition of a second identity" (Brown 1987, 128). In consequence, we try our best to avoid any classroom activities or devices that might convey the impression that we are trying to *replace* one language and culture ("identity") with another. Rather, we want our students to experience the advantages—the flexibility and power—that come from the acquisition of two languages, two identities. We may even try to provide some classroom opportunities for our students to "give voice to" both their first and second identities through the medium of their second language.

Such was my orientation as I set about examining our subjects' responses. My first reaction was one of pleasant surprise to find how readily the deaf students accepted the concept of voice. In this, and in the wide range of interpretations they gave to the concept, they behaved very much like the hearing students I had surveyed at Georgetown. What makes the graceful adaptiveness of the deaf students of particular interest, of course, is that they are accommodating to a metaphor originating in the hearing community. But do they, at the same time, find ways to apply the voice concept to their own special culture, that is, in a sense express *themselves* politically? We have already pointed out that some of our subjects indeed do: "Voice can tell [i.e., inform] the people who do not have [the] kind of thing we have such as deafness" (Bruce); "I think that the voice might be a sign [i.e., be expressed through signing]" (Patino); "[The voice of the deaf person] bridges the worlds of the other [i.e., the hearing person]" (Lang).

What I have learned from our admittedly small-scale study, then, is that the voice metaphor appears to be sufficiently "robust" to be meaningful even to deaf students. Were I teaching communication skills to such students, I would surely wish to assign them a writing task similar to that reported here, with the expectation that it would prove pedagogically most useful to me and quite likely self-revelatory to them.

Bonnie Meath-Lang

The students whose voices created this paper reach out to me from a distance. It is difficult for me now, living in the everyday of new classes, to achieve the immediacy and particularity of the day-to-day concerns of that classroom community—the urgent notes, the media events, the clothes, the latest campus crisis coloring our words. What I do remember most about that period of posing the question and writing a first version of this paper was an intense examination of my own history as a student and academic. In my various re-creations of the past, it seemed that I was alternately losing and finding my voice as often as one might lose an umbrella or recover a single glove.

There were two overriding reasons for this plunge into introspection. First, learning from the students' experiences and my own could prevent me from becoming an accomplice in the silencing of young writers spoken of in mainstream work, such as that of Peter Elbow and Ken Macrorie, and in work centering on oppressed groups, such as that of Paulo Freire and Mary Belenky. Put more directly and personally, from a feminist and qualitatively oriented perspective, I did not want to put students through what I had gone through in learning to write. The second goal of this reflection was addressing an uneasiness with my own and others' notion of voice. I had been developing a sense that voice is a far more stable phenomenon than it is, that we all have some authentic voice trapped between our personalities and our inhibitions, fighting to get loose from the constraints of arcane, field-demanding discourses. While I could not deny the latter part of that statement, the notion of a single, true voice was becoming less convincing to me. I looked to the students' texts again with both issues in mind.

As I read and reread the students' words, and noted how they moved, within their essays, among the categories of muse, medium, and message, it occurred to me that there is a danger—danger, yes, but of a restricted sort—in destroying the voices of students. We have little access to the students' muse—be it conscience, a lover, a model writer, a god—and thus have negligible effect on this source of energy. This voice, these students tell us, is known in a particular, relational way to the person who follows it. On the other hand, the medium or personality is, if we are alert, a rich resource—even when teaching specific types of professional writing. In recent technical and professional writing classes, students and I have "tried on" other voices—those of parents, teachers, friends—to effect, and contrasted them with the demands of a professional situation. In this context, the "technical" language becomes only another of our voices. It is the message, ultimately, where we teachers must be most cautious and respectful. When we are making suggestions concerning style, grammar, and word choice, we need to have consistent dialogue with students, so not to tamper with the meaning of the message. The current movement to writing conferences is a positive safeguard toward enhancing, versus neutralizing or destroying, the voice-as-message.

As for the issue of the stability of voice, last week I received a letter from Ms. Bruce, who is now studying fashion and modeling. As engaging as her piece on the play "One Voice" in this essay is, her present voice has grown as she has grown and moved beyond us. She has new muses, I suspect, the rhythms of a new place and profession in her words, and new messages to send and ponder. Mikhail Bakhtin (1984) tells us that "the world is full of other people's words" (200–1), and the students we have met in this paper are experiencing them even as I write this. These days, I am much more comfortable in that double-voiced, multiple-voiced universe of Bakhtin's. For he acknowledges that we develop, compromise, and even masquerade our voices from necessity. All that we can lose, then, is the desire to examine them.

John A. Albertini

As a student of literacy, I was struck by the prominence and importance of writing in these students' personal and educational lives. Their writing supports Maxwell's (1985) claim that low levels of educational literacy as measured by standardized tests reflect neither the cultural significance nor actual use of literacy in the deaf community. In her extensive interviews, she found that writing was important for communication among deaf people as well as between deaf and hearing people. In addition, she found that hearing parents of deaf children lacked this cultural perspective and that both hearing and deaf teachers neglected it. The students contributing to this report come from a later generation than Maxwell's respondents. Yet, they come from similar backgrounds and share a traditional, school-based conception of literacy. The paradox of working with these students is that they view themselves as incompetent writers, yet when addressed as writers, they produce thoughtful and compelling descriptions of their experience.

For the classroom, their views provide a text for the further investigation of voice. After showing selections from this report to a recent class, one student extended the metaphor to body language and gesture. In a short piece on "voice" written for this class, Tod Carter describes an encounter with a Mexican street vendor who wants to sell him a blanket. The customer is deaf and does not speak Spanish; the vendor is hearing and does not speak English. Once the vendor realizes the double communication barrier, "His voice became [a mixture of] body language and gestures at the same time as his voice sounds [went] silent. His gestures are clearly to communicate with me. We bargained in the gestures to get the better deal." In this piece, Mr. Carter suggests a visual correlate to what Peter Elbow has called "audible voice" in writing (see chapter 1, this volume). Three students in this report noted that individual personality could be expressed in sign as well as in speech and writing. Mr. Carter is suggesting a more general construct:

"visual voice." The vendor used a set of postures and gestures determined by situation and culture.

For me as a writer, the project has raised new questions about my own voice or repertoire of voices. The original questions galvanized our interest; the student texts and a common purpose provided the focus for collaboration. Yet, a recurrent question has been which voice(s) to use in writing the various drafts of this paper; and trying to make our voices speak as one proved difficult. The present volume has provided a context for this final version: a compromise, perhaps, between "collective voice" and "collected voice."

Works Cited

Albertini, John A., and Bonnie Meath-Lang. 1986. "An Analysis of Student-Teacher Exchanges in Dialogue Journal Writing." *Journal of Curriculum Theorizing* 7: 153–201.

Bakhtin, M. M. 1984. *Problems of Dostoevsky's Poetics*. Edited and translated by Caryl Emerson. Manchester, England: University of Manchester.

Belenky, Mary Field, Blythe McVicker Clinchy, Nancy Rule Goldberger, and Jill Mattuck Tarule. 1986. *Women's Ways of Knowing: The Development of Self, Voice, and Mind*. New York: Basic Books.

Berent, G. P. 1983. "Control Judgements by Deaf Adults and by Second Language Learners." *Language Learning* 33: 37–53.

Brown, H. Douglas. 1987. *Principles of Language Learning and Teaching*. 2nd ed. Englewood Cliffs, NJ: Prentice-Hall.

Burnham, C. C. 1989. *Writing from the Inside Out*. New York: Harcourt, Brace, Jovanovich.

Elbow, Peter. 1981. *Writing with Power: Techniques for Mastering the Writing Process*. New York: Oxford University Press.

———. 1985. "The Shifting Relationships between Speech and Writing." *College Composition and Communication* 36.3 (October): 283–303.

———. 1989. "The Pleasures of Voice in the Literary Essay: Explorations in the Prose of Gretel Ehrlich and Richard Selzer." In *Literary Nonfiction: Theory, Criticism, Pedagogy*, edited by Chris Anderson, 211–34. Carbondale: Southern Illinois University Press.

Eliot, T. S. 1957. "The Three Voices of Poetry." In *On Poetry and Poets*, 89–102. London: Faber & Faber.

Gilligan, Carol. 1982. *In a Different Voice: Psychological Theory and Women's Development*. Cambridge, MA: Harvard University Press.

Goldberg, J. P., and M. B. Bordman. 1974. "English Language Instruction for the Hearing Impaired: An Adaptation of ESL Methodology." *TESOL Quarterly* 8: 263–70.

Langston, C., and M. Maxwell. 1988. "Holistic Judgement of Texts by Deaf and ESL Students." *Sign Language Studies* 60: 295–312.

Macrorie, Ken. 1985. *Telling Writing*. Upper Montclair, NJ: Boynton/Cook.

Maxwell, M. 1985. "Some Functions and Uses of Literacy in the Deaf Community." *Language in Society* 14: 205–21.

Meath-Lang, Bonnie, F. C. Caccamise, and John A. Albertini. 1982. "Deaf Students' Views on Their English Language Learning." In *Interpersonal Communication and Deaf People*, edited by H. Hoemann and R. Wilbur, 295–327. Washington, D.C.: Gallaudet University Press.

Moffett, James 1981. *Active Voice: A Writing Program Across the Curriculum*. Upper Montclair, NJ: Boynton/Cook.

Moores, Donald F. 1978. *Educating the Deaf: Psychology, Principles, and Practices*. Boston: Houghton-Mifflin.

Morrissey, Patricia A. 1991. *A Primer for Corporate America on Civil Rights for the Disabled*. Horsham, PA: LRP Publications.

Murray, Donald M. 1985. *A Writer Teaches Writing*. Boston: Houghton-Mifflin.

Padden, Carol, and Tom Humphries. 1988. *Deaf in America: Voices from a Culture*. Cambridge, MA: Harvard University Press.

Peyton, Joy Kreeft. 1988. "Dialogue Writing—Bridge from Talk to Essay." In *Dialogue Journal Communication: Classroom, Linguistic, Social and Cognitive Views*, edited by Jana Staton, Roger W. Shuy, Joy Kreeft Peyton, and L. Reed, 88–106. Norwood, NJ: Ablex.

———. 1989. "Cross-Age Tutoring on a Local Area Computer Network: Moving from Informal Interaction to Formal Academic Writing." *The Writing Instructor* 8: 57–67.

Ruiz, Richard. 1989. "The Empowerment of Language-Minority Students." In *Empowerment through Multicultural Education*, edited by Christine E. Sleeter, 217–27. Albany: State University of New York Press.

Shaughnessy, Mina P. 1977. *Errors and Expectations: A Guide for the Teacher of Basic Writing*. New York: Oxford University Press.

Shuy, Roger W. 1988. "The Oral Language Basis for Dialogue Journals." In *Dialogue Journal Communication: Classroom, Linguistic, Social and Cognitive Views*, edited by Jana Staton, Roger W. Shuy, Joy Kreeft Peyton, and L. Reed, 73–87. Norwood, NJ: Ablex.

Spender, Dale. 1985. *Man-Made Language*. 2nd ed. London: Routledge & Kegan Paul.

Swisher, M. V., B. Butler-Wall, and A. Stavans. 1988. *Written Errors of Deaf Students, ESL, SED, and Natives*. Paper presented at the 22nd Annual TESOL Convention. Chicago, Illinois. March.

Todorov, Tzvetan. 1984. *Mikhail Bakhtin: The Dialogical Principle*. Minneapolis: University of Minnesota Press.

Vanett, L., and D. Jurich. 1990. "The Missing Link: Connecting Journal Writing to Academic Writing." In *Students and Teachers Writing Together: Perspectives on Journal Writing*, edited by Joy Kreeft Peyton, 21–33. Alexandria, VA: Teachers of English to Speakers of Other Languages.

Vygotsky, Lev. 1962. *Thought and Language*. Edited and translated by Eugenia Hanfmann and Gertrude Vakar. Cambridge, MA: MIT Press.

Welty, Eudora. 1983. *One Writer's Beginnings*. New York: Warner.

12 Varieties of the "Other": Voice and Native American Culture

Tom Carr
University of Colorado

While I stood there, I saw more than I can tell, and I understood more than I saw; for I was seeing in a sacred manner the shapes of all things in the spirit, and the shape of all things as they must live together like one being.

—Black Elk (Ogalala Sioux)

In our intercourse with the Indians it must always be borne in mind that we are the more powerful party.... We ... claim the right to control the soil which they occupy. And we assume that it is our duty to coerce them, if necessary, into the adoption and practice of our habits and customs.

—Columbus Delane,
"Report of the Secretary of the Interior," 1872,
3–4. (Spicer 1969, 235)

Two writers; two languages; two cultures with very different world-views: both focused on what passes for the same experience. What we have begun more fully to appreciate of late, however, is that this experience has not been, and is not, universal, is not the same for its diverse participants, all our myths notwithstanding. This is especially true for the Indian. Traditionally, of course, what we have known of Native American cultures has come from poorly handled political dealings, superstitious colonial folklore, and primitive anthropological ethnographies of the nineteenth and early twentieth centuries. Through these sources of misinformation, those in the mainstream culture have created an Indian that was a better match *for* their needs than *to* the people and the cultures being "otherized," being portrayed alternately as sub-human and as special-human. The effect of both portrayals not only diminished the Indian, but distorted and silenced native peoples and their cultures.

The primary focus of this essay will be to examine the history of this "otherization" of the Native American peoples by Western society, as well as to link this otherization to the concepts of silence, appropriation, and voice.

The Concept of the Other

"Otherization" is a process that has been applied to various peoples in addition to Native Americans. In his text *Anthropology and the Western Tradition,* Jacob Pandian (1985) attributes many Western constructs to the Judeo-Christian view of the dichotomized self. In this tradition there is both the divine *true self* representing godliness and cultural correctness, and the *untrue self* representing the darker side of human experience. Pandian claims that this view of human nature "rejects the enactment of the complexity of the human condition in its representation of divinity" (124). According to Pandian, then, in this simplistic view the true self was associated with godliness while anything that did not correspond with the divine being was perceived as less than human. This view of man was in turn projected out of the individual self into elements of the surrounding environment. Nothing was spared this treatment; plants, animals, all things in nature—everything— became either good or evil. And as the explorers and missionaries of the Western cultures embodying this tradition began their domination over the rest of the world, they applied this dichotomous typology to the non-Christian peoples they encountered.

During this period, the image of the Native North American provided Europe with a romantic symbol of the settling of the North American continent (Mead 1960, 3). But even in this romanticizing, the American Indian came to be seen negatively—as non-Christian, less-than-human *other*—uncivilized, disorderly, bloodthirsty, and cannibalistic (Pandian 1985, 65). In the increasingly dichotomized worldview of colonial Europe, the American Indian became the symbol of the savage other. Pandian writes:

> The symbol of the savage has a long history: the concrete form of the savage was, at one time, the primal man, and it changed from the wild man of the forest during Medieval times to the Native Americans during colonial times. . . . The connotations of the savage include the positive noble savage and the negative ignoble savage. As an aid in conception, the symbol was used to conceive

of irrationality, disorder, chaos, and so on; and as a model for action, the symbol made it legitimate to take away the land of the Native Americans. (38)

Not only did this attitude make it legitimate to take Indian land, but it also allowed the Europeans to take Indian lives as well. As the Puritans explained, they rationalized slaughter of the Pequot tribe by calling on God: "God had hardened their hearts to the task and deafened their ears to the children's screams" (Ziff in Hinsley 1989, 169).

For almost 500 years this dichotomized worldview has prevailed. Recently, however, we see the beginnings of a more self-critical and relativistic orientation toward Native American culture. It is clear, for instance, that a fascination with elements of native culture by contemporary nonnative peoples permeates much of the popular media of Western society. In literature, theater, music, radio, and film—*Dances with Wolves* being one of the latest examples—we have witnessed another romantization of the Native American. How did this fascination come about and how does it relate to otherization, appropriation, and voice?

As it turns out, anthropology has a great deal to do with all three. Understanding this, and articulating the ways that Native Americans have been otherized, can assist students who wish to work with and understand native writers in a respectful and relativistic fashion, while at the same time dramatizing some of the key issues in voice.

The Influence of Museumification

During the second half of the nineteenth century, many Americans felt a need to understand the Native Americans (Bunzel 1960, 153), and this need was expressed in the context of the founding of several museums, both public and private. At Harvard in 1866, realizing the museum's potential for research and education, George F. Peabody founded the Peabody Museum. Two years later in 1868, the American Museum of Natural History was established in New York (Bunzel 1960, 276–77).

About the same time that these museums were being founded, there emerged the American school of cultural anthropology. Under the direction of Franz Boaz, a generation of American anthropologists settled down for what they considered a "holistic" examination of native cultures. Their aim was to record the quickly vanishing past and document the difference between cultures: between Zuni and Hopi, or Blackfoot and Crow (Mead 1960, 8). Unlike many European scholars, Boaz and his students recognized the legitimacy of the histories of nonliterate peoples around the world, including those in his own backyard. But these anthrolopologists were plagued by the general attitude of mainstream culture toward the Indian, who was still being either killed off or displaced to reservations by post-Civil War administrations. Given these political occurrences, many anthropologists felt the need to create quickly as many ethnographies of the vanishing peoples as they could.

Yet these anthropologists were only a part of what became the museumification of the Native American. Curtis M. Hinsley, in his essay "Zunis and Brahmins" (1989), tells us that anthropologists, journalists, philanthropists, and politicians worked together to bring about what became the *dehistorization* of native peoples. This process involved world fairs, sideshows, publications, and museums. Hinsley argues that America's museums resolved the moral dilemma faced by anthropologists by declaring and demonstrating that the end of Indian history had been reached (170), thus legitimizing the gathering of Indian materials, the taking away of the artifacts defining them. In her introduction to *The Golden Age of American Anthropology* (1960), Margaret Mead claims that anthropologists realized the Indian's situation and that the "Indian cultures had no chance of survival" (3), so while their intentions might have been benign, the effects of this gathering were not.

Of course it wasn't simply the collection of the artifacts that played a significant role in dehistoricizing the Indian. It was the way the collection was created and the analogues used to contextualize the exhibits and "make sense" of them. Mead, for instance, explains that the Indian artifacts collected by museums were treated like biological specimens. Earth lodges were compared to anthills or beaver dams, not to the homes of early Greeks or American settlers (11). And the exhibits were organized along a cultural developmental scale inhabited by Western values, so that the Indians were not presented as different (or superior) so much as primitive and inferior compared with the West (Pandian 1985, 59). Through museumification, the Indian thus become an other of the past, charming and noble perhaps, but not "civilized."

Romantic Nostalgia

Other dehistorizations were rooted in both nostalgia and the anthropologist's willingness to make theatre out of what was supposedly science. In the year 1879, anthropologist Frank Hamilton Cushing was left at the Zuni Pueblo to stay for a few months of in-depth study. He stayed twenty-nine months, until February of 1882. Cushing spent many of his early months acquainting himself with Zuni language and culture (Hinsley 1989, 176). He also experienced a degree of acculturation at the hands of the Zuni, who told him this was to help "harden his meat." From here he went on to become the Bow Priest and "First War Chief of the Zunis" (176–79).

During the years of Cushing's stay with the Zunis, the romance of the Pueblo Indian and his land was still growing. In 1881, Boston *Herald* reporter Sylvester Baxter and artist Willard Metcalf set off to look for romantic magazine material, found the Zuni, and chose to tell about Cushing's work at the Zuni Pueblo. Subsequent articles and illustrations showed aspects of Zuni life as well as Cushing's famous trip to the Atlantic Ocean.

In February of 1882 Cushing left Zuni for the Atlantic with five Native American "pilgrims." The following tour would take them to a number of U.S. cities, most importantly Boston, where they would be introduced to such phenomena as dinner clubs, theaters, churches, and modern industry. Hinsley characterizes the tour as close to a circus: "Cushing brought rich traveling theater eastward in 1882, a year before William F. Cody first took his Wild West show on tour" (180).

Cushing's Indian tour was accepted by most New Englanders with open romantic fascination. People went to theater shows performed for the Zunis so that they might watch the Zunis themselves. Support of Cushing's work was widespread. Ironically, part of Cushing's Zuni tour was supported by Edward Everett Hale, a preacher and popular writer of nineteenth-century optimism who believed that the destiny of America required an empty landscape. He saw the American West as a moral emptiness, a place for "Trying the experiments of a new Christian order" (Hale 1900, in Hinsley 1989, 188–91).

When it was all over, Charles P. Lummis observed that Cushing's work was "the cleverest thing that has ever been devised and carried out by a scientific student anywhere" (Lummis, in Hinsley 1989, 181). This "cleverness" addresses the idea of the romantic fascination of the anthropologist with his subject and masks the ill-conceived nature of this academic enterprise. Although anthropology was promoted as a science, one of its brightest pupils showed himself as a dramaturge, creating a "history [that] became theater, and an anthropology [that] became myth" (Hinsley 1989, 204). Of course, lost in this exercise was an Indian whose otherization provided entertainment for the mainstream, a curiosity who could be examined in person as well as in museums.

The Golden Age of Anthropology

The next period of romance associated with Native Americans came during the late 1800s, when settlers began moving onto the Great Plains. Many were fascinated with the wide-open spaces, the herds of buffalo, and the nomadic peoples that moved seemingly aimlessly and leisurely across the land. But once again, as conflicts began to arise, it was the Indian who lost home and place. By the end of the century, most of the tribes had been either destroyed or restricted to reservations. Dismay and depression settled over those who survived the ordeal.

Anthropologist Ruth Bunzel (1960) points out that the Plains Indian ethnographers could not, as Cushing did, sink themselves into a culture; the culture of the past did not exist. Their job therefore was to learn what was possible from the old people who could still remember. Many of America's most famous anthropologists participated in these studies: Kroeber, Wissler, Lowie, and Radin. These men were often faced with great frustrations due to the general apathy of the Indians as well as the difficulty in finding willing and reliable informants (Bunzel 1960, 340–41).

It was during these studies that many of the more typically American practices of taking ethnographies were developed. Studies became increasingly emic (informant) oriented, with the one-on-one interview becoming the most valuable tool. Bunzel contends that these men who came to study the vanishing Plains Indians were not motivated by moral responsibility or romantic notions. She states that they were the trained professionals anthropologists aspired to be, interested in the collection and evaluation of data (340).

Mead goes further, crediting the Native American for this progress in anthropological method, for if there had been no Native Americans, American anthropology would have taken on a much different, probably European and theoretical, style. She also defends the motives of the Golden Age scholars. She asserts that this period brought a tradition of objectivity that could better coexist with a new anthropology that was committed to more immediate human concerns, as reflected in the theoretical work of Ruth Benedict's *Patterns of Culture* (1934).

A Final Romance

The final period of romance associated with the Native American began sometime around World War II and continues through today. It is based in part on an enlarged version of what James A. Clifton calls the development of the romantic Indian narrative. In "Cultural Fictions" (1990), he explains that this narrative is transmitted across time and space in all forms of media: literature, oral histories, films, and ethnographies. He states that "case studies by anthropologists . . . about the cultures of native peoples . . . are one significant kind of exposition" (19).

The traditional narrative tells the tragic story of the righteous Indian in North American history. It also helps to create a place for living Native Americans in modern moral orders and political systems (20). But even in light of this narrative, the typical mass-media portrayal of the Indian during the 1940s, 1950s, and 1960s was both negative and stereotypical.

Of all of the forms of media affecting public opinion since the 1940s, it is undoubtedly the western film genre that has had the most influence. The western film genre is somewhat of a Utopia, projecting stories with strong romantic idealism. Clear dichotomies exist: good vs. evil, law vs. outlaw, and settler vs. savage wilderness (Sharrett 1991, 91). Here again we see the contrasts that are so common in Western thought: we and the other. Most often in these films good arrives in the form of the white settler or the U.S. Cavalry fighting the evil, savage Indians. But from the 1970s through the present we have seen something of a turn. Films like *Little Big Man* and *Windwalker* began to show a more realistic and prouder image of the Indian. Kevin Costner's 1990 film *Dances with Wolves* represents the most romanticized portrayal of a Native American cultural group on film, as well as an honest look at the nature of the cultural conflict that took place, though the less popular *Black Robe* seems both less romantic and closer to an accurate rendering of the experience.

Costner's character Lt. John Dunbar resembles an anthropologist, like Cushing, who is acculturated into the tribal society. And like Cushing, Dunbar would like to stay in his adopted society but cannot, due to political pressures and his constant liminality within the group. Even though *Dances with Wolves* is a brilliantly emotional film, it is of course important to remember that is a creation, a cultural fiction, in much the same way that earlier representations of the Indian have been. As Costner explains,

> It is a romantic look at a terrible time in our history, when expansion in the name of progress brought us very little and, in fact, cost us deeply. (1990, viii)

This brings us back to our current dilemma. While works such as Costner's film are popular and well received among many native groups, they still serve to propagate the myths and ideologies associated with the western tradition. Andrew Wiget (1984; 1992) warns us that we must be aware of the temptation to inappropriately utilize this cultural identity, as has been done by "white shamans" such as Jerome Rothenbery and James Koller. Wiget contends that the "beads and feathers" orientation, even when it seems to be positive, makes it difficult for Native American writers and artists to work outside of this genre and have their work accepted. Some even go as far to say that westernized appropriation of traditional language and imagery is a "naked form of cultural imperialism" (Hobsen 1981).

In sum, we need to understand that what we create are fictions or inventions, no matter how objective we try to be. Pandian (1985) points out that if an ethnography is an invention, just as James Clifton (1990) calls the Indian narrative a fiction (28), then these fictions are subject to theoretical treatment and debate (85). Moreover, as Clifton points out, we must realize that we are all inventions—whites, Indians, all peoples—culturally constructed categories of humans (Clifton 1990, 25). In other words, we are all human others. Using this as a starting point enables us to begin to understand the other by asking rather than by assuming, by measuring what we take to be certainty.

The Role of Language

There is one last "otherizing" factor to consider when examining groups of people who have been silenced for so long, that of language itself. Although there is great debate as to the exact nature of the language/culture relationship, let us agree for the sake of this argument that, as Peter Farb states, "no linguist today doubts that language and culture interpenetrate one another" (1968, 58).

In the case of Native Americans, silence was realized in the form of social oppression. But there were also language barriers and misconceptions. These problems, again, are rooted in the Western habit of dichotomization. In the past, as indicated earlier, Western scholars have tended to divide all cultures into technologically advanced and primitive categories, with the result that people often believe that the more "primitive" cultures have equally primitive languages. Yet anthropological studies have shown that technologically unsophisticated societies are no less capable of expressing just as wide a variety of ideas and concepts as more advanced societies (Ferraro 1990, 51).

It has already been pointed out that Native American cultures were considered to be much less technologically sophisticated than European societies. Now consider the fact that there were as many as 1,000 distinct Native American languages, most of which were not written. Combine this language factor with the basic ideological difference between the two cultures, and it becomes clear why miscommunication was so common and why it still continues: mainstreamers ignored these languages. It also helps us to understand why many of these languages have only recently been utilized by their own native speakers to communicate ideas to the rest of contemporary American society.

Andrew Wiget points out that Native American writers, having been displaced from reservation life and having lost their native languages, are "compelled to create a bicultural identity in art through a foreign tongue." And he adds that because of this biculturalism, each Native American writer is providing the audience with "invaluable personal and cultural insights on issues of such importance that all of us would be diminished if these voices went unheard" (Wiget 1992, 600). Recovering the native languages, from which many writers have in effect been divorced, is a task that most Indian writers must face.

Related to this is a second problem for the Native American writer: hearing Indian voices is difficult for mainstream peoples, precisely because those peoples are inclined to permit only a certain Indian voice, one that confirms what they expect to find. According to Wiget (1992), Native American writers must negotiate a relationship among authority, authorship, and audience peculiar to them, given that audiences influence what writers can compose, how they are read, and even whether Indians can write as Indians "apart from the Anglo-authored discourse of Indianness." His conclusion, not unlike Alice Walker's in "The Black Writer and the Southern Experience" (1990 [1970]), is that Indian writers can write in multiple voices, drawing on the literary resources of both voices and on two "distinct fields of action, of meaning-making." Although Wiget here is addressing the particular difficulty of artists as opposed to nonfiction writers, what holds true for the one seems to hold true for both. Another difficulty for the Indian writer, then, is to confound and confront the notion of voice brought to the text by the reader, to carve out a space within the Anglocized discourse for a different voice, an Indian voice.

Our philosophy of voice, of how we live and communicate, presents a third difficulty. Wiget, in his essay "Sending a Voice: The Emergence of Contemporary Native American Poetry" (1984), states that although Native American writers associate themselves with particular landscapes, they are so rooted in the land that their voice is as much a part of the shared tribal history as it is a manifestation of a unique personal experience (599). The nature-centered tribal self of the Indian seems more like the communitarian ethos of the Asian American writer (see Powers and Gong, this volume) than the individual self of the West. In other words, the very nature of the self in Native American culture is a radical departure from what most readers bring to the page.

Connecting to the Classroom

So what have we learned from all of this with regard to the teaching of voice in writing? In their essay "What Educational Difference Does your Theory of Language Make?" Jerome Harste and Kathy Short (1988) note that, given the nature of our democratic society, it is important that conceptions of literacy begin with hearing everyone's voices, especially those from groups who have been previously silenced. Native Americans represent one of the largest silenced populations since the domination of Europe over North America began in the 1500s. And even though it may be difficult for many to deal with the tragedy of the cultural collision that occurred between Native Americans and Europeans, one cannot ignore the unique opportunities for cultural insight that can be gained by studies of those times as well as by listening to the voices of those people who for so long have not been heard.

In order to hear those voices and to understand the construction that is voice, certain guidelines are helpful:

1. Students should understand that any writer's voice takes place within a certain culture, one they may approach as an other themselves. We are all others, given the appropriate context, which means that instead of hearing what we think we are expressing, our audience may simply be learning and/or confirming what they expect or what their discourse permits.

2. When seeking to understand a culture that is different than our own, the comparisons we use to illustrate what we see will shape *what* we see, as in the case of the Indian huts being compared to animal houses instead of Greek palaces.

3. Students will understand that many, if not most, people in contemporary American society have multiple levels of membership within the larger community, and therefore multiple voices as well. This should help students understand that they may write in multiple voices. Native Americans, like other groups such as Asian Americans, present a special case of this multiple membership.

4. Writers need to be careful not to inappropriately draw on someone else's cultural heritage, nor to romanticize or overgeneralize it.

5. There is a great deal to learn from Native American cultures, about being human, about living. Allowing Indian voices to be heard and heeding some of the advice they offer can help all of us better write and better live.

Works Cited

Benedict, Ruth. 1934. *Patterns of Culture*. New York: Houghton-Mifflin.

Bunzell, Ruth. 1960. Chapter notes for *The Golden Age of American Anthropology*. New York: George Braziler.

Clifton, James A. 1990. "Cultural Fictions." *Society* (May/June): 19–28.

Costner, Kevin, Michael Blake, and Jim Wilson. 1990. *Dances with Wolves: The Illustrated Story of the Epic Film*. New York: Newmarket Press.

Farb, Peter. 1968. "How Do I Know What You Mean?" *Horizon* 10(4): 52–57.

Ferraro, Gary P. 1990. *The Cultural Dimension of International Business*. Englewood Cliffs, NJ: Prentice-Hall.

Garbarino, Merwyn S. 1977. *Sociocultural Theory in Anthropology*. Prospect Heights, IL: Waveland Press.

Harste, Jerome C., and Kathy G. Short. 1988. "What Educational Difference Does Your Theory of Language Make?" Unpublished paper.

Hinsley, Curtis M. 1989. "Zunis and Brahmins: Cultural Ambivalence in the Gilded Age." In *Romantic Motives: Essays on Anthropological Sensibility*, edited by George W. Stocking Jr., 169–203. Madison: University of Wisconsin.

Hobsen, Geary. 1981. "The Rise of the White Shaman as a New Version of Cultural Imperialism." In *The Remembered Earth*, 100–8. Albuquerque: University of New Mexico Press.

Mead, Margaret. 1960. "Introduction." In *The Golden Age of American Anthropology*, 1–12. New York: George Braziler.

Pandian, Jacob. 1985. *Anthropology and the Western Tradition: Toward an Authentic Anthropology*. New York: Waveland Press.

Sharrett, Christopher. 1991. "The Reel World: The Western Rides Again." *USA Today* 120(2554): 91.

Spicer, Edward H. 1969. *A Short History of the Indians of the United States*. Malabor, FL: Robert E. Krieger.

Walker, Alice. 1990 [1970]. "The Black Writer and the Southern Experience." Rpt. in *In Depth: Essayists for Our Time*, edited by Carl H. Klaus, Chris Anderson, and Rebecca Blevins Faery, 690–94. New York: Harcourt, Brace, Jovanovich.

Wiget, Andrew. 1984. "Sending a Voice: The Emergence of Contemporary Native American Poetry." *College English* 46.6 (October): 598–609.

———. 1992. "Identity, Voice, and Authority: Artist-Audience Relations in Native American Literature." *World Literature Today* 66(2): 258.

13 East Asian Voice and the Expression of Cultural Ethos

John H. Powers
Texas A&M University

Gwendolyn Gong
Texas A&M University

The metaphor of voice has enriched traditional studies of written discourse by enabling linguists, rhetoricians, literary critics, and students of composition to "hear" in their imaginations the writer of a piece of discourse. By conjuring up a mental picture of the writer as a "speaker," readers and researchers have also used the metaphor of voice as a vehicle for understanding the ethos—that is, the character—of the writer as it is projected into the written text. Because the ethos expressed in a communicator's utterance arises from the interplay between the individual's unique experiences and the culturally shared experiences provided by the community within which the individual lives, an important component of every communicator's voice reflects the cultural ethos acquired during social interaction within the larger cultural community. Therefore, to fully understand an individual's spoken or written utterances, we need to understand the contribution of cultural ethos to creating the communicator's distinctive individual voice.

In this essay, we will explore the distinctive cultural ethos reflected in the East Asian[1] communicator's voice. We have chosen to focus on East Asian voice in particular because it clearly illustrates the general relationship between a communicator's personal voice and cultural ethos and because East Asian voice will be especially important for Americans to understand in the twenty-first century. For whether or not the center of economic power shifts to East Asia, as some have predicted, oral and written communication between Americans and East Asians will surely continue to accelerate in the decades to come.

Voice is both a literal phenomenon and a metaphor used to understand a writer's ethos; consequently, we have organized this essay into four sections. First, we examine the nature of voice as a literal phenomenon having a number of specific, observable elements that help inform the metaphor. Second, we discuss the relationships between the elements of the literal human voice and the ways in which they can express an individual's cultural ethos or character. Next, we briefly review some key speech communication scholarship on East Asian communication and ethos, identifying some representative perspectives on routine oral communication that might contribute to a fuller understanding of the cultural ethos expressed in an East Asian's written communication. Finally, we conclude by discussing some possible implications of this work for the study of the cultural voice in East Asian written communication.

Voice as a Literal Phenomenon

To speak literally of the human voice is to treat it, first, as an acoustic event. Our lungs force air past our vocal cords, creating a complex sound wave that is shaped and divided into units through well-known resonation and articulation processes. The resulting sound wave carries information concerning such things as how speakers group their ideas together into phrases, clauses, sentences, and larger discourse, how they feel about those ideas and the other communicators, and how an utterance is to be taken within its pragmatic context (e.g., literally versus ironically). Even the speaker's degree of fatigue seems to be represented in the sound wave. This information is conveyed by such acoustic attributes of the speech stream as its volume, rate, resonance, rhythm, pitch, stress, types of pauses and hesitations, as well as the speaker's use of vocal variety and vocal climax (e.g., see Atkinson 1984).

Can such acoustic features be used to differentiate the voice of speakers from different cultural backgrounds? The answer is obviously, "yes," as anyone who has ever heard a "foreign accent" can attest. Nonnative speakers usually bring their own phonetic structures with them as they learn a new language. Phonemic distinctions, stress patterns, speech rates, and oral rhythms can all express the cultural background of the speaker. Moreover, as Ekman and Friesen report in "The Repertoire of Nonverbal Behavior: Categories, Origins, Usage, and Coding" (1969), different cultural communities also adopt different "display rules" for how they express a variety of feelings. Thus, given a certain spontaneous feeling, one culture might learn to *deintensify* its expression, while others might be taught to *overintensify, neutralize,* or even be *deceptive* concerning the actual feelings experienced. An insider trained in the display rules of the group would, therefore, be likely to understand the voice of the communicator while an outsider might misunderstand because a different set of display rules is applied to making the interpretation.[2] For those who know the appropriate cultural display rules, interpreting the acoustic portion of the individual's voice provides a rich resource for understanding an individual's cultural and personal ethos.

When speech is transcribed into writing, most of this acoustic information is lost—although in alphabetic writing systems the essential "sound image" of the word is retained. Alliteration, assonance, and rhyme are obvious examples of how a word's sound image can be used expressively in writing as well as speech. Furthermore, there are many punctuation conventions—such as commas, periods, dashes, colons, and semicolons—that allow writers to employ some of the acoustic resonance of the spoken voice. In addition to its acoustic aspect, however, the literal human voice also has a verbal aspect whose ethical expressiveness is more easily translated into the metaphorical voice of the written text.

When we consider the verbal aspect of human voice, we are talking about both the propositional *content* of what is said and the *manner* in which that content is presented. Because to speak is to select words and arrange them in patterns that project the patterns of our thoughts, the verbal component of voice has a number of facets that reflect the complexity of the communication process. Among the many elements that define an individual's "verbal voice" are the following: (1) the topics the person chooses to talk about in the first place; (2) the propositions advanced as true or denied as false concerning that topic; (3) the way the utterance is organized globally in terms of its information flow from beginning to end; (4) the assumptions that are made concerning what need not be said (the "taken-for-granted"); (5) the preferred discourse forms (narrative, description, exposition, definition, statistics, examples, etc.) used to develop the central propositions; (6) the syntactical choices (sentence forms and rhetorical schemes) used to express the propositional content; (7) the lexical items selected to label or express specific concepts and ideas; and (8) the "sound images" of the individual words, especially as they interact with one another to create alliterative, rhyming, and other acoustic patterns and effects. When we combine the verbal with the acoustic elements of the individual's literal voice, it becomes apparent just how rich the metaphor of voice in written texts is.

Voice as the Expression of Cultural Ethos

The acoustic and verbal aspects of the human voice are all well known and need merely be mentioned here by way of reminder. They are usually included as aspects of a communicator's personal style (Norton 1983). However, the voice is also richly expressive of the ethos of the individual communicator and the cultural traditions within which the communicator interacts. For, as we are using the term, *ethos* is one's character—one's personal sense of values. And it is through the window of the communicator's acoustic and verbal voice that others can most readily observe the communicator's ethical character or system of values.[3] Why is this so? *Ethos* as we view it concerns our *choices* and the *values* those choices reflect. Aristotelian in nature, this approach relates the concept of ethos rather directly to the human voice because, whenever we speak or write, we are constantly making choices about such things as the topics we will discuss, the things we will say about them, the way we will organize and support our ideas, and the words we will use to encode those ideas. These choices give voice to our character because they are made against a backdrop of things we *could* have said but didn't. For we all have at our disposal a range of possibilities, an extensive repertoire of acoustic and verbal options, concerning what to express and how it might be voiced.[4]

However, no individual selects what to say from the infinite variety of what *might* be said. Our personal verbal repertoires are not unlimited. For example, no one is likely to know all of the lexemes of English, let alone all of the lexemes available within all of the world's ancient and contemporary languages. At our best, most people know only a small handful of languages well enough to use them for social communication. This is where the cultural elements of our voice come into play—by laying down a foundation of acoustic and verbal options for our use. Every child is born into a cultural group or community that has already narrowed the repertoire of acoustic and verbal options from which the child might choose. This results because, historically, the community of speakers has already made numerous choices concerning what to value and how to organize it into meaningful categories. For example, in his essay "How Shall a Thing Be Called?" Roger Brown (1958) asserts that many of these choices are codified in our labeling practices and are passed spontaneously from generation to generation as we learn what to call the various things we experience in daily life. Most things have several different labels by which they might be called—with each label reflecting a somewhat different conceptual emphasis, place in a hierarchical organizing scheme, and, of course, value (Markman 1989; Keil 1989).

So, every time we choose a label from the culturally provided repertoire of options, we are voicing our personal ethos because the label chosen was selected from a number of competitors that would each have expressed a somewhat different set of values. Granted, these choices are usually unconscious, habituated ones. However, unless we coin a new term, or adopt a lexeme from another culture, our acoustic and verbal choices reflect the general voice *of* our culture at the same time they voice our personal ethos as a member *within* that culture (cf. Bakhtin 1981). For our personal voice is always forged from the resources and options available in the larger repertoire of our cultural voice.

In addition to the culturally provided repertoire of lexical items from which we choose in creating our personal voice, other aspects of our personal voice, such as our specific beliefs—the propositions we espouse—have a strong grounding in the voice of the culture. For example, every group seems to have its own set of proverbs and "words of wisdom" that parents recite to their children as "memorable messages" meant to apply to various recurring situations (Knapp, Stohl, and Reardon 1981). "If you can't say something nice, don't say anything at all," "A bird in the hand is worth two in the bush," and "A rolling stone gathers no moss" are all examples of such cultural "truisms" that help formulate an individual's personal ethos. Similarly, every culture has a storehouse of mythic stories that encapsulate the values the community espouses (Bormann 1985). And recently, family stories (Stone 1988) and other personal narratives of various sorts (Bennett 1978; Riessman 1990; McLaughlan, Cody, and Read 1992) have been examined for their ability to convey a set of shared values and beliefs. Even the metaphors the culture employs to understand "the way things are" are part of the culture's collective voice (Lakoff and Johnson 1980). As these examples reveal, then, a cultural community has numerous resources for use in laying down the foundations for the individual's voice and the more particular ethos it represents.

Voice and East Asian Ethos

If it is true that the verbal choices we make reveal our ethical character as a member of a cultural community, then the voice of different cultural communities should be readily detectible in the communication choices of its individual members. With that in mind, we turn next to a discussion of the cultural ethos expressed in East Asian voice, especially as reported in studies of the oral communication in such East Asian nations as China, Korea, and Japan. To accomplish our goal, this section is divided into two parts. The first surveys the available speech communication research in this area and the second identifies a number of broad features that characterize East Asian voice.

Studies in the Speech Communication Tradition

A number of scholars in the speech communication discipline have studied the communication practices occurring in a variety of East Asian nations—especially China (Chang 1992; Chang and Holt 1987; Cheng 1987; Oliver 1961), Korea (Park and Kim 1992; Yum 1987a, 1987b; Oliver 1959), and Japan (Ishii 1992; Klopf 1991; Di Mare 1990; Barnlund and Araki 1985; Ting-Toomey 1986; Doi 1973). By all accounts, the most fundamental contributor to the development of a distinctive East Asian voice appears to be Confucianism—whose principles were first formulated in China around 500 B.C. and subsequently carried east to Korea and then to Japan.

Confucianism provides a coherent philosophy of human nature and action—a philosophy that was taught in the schools as the "official" philosophy of China for over two millennia, and elsewhere in East Asia for extensive periods.[5] In "The Impact of Confucianism on Interpersonal Relationships in Korea" (1988), Yum explains that "Confucianism is a philosophy of human nature which considers proper human relationships as the basis for society"[6] (377). And according to Hui-Ching Chang, in "From Words to Communication: Some Philosophical Implications for Chinese Interpersonal Communication" (1992), the fundamental ideal of the Confucian system of thought holds that "when people arrive at a match between their proper place in society and their behavior ... individual, family, and governmental processes will evolve in an orderly and proper manner" (2). Thus, the foundation of human motivation in Confucian terms is right conduct based on the social relations one is involved in.[7] If everyone relates *properly* to one another on the individual level, Confucianism holds, all higher levels of social structure will naturally take care of themselves. Accordingly, Confucius proposed a code of precepts to guide proper conduct within "the five basic human relationships: loyalty between king and subject, closeness between father and son, distinction in duty between husband and wife, obedience to orders between elders and youngers, and mutual faith between friends" (Yum 1988, 376).

Confucian principles and precepts are made manifest in many aspects of contemporary East Asian verbal voice: what it is proper to talk about, the degree of directness permitted in the talk, the assumptions made about human nature and motivation when explaining human action, what constitutes right and wrong communicative behavior in various social settings, and even the vocabulary used to discuss many concrete topics. For example, Chang (1992), Chang and Holt (1987), Oliver (1969), Yum (1988), and Cheng (1987) all explore specific lexical items and the basis of their underlying concepts in Confucist thought. Confucian philosophy is not, of course, the only contributor to East Asian voice—even in China. For example, in addition to Confucius's own writings, there is a long tradition of Confucian scholarship that develops the original Confucian tenets and adapts them to changing historical circumstances (Oliver 1969; Cheng 1987). Furthermore, China produced other philosophies, such as Taoism (Oliver 1961; Reynolds 1969) and a form of Buddhism (Cheng 1987; Chang 1992) that contribute their own elements to East Asian voice. And as Confucianism, Taoism, and Chinese Buddhism each moved eastward into Korea and Japan, they met indigenous cultures that made distinctive adaptations of their central tenets as they incorporated them into their own cultural ethos. Currently, Western ideas, especially capitalist economic ideas and popular culture, are gaining influence and are being incorporated into the larger cultural ethos. So, while the Korean and Japanese cultural voices have a definite Confucist flavor, they also have their own distinctive ethos that differentiates them from both China and one another. In Korea's case this involved 500 years of neo-Confucian development during the Yi dynasty (1392–1910), where at least five different schools of thought (Oliver 1959) contributed to the development of contemporary Korean voice (Lee 1987). And in Japan, Buddhism has become a major influence in the expression of a distinctively Japanese ethos.

Perspectives That Reflect East Asian Ethos

Given the speech communication research on cultural ethos, what are some specific findings that these scholars report in their research? While it is impossible to identify and summarize every noteworthy discovery in this literature, it is possible and helpful to explain a number of key perspectives that, according to most cultural speech scholars, commonly reflect East Asian voice and ethos. Toward that end, we present the following perspectives on human relationships and communication that East Asian speakers may consider important when they engage in speech acts (Yum 1988):

PERSPECTIVES ON HUMAN RELATIONSHIPS

Particularistic View

To say that East Asians hold a particularistic view of human relationships means that they see every communicative situation and interaction as distinctive. As a consequence, East Asians analyze their audiences according to their status or rank, age, gender, and context, framing their utterances accordingly. In contrast, Americans generalize rather than particularize in their human relationships.

For example, Americans consider it appropriate to adhere to general and objective rules when speaking to others. In an office setting in the U.S., an American speaker might address everyone he or she meets in the same way, uttering a conventional speech act such as "good morning." This individual might even initiate a casual conversation with a virtual stranger.

An East Asian speaker, however, would take a different tack. He or she would probably not initiate conversations with strangers, and certainly would consider it inappropriate to offer a conventional speech act—a simple morning greeting—to acquaintances as well as strangers in the same way. For East Asians, people should be approached and addressed according to appropriate protocol. For example, in business situations, East Asians would greet others in this order: the higher-ranked person before the lower-ranked one; the older person before the younger one; the woman before the man. This particularized perspective is reinforced in most Asian languages as well. For example, words that indicate family relationships such as aunt, uncle, brother, grandmother, grandfather, and so on illustrate how pervasive this particularized view is. In Chinese, if you were to address your sister, you would not use a general word for *sister*; instead, you would consider your relationship to this sibling (i.e., is she older or younger than you are) and then choose either *day-day*, the word for *older sister*, or *dee-dee*, the word for *younger sister*.

As this illustration clarifies, East Asians determine appropriate forms of address according to others' position or rank, age, gender—particularistic considerations that are also often reflected in their language. American egalitarianism in speech acts would seem awkward for East Asians, contradicting their view of human relationships: Confucian ethics hold that all human relationships are not equal.

Long-Term and Asymmetrical Reciprocity

When East Asians establish relationships, they view them as long-term associations that will require all involved to nurture the relationship continually. For example, an East Asian may invite colleagues at work to have dinner at a restaurant with his or her family. The guests are perceived as extended members of the family, and they are not allowed to pay for any portion of the bill. Why? It is important for the professional relationship to be strengthened by the social and family interaction. In fact, this notion reinforces both the philosophical tenets of community, family, and teams that Asian corporations tout; no one is disenfranchised from the company, so to speak. Obviously, this perspective leads to obligation. In our example, guests don't contribute to paying for dinner; thus an automatic and natural asymmetrical relationship is created. According to Yum (1988), "Under this system of reciprocity, the individual does not calculate what he or she gives and receives. To calculate would be to think about immediate personal profits, which is the antithesis of the principle of mutual faithfulness" (379). Once a relationship is established, it is viewed as a lasting association, similar to family ties: one has blood relatives forever, and one always takes care of them as best as he or she can.

Ingroup/Outgroup Distinction

The ingroup/outgroup perspective is related to the idea that long-term associations translate into extended family ties. As a result, when East Asians establish human relationships, they expand their own and others' ingroup community. Again, this perspective underscores the sense of belonging and membership for individuals.

Role of Informal Intermediaries

East Asians consider their membership in the "ingroup" favorably. To become acquainted with others, however, East Asians need an intermediary (i.e., another person who knows both them and the other party) to introduce them. The Confucian notion of propriety would be violated were they to presume to introduce themselves directly to another individual.

Shared Personal and Professional Social Interaction

All of the views identified in this section reflect a strong belief in shared personal and professional social interaction. East Asians prefer to work with individuals whom they also know at a human level. For example, a business executive from Japan may prefer to enter into a partnership with a company in the U.S. based on his or her American executive counterpart's quality as a colleague as well as a human. Would this East Asian choose to get to know this individual if business had not brought them together? For East Asians, the best business or work associations are those that they would and could extend to the personal, human level.

PERSPECTIVES ON HUMAN COMMUNICATION

Emphasis on Process

For Americans, speech acts are judged as successful when they elicit the intended response. As such, speaking can be perceived as very product oriented. For East Asians, on the other hand, the process of speaking is more important than the outcome. Confucian philosophy places great value on nurturing and maintaining relationships, so a premium is put on the ongoing process of communicating rather than the end product.

Emphasis on Indirect Communication

Indirect communication (i.e., metaphors, innuendoes, hints, irony) enables East Asians to maintain the Confucian principles of politeness and deference. That is, by asking or responding to other people indirectly, East Asians privilege their audience instead of themselves.

For example, suppose an American in China asked a shopkeeper directions to a particular restaurant that a friend had frequented last summer and that had recently burned down. The shopkeeper would probably respond by recommending another restaurant, one that might not even be located in the vicinity of the one you inquired about.

What's going on? The Chinese speaker is respecting you by politely helping you save face: by directing you to another eatery, the shopkeeper avoids embarrassing you and telling you bad news. While the American speaker may have preferred the direct speech act (i.e., "The restaurant burned down last week; if you go there, don't expect to eat there."), the Chinese speaker would consider that response rude. This emphasis on indirect communication thus provides this East Asian speaker a thoughtful and effective rhetorical strategy.

Emphasis on the Audience

Like Americans, East Asian speakers tend to consider the audience's responses to their utterances as extremely important. But there is one fundamental difference. For American speakers, what a speaker has to say is primary. As a consequence, Americans focus on strategies for communicating messages, for establishing credibility, and for enhancing the presentation of the messages. These are all tasks that are speaker or sender centered. For East Asians, the primary concern is how the audience will interpret the message. Interestingly enough, "In North America, an effort has been made to improve the effectiveness of speakers through such formal training as debate and public speaking, whereas in East Asia, the effort has been on improving the receiver's sensitivity" (Yum 1988, 385).

East Asian Ethos and Written Communication Research

As documented by speech communication scholars, these cultural perspectives that influence and shape East Asian ethos have significant implications for researchers, teachers, and students of written communication. First of all, this extant research conducted in this sister discipline provides writing researchers with a broad spectrum of methodologies, ranging from social science to naturalistic approaches, to employ in the study of written texts. By examining the research methodologies used by speech communication scholars, writing researchers can seek to replicate certain studies in terms of written texts to determine how East Asian ethos is developed and how oral versus literate cultural ethos compare and contrast. In addition, writing researchers can focus on intercultural writers and texts, subjects long overdue for study. At present, most research conducted in this area is isolated, dedicated primarily to the fields of linguistics and education (i.e., English as a second language and bilingual education programs). This compartmentalized view of knowledge about other cultures as they relate to English needs to be broadened. In our contemporary and dynamic world, our every reality—economical, social, ethical, educational, health, cultural—is global rather than local in nature. So indeed should our research reflect a more dynamic, integrated, and global view of written language.

The research on East Asian ethos can also benefit writing teachers and their students of all cultures and backgrounds. By understanding the rhetorical strategies, the rationale East Asian speakers and writers use, and the cultural voice of their students, teachers can better instruct and guide their Asian students in Western communication situations. When East Asians are aware of the contributing factors that cause them to communicate in certain ways, they can analyze their rhetorical situations more purposefully and, in turn, adapt their strategies to correspond accordingly. In this way, Western teachers and students can acknowledge and respect the cultural ethos of East Asians, and vice versa. East Asians can realize that their cultural ethos is not incorrect; as is true with any strategy, certain cultural perspectives may be used more appropriately in some contexts than others. Exploring when and how East Asian speakers and writers need to adapt their communication strategies thus becomes a major teaching objective.

The study of East Asian ethos in written texts can further our understanding of cultural voices—"theirs" as well as our own. Ethos suggests the character and nature of the writer, and it is this "center," replete with cultural perspectives about that individual's world, which research in this area can shed light on. To understand others and their cultural ethos better enables us to understand ourselves and our own cultural ethos.

Speech communication researchers in the area of intercultural studies have forged the way for writing specialists, but despite their head start, they are still being challenged to increase their efforts. For example, in a 1987 *Rhetoric Society Quarterly* essay, "Teaching East Asian Rhetoric," J. Vernon Jensen (1987b) reprimands his colleagues in speech communication for their failure to expand their attention to Asian rhetoric:

> Our profession since its origin has dutifully analyzed the rhetoric of Greece, Rome, Britain, and the United States, but has ignored over half of the globe. We have exhausted ourselves probing the Western rhetorical heritage, which honors verbal expression, reason, cause and effect linear linkages, directness, clear organization, unadorned style, and the debating of opposing views so that truth will emerge more purely from the clash. We have overlooked the rhetorical heritage of the East, which honors non-expression, silence, the nonverbal, the softness and subtlety of ambiguity and indirectness, the insights of intuition, and the avoidance of clash of opinion in order to preserve harmony. We have not fully appreciated communication which highly values reasoning from authority and example, which relies heavily on analogy and metaphor. With our devotion to individualism we have not fully appreciated communicative behavior which puts group above the individual, which greatly respects relationships with others based on age, relative status, and tradition. (135)

Jensen admits that intercultural communication research—spanning over forty years—has increased dramatically over the past twenty years, but he contends the effort falls short. He thus calls for more studies of East Asian rhetoric as well as the development of more naturalistic research methodologies.

If Jensen can challenge his colleagues in speech communication to conduct and support more intercultural research, indeed researchers of written communication would do well to accept the challenge. How much intercultural research (i.e., theoretical, empirical, naturalistic, pedagogical) of Asian writing and writers have composition scholars conducted? How have writing researchers added to knowledge concerning Asian rhetoric—be it spoken or written, or the relationship between Asian speech and writing expressed in English or in some other language? And, in terms of our essay's focus on the metaphor of voice, what do we gain or lose when we view voice in written texts as cultural ethos? These questions represent only the beginning of a long list of inquiries that have yet to be addressed by writing researchers.

Research in this area can help writing teachers narrow the gap between two cultures and voices, as three recent essays demonstrate. In "From Silence to Words: Writing as Struggle," Min-zhan Lu (1987) recounts how the conflict between two languages—Standard Chinese (the language of home and the language of school) and English (the language of the Bourgeois)—influenced her ways of reading and writing as she grew up in China. In "The Classroom and the Wider Culture: Identity as a Key to Learning English Composition," Fan Shen (1989) explains the experience of negotiating between "my Chinese identity with an English identity dictated by the rules of English composition" (459). And Carolyn Matalene (1985) identifies and describes differences between Chinese and American rhetoric so that we can become more effective writing teachers. These essays represent important contributions to scholarship on Asian rhetoric and voice, but more research is warranted.

This essay and the following selected bibliography serve as our call for written communication researchers to advance studies on East Asian rhetoric, starting with examinations of East Asian voice and cultural ethos in written texts. For far too long, writing scholars, teachers, and students have assumed rhetoric and voice to refer only to discourse of the Western world. We hope that this essay will challenge and eventually change that view.

Notes

1. Although China, Korea, and Japan each have their own distinctive ethnic voice as well, these three cultures are generally grouped together as "East Asian" for a number of reasons: their close geographical proximity, their long use of the Chinese ideographic writing system, and a shared intellectual tradition based on the role that Confucianism, Taoism, and the Chinese adaptation of Buddhism have played in providing a foundations for their social communication practices (Jensen 1987a; 1987b). For example, Oliver (1959) writes that "because all scholarship in Northeast Asia was conducted in Chinese ideograms, there is a strong communal relationship among the Confucian sects of China, Korea, and Japan" (364). This cultural connection continues even today because, although both Japan and Korea have adopted phonetic (alphabetic) writing systems, they each supplement their alphabetic writing systems with the use of over a thousand relatively independent Chinese characters apiece.

2. In treating men and women's speech as arising from different cultural styles, Deborah Tannen (1986; 1990) analyzes several acoustic aspects of voice that can readily be misunderstood by "outsiders" to the culture of the other sex.

3. The examples in this discussion will concern only the verbal voice. However, for students of oral voice, the relation of the voice to one's ethos is no less compelling. The reason an individual's ethos is so closely identified with his or her acoustic voice is that the act of speaking arises from so many bodily resources that it may legitimately be called a "total bodily act." Our entire being participates. For example, Langer (1954) writes: "Speech is a highly specialized activity in human life.... Verbal utterance is the overt issue of a greater emotional, mental, and bodily response, and its preparation in feeling and awareness or in the mounting intensity of thought is implicit in the words spoken. Speech is like a quintessence of action" (314). Similarly, Ong (1967) emphasizes the relation of the spoken word as a special sensory key to viewing an individual's "interiority," because "sound has to do with interiors as such" (117). Contrasting the sense of hearing with that of sight, Ong writes, "sight presents surfaces (it is keyed to reflected light; light coming directly from its source, such as fire, an electric lamp, the sun), rather dazzles and blinds us ..." (117).

4. Because everything we say reflects a choice we have made "under the circumstances," we, of course, reveal our values as they relate to the continuously shifting pattern of rhetorical situations we encounter. However, the important point is that, under most circumstances (external compulsion and ritual litany being possible exceptions), we are free to have chosen differently—a different topic, approach, or lexeme, and so forth. Because even silence is a choice, our voice represents a constant display of our personal ethos.

5. In explaining the deep influence of Confucianism in East Asia, Yum (1988) writes: "One reason that Confucianism has had such a profound impact

[in East Asia] is because it was adopted as the official philosophy of the Yi dynasty for 500 years in Korea, and of the Tokugawa shogunate in Japan for 250 years, as well as in many dynasties in China" (376).

6. In contrast, the Western (especially American) ethos tends to celebrate the relatively isolated individual. Human relationships are treated more an inconvenient necessity than a virtue to be sought as the foundations for society.

7. Calling the Confucian approach to motivation the Four-Seven Thesis, Oliver (1959) says there were four principles from which right conduct was thought to arise: "(1) charity [humanism], (2) duty to neighbors [faithfulness], (3) propriety, and (4) wisdom [or a liberal education]" (367). (The alternate phrasings are found in Yum [1988, 377], and are included to give a little more of the flavor of the concepts.) "Opposing these four principles of right conduct," Oliver continues, "were the seven passions: joy, anger, sorrow, fear, love, hatred, and desire" (367).

Works Cited

Atkinson, Max. 1984. *Our Masters' Voices: The Language and Body Language of Politics*. London: Methuen.

Bakhtin, M. M. 1981. *The Dialogic Imagination: Four Essays*. Edited by Michael Holquist and translated by Caryl Emerson and Michael Holquist. Austin: University of Texas Press.

Barnlund, Dean C., and Shoko Araki. 1985. "Intercultural Encounters: The Management of Compliments by Japanese and Americans." *Journal of Cross-Cultural Psychology* 16: 9–26.

Bennett, W. Lance. 1978. "Storytelling in Criminal Trials: A Model of Social Judgment." *Quarterly Journal of Speech* 64: 1–22.

Bormann, Ernest G. 1985. *The Force of Fantasy: Restoring the American Dream*. Carbondale: Southern Illinois University Press.

Brown, Roger. 1958. "How Shall a Thing Be Called?" *Psychological Review* 65: 14–21.

Chang, Hui-Ching. 1992. "From Words to Communication: Some Philosophical Implications for Chinese Interpersonal Communication." Paper presented at the Speech Communication Association. Chicago, Illinois. October.

———, and G. Richard Holt. 1987. "More than Relationship: Chinese Interaction and the Principle of *Kuan-Hsi*." *Communication Quarterly* 39: 251–71.

Cheng, Chung-Ying. 1987. "Chinese Philosophy and Contemporary Human Communication Theory." In Kinkaid, 23–43.

Di Mare, Leslie. 1990. "*Ma* and Japan." *Southern Communication Journal* 55: 319–28.

Doi, L. Takeo. 1973. "The Japanese Patterns of Communication and the Concept of *Amae*." *Quarterly Journal of Speech* 59: 180–85.

Ekman, Paul, and Wallace V. Friesen. 1969. "The Repertoire of Nonverbal Behavior: Categories, Origins, Usage, and Coding." *Semiotica* 1: 49–98.

Ishii, Satoshi. 1992. "Buddhist Preaching: The Persistent Main Undercurrent of Japanese Traditional Rhetorical Communication." *Communication Quarterly* 40: 291–397.

Jensen, J. Vernon. 1987a. "Rhetoric of East Asia—a Bibliography." *Rhetoric Society Quarterly* 17: 213–31.

———. 1987b. "Teaching East Asian Rhetoric." *Rhetoric Society Quarterly* 17: 135–49.

Keil, Frank C. 1989. *Concepts, Kinds, and Cognitive Development*. Cambridge, MA: MIT Press.

Kinkaid, D. Lawrence, ed. 1987. *Communication Theory: Eastern and Western Perspectives*. San Diego: Academic Press.

Klopf, Donald W. 1991. "Japanese Communication Practices: Recent Comparative Research." *Communication Quarterly* 39: 130–43.

Knapp, Mark L., Cynthia Stohl, and Kathleen K. Reardon. 1981. "'Memorable' Messages." *Journal of Communication* 31: 27–41.

Lakoff, George, and Mark Johnson. 1980. *Metaphors We Live By*. Chicago: University of Chicago Press.

Langer, Susanne K. 1954. *Feeling and Form*. New York: Charles Scribner's Sons.

Lee, Sang-Hee. 1987. "The Teachings of Yi Yulgok: Communication from a Neo-Confucian Perspective." In Kincaid, 101–14.

Lu, Min-zhan. 1987. "From Silence to Words: Writing as Struggle." *College English* 49.4: 437–48.

Markman, Ellen M. 1989. *Categorization and Naming in Children: Problems of Induction*. Cambridge, MA: MIT Press.

Matalene, Carolyn. 1985. "Contrastive Rhetoric: An American Writing Teacher in China." *College English* 47.8: 789–808.

McLaughlan, Margaret L., Michael J. Cody, and Stephen J. Read, eds. 1992. *Explaining One's Self to Others: Reason-Giving in a Social Context*. Hillsdale, NJ: Lawrence Erlbaum.

Morson, Gary Saul, ed. 1986. *Bakhtin: Essays and Dialogues on His Work*. Chicago: University of Chicago Press.

Norton, Robert. 1983. *Communicator Style: Theory, Application, and Measures*. Beverly Hills: Sage.

Oliver, Robert T. 1959. "The Confucian Rhetorical Tradition in Korea during the Yi Dynasty (1392–1910)." *Quarterly Journal of Speech* 45: 363–73.

———. 1961. "The Rhetorical Implications of Taoism." *Quarterly Journal of Speech* 47: 27–35.

———. 1969. "The Rhetorical Tradition in China: Confucius and Mencius." *Today's Speech* 17: 3–8.

Ong, Walter J. 1967. *The Presence of the Word: Some Prolegomena for Cultural and Religious History*. New York: Simon and Schuster.

Park, Myung-seok, and Moon-soo Kim. 1992. "Communication Practices in Korea." *Communication Quarterly* 40: 398–404.

Reynolds, Beatrice K. 1969. "Lao Tzu: Persuasion through Inaction and Non-Speaking." *Today's Speech* 17: 23–25.

Riessman, Catherine Kohler. 1990. *Divorce Talk: Women and Men Make Sense of Personal Relationships.* New Brunswick, NJ: Rutgers University Press.

Shen, Fan. 1989. "The Classroom and the Wider Culture: Identity as a Key to Learning English Composition." *College Composition and Communication* 40.4: 459–66.

Stone, Elizabeth. 1988. *Black Sheep and Kissing Cousins: How Our Family Stories Shape Us.* New York: Times Books.

Tannen, Deborah. 1985. "Cross-Cultural Communication." In *Handbook of Discourse Analysis: Discourse Analysis in Society,* vol. 4, edited by Teun A. van Dijk, 203–15. London: Academic Press.

———. 1986. *That's Not What I Meant! How Conversational Style Makes or Breaks Your Relations with Others.* New York: William Morrow.

———. 1990. *You Just Don't Understand: Women and Men in Conversation.* New York: William Morrow.

Ting-Toomey, Stella. 1986. "Japanese Communication Patterns: Insider versus the Outsider Perspective." *World Communication* 25: 113–26.

Yum, June Ock. 1987a. "Korean Philosophy and Communication." In Kincaid, 71–86.

———. 1987b. "The Practice of *uye-ri* in Interpersonal Relationships in Korea." In Kincaid, 87–100.

———. 1988. "The Impact of Confucianism on Interpersonal Relationships and Communication Patterns in East Asia." *Communication Monographs* 55: 374–88.

Appendix: East Asian Voice and the Expression of Cultural Ethos: A Selected Bibliography

General References

Atkinson, Max. 1984. *Our Masters' Voices: The Language and Body Language of Politics.* London: Methuen.

Becker, Carl. 1986. "Reasons for Lack of Argumentation and Debate in the Far East." *International Journal of Intercultural Relations* 10: 75–92.

Bennett, W. Lance. 1978. "Storytelling in Criminal Trials: A Model of Social Judgment." *Quarterly Journal of Speech* 64: 1–22.

Bormann, Ernest G. 1985. *The Force of Fantasy: Restoring the American Dream.* Carbondale: Southern Illinois University Press.

Brown, Roger. 1958. "How Shall a Thing Be Called?" *Psychological Review* 65: 14–21.

Brown, William J. 1992. "Culture and AIDS Education: Reaching High-Risk Heterosexuals in Asian-American Communities." *Journal of Applied Communication Research* 20: 275–91.

Casmir, Frederick L. 1987. *International, Intercultural Communication: Selected Annotated Bibliography*. Annandale, VA: SCA.

Chua, Elizabeth G., and William B. Gudykunst. 1987. "Conflict Resolution Styles in Low- and High-Context Cultures." *Communication Research Reports* 4: 32–37.

Cushman, Donald P., and D. L. Kinkaid. 1987. "Introduction and Initial Insights." In *Communication Theory: Eastern and Western Perspectives*, edited by D. Lawrence Kincaid, 1–22. San Diego: Academic Press.

Dance, Frank E.X. 1981. "The Tao of Speech." *Central States Speech Journal* 32: 207–11.

Ekman, Paul, and Wallace V. Friesen. 1969. "The Repertoire of Nonverbal Behavior: Categories, Origins, Usage, and Coding." *Semiotica* 1: 49–98.

Ellingsworth, Hubert W. 1963. "Anthropology and Rhetoric: Towards a Culture-Related Methodology of Speech Criticism." *Southern Speech Communication Journal* 28: 307–12.

———. 1969. "National Rhetoric and Inter-Cultural Communication." *Communication Quarterly* 17: 35–38.

Gudykunst, William B. 1987. "Cross-Cultural Comparisons." *Handbook of Communication Science*, edited by C. R. Berger and S. H. Chaffee, 847–89. Newbury Park, CA: Sage.

———, and Tsukasa Nishida. 1984. "Individual and Cultural Influences on Uncertainty Reduction." *Communication Monographs* 51: 23–36.

———, and Tsukasa Nishida. 1986a. "Attributional Confidence in Low- and High-Context Cultures." *Human Communication Research* 12: 525–49.

———, and Tsukasa Nishida. 1986b. "The Influence of Cultural Variability on Perceptions of Communication Behavior Related with Relationship Terms." *Human Communication Research* 13: 147–66.

———, and Stella Ting-Toomey. 1988. *Culture and Interpersonal Communication*. Newbury Park, CA: Sage.

Hamill, James F. 1990. *Ethno-Logic: The Anthropology of Human Reasoning*. Urbana: University of Illinois Press.

Hofstede, Geert. 1980. *Culture's Consequences*. Beverly Hills: Sage.

Jensen, J. Vernon. 1987a. "Rhetoric of East Asia—A Bibliography." *Rhetoric Society Quarterly* 17: 213–31.

———. 1987b. "Teaching East Asian Rhetoric." *Rhetoric Society Quarterly* 17: 135–49.

Jensen, Richard J., and Cara J. Abeyta. 1987. "The Minority in the Middle: Asia-American Dissent in the 1960s and 1970s." *Western Journal of Speech Communication* 51: 402–16.

Keil, Frank C. 1989. *Concepts, Kinds, and Cognitive Development*. Cambridge, MA: MIT Press.

Kinkaid, D. Lawrence, ed. 1987. *Communication Theory: Eastern and Western Perspectives*. San Diego: Academic Press.

Knapp, Mark L., Cynthia Stohl, and Kathleen K. Reardon. 1981. "'Memorable' Messages." *Journal of Communication* 31: 27–41.

Lakoff, George, and Mark Johnson. 1980. *Metaphors We Live By*. Chicago: University of Chicago Press.

Langer, Susanne K. 1954. *Feeling and Form*. New York: Charles Scribner's Sons.

Markman, Ellen M. 1989. *Categorization and Naming in Children: Problems of Induction*. Cambridge, MA: MIT Press.

Martini, Marianne, Ralph R. Behnke, and Paul E. King. 1992. "The Communication of Public Speaking Anxiety: Perceptions of Asian and American Students." *Communication Quarterly* 40: 279–88.

McLaughlan, Margaret L., Michael J. Cody, and Stephen J. Read, eds. 1992. *Explaining One's Self to Others: Reason-Giving in a Social Context*. Hillsdale, NJ: Lawrence Erlbaum.

Moerman, Michael. 1988. *Talking Culture: Ethnography and Conversation Analysis*. Philadelphia: University of Pennsylvania Press.

Norton, Robert. 1983. *Communicator Style: Theory, Application, and Measures*. Beverly Hills: Sage.

Oliver, Robert T. 1974. "Asian Public Address and Comparative Public Address." *Speech Teacher* 23: 101–8.

————. 1989. *Leadership in Asia: Persuasive Communication in the Making of Nations, 1850–1950*. Newark: University of Delaware Press.

Ong, Walter J. 1967. *The Presence of the Word: Some Prolegomena for Cultural and Religious History*. New York: Simon and Schuster.

Riessman, Catherine Kohler. 1990. *Divorce Talk: Women and Men Make Sense of Personal Relationships*. New Brunswick, NJ: Rutgers University Press.

Stone, Elizabeth. 1988. *Black Sheep and Kissing Cousins: How Our Family Stories Shape Us*. New York: Times Books.

Tannen, Deborah. 1985. "Cross-Cultural Communication." In *Handbook of Discourse Analysis: Discourse Analysis in Society*, vol. 4, edited by Teun A. van Dijk, 203–15. London: Academic Press.

————. 1986. *That's Not What I Meant! How Conversational Style Makes or Breaks Your Relations with Others*. New York: William Morrow.

————. 1990. *You Just Don't Understand: Women and Men in Conversation*. New York: William Morrow.

van Dijk, Teun A. 1987. *Communicating Racism: Ethnic Prejudice in Thought and Talk*. Newbury Park, CA: Sage.

Chinese Voice and Ethos

Bloom, Alfred. 1981. *The Linguistic Shaping of Thought: A Study in the Impact of Language on Thinking in China and the West*. Hillsdale, NJ: Lawrence Erlbaum.

Chang, Hui-Ching. 1992. "From Words to Communication: Some Philosophical Implications for Chinese Interpersonal Communication." Paper presented at the Speech Communication Association. Chicago, Illinois. October.

————, and G. Richard Holt. 1987. "More than Relationship: Chinese Interaction and the Principle of *Kuan-Hsi*." *Communication Quarterly* 39: 251–71.

Chang, Shau-Ju. 1991. "Chinese Compliment and Compliment Response—A Qualitative Study." Paper presented at the 8th Annual Intercultural and International Communication Conference. Miami, Florida. February.

Cheng, Chung-Ying. 1987. "Chinese Philosophy and Contemporary Human Communication Theory." In Kinkaid, 23–43.

Chu, Godwin C. 1977. *Radical Change through Communication in Mao's China.* Honolulu: University of Hawaii Press.

———. 1978. *Revolutionary Language and Chinese Cognitive Processes.* Honolulu: Papers of the East-West Communication Institute.

———, and Leonard Chu. 1981. "Parties in Conflict: Letters to the Editor of the *People's Daily.*" *Journal of Communication* 31: 74–91.

Crew, Louie. 1987. "A Comment on 'Contrastive Rhetoric: An American Writing Teacher in China'" *College English* 49.7: 827–30.

Cushman, Donald P. 1987. "Contemporary Chinese Philosophy and Political Communication." In Kincaid, 57–70.

Fu, James S. 1987. "Communication in Chinese Narrative." In Kincaid, 45–56.

Gong, Gwendolyn. 1994. "When Mississippi Chinese Talk." In *Our Voices: Essays in Culture, Ethnicity, and Communication,* edited by Alberto Gonzalez, Marsha Houston, and Victoria Chen, 92–99. Los Angeles: Roxbury.

Günthner, Susanne. 1992. "The Construction of Gendered Discourse in Chinese-German Interactions." *Discourse and Society* 3: 167–92.

Jerstad, Luther G. 1967. "Buddhist Proselytization in the Tibetan Drama *Drowanzangmu.*" *Western Journal of Speech Communication* 31: 199–210.

Lee, Chin-Chuan. 1981. "The United States as Seen through the *People's Daily.*" *Journal of Communication* 31: 92–101.

Lik, Kuen Tong. 1976. "The Meaning of Philosophical Silence: Some Reflections on the Use of Language in Chinese Thought." *Journal of Chinese Philosophy* 3: 169–83.

Lu, Min-zhan. 1987. "From Silence to Words: Writing as Struggle." *College English* 49.4: 437–48.

Ma, Ringo. 1990. "An Exploratory Study of Discontented Responses in American and Chinese Relationships." *Southern Communication Journal* 55: 305–18.

———. 1992. "The Role of Unofficial Intermediaries in Interpersonal Conflicts in the Chinese Culture." *Communication Quarterly* 40: 269–78.

Matalene, Carolyn. 1985. "Contrastive Rhetoric: An American Writing Teacher in China." *College English* 47.8: 789–808.

Merriam, Allen R. 1981. "Charismatic Leadership in Modern Asia: Mao, Gandhi, and Khomeni." *Asian Profile* 19: 389–400.

O'Hair, Dan, Michael J. Cody, Xiao-Tian Wang, and Edward Yi Chao. 1990. "Vocal Stress and Deception Detection among Chinese." *Communication Quarterly* 38: 158–69.

Oliver, Robert T. 1961. "The Rhetorical Implications of Taoism." *Quarterly Journal of Speech* 47: 27–35.

———. 1966. *Leadership in Twentieth-Century Asia: The Rhetorical Principles and Practices of the Leaders of China, Korea, and India, from Sun Yat-Sen to Jawaharal*

Nehru. University Park, PA: Center for Continuing Liberal Education, University of Pennsylvania.

————. 1969. "The Rhetorical Tradition in China: Confucius and Mencius." *Today's Speech* 17: 3–8.

————. 1971. *Communication and Culture in Ancient India and China.* Syracuse, NY: Syracuse University Press.

Pierson, Herbert D. 1992. "Communication Issues during a Period of Radical Transition: The Case of Hong Kong." *Communication Quarterly* 40: 382–90.

Pye, Lucian W. 1986. *Chinese Commercial Negotiating Style.* Yarmouth, ME: Intercultural Press.

Reynolds, Beatrice K. 1969. "Lao Tzu: Persuasion through Inaction and Non-Speaking." *Today's Speech* 17: 23–25.

————. 1976. "Mao Tse-Tung: Rhetoric of a Revolutionary." *Central States Speech Journal* 27: 212–17.

Rogers, Everett M., Xiaoyan Zhao, Zhongdang Pan, and Milton Chen. 1985. "The Beijing Audience Study." *Communication Research* 12: 179–208.

Schneider, Michael J., and W. Jordan. 1981. "Perceptions of the Communicative Performance of Americans and Chinese in Intercultural Dyads." *International Journal of Intercultural Research* 5: 175–91.

Shen, Fan. 1989. "The Classroom and the Wider Culture: Identity as a Key to Learning English Composition." *College Composition and Communication* 40.4: 459–66.

Thomas, Gordon K. 1986. "A Comment on 'Contrastive Rhetoric: An American Writing Teacher in China.'" *College English* 48.8: 844–45.

Waley, Arthur, trans. 1938. *The Analects of Confucius.* London: George Allen & Unwin.

Walsh, James F., Jr. 1986. "An Approach to Dyadic Communication in Historical Social Movements: Dyadic Communication in Maoist Insurgent Mobilization." *Communication Monographs* 53: 1–15.

Wang, James C.F. 1977. "Values of the Cultural Revolution." *Journal of Communication* 27: 41–46.

Korean Voice and Ethos

Dreher, John, and James I. Crump, Jr. 1952. "Pre-Han Persuasion: The Legalist School." *Central States Speech Journal* 3: 10–14.

Lee, Sang-Hee. 1987. "The Teachings of Yi Yulgok: Communication from a Neo-Confucian Perspective." In Kincaid, 101–14.

Oliver, Robert T. 1959. "The Confucian Rhetorical Tradition in Korea during the Yi Dynasty (1392–1910)." *Quarterly Journal of Speech* 45: 363–73.

Park, Myung-seok. 1979. *Communication Styles in Two Different Cultures: Korean and American.* Seoul: Han Shin.

————, and Moon-soo Kim. 1992. "Communication Practices in Korea." *Communication Quarterly* 40: 398–404.

Yum, June Ock. 1987a. "Korean Philosophy and Communication." In Kincaid, 71–86.

————. 1987b. "The Practice of *uye-ri* in Interpersonal Relationships in Korea." In Kincaid, 87–100.

————. 1988. "The Impact of Confucianism on Interpersonal Relationships and Communication Patterns in East Asia." *Communication Monographs* 55: 374–88.

Japanese Voice and Ethos

Barnlund, Dean C. 1989. *Communication Styles of Japanese and Americans: Images and Realities*. Belmont, CA: Wadsworth.

————, and Shoko Araki. 1985. "Intercultural Encounters: The Management of Compliments by Japanese and Americans." *Journal of Cross-Cultural Psychology* 16: 9–26.

Becker, Carl. 1983. "The Japanese Way of Debate." *National Forensics Journal* 1: 141–47.

Beninger, James R., and D. Eleanor Westney. 1981. "Japanese and U. S. Media: Graphics as a Reflection of Newspapers' Social Role." *Journal of Communication* 31: 14–27.

Di Mare, Leslie. 1990. "*Ma* and Japan." *Southern Communication Journal* 55: 319–28.

Doi, L. Takeo. 1973. "The Japanese Patterns of Communication and the Concept of *Amæ*." *Quarterly Journal of Speech* 59: 180–85.

Fisher, J. L., and Teigo Yoshida. 1968. "The Nature of Speech According to Japanese Proverbs." *Journal of American Folklore* 80: 34–43.

Gudykunst, William B., Lori L. Sodetani, and Kevin T. Sonoda. 1987. "Uncertainty Reduction in Japanese-American/Caucasian Relationships in Hawaii." *Western Journal of Speech Communication* 51: 256–78.

Haglund, Elaine. 1957. "Japan: Cultural Considerations." *International Journal of Intercultural Research* 8: 61–76.

Hammer, Michael R., and Judith N. Martin. 1992. "The Effects of Cross-Cultural Training on American Managers in a Japanese-American Joint Venture." *Journal of Applied Communication Research* 20: 161–83.

Hatlen, Theodore W. 1954. "Visit to the Japanese Noh Drama Theatre." *Western Journal of Speech Communication* 18: 231–35.

Hirokawa, Randy Y. 1987. "Communication within the Japanese Business Organization." In Kincaid, 137–50.

Ishii, Satoshi. 1973. "Characteristics of Japanese Nonverbal Communicative Behavior." *Journal of the Communication Association of the Pacific*, n.v.: n.p.

————. 1992. "Buddhist Preaching: The Persistent Main Undercurrent of Japanese Traditional Rhetorical Communication." *Communication Quarterly* 40: 291–397.

————, and Tom Bruneau. 1991. "Silence and Silences in Cross-Cultural Perspective: Japan and the United States." In *Intercultural Communication: A Reader*, 6th ed., edited by Larry A. Samovar, and Richard E. Porter, 314–19. Belmont, CA: Wadsworth.

Iwao, Sumiko, Ithiel de Sola Pool, and Shigeru Hagiwara. 1981. "Japanese and U. S. Media: Some Cross-Cultural Insights into TV Violence." *Journal of Communication* 31: 28–36.

King, Stephen W., Yuko Minami, and Larry Samovar. 1985. "A Comparison of Japanese and American Perceptions of Source Credibility." *Communication Research Reports* 2: 76–79.

Kitao, K. 1980. "Difficulty of Intercultural Communication between Americans and Japanese." *Journal of Communication Association of the Pacific* 9: 24–34.

Klopf, Donald W. 1991. "Japanese Communication Practices: Recent Comparative Research." *Communication Quarterly* 39: 130–43.

Kume, Teruyuki. 1985. "Managerial Attitudes toward Decision-Making: North America and Japan." *International and Intercultural Communication Annual* 9: 231–51.

Kuroda, Yasumasa. 1965. "Newspaper Reading and Political Behavior in a Japanese Community." *Journal of Communication* 15: 171–81.

Lomas, Charles W. 1946. "Public Discussion in Japan—Index to Democracy." *Quarterly Journal of Speech* 32: 311–16.

———. 1949. "The Rhetoric of Japanese War Propaganda." *Quarterly Journal of Speech* 35: 30–35.

Matsumoto, David. 1991. "Cultural Influences on Facial Expression of Emotion." *Southern Communication Journal* 56: 128–37.

McCrosky, James C., William B. Gudykunst, and T. Nishida. 1985. "Communication Apprehension among Japanese Students in Native and Second Languages." *Communication Research Reports* 2: 11–15.

Mitsubishi Corporation. 1988. *Tatemæ and Honne: Distinguishing between Good Form and Real Intention in Japanese Business Culture.* New York: Free Press.

Morrison, John L. 1972. "The Absence of a Rhetorical Tradition in Japanese Culture." *Western Journal of Speech Communication* 36: 89–102.

Nakagawa, Gordon. 1990. "'What Are We Doing Here with All These Japanese?' Subject-Constitution and Strategies of Discursive Closure Represented in Stories of Japanese American Internment." *Communication Quarterly* 38: 388–402.

Neulien, James W., and Vincent Hazelton, Jr. 1985. "A Cross-Cultural Comparison of Japanese and American Persuasive Strategy Selection." *International Journal of Intercultural Research* 9: 389–404.

Nishida, Hiroko. 1985. "Japanese Intercultural Communication Competence and Cross-Cultural Adjustment." *International Journal of Intercultural Research* 9: 247–69.

Nishiyama, Kazuo. 1971. "Interpersonal Persuasion in a Vertical Society—The Case of Japan." *Speech Monographs* 38: 148–54.

Nomura, Naoki, and Dean C. Barnlund. 1983. "Patterns of Interpersonal Criticism in Japan and the United States." *International Journal of Intercultural Research* 7: 1–18.

Nordstrom, L. 1979. "Zen and the Nonduality of Communication: The Sound of One Hand Clapping." *Communication* 4: 15–27.

Ogawa, Dennis M. 1979. "Communication Characteristics of Asian Americans in Urban Settings: The Case of the Honolulu Japanese." In *Handbook of Intercultural Communication,* edited by Molefe Kete Asante, Eileen Newmark, and Cecil A. Blake, 321–37. Beverly Hills: Sage.

Okabe, K. 1987. "Indirect Speech Acts of the Japanese." In Kincaid, 127–36.

Okabe, Roichi. 1973. "Yukichi Fukusawa: A Promulgator of Western Rhetoric in Japan." *Quarterly Journal of Speech* 59: 186–95.

———. 1979. "*Yuben* in the Early Twentieth Century: A Case Study in the Promulgation of Western Rhetoric in Japan."" *Journal of the Communication Association of the Pacific* 7: 1–11.

———. 1983. "Cultural Assumptions of the East and West: Japan and the United States." In *Intercultural Communication Theory,* 21–44. Beverly Hills: Sage.

Sloan, Thomas O. 1957. "Public Recitation in Japan." *Quarterly Journal of Speech* 43: 394–98.

Ting-Toomey, Stella. 1986. "Japanese Communication Patterns: Insider versus the Outsider Perspective." *World Communication* 25: 113–26.

———. 1988. "Rhetorical Sensitivity Style in Three Cultures: France, Japan, and the United States." *Central States Speech Journal* 39: 28–36.

Tsujimura, Akira. 1987. "Some Characteristics of the Japanese Way of Communication." In Kincaid, 115–26.

Yamada, Haru. 1992. *American and Japanese Business Discourse: A Comparison of Interactional Styles.* Norwood, NJ: Ablex.

14 Voice and the Naming of Woman

Susan Brown Carlton
Pacific Lutheran University

As the introduction to this volume makes clear, the metaphor of "voice" dominates composition studies. It is likewise difficult to imagine a feminism devoid of the metaphor of voice. Four titles deliver four variations: *Silences* (Olsen 1972) laments the material and intellectual conditions that prevent women from voicing their experience. *In a Different Voice* (Gilligan 1982) analyzes the discourse of ethical decision making, locating the gendered voices of objective justice and subjective care and praising the conciliatory, nurturing language culturally marked by and for women. "The Laugh of the Medusa" (Cixoux 1983) advocates the disruption of language codes as a counter to woman's imprisonment in an alien discourse. *Talking Back* (hooks 1989) valorizes a particular mode of voice, engaged and contestatory, to interrogate difference. Each of these feminisms draws energy from a metaphor of woman as an entity that cannot take for granted the efficacy of speech.

One explanation for the dominance of metaphors of voice in feminism and in composition studies is that both the student writer and the woman find their "voicing" of opinion, experience, analysis, and passion restricted because of their positions in the social order. A second possibility which we might add to the first is that "voice" necessarily invokes the point of intersection between the body, living in a space and through a time, and the cultural order, with immense resources for sustaining, restricting, or destroying the body. Language is always already socially coded, but "voice," though available for a reading, sometimes sidesteps semiotics. Provoked by pain or joy, voices reiterate dimensions of our experience that appear to exceed the patterning of a particular, given cultural order. And at the same time, voice marks the extreme of individuation in a culture which honors the individual subject as a primary unit of analysis: Each of us can be tracked down and identified as singular through a pattern of soundwaves. These experiences of tension between the sense of an uncoded, unknowable,

extralinguistic excess and the sense of a linguistically coded individuation, between a body trapped in time and a social order that from the
vantage point of the body seems always to exceed it, are hardly restricted to women and to writers, but they pose particular kinds of
issues for women and for writers.

It is one such issue that I will explore further here, framing my
discussion in the language of "voice": the naming of woman/women.
I will review three positions that have been elaborated in response to
this issue and then delineate the limitations on "voice" that emerge
when these three positions are aligned in a narrative of progress with
one triumphing as the "higher" insight, or in the language of problem
solving in which one theory "corrects" another, or in a dialectical encounter in which two opposed positions are transcended to create a
superior theory. My focus, then, is less on the limitations of particular
theorists or theories than on the limitations of a dominant mode of
academic discourse. My primary aim is to reformulate the metaphysical
and historical impasses of the naming of woman/women as a rhetorical
event confronted by writers and rhetors.

In elaborating on how rhetoric and composition studies can contribute to feminist theory, I am responding to a project initiated by Susan
Jarratt in *Rereading the Sophists: Classical Rhetoric Refigured* (1991b).
There, Jarratt locates congruences between the Sophists' rhetorical theory and feminist theories, including Linda Alcoff's theory of positionality (66–70). While I concur with Jarratt that Alcoff's theory is an
important resource for rethinking feminism as a rhetorical field of inquiry and action, I wish to critique the discursive frame of Alcoff's
argument, a frame that is at odds with her strongest insights. In addition to examining that frame, I juxtapose Alcoff's philosophical discussion with Denise Riley's (1988) historical inquiry, and I resituate the
work of both Alcoff and Riley in the light of feminist composition
theory. My central claim is that what Alcoff calls an impasse could be
renamed as a misrecognized rhetorical multiplicity that cannot be transcended but must be worked through over and over.

As I examine three positions on the issue of the naming of
"woman/women," I will adopt Alcoff's terms because they usefully
identify the positions as linguistic ones: each rests on a different assumption about how language intersects with our material and historical existence. Alcoff names one position "essentialist": that is, it assigns
to "woman" a particular set of attributes, attitudes, and responses
which are assumed to be more or less invariant. The name "woman"
identifies a territory where women live and a distinctive set of practices
and problems that are necessarily put into play when one answers to

the name of woman. To call this position essentialist is to charge it with restricting women's options for redefining the category of gender. Alcoff did not initiate the critique of feminist essentialism. But Alcoff's version is a particularly cogent one for our purposes, for in her attempts to define feminist essentialism, she is required to mark off as flawed, failed, and anti-progressive an immense expanse of feminist work, namely all work that can be categorized as "cultural feminism." As this term makes clear, her definition of essentialism is not limited to biological determinism; gender can be acknowledged as socially constructed, yet still assigned the power of limiting the cultural role of women to specified dimensions.

Thus the essentialist charge can be leveled against cultural feminists simply because of "their emphasis on building a feminist free-space and woman-centered culture," a point formulated by Alice Echols and approvingly summarized by Alcoff (1988, 264). The terms of Alcoff's dismissal of cultural feminism are familiar to readers of academic prose in any discipline: acknowledgement of a movement's contributions is followed by consignment of that movement to the errors of a past that we must divest ourselves of if future work is to be instigated:

> After a decade of hearing liberal feminists advising us to wear business suits and enter the male world, it is a helpful corrective to have cultural feminists argue instead that women's world is full of superior virtues and values. . . . Herein lies the positive impact of cultural feminism. And surely much of their point is well-taken, that it was our mothers who made our families survive, that women's handiwork is truly artistic, that women's care-giving really is superior to male competitiveness.
>   Unfortunately, however, the cultural feminist championing of a redefined "womanhood" cannot provide a useful long-range program for a feminist movement and, in fact places obstacles in the way of developing one. . . . To the extent cultural feminism merely valorizes genuinely positive attributes developed under oppression, it cannot map our future long-range course. (266)

I find the charges leveled by Alcoff against cultural feminism to be misplaced. However, before I elaborate on why I find this dismissal so troubling, I want to turn to the second feminist position on naming critiqued by Alcoff, the nominalist position assumed by poststructuralists.

Alcoff's choice of the term "nominalism" emphasizes that the poststructuralist assumptions about the naming of woman are formulated within a theory about the relationship between language and lived experience. While modern nominalists assign to words the power to group entities together on the basis of perceived likenesses, they share with the medieval nominalists the assumption of a radical discontinuity between names and the entities or qualities those names label. However meaning-laden a term may be within a particular language, it never can bridge the gap between the universalist demand that naming stabilize meaning and the concrete experience of a limitless differential potential between two supposedly "like" entities. Whereas an essentialist feminism wants to assume the power to redefine "woman" so as to overturn misogynist or paternalistic definitions that would consign her to the categories of devil or child, a nominalist feminism refuses to name woman because any "definitive category of 'woman'" takes on meaning in relation to 'man' (269). According to Alcoff, this radical refusal severely restricts feminist discourse: feminists can either endlessly reaffirm the undecidability of naming, or they can, following Kristeva's suggestion, speak only to negate every formulation of the category of woman (270); no positive, action-inducing discourse can be elaborated, only an endless oscillation between undecidability and negation.

As with the cultural feminists, Alcoff affirms dimensions of poststructuralism, namely the historicizing of subjectivity and the recognition of gender's embeddedness in linguistic and cultural processes. Yet nominalism, she believes, so disengages gender from any basis in the lived experience of women that ultimately it can only erase the category's political significance:

> A nominalist position on subjectivity has the deleterious effect of de-gendering our analysis, of in effect making gender invisible once again. . . . If gender is simply a social construct, the need and even the possibility of a feminist politics becomes immediately problematic. What can we demand in the name of women if "women" do not exist and demands in their name simply reinforce the myth that they do? (272)

Alcoff's discussion of poststructuralism could be critiqued on several grounds, but her summary is preferable to a more nuanced presentation in that it coincides with a very common reading of poststructuralism, a reading which defines poststructuralism as a form of political paralysis. What is valuable for my purpose here is her own reference to voice: she defines the difference between cultural feminist essentialism and poststructuralist nominalism as a difference in voicing. The essentialist affirms self-naming; the nominalist resists.

Alcoff's theory of positionality is presented as the solution to the essentialism/nominalism dilemma. "Positionality" theory is based on the classical structuralist observation that "identity" is not an essence inherent in entities but a product of that entity's placement within a set of relations. But Alcoff, elaborating on the work of de Laurentis, adds temporality and agency to structuralist relationality: women rethink, revise, and reinterpret the cultural and historical relationships that produce their identity and subjectivity, and those relationships constitute a context that is fluid, historicized, "constantly moving" (286). Susan Jarratt has recognized that what Alcoff has discovered is the rhetorical stance as defined by Sophistic rhetoric (Jarratt 1991b, 70).

Alcoff's conclusion, recontextualized as a variety of rhetoric, offers a frame for defining feminism as a question of "voice," more specifically as an active choice among options for voicing. What I find troubling in Alcoff's presentation is her lack of self-reflexivity. The insights of her theory of positionality surely indicate that essentialism and nominalism are not doctrines to be transcended, but rhetorical options for voicing two positions occupied by women—not by two different groups of women but by each woman as she moves through the various contexts of her life.

In my introductory paragraph, I claimed that the metaphor of "voice" draws energy from a definition of woman as the entity that cannot take for granted the efficacy of speech. The power of Alcoff's formulation lies in her evocation of the precariousness of choosing a language: the efficacy of affirming woman is undercut by that affirmation's constitutive power to reiterate a single definitional cell for woman; the efficacy of negating woman so as to escape that definition is undercut by an indeterminacy that reduces women to a language without political power.

That precariousness of choosing a language also dominates "Am I That Name?" in *Feminism and the Category of History* (Riley 1988), and we find there as well the other dimension of voicing addressed in my introduction, the relationship between the body and cultural coding. Denise Riley reconstructs the history of feminism as the history of choosing between arguments of an essential difference between male and female and arguments that the difference can be erased. In the following summary of Riley's text, I organize the feminist arguments she documents into the two categories of essentialism and nominalism, though Riley herself never uses these terms. She organizes feminist discourse in terms of arguments for special virtues and arguments for equal status. By imposing other terms on Riley's schema, I am not claiming that each term sustains a constant definition through history, but I do claim that each term delineates a rhetorical stance regarding the stability of the category of gender: essentialist arguments demand recognition of women's special virtues and distinctive needs and interests; nominalist arguments attempt to divest sexual differentiation of normative power.

Riley explains that from the twelfth to the seventeenth centuries, it was possible to argue "that the soul before God had no sex" (43). I would label this a variety of nominalism: the bifurcation of male and female is assigned a purely temporary reality that dissolves in the face of a higher discourse. Riley also documents that during these same centuries, women attempted to praise their own "essential beings" to counter misogynist attacks and to establish spheres of experience in which they were empowered through their particular, sex-specific virtues. In the course of the eighteenth century, women lost ground in that the medieval and Renaissance theological recognition of spiritual equality before God ceased to have much salience. As the argument for a sexless soul lost its cogency, the gender coding of a rationality distinct from nature leaves no space for the possibility of dissolving the male/female distinction. There cease to be any ungendered regions of the soul: "The whole meaning of 'woman' had been transformed once the concept of the female person as thoroughly sexed through all regions of being had become entrenched" (43). And that meaning pinned woman relentlessly to a single sphere of activity, the domestic. I do not mean that women in fact only lived within that sphere, but that the language could only code women's ventures outside the domestic sphere as transgressions of nature and reason.

The response of nineteenth-century feminists again diverges along the two trajectories of nominalism and essentialism. Some argue for "women" as a historical rather than a natural category and so available for redefinition. Other feminists reiterate the definitions which pin woman to the private sphere of the family but attempt to coerce that sphere to flood the social world:

> If women's sphere was to be the domestic, then let the social world become a great arena for domesticated intervention, where the empathies supposedly peculiar to the sex might flourish on a broad and visible scale. (46)

Both discourses attempted to allow women to enter the category of humanity, the one by means of an equality preceding sexualization, the other by means of a set of sex-determined attributes worthy of praise. Neither discourse had easy success, as the exclusion of women from political power was sustained through a restriction of voting rights that overpowered the discourse of suffragists throughout the nineteenth century and into the twentieth.

As Riley reflects on the implications of her history for contemporary feminism, she refuses to synthesize the two positions. Rather, she urges us to deploy two discourses: one, a discourse stabilizing "women" as a category so that women can engage in the political activism necessitated "as long as sexual division is a bifurcation of the discursive world" (101), the other a discourse which proclaims "that it is neither possible nor desirable to live solidly inside any sexed designation" (112).

Perhaps it is now clearer why I have chosen to broaden the terms "essentialism" and "nominalism" to accommodate Riley's historical insights. To do so highlights the alternative path which Alcoff did not explore: the inclusion of cultural and poststructuralist feminism in an account of the stances, or to modify one of Alcoff's phrases, the activist points of departure (283–84) available for contemporary feminist discourse and practice. Riley's historical perspective provides her readers with a specification of the material, epistemological, and ideological circumstances which earlier feminisms both responded to and helped shape. This specificity is missing in Alcoff's summaries of essentialist and nominalist feminisms, which are presented as failed responses to a question about naming which is in fact Alcoff's question, and not the problematic which those feminisms were both confronting and constructing.

Still, Alcoff's conclusion recontextualized as a variety of rhetoric offers compositionists a theoretical instrument for viewing feminism as an active choice among options for voicing the name of woman/ women. And when we juxtapose to her insights those of Riley, a pragmatic response to the essentialist/nominalist question begins to take shape:

> And while there is indeed a phenomenology of inhabiting a sex, the swaying in and out of it is more like ventures among descriptions than like returns to a founding sexed condition. So to speak about the individual temporality of being a woman is really to speak about movements between the many temporalities of a designation. . . . Some characterization or other is eternally in play. The question then for a feminist history is to discover whose, and with what effects. (98)

The preceding discussion moves us onto a discursive terrain familiar to composition theorists: it becomes possible to ask about the production of discourses under the circumstances faced by rhetors and writers, the matrix of pressures from already voiced designations contending with the not-yet-formulated terms from which new constructions might emerge. What might feminist compositionists contribute to the essentialist/nominalist impasse once it is reconfigured as "ventures among descriptions"? I would suggest that we are in a position to elaborate multiple rhetorics that specify more fully the circumstances within which a given designation is likely to produce effective discourse and that expand the range of available definitions for that never-innocent term, "effective."

To illustrate my claim, I will conclude with a review of three articles in feminist composition theory. I wish to transpose Alcoff's taxonomy of essentialist, nominalist, and positionalist categories into a taxonomy of rhetorics. What does one ask of a rhetoric? Not that it provide a final, fixed, explanatory matrix within which all phenomena can be placed, assessed, and judged, but that it (1) provoke and shape a particular variety of discourse and (2) teach explicitly or implicitly the features and powers of a type of discourse, thereby demystifing discourse production so that it might be available to all who need it. In this case, then, I want to specify a set (open, not closed) of rhetorics which feminists might avail themselves of: a rhetoric of advocacy which operates within the essentialist problematic, a rhetoric of radical possibility which embraces nominalism, and a rhetoric of intervention that articulates subject positions and contexts. The three articles I review were not written as rhetorics, but each article can perform a kind of feminist rhetorical "work" because its discourse is shaped by a coherent set of concerns. I should add that while for purposes of elucidation it is convenient to align each article with a rhetoric focused on one of these three tasks, I do not believe that a given text is always tied to a discrete rhetoric, either the ones that I identify here or others that perform other kinds of discursive work. There is no reason at all to assume that essentialism, nominalism, and positionality do not collide within a single text. Quite the contrary. But by isolating each as a task and a rhetoric, we can undertake the specifically compositionist task of multiplying effective feminist textual production and reception.

Composing as a Woman—A Rhetoric of Advocacy

Flynn's essay (1988) is initiated by a series of linkages made between women and attributes ascribed to them: women are nurturing, committed to service and to repetitive, unending work, and experienced in the expressive genres of the private sphere. This image of woman is then linked to the field of composition as a whole, first in a positive sense, to indicate the praiseworthiness of the field, and then in a critical sense, in that in answering to a female identity, composition is marginalized and denied its rightful authority. Flynn then reviews feminist texts in other disciplines that have explored gender differences in contemporary culture, differences in the subject's sense of self, style of personal interaction, and mode of moral and intellectual problem resolution. In her review of Belenky et al., the metaphor of "voice" is used to trace women's intellectual development from silence, "selfless and voiceless" (427), through identification with a group deemed more knowledgeable, to an integration of intuitively derived wisdom with group-sanctioned knowledge. Then the contrastive male/female patterns are verified as relevant to composition teaching, first because they emerge in student texts and hence show us how students "know," and then because they allow gender to be introduced to students as a category of analysis and inquiry.

Flynn's essay could be described as the product of a rhetoric of advocacy: that is, the three goals of advocating women, composition as a field of knowledge, and student-centered (as opposed to subject matter-centered) pedagogy are skillfully intertwined. The essay invites identification at every turn: the female composition teacher can locate a positive image of herself, her female students, and her profession; the male composition teacher must choose between identifying himself as "female," no doubt a problematic undertaking, or identifying himself as "male" and resistant to the values Flynn praises. Yet the essay is clearly conciliatory toward its male readers: student essays written by males are accorded respect and in all her presentations of male modes of thinking, Flynn adopts the neutral tone of the unbiased researcher.

Within Alcoff's schema, we would have to reject this essay as hopelessly caught in the coils of essentialism. The focus is on countering devaluation of women's work, women's lives, and women's texts through positive reassessment of attributes ascribed to women. The validity of male/female as a bifurcation of the whole field of the human is not contested. Perhaps we could even concede that an array of traditional cultural assumptions about gender remain uncontested. But what the article does bring into focus are two fundamental concerns of feminism: that gender is one dimension of human experience that is formative of practices and that the greater privilege and respect accorded male experience has restricted our understanding of our encounters with human behavior and products in every dimension of activity. Unless we are willing to accord the collectivity of women specificity, we cannot work as advocates for women's experience or, perhaps more importantly within composition studies, make it possible for women students to become their own advocates through revisioning their experience.

In a footnote, Alcoff, who has earlier in her article charged Mary Daly with essentialism because she creates a space for female culture, notes how she has profited from Daly's discussion of "internalized oppressive mechanisms" and how women might resist them (Alcoff 1988, 284). How could Daly possibly have identified these mechanisms without essentializing woman? In relegating cultural feminism to the past, in denying cultural feminism a viable role in the present and future, we would assume that our colleagues and our students have lived our past, have for example successfully resisted "internalized oppressive mechanisms" (something I for one am still working on) and are ready to break through to build the gender-free culture of the future. I have no objection to Utopian visions, but surely constructing them does not require jettisoning modes of feminist discourse designed to do other kinds of work.

For compositionists, the devaluing of women is very much tied to the question of professional status and working conditions. Composition's association with female attributes and female marginality is long-standing and complex (Holbrook 1991). Flynn's linkage of the two here should serve to remind us that we have a particular stake in not dismissing cultural feminism and in learning all that we can about the rhetoric of advocacy, the need for which has in no way diminished.

A Rhetoric of Radical Possibility— Worsham on Écriture Féminine

Since "écriture féminine" is one of those feminisms often charged with essentialism, my choice of this essay to represent nominalism might seem misdirected. However, it is not écriture féminine's relationship to the essentialism/nominalism debate that interests me here. I want instead to show Lynn Worsham's 1991 enactment of a rhetoric rethinking "gender."

I adopt the term "rhetoric of radical possibility" from Barbara Biesacker's "Rethinking the Rhetorical Situation from Within the Thematic of Différance" (1989). Biesacker advocates deconstruction because it "enables us to read symbolic action in general and rhetorical discourse in particular as radical possibility" (111) and allows us to participate in the postmodern rejection of "essentializing and universalizing claims" (126). But in her conclusion she suggests that while deconstruction is one important way to reread the rhetorical situation because it opens

up new possibilities for understanding how texts and subjects are formulated, deconstruction does not replace traditional conceptions of
rhetoric (127). Deconstructive readings of texts and audiences are always possible, because texts, audiences, and situations are always in a
process of "becoming rather than Being" (127). If we wish "to discern
the considerable heterogeneity of the social sphere and the formidable
role that rhetoric plays in articulating this heterogeneity" (126), then
deconstruction is certainly available for appropriation. By presenting
deconstruction as an always available option, Biesacker avoids the
philosophical gesture that would move from affirmation of becoming
to rejecting all work that wishes to fix existing models of identity for
nondeconstructive readings.

For Biesacker, and for Worsham, as we shall see shortly, the concern
is to make a space for a rhetoric of radical possibility. To be "taxono-
mized," limited to some purposes and not to others, might be precisely
the kind of appropriation they had hoped to avoid. In other words, I
can find some evidence in Biesacker's text and extensive evidence in
Worsham's for a lack of sympathy with my reading strategies and my
view of the relationship between deconstruction or écriture féminine
and the contexts of rhetoric and composition studies. (It seems only fair
to point out that there is a tension between my contextualization of a
rhetoric of possibility and theirs, but I will have to leave that tension
unexplored here.)

First, what is a rhetoric of radical possibility? I will not try to recapitulate Biesacker's excellent discussion of one dimension of such a
rhetoric, "the complicated attempt to form a unity out of a division"
(112), since her remarks on audience are more germane to my concerns
here. She contrasts the traditional view of audience as "fixed essences
encounter[ing] variable circumstances" (123) with a deconstructive
view:

> If the subject is shifting and unstable . . . then the rhetorical
> event may be seen as an incident that produces and reproduces
> the identities of subjects and constructs and deconstructs linkages
> between them. . . . From within the thematic of différance we
> would see the rhetorical situation neither as an event that merely
> induces audiences to act one way or another or as an incident that,
> in representing the interests of a particular collectivity, merely
> wrestles the probable within the realm of the actualizable. Rather
> we would see the rhetorical situation as an event that makes
> possible the production of identities and social relations. (126)

Here we see an excellent definition of a rhetoric of advocacy which
"in representing the interests of a particular collectivity . . . wrestles the

probable within the realm of the actualizable." A rhetoric of radical possibility might be said to wrestle with the not-yet-thought in the realm of the yet-to-be-actualized. Worsham locates écriture féminine on the edge of that realm of the unthought operating in opposition to the "epistemological attitude." An epistemic stance subjects symbolic action to scrutiny in order to interpret, to assign meaning; compositionists who assume such a stance attempt to locate the sources of coherence for particular kinds of discourse and then construct pedagogies to impart interpretive and productive powers to students. Worsham objects to composition's attempts to "apply" the resources of écriture féminine to such a project. The epistemic stance bars access to the realm of the not-yet-thought, and for that reason is incompatible with the procedures of écriture féminine: refusal, mimicry, laughter, audacious disruptiveness. These are the procedures of any avant-garde, but écriture féminine distinguishes itself from other avant-garde movements in that it is the voice of woman that instantiates disruptiveness of interpretive codes: woman voicing a nonmasculinist logic, not to fix a new identity for woman or assign to her a higher value, but to pursue a discourse production that cannot be decoded or encoded within the confines of the present gender system.

According to Worsham, écriture féminine argues that the standards by which discourse is judged, standards of unity, univocal meaning, coherence, are based on a logic that is isomorphic with the male body. An alternative logic isomorphic to the female body would make operative the multiplicity, indeterminate meaning, and heterogeneity that runs through all discourse. The feminine is not an attribute of female-gendered individuals, but a particular kind of energy that the social order attempts to contain so as not to be confronted with the radical uncertainty of unknown, extradiscursive realms. Paradoxically, the extradiscursive is not "outside" language but runs through it: it is the space of the not-yet-formulated, which always threatens to be the space of the unformulateable.

Thus écriture féminine affirms the nominalist insight that there is a radical disjunction between words and meaning, as well as the postmodern insistence that certain stylistic "excesses" put us on the track of that disjunction. I would argue that écriture féminine as Worsham presents it constitutes a kind of rhetoric for the disassembly of phallocentric discourse, and also a rhetoric for new assemblies that can constitute new "identities and social relations," but cannot predict or dictate the new forms that such identities and social relations might take: one could, however, be certain that whenever the unity-coherence logic is challenged, the logic of male/female division is undermined.

Though I do not share Worsham's disdain for the epistemological attitude, I would concur with her critique of compositionist theories that equate all discourse production with the "mastery" of the unknown, the speedy translation of non-sense into a common sense. A rhetoric of radical possibility interrupts this operation to replace it with an unrestricted confrontation with "the enigmatic other that exceeds and threatens every system of meaning, including individual identity" (83). Both Worsham and Biesacker see that moment of confrontation as embedded in the act of discourse production. For feminists, that embeddment assures that in writing, as in other modes of voicing, the attempt to make gender "mean" can always be undermined.

Interventionist Rhetorics—Jarratt on the Politics of the Classroom

But it is not always possible, and certainly often not desirable, to engage in an unrestricted confrontation with "the enigmatic other." And advocacy of an already defined collectivity, such as we have seen in Flynn's work, leaves unexamined the complexities of the way that identity is conferred through participation in that collectivity. Alcoff's theory of positionality can be of help here. Jarratt's feminist analysis of the politics of teacher-student relations develops options for intervening in the production of gender, race, and class distinctions, options that rhetorics of advocacy and radical possibility are unable to explore. Jarratt does not cite Alcoff in this particular article, but her analysis of the positioning of male and female composition teachers and students is consistent with Alcoff's principles of positionality.

Jarratt (1991a) critiques feminist and compositionist pedagogies that attempt to construct conflict-free classrooms. Her critique rests on her analysis of the differing resonances of marginalized and dominant voices. A feminist pedagogy such as that of Gearhart (1979), who advocates total acceptance of all points of view expressed in the classroom, and a composition pedagogy such as that of Elbow, who advocates that students take on an attitude of total receptivity toward one another's opinions, places individuals at risk: Gearhart's pedagogy cannot help women, people of color, or working-class, lesbian, and gay students to strategize how to speak with authority in patriarchal culture; and when a classroom is dominated by male, white, heterosexual, middle-class voices, Gearhart's pedagogy would leave the power relations between dominant and marginalized groups intact and unexplored. Elbow's call for total receptivity might be valuable for male students who are unlikely to be practiced in taking noncombative stances, but women students are hardly in need of yet another forum in which to listen, accept, wait, and comply.

Jarratt then insists that we complicate the category of "students," seeing them not simply as the disempowered in contrast to an authority figure named "teacher," but as a heterogeneous collection of subjectivities with different histories of speaking, listening, responding, and asserting. The "teacher" category also becomes more differentiated: the woman teacher, for example, surely evokes the conflicted responses directed toward mothers in our culture (113). And the spaces for interaction are also differentiated: Jarratt cites Treblicot's (1988) "principle of non-persuasion," which can sustain nonconflictual discourse in situations in which coercive, patriarchal relations are not operative but recognizes that a different principle must be deployed in forums in which women must act within a power structure that favors confrontational, authoritative voicing.

Jarratt locates strong similarities between Treblicot's discourse theory and Sophistic rhetoric:

> When "wimmen" meet to talk in nonhierarchical and noncompetitive communication situations, they tell stories—past, present, and future—and plan action. In a telegraphic way, Treblicot proposes a version of Sophistic rhetoric, *the art of representing the past and present so as to suggest a course of action for the future.* (115; emphasis added)

Here Jarratt's phrasing captures the value of interventionist rhetorics: they review the past and present conditions so as to intervene in those conditions to initiate change in practices. And since intervention necessarily produces resistance, Jarratt turns to Kathleen Weiler's (1988) and bell hook's (1989) pedagogical theories. Both argue for productive conflict: by confronting conflict, students and teachers acknowledge the social forces that sustain inequalities. The inequalities to be explored are inequalities of position: since positioning is relational, transforming inequalities becomes at least thinkable (Jarratt 1991a, 119).

In her concluding remarks, Jarratt emphasizes the interventionist possibilities generated by contention over unequal positioning. Each participant confronts not simply another participant, but the conjunction of private and public realms in discourse. Composition classrooms can go beyond offering students and teachers the possibility of examining how power is allocated and who is allowed to exercise it. They can become sites for intervention in those power allocations, if the focus of discursive practice shifts from the "expression" of an already formulated individual to the production of realignments of our commitments across private and public spheres. Jarratt suggests that argument is an indispensable mode of voicing in interventionist rhetorics.

What is at stake in reformulating the essentialist/nominalist/positionalist triad as a taxonomy of rhetorics? One concern is to reconstruct a philosophical impasse as a map of rhetorical options available for voicing the feminist stance. A second concern is that when academic discourse norms universalize any mode of voicing, alliances among constituencies come apart or remain unformed because no single mode of voicing can ever accommodate the myriad discourse situations confronting feminists. The complex interweaving, undoing, and reweaving of situations, identities, and discourses is at the center of composition studies. Acknowledging the multiplicity of feminist voicing, we can move among rhetorics of advocacy, possibility, and intervention . . . and imagine rhetorics that remain as yet unformulated. Venturing among descriptions to discover whose characterizations are "in play", and with what effect: Riley's definition of feminist history is also a definition of the reading and writing subject that engages composition studies. In a sense, feminist philosophy and history have discovered the inescapability of rhetoric, but have yet to explore its implications. Therein lies a project for feminist compositionists: to reconstruct feminist philosophical impasses as a map of rhetorical options.

Works Cited

Alcoff, Linda. 1988. "Cultural Feminism versus Poststructuralism: The Identity Crisis in Feminist Theory." In *Reconstructing the Academy: Women's Education and Women's Studies,* edited by Elizabeth Minnich, Jean O'Barr, and Rachel Rosenfeld, 257–88. Chicago: University of Chicago Press. Rpt. from *Signs* 13 (1988): 405–36.

Biesacker, Barbara A. 1989. "Rethinking the Rhetorical Situation from Within the Thematic of Différance." *Philosophy and Rhetoric* 22: 110–30.

Cixoux, Helene. 1983. "The Laugh of the Medusa." Translated by Keith Cohen and Paula Cohen. In *The Signs Reader: Women, Gender, and Scholarship,* edited by Elizabeth Abel and Emily K. Abel, 279–99. Chicago: University of Chicago Press.

Daly, Mary. 1978. *Gyn/ecology: The Metaethics of Radical Feminism.* Boston: Beacon.

de Laurentis, Teresa. 1984. *Alice Doesn't.* Bloomington: Indiana University Press.

———, ed. 1986. "Introduction." In *Feminist Studies/Critical Studies.* Bloomington: Indiana University Press.

Echols, Alice. 1983. "The New Feminism of Yin and Yang." In *Powers of Desire: The Politics of Sexuality,* edited by Ann Snitow, Christine Stansell, and Sharon Thompson, 439–59. New York: Monthly Review Press.

Elbow, Peter. 1986. "Methodological Doubting and Believing: Contraries in Inquiry." In *Embracing Contraries: Explorations in Learning and Teaching,* 254–300. New York: Oxford University Press.

Flynn, Elizabeth. 1988. "Composing as a Woman." *College Composition and Communication* 39.4 (December): 423–35.

Gearhart, Sally Miller. 1979. "The Womanization of Rhetoric." *Women's Studies International Quarterly* 2: 195–201.

Gilligan, Carol. 1982. *In a Different Voice: Psychological Theory and Women's Development,* Cambridge, MA: Harvard University Press.

Holbrook, Sue Ellen. 1991. "Women's Work: The Feminization of Composition." *Rhetoric Review* 9: 201–29.

hooks, bell. 1989. *Talking Back: Thinking Feminist, Thinking Black.* Boston: South End Press.

Jarratt, Susan C. 1991a. "Feminism and Composition: The Case for Conflict." In *Contending with Words: Composition and Rhetoric in a Postmodern Age,* edited by Patricia Harkin and John Schilb, 105–23. New York: Modern Language Association of America.

————. 1991b. *Rereading the Sophists: Classical Rhetoric Refigured.* Carbondale: Southern Illinois University Press.

Olsen, Tillie. 1972. *Silences.* New York: Dell.

Riley, Denise. 1988. "*Am I That Name?*" *Feminism and the Category of Women in History.* Minneapolis: University of Minnesota Press.

Treblicot, Joyce. 1988. "Dyke Methods or Principles for the Discovery/Creation of the Withstanding." *Hypatia* 3: 1–13.

Weiler, Kathleen. 1988. *Women Teaching for Change: Gender, Class, and Power.* South Hadley, MA: Bergin & Garvey.

Worsham, Lynn. 1991. "Writing against Writing: The Predicament of *Écriture Féminine* in Composition Studies." In *Contending with Words: Composition and Rhetoric in a Postmodern Age,* edited by Patricia Harkin and John Schilb, 82–104. New York: Modern Language Association of America.

15 Voicing the Self: Toward a Pedagogy of Resistance in a Postmodern Age

Randall R. Freisinger
Michigan Technological University

Had I consciously tried, I don't think I could have assembled in one title four terms in composition studies that are very much more problematic, definitionally complex, and ideologically loaded than *voice, self, postmodernism,* and *resistance.* All four have undergone considerable scrutiny in recent years and have been the source at times of heated debate. In what follows, I want to explore each of these four terms, albeit necessarily in a summary fashion that omits much of the detail in the rich discourse surrounding them. At the same time I want to provide some links among these terms that might help restore certain pedagogical practices to a place of esteem. The terms *voice* and *self,* for example, I want to link together in the familiar phrase *authentic voice,* a concept we now associate with the 1960s and early 1970s when such assignments as freewriting and the personal, autobiographical essay were central to most writing curricula. I believe this personal writing pedagogy, for which Ken Macrorie, Donald Murray, James Britton, and Peter Elbow have been primarily responsible (and more lately attacked), has been a valuable but increasingly neglected tool for teaching students how to write, how to "voice" themselves, how to locate themselves within the complex network of surrounding institutions and culture. My central argument in what follows is that teachers of writing need to reexamine and revise the lessons of this Authentic Voice pedagogy and seek to incorporate them into the increasingly influential assumptions of postmodernism if schools are to provide students with a truly liberating education and society itself with a more equitable distribution of power.

The link between self and voice I stipulated above is certainly nothing new, and I felt the stipulation necessary only because both terms and the linkage itself have been severely interrogated, indeed dismissed, in the more recent postmodern climate of socially constructed selves and dialogic voices, a consequence I will take up later and one which needs to be reconsidered. If the Authentic Voice school seems naïve and simplistic to many these days, such was not always the case. In the 1960s and early 1970s, when the New Criticism still held a steady course in my doctoral program and when governmental hypocrisy and institutional oppression, including that of the university, were as commonplace as the daily reports of atrocities in the Viet Nam War, I can well remember the names of Macrorie and Elbow being literally evoked in conspiratorial whispers by graduate students or raged against and/or mocked by professors in the faculty lounge. In an age of sham and cant, the very idea of authenticity, with its existential resonances, was vastly appealing to many of us who were just beginning our professional lives and who were just beginning to glimpse the possibility that teaching composition was not so clearly the trench work we had been brought up to believe. Furthermore, many of our students were extremely responsive to the simple idea that they could give voice in powerful words and images to what *they* thought really mattered, that in fact first-year English might not be a game of "psyche out the professor" after all but a legitimate opportunity to explore self and tell some long-repressed truths. Many of us spent hours running from cubicle to cubicle, reading to each other the seemingly amazing things our once lip-locked students had suddenly blurted out. We all felt as if we had just witnessed the angel bid Caedmon sing or a little like Galileo staring at newly discovered planets.

And when, in the late 1970s, I began my work in writing across the curriculum with Art Young and Toby Fulwiler at Michigan Tech, I read James Britton's *Language and Learning* (1970) and later his *The Development of Writing Abilities (11–18)* (1975) and immediately found in both texts corroboration for Macrorie and Elbow in Britton's central claims that what he called expressive writing—writing for the self—was the matrix out of which more formal modes of writing naturally evolved and that a writer had to "get it right with the self" before getting it right with his or her ultimate audience. Doing workshops for faculty at my own university and for groups at other universities around the country, I was constantly amazed at how threatening and controversial this notion of expressive writing was. Faculty, particularly those from English departments, regarded those of us who directed such workshops as subversives, although they were usually not quite certain why, except that we didn't have enough to say about mechanics and grammar and were somehow into "touchy-feely" stuff inappropriate to the rigors of a "real" university education.

As a way of proceeding, let me first examine three of the four terms I mentioned above—voice, self, and postmodernism—by briefly looking at the history of each and considering some of the problems each term raises for writing teachers. It will quickly become evident that it is impossible to separate these terms. They are, by now at least, in almost constant "dialogue" with one another, and to "voice" one of them inevitably prompts vocalizations from the others. Finally, I will try to unite these three terms in order to argue for a theory of education based on resistance and aspiring to bring about a more just society.

Self

To the traditionalist, this term seems commonsensical, a self-evident part of a long and honored tradition of humanistic learning existing at least since the Oracle at Delphi, over whose entryway was inscribed the famous imperative, "Know Thyself." From that point, through the trivium and quadrivium of the Greeks and Romans, through medieval scholasticism, Renaissance humanism, Romantic celebration of the ego, Arnoldian faith in the best that has been thought and said, right through T. S. Eliot's "tradition" and, most recently, in the renewed emphasis on acculturation sought by the Bennett-Bloom-Hirsch contingent, the Western liberal humanist tradition has accepted belief in a central core of stable, unified, transcendent, even transcultural self, a belief which served as a matrix out of which definitions of citizenship and ethical behavior and creativity are thought to evolve. Following the powerful assertion of individual selfhood accompanying the Enlightenment, nineteenth-century Romanticism made self the centerpiece of its philosophy. Poets in both England and America celebrated the personal over the universal, clearly manifested in these famous lines from Whitman's "Song of Myself": "I celebrate myself, and sing myself, / And what I assume you shall assume / For every atom belonging to me, as good belongs to you." Whitman's celebration states a premise vital to Romantic theory and to neo-Romantic attitudes which resurfaced after the twentieth-century break with Modernism. Contemporary American poet Galway Kinnell reiterates this theme in his essay "Poetry, Personality, and Death" when he says, "We [many American poets] move toward a theory in which the poet seeks an inner liberation by going so deeply into himself [sic]—into the worst of himself as well as the best—that he suddenly finds he is everyone" (1984, 75). The personal is, in other words, ultimately universal. Poet Alberta Turner echoes

Kinnell's claim when she says, in "Not Your Flat Tire, My Flat Tire: Transcending the Self in Contemporary Poetry" (1980), that poets

> are working on the same assumption that has always underlain both the making of fictional characters and the telling of autobiography—that the universally common experiences created by human psychology, physiology, and history ensure that any cluster of specific, concrete details of any single human being's experience can be made to evoke similar responses from all human beings. . . . It is this problem of presenting the data of one unique self so that other unique selves will recognize it as their own that poses the chief artistic challenge to contemporary poets who probe their own selves for the sake of transcending the individual in order to reveal the universal self. (135–36)

It was not until Victorian times, with the rise of urban life and industrial capitalism, that faith in the universal or transcendent self—one that is firmly anchored and unchanging—began to waver. Matthew Arnold, ironically the avatar of a unitary culture founded on a stable concept of self, gives us one of the first serious signals of a destabilized self in his poem "The Buried Life": "But often, in the world's most crowded streets, / But often, in the din of strife, / There arises an unspeakable desire / After knowledge of our buried life; / A thirst to spend our fire and restless force / In tracking out our true, original course." But the desire, Arnold tells us, is nearly futile: "And many a man then in his own breast delves, / But deep enough, alas! none ever mines." We try, Arnold says, "in vain to speak and act / our hidden self," although finally he concedes that only in rare moments, through the transforming power of love, can we possibly discover our deeply embedded self. Arnold's fear is not so much that self doesn't exist, but rather that it rests beneath too many masks for us to have much success in reaching it.

When, a century later, John Barth opens his 1958 novel, *The End of the Road*, with his protagonist's equivocal introduction—"In a sense, I am Jacob Horner"—we know things have only worsened. Camus had already capped off a growing sense of alienation in modern times by telling us, in *The Myth of Sisyphus* (1955), "Forever I shall be a stranger to myself and to the world" (15). Wylie Sypher documented the results of this alienation in his 1962 study entitled *Loss of the Self in Modern Literature and Art*, showing how the self had become anonymous, a victim of a collective, technological, vastly impersonal society. Shaken as the faith in self has been in our century's literature, this faith has never been entirely silenced. In American literature, especially in contemporary poetry, the self remains with us, sometimes a solace, sometimes a burden, but ultimately inescapable, even mythic, rooted in our very collective psyche. Consider, for example, Stephen Dobyns, whose voice through most of his major books of poems remains as recognizable as the concern for self in his poem "How You Are Linked," from his recent collection, *Body Traffic* (1990). After beginning the poem on a note of estrangement—"There are days when you wake and your body / feels too long or too short, like a shirt shrunk in the wash ..."— Dobyns tells us: "you decide / that the body you are wearing belongs to someone / you knew as a child. ...." This child turns out to be someone the "you" of the poem abused repeatedly, and the imagined or real exchange of bodies serves as a form of atonement. In a dream the two meet, make amends, and the "you" awakes inside his own body again, and runs off joyously to repeat his same old mistakes until the world once again slams him into a stranger's body:

> Who's this? you say, / as if it were some stray beauty, the seduced / victim of late night desire. But hidden within / this newcomer lurks only yourself: the monster, / the treasure, the curiosity you have passionately / tried to decipher for all the years of your life. (34–38)

In the poetry of women, this quest for self has been especially strong. Citing the work of Sylvia Plath, Denise Levertov, Anne Sexton, Adrienne Rich, Diane Wakoski, Muriel Rukeyser, Gwendolyn Brooks, and Margaret Atwood, Sandra Gilbert, in a 1984 essay entitled "My Name Is Darkness: The Poetry of Self-Definition," argues that "the self-defining confessional genre, with its persistent assertions of identity and its emphasis on a central mythology of the self, may be (at least for our own time) a distinctively female poetic mode" (99). The female poet, Gilbert says, "writes in the hope of discovering or defining a self, a certainty, a tradition, an ontology of selfhood, some irreducible and essential truth about her own nature" (100, 102–3).

Voice

The concept of voice is so pervasive in our culture, either in its literal or its metaphoric sense, that it is easy enough not even to take note of it. At a recent lecture on my campus, Native American activist Donald Grinde, in providing an indigenous perspective on the Christopher Columbus myth, said toward the end of his speech that after the final defeat and humiliation at Wounded Knee, Indian peoples were *silenced*, that they became *voiceless*. A few weeks later, at the Episcopal church I attend, our priest was speaking of the plight of children in America, specifically the astonishing degree of hunger and poverty that afflict roughly one out of five children in one of the world's most materially rich societies. He urged us all to speak out, to write our elected officials, to bring an end to the relative silence in America on this subject. By so doing, he concluded, we would be lending our voices to those whose voice had been stilled. In a recent issue of *College English*, Barbara Henning (1991), in an essay on basic writing instruction in the urban university, criticizes a number of pedagogical practices, including that of the Authentic Voice school, which has focused too much, Henning argues, on individualism. She characterizes basic writing students as "socially excluded, students who are 'selfless' and 'voiceless' because their experience and language do not allow them to construct a recognizable *mainstream* self and voice" (680). Feminists, after hundreds of years of being silenced, have acquired a voice, and the emerging men's movement is now seeking to help men regain their "real" voice, the one that allegedly lies beneath the false voices imposed by centuries of patriarchy. In short, the concept of voice saturates our public and private discourse, and, as writing teachers, we need not only to recognize this saturation but also to appropriate the best of the traditional aspects of this concept or create new perspectives if we are to adjust our curricula to fit a postmodern age. Let me begin with the notion of authentic voice, my ultimate aim being to recontextualize the concept, moving it out of its Romantic matrix and adapting it for our current needs.

Authentic voice is most likely an inheritance of our oral tradition and has long been regarded as a manifestation of this ontology of selfhood. As C. M. Bowra has demonstrated in his study of the origins of poetry, *Primitive Song* (1963), ancient communities were held together by the power of this authentic voice reciting or singing the history and rituals of the tribe, and voice initially evoked an individual's mystical connection to the Divine or the Muse. That conception fell into disfavor in the rationalistic wake of the Enlightenment, but it came back with the advent of Romanticism in late eighteenth-century Europe. Voice became closely linked metaphorically with breath itself, the breath of some transcendent Power playing upon the soul of the poet like wind on the strings of an aeolian harp, and the resulting music was truth spoken, as Wordsworth asserted in the famous Preface to his and Coleridge's *Lyrical Ballads* (1965 [1798]), in a natural voice to ordinary people who "convey their feelings and notions in simple and unelaborated expressions" (735).

Under the combined influence of Modernism and the New Criticism, authentic voice again went, like Xanadu's sacred river Alph, underground for a while, only to surface again in the 1950s and early 1960s in the spontaneous prose of Kerouac, Ginsberg's *Howl,* and Lowell's *Life Studies.* This was the beginning of the so-called Confessional movement (including poets such as the aforementioned Sexton and Plath), and much of the discourse dealing with the literature of the last four decades has been dominated by a commitment to voice. We know (or at least believe we know) a particular author by his or her distinctive voice. We read of prizes for "new voices." Young creative writers are told repeatedly that they must keep working at their craft until they "find their voice," which is regarded as a form of verbal equivalent for the physical presence of the author and as a lens to his or her authentic self. Poet and critic Jonathan Holden remarks in his *The Rhetoric of the Contemporary Lyric* (1980) that "the art of poetry consists mainly of the art of infusing feeling into language so that, without the aid of external devices such as the author's actual voice in performance, language on a silent page can attain the power and immediacy of a singing voice in the ear of the reader" (135). And in *Style and Authenticity in Postmodern Poetry* (1986), Holden, locating the origin of the word "authenticity" in the Greek *authentes* ("one who does anything with his own hand"), concludes that our sense of value in a well-made poem

> is intimately connected with our sense that it is not mass produced, not stamped out by machine, that the decisions which went into its shaping were not those of a committee, a corporation ... but ... of a single, passionate individual—the author—acting alone ... us[ing] the best materials available: human experience noticed in language ... bear[ing] the unmistakable mark of individual craftsmanship. (184)

Contemporary literature quickly found an ally in the emerging discipline of composition studies, which in the 1960s and early 1970s began to shift its emphasis from product to process, from the composed to the act of composing. Donald Stewart, in the preface to his 1972 text *The Authentic Voice: A Pre-Writing Approach to Student Writing,* makes clear a pedagogical intent which had already begun to dominate writing instruction. Stewart asserts his conviction that "the primary goal of any writing course is self-discovery for the student and that the most visible indication of that self-discovery is the appearance, in the student's writing, of an authentic voice" (xii). In his introduction he defines self-discovery as "the process of acquiring both a more objective and a psychologically deeper sense of the person you are ... beyond the complex of roles you play in life" (1). Authentic voice, he claims, "is a natural consequence of self-discovery" (2). Stewart, along with many others, assumed, in other words, that each student had a unique self and voice, but exactly *how* these resources were to be tapped remained somewhat unclear, although a variety of prewriting or invention strategies, including freewriting and journals, were advanced as the best tools for helping students discover their authentic selves. One spin-off of this emerging philosophy was the "talk-write" school, which attempted to get students to draw upon the "natural resources" of speaking as they began to write. If students would bring *their* reality into the classroom and into their writing, readers would, according to Lou Kelly, in *From Dialogue to Discourse: An Open Approach* (1972), "hear a *voice*—carried from speaker to listener by inanimate symbols, carried by words on a piece of paper ... a very audible voice. A voice that is alive with the sound of you" (145).

Probably the two most prominent of the Authentic Voice advocates have been Ken Macrorie and Peter Elbow, both of whose positions are so well known that I need touch only briefly upon them here. Macrorie's ideas came from a variety of publications that made many of us rethink our pedagogical legacy. Both *Uptaught* (1970b) and *A Vulnerable Teacher* (1974) were strong influences on me personally, but probably the most widely influential, on both secondary and college writing teachers, was *Telling Writing* (1970a), which in effect outlined what seemed at the time a radical pedagogy based on freewriting, journals, "telling facts," and "fabulous realities." Throughout the text Macrorie insists on truth telling and avoiding the poisonous bite of the "Engfish" (institutional language or language that conceals rather than reveals self). Early in the book, Macrorie asserts that "all good writers speak in honest voices and tell the truth" (5). Not *the* truth, he admits ("whoever knows surely what that is" [5]), "but some kind of truth" (5). Later on in the book, Macrorie connects truth to voice, a linkage which is discovered in an almost Zen-like manner during freewriting: "In freewriting a person frequently finds that his pen or typewriter seems to have taken over the job of writing and he [sic] is sitting there watching the words go down on paper" (148). "Finding the right voice," he tells the student reader, "will help you *write* better than you ever thought yourself capable of writing" (149). Not only will voice reveal truth, Macrorie insists, but it will also provide unity and coherence to one's writing. Macrorie ends his discussion of voice by admitting (and anticipating later critiques) that, "[l]ike everyone else who has ever spoken a word ... you have at your command a number of *different* voices [italics mine]. Use them" (157).

The influence of Macrorie on Elbow was immediately apparent. At the end of the preface to his by now classic text, *Writing without Teachers* (1973), Peter Elbow says that his book "wouldn't have been possible without the example and support of Ken Macrorie" (x), so we should

rightly expect to find strong parallels and similar pedagogical principles, and of course we do. We also find an emphasis on the liberating
power which authentic voice can make available to inexperienced writers. Elbow notes early in the book:

> In your natural way of producing words there is a sound, a tex-
> ture, a rhythm—a voice—which is the main source of power in
> your writing. I don't know how it works, but this voice is the force
> that will make a reader listen to you, the energy that drives the
> meaning through his [sic] skull. . . . [I]t's the only voice you've got.
> It's your only source of power. (6–7)

During the course of Elbow's advocacy of freewriting exercises and
teacherless writing groups, the word "magic," or synonyms for it, occurs a number of times, and this is an echo of the telling statement in
the just-quoted passage: "I don't know how it works." Authentic voice
is, for most of those who advocate it, somehow natural, innate, magical,
unavailable for empirical verification or rational explanation.

This theme is developed at greater length in Elbow's *Writing with
Power: Techniques for Mastering the Writing Process* (1981), a book held
together by three themes: (1) that the composing process must be privileged and separated from the critical faculty; (2) that every person has
innate skill with written language; and (3) that his "cookbook" strategies for improving writing should be followed by novice writers until
these "recipes" have been so internalized that these writers can take
charge of their own writing. Early in the text he admits that voice is
hard to talk about and is probably best learned through consciously
imitating a voice the writer finds compelling. But in a later chapter,
Elbow tackles the issue head on, using metaphors drawn from music to
try to articulate what he has already admitted may not be explainable:
According to him, we each have a chest cavity unique in size and shape
so that "each of us resonates to one pitch alone" (282). A few people, he
grants,

> sing with ringing power, but no one seems to understand how
> they manage this, not even they. In this metaphorical world, then,
> even if we figure out the system, we are stuck. If we want to be
> heard we are limited to our single note. If we want to sing other
> notes, we will not be heard. (282)

It's important to notice how self and voice dovetail at this point for
Elbow and the many teachers who have embraced his teaching philosophy, and it is equally important to attend to the assumption of a stable,
unique self, an essence, that underlies this concept of voice. Elbow
admits that writers may eventually be able to sing other notes after

extensive practice, but they will only be able to do so if they are "willing to start off singing [their] own single tiresome pitch for a long time and in that way gradually teach the stiff cells of [their] bodies to vibrate and be flexible" (282).

In a section entitled "How I Got Interested in Voice," Elbow chronicles his experience with student writing and his intuitive sense that some passages were somehow more "real." Furthermore, as he identified such passages to students and encouraged them to work more in that voice, their writing became more powerful and more connected to their sense of self. So Elbow decided he wanted to work out a "fuller theory of voice. For the power I am seeking, some people use words like *authenticity* or *authority*. Many people call it *sincerity*. . . ." Elbow himself prefers the word *juice* "because I'm trying to get at something mysterious and hard to define. 'Juice' combines the qualities of *magic potion, mother's milk,* and *electricity*. Sometimes I fear I will never be clear about what I mean by voice" (286). At this point Elbow reproduces a note sent to him by Ellen Nold after he had apparently struggled to articulate his theory at a meeting of writing teachers. The note is telling and worth quoting in full, but I'll limit myself to her concluding sentences. After linking voice to notions of Quality found in Eastern thought, she advises:

> Don't try to explain it to rationalistic people in rationalistic terms! It is something that ultimately cannot be explained to anyone who hasn't heard. And those who have heard will forgive you for the inadequacy of your words. (287)

Despite her advice, Elbow continues nevertheless, later pausing over the phrase "real self": "Real self. Real voice," he exclaims, "I am on slippery ground here. There are layers and layers" (293). Perhaps Elbow was already anticipating the first snipings of postmodernism, but these snipings, which have now grown into a constant fusillade, have not deterred Elbow. He has continued to explore the concept of voice and its relation to power, an exploration in the face of considerable opposition for which, as I shall finally argue, we should continue to be grateful.

Postmodernism

What the Divine has joined together, let no one tear asunder: So might the proponents of Authentic Voice proclaim, given their attraction to the mystery, the Power, the holistic (perhaps even holy) as well as interdependent nature of self and voice. But postmodernism has, as part of its ambitious agenda, performed just such a sundering, attacking both concepts individually as well as denying their interdependence. It is not within the scope of this essay to undertake a thorough examination of this complex and multifaceted term, but I might begin with some form of working definition before I turn to postmodernism's serious challenge to concepts of voice and self.

Steven Conner's *Postmodernist Culture: An Introduction to Theories of the Contemporary* (1989) is a wide-ranging study of the impact of postmodernist thought on the university, on architecture and the visual arts, on literature, television, video, and film, on pop culture and on cultural politics. In his initial chapter, Conner locates the basic feature of this relatively new perspective in "the fact that there no longer seems to be access to principles which can act as criteria of value for anything else . . . there are no absolute grounds of value which can compel assent" (8). And, Conner continues, "the postmodern condition . . . manifests itself in the multiplication of centres of power and activity and the dissolution of every kind of totalizing narrative which claims to govern the whole complex field of social activity and representation" (9). There is, however, Conner notes, irony in

> the degree of consensus in postmodernist discourse that there is no longer any possibility of consensus, the authoritative announcements of the disappearance of final authority and the promotion and recirculation of a total and comprehensive narrative of a cultural condition in which totality is no longer thinkable. (10)

Citing Fredric Jameson's influential essay "Postmodernism and Consumer Society" (1985), Conner summarizes Jameson's list of stylistic features that characterize postmodernism:

> its fondness for pastiche, for the "flat" multiplication and collage of styles, as opposed to the "deep" expressive aesthetic of unique style characteristic of modernism, and its retreat from the unified personality to the "schizoid" experience of the loss of self in undifferentiated time. (44)

Jameson, Conner observes, sees part of the postmodern condition as stemming from

> the tendency in contemporary social life towards the fragmentation of linguistic norms, with each group coming to speak a curious private language of its own, each profession developing its private code or dialect, and finally each individual coming to be a kind of linguistic island, separated from everyone else. (44)

A very good analysis of the effects of postmodernism on the concept of self is Kenneth Gergen's recent study, *The Saturated Self: Dilemmas of*

Identity in Contemporary Life (1991). Gergen, a psychologist, is uneasy with the term *postmodern* because of its multiple uses and because of its faddish and ubiquitous presence in so many different forms of discourse. "Still," Gergen concludes, "there seems to be a corpus of coherently related ideas and images surrounding the use of the term . . . and it would be a mistake to let the term slip away before examining its fuller significance" (xi). Gergen's basic argument is that postmodernism has resulted from what he calls the "century's technologies of saturation" (xi). The overall message of his book, Gergen insists, is optimistic, though before he can get to that optimism he admits many readers will, "as succeeding chapters cast one aspect of the Western sensibility after another into the void," feel as if they have been through a "journey into hell" before he is able to move them at last beyond "the abyss of despair" (xii). "[T]here is little hope that the past can be recovered," Gergen concludes. "Our best option, then, is to play out the positive potentials of this postmodern erasure of the self" (xiii).

Gergen's strategy is first to "take stock of our cultural inheritance" (16) by tracing the history of the self through its Enlightenment, Romantic, and Modern phases. The Enlightenment and Modernism both shared an emphasis on rationalism and scientific proof, while Romanticism stressed the unconscious, or "deep interior" (20), and developed a vocabulary of

> passion, purpose, depth, and personal significance. . . . It fosters a belief in deep dynamics of personality—marriage as a "communion of souls," family as bonded in love, and friendship as a lifetime commitment. Because of Romanticism we can trust in moral values and an ultimate significance to the human venture. (27)

For many, Gergen claims, "the loss of such a vocabulary would essentially be the collapse of anything meaningful in life" (27).

Gergen views Modernism as a return to Enlightenment values. Its great narrative is that of progress, of continuous upward movement provided by the leadership of science. Driving this upward movement is "a quest for essence . . . a fundamental thing-in-itself" (32–33), and its fundamental metaphor is that of the machine, and the Romantic obsession with the "deep interior," essentially unreachable, is now replaced by the "accessible self," one open to observation, rational analysis and, if needed, correctable, even, in fact, reproducible, much as machines themselves can be designed and manufactured. The modernist self, Gergen summarizes,

> is knowable, present in the here and now, just slightly below the surface of his [sic] actions. He is not likely to be transported by

sudden inspiration, be smitten by some great passion, or give
way to a rush of suicidal urges. Rather, he is flexible and trustworthy.... The modernist self is not likely to have his reason clouded
by intense emotional dramas.... With proper molding, and the
help of science, we can create the future of our dreams. It is this
modernist place in the sun that we shall find eclipsed by the rise
of postmodernism. (47)

In this postmodern world, Gergen claims, we are immersed in the
opinions and values of others by means of what he calls *the technologies
of social saturation* to the point that our self is ultimately erased, repopu-
lated with the multiple relationships we experience until there is finally
the onset of a multiphrenic condition "in which one begins to experience the vertigo of unlimited multiplicity" (49). These technologies of
social saturation include jet travel, photocopy and fax machines, computers, telephones, films, television, VCRs, electronic mail, on-line information services, and satellite communications leading to global
linkages, and fiber optics. Consequently, the world shrinks. Our sense
of time and place is altered. Everything is accelerated. We are capable
of many more and even nearly simultaneous relationships. We begin to
experience "a populating of the self, the acquisition of multiple and
disparate potentials for being." It is this process of self-population for
Gergen that "begins to undermine the traditional commitments to both
romanticist and modernist forms of being" (69). "A multiphrenic condition emerges," Gergen claims, "in which one swims in ever-shifting,
concatenating, and contentious currents of being. One bears the burden
of an increasing array of oughts, of self-doubts and irrationalities....
[T]he way is open for the postmodern being" (80).

Following a chapter on the erosion of Truth and the rise of relativism,
especially in the academy, Gergen turns to the emergence of postmodern culture. He cites the breakdown of rational order, the challenge to
all claims to authority, the blurring of genres in architecture, literature,
and music, the free play in the visual arts. Traditional categories collapse, objective knowledge seems illusionary, and the relativity of postmodernism leads to a sense that all facets of culture and history are
socially constructed, contingent on the particularities of time and place.
It is only a small move to seeing the self as merely another example of
the socially constructed. Finally, Gergen concludes,

> With postmodern consciousness begins the erasure of the category
> of self. No longer can one securely determine what it is to be a
> specific kind of person—male or female—or even a person at all.
> As the category of the individual fades from view, consciousness
> of construction becomes focal. We realize increasingly that who
> and what we are is not so much the result of our "personal es-

sence" (real feelings, deep beliefs, and the like), but of how we are constructed in various social groups. . . . [O]ne acquires a pastiche-like personality. Coherence and contradiction cease to matter as one takes pleasure in the expanded possibilities of being in a socially saturated world. (170)

I have barely done justice to this part of Gergen's analysis, but before I move on, a few words about the implications of Gergen's postmodern, saturated self on the notion of authentic voice. The word *voice* shows up a number of times in Gergen's treatment of self, but as one might well expect, his sense of that word differs considerably from the meaning ascribed to it by the Authentic Voice theorists. The proliferation of communication technologies exposes us to a virtual host of other voices, many of which we consciously or unconsciously incorporate into our own. Thus it is *voices* Gergen stresses, not any single unique voice. In examining the academy's encounter with deconstruction, for example, Gergen makes the by now predictable critique of language which denies referentiality and makes language a system of differences:

> Its structure preexists any single individual, and if sense is to be made, the individual must essentially participate in the communal conventions. Thus, individuals are not the intentional agents of their own words, creatively and privately converting thoughts to sounds or inscriptions. Rather, they gain their status as selves by taking a position within a preexisting form of language. (110)

There can be no *I*, only *we*, and the self perforce must exit, leaving behind a polyphony of voices. Pluralism predominates in the arts, and consciousness of unitary form is replaced by free play of mixed forms. Speaking of architecture, Gergen notes that "the postmodern building is designed to speak in multiple vernaculars" (115), a reflection of the pastiche motif cited earlier. Later, underscoring the dramatic increase in relationships which one is able to maintain in a socially saturated world, Gergen observes, "In the case of 'Who am I?' it is a teeming world of provisional possibilities" (139), not the stable sense of self implied by the imperative of the Oracle at Delphi. The intense competition of voices, Gergen maintains, challenges the notion of the thing (or person) in itself. We as individuals are an assemblage of voices, and

> if each voice portrays the individual a little differently, then the very idea of an "isolated self," independent of the voices themselves, begins to teeter. . . . As the chorus of competitive voices builds, "the person" as a reality beyond voice is lost. There is no voice now trusted to rescue the "real person" from the sea of portrayals. (140)

In making his case for the positive side of postmodernism, Gergen notes the ways in which any language bears with it the traces or remnants of languages from subcultures and from previous historical eras, and he cites the *heteroglossia* of Russian literary theorist Mikhail Bakhtin to help him conclude:

> In this sense, postmodernism invites a heteroglossia of being, a living out of the multiplicity of voices within the sphere of human possibility. There is little reason to suppress any voice. Rather, with each new vocabulary or form of expression, one appropriates the world in a different way, sensing aspects of existence in one that are hidden in another, opening capacities for relatedness in one modality that are otherwise hindered. (247)

It remains to be seen how accurate is Gergen's assessment of the positive potential in postmodernism. As we know, voices still are being silenced, despite the rose-tinted view Gergen provides us. Is it possible, within this multiplicity of voices, to empower those who yet have no voice? Postmodernism must allow for that liberation if it is to realize its full pedagogical potential.

So this postmodern critique of self and voice leaves us in a bit of a bind. On the one hand, the stable, transcendent self has been erased. On the other, postmodern theories posit a kind of lacuna, or empty space, at the center of the human organism, a space to be filled by language-mediated social experience and the agendas of ideological apparatuses. Such an either/or vision is, of course, oversimplified, reductive. The liberal humanist view *is* nostalgic, and it is seriously flawed by its inability to respond to the ideological critiques of Marxist and post-structuralist theory, e.g., that a stable self is illusory, that individuals are products of specific times and circumstances and unwittingly manipulated by powerful institutionalized interests beyond their control, that language cannot and never has been able to serve as a bridge between elusive subjective life and so-called objective reality. These latter theories, on the other hand, are incomplete because ultimately they are deterministic and pessimistic about human nature, reducing it to a passive and helpless entity and failing to posit a view of self (or human agency) which can allow for resistance to the repressive and dominatory mechanisms of economic, political, and educational systems. What we need is a theory of self which synthesizes these two theoretical extremes and offers hope for change, a kind of Archimedean notion of self which gives individuals a place to stand, a point of leverage by which they can move their world.

And it is this lack of such a point of leverage in current theory that makes this intensified attack on earlier versions of self matter to writing teachers who want to empower their students, not just in the sense of helping them get a job or enabling them to achieve upward social mobility, but in the more ambitious sense of equipping them to be active agents in the cause of social justice. A too-quick acceptance of poststructuralist theories is presently undermining useful pedagogical approaches prematurely, especially the expressive and personal writing most often associated with the Authentic Voice school. Consider, for example, the current challenge to personal writing resulting from post-modernist assumptions that have served to delegitimate the self. A useful illustration is James Berlin's 1988 *College English* article, "Rhetoric and Ideology in the Writing Class." As he has elsewhere, here Berlin classifies major rhetorical theories, identifies the ideological assumptions of each, and argues for his own preference. In this particular essay he identifies three current and competing rhetorical theories: Cognitive, Expressionistic, and Social-Epistemic. Using Goran Therborn's formulation of ideology as his framework, Berlin argues against Cognitive and Expressionistic theories in order to make a case for the Social-Epistemic.

I am interested here in his attack on Expressionistic rhetoric, because he lays the groundwork for subsequent challenges to personal writing and pedagogies seeking "authentic voice," the rhetoric, in other words, of Ken Macrorie, Peter Elbow, Walker Gibson, William Coles, Jr., and Donald Murray. After tracing the roots of this rhetoric in the early years of this century, Berlin rejects it for its false epistemology, one located in a central self. For Expressionists, writing is valued as "an art, a creative act in which the process—the discovery of the true self—is as important as the product—the self discovered and expressed" (484). Berlin grants that, unlike the Cognitive school, Expressionistic rhetoric embraces as one of its primary aims a critique of a dominant and corrupt society. Unfortunately, Berlin concludes, the Expressionists' epistemology is its own worst enemy, defining resistance in purely individual rather than collaborative and social terms—this seems a valid critique and one I want to pursue later. Expressionists, according to Berlin, believe

> [t]he only hope in a society working to destroy the uniqueness of the individual is for each of us to assert our individuality against the tyranny of the authoritarian corporation, state, and society. Strategies for doing so must of course be left to the individual, each lighting one small candle in order to create a brighter world. (487)

This commitment to the epistemology of individual self, Berlin concludes, ironically allows the Expressionists to be co-opted by the very ideology they would subvert, an ideology rooted in "individualism, private initiative, the confidence for risk taking, the right to be contentious with authority (especially the state)" (487). Such private vision easily enough defers collective action, and self-expression is too often deflected into various forms of consumer behavior since the appeal to individuality lies at the heart of so much commodity advertising.

After making a case for Social-Epistemic rhetoric built in good measure on a social-constructionist epistemology, and after claiming for this rhetoric the power of critiquing the dominant culture without being co-opted, Berlin presents the pedagogy outlined in Ira Shor's Critical Teaching and Everyday Life (1987) as a model application of Social-Epistemic rhetoric. Oddly enough, Shor's practices are aimed, according to Berlin, at externalizing false consciousness and "changing students," Shor is quoted as saying, "from re-active objects into society-making subjects" (491). Unfortunately, the notion of "false consciousness," essentially Marxist in origin, has been problematic and ultimately rejected precisely because it has been interpreted as implying a true consciousness, a humanistic core self, underneath accumulated layers of capitalist-induced domination, a "full" or "true" consciousness which will surface when ideology disappears. Paul Smith, in Discerning the Subject (1988), summarizes the Marxist perspective well for our purposes:

> [H]is [Marx's] formulations take for granted that there *is* some essential humanity, but that it cannot yet be theorized since "society does not consist of individuals, but expresses the sum of interrelations within which these individuals stand" [Smith is citing Marx here]. . . . Thus, concrete individuality does not exist in the current conditions of alienation but rather is smothered beneath the weight of these real conditions. In other words, subjectivity [or self] can currently have no force and no effect, and can only await its fulfillment, exactly, in the destruction of capitalism and the building of socialism/communism. (6–7)

Smith goes on to note that Marx engages in a utopian ploy which

> effectively deprivileges the very real existence experienced by the subject/individual only as a currently unrealized form of exactly that lure which has been offered by traditional notions. . . . Marxism looks forward to bringing about an "individual," exactly, whose unalienated activity "will coincide with material life, which corresponds to the development of individuals into *complete* individuals." (p. 7; again, Smith quotes Marx; the italics are Smith's)

In fairness, the practices of Shor which Berlin refers to do include a notable number of assignments that rely on personal, autobiographical, and expressive forms of writing. My purpose is not to devalue Shor's work but rather to point to an inconsistency in Berlin's argument. To Berlin's credit, he argues for a theory that *will* promote resistance, but his characterization of Expressionistic rhetoric seems, to me at least, oversimplified and incomplete, and his pedagogical solution seems tainted by the same epistemological problem that he says haunts the Expressionists.

Lester Faigley, in a recent *CCC* essay entitled "Judging Writing, Judging Selves" (1989), offers us another critique of personal or autobiographical writing, and, like Berlin, his attack is grounded in social constructionist assumptions about the way ideology operates to construct the social self. Faigley manages to avoid the predicament Berlin created for himself when the latter invoked the humanist Marxism of Ira Shor's pedagogy. Faigley does this mainly by relying on Louis Althusser's revisionist view of Marxism, a view which posits that "subjects" or selves are interpellated or summoned to play roles within an ideological structure and that this ideology never disappears; thus there can be no utopian future moment when false consciousness falls away and we live as full humans within an ideology-free society. Whether or not one would automatically live a "full" life in a society free of ideology, or whether the latter is even possible—both of these claims are debatable, but that seems to be the line of traditional Marxist logic—Faigley, like most commentators on Althusser, notes the pun inherent in Althusser's use of the term "subject":

> People are subjected to dominant ideologies, but because they recognize themselves in the subject-positions that discourses provide, they believe they are subjects of their own actions . . . people fail to see that the subject-positions they occupy are historically produced, and they imagine that they are freely choosing for themselves. (403)

Faigley's real target is a 1985 book by William Coles, Jr., and James Vopat called *What Makes Writing Good*. For this book, forty-eight well-known teacher-scholars submitted pieces of student writing that they felt demonstrated excellence, along with a commentary explaining their choice. Faigley, puzzled by the high number of personal experience essays, observes, "I have no simple explanation for the strong preference for autobiographical essays" (404). In the commentaries, furthermore, he is troubled by the appearance of such characterizations as "honest," "authentic voice," and "integrity," and in both the commentaries and several of the student essays he detects the "assumption that individuals possess an identifiable 'true' self and that the true self can be expressed in discourse" (405). And Faigley goes on to say, borrowing heavily from current ideologically based theory, "To ask students to write authentically about the self assumes that a rational consciousness can be laid out on the page. That the self must be interpellated through language is denied" (409–10). Faigley concludes that teachers of writing "are still very much concerned with the self" (410), a concern he clearly believes is inadvisable because it dupes students and teachers alike into believing that discovering authentic self is somehow empowering. "[We must]," he concludes, "teach our students to analyze cultural definitions of the self, to understand how historically these definitions are created in discourse, and to recognize how definitions of the self are involved in the configuration of relations of power" (411). I don't at all disagree with Faigley about *what* we must teach our students; the how is a different matter altogether. Furthermore, I believe the pedagogy he advocates is incomplete in that it fails to provide students with any point of Archimedean leverage. If we follow his pedagogy, we inform students of the ways in which ideology defines them and forces certain subject-positions upon them, but we fail to provide them with any significant sense of self which might serve as grounds for resistance and liberatory behavior. And in the process, by virtue of the way we locate ourselves with respect to them in terms of authority, we enact an ideology that further denies such a grounding to them.

Up to this point I have summarized briefly the concepts of self and voice in the Western tradition, both of which seem to have arrived at dead ends in postmodern versions of subjectivity. I have also asserted that the concept of self implicit in the Authentic Voice school, all but abandoned by composition theorists under the influence of postmodernism, still offers considerable potential sustenance to writing teachers who seek to design a liberatory pedagogy and work with their students to bring about a more just society. Let me now turn to theoretical work, some of it fairly "old" by this time and some of it still in process, that is beginning to map out a more positive view of knowledge and education and their potential for effecting social transformation.

To begin with, this positive view must be rooted in a concept of human agency. Human agency does not mean human "actor," for such a definition too easily reduces to a sense of assuming roles, much as an actor does. And that sense of the term shares too much in common with the concept of constructed or assigned parts in the social drama. At the heart of human agency is the ability to take action, sometimes in harmony with and sometimes against socially accepted values. Only when such action is possible is a theory of resistance feasible. For my purposes, human agency and self are roughly synonymous, though in what follows I intend to distinguish between these two roughly synonymous terms, on the one hand, and the traditional Romantic concept of self characterized earlier. Facets of the positive theory I advocated above have been available for some time in perspectives which have attempted to synthesize both the individual and social contributions of knowledge and to regard the link between the self and the social as interdependent or transactional. The work of Piaget, specifically his organic view of knowledge and the attendant theories of assimilation and accommodation, is one such facet. Piaget argues that organisms adapt to their environment by first assimilating the new and often frightening experience into their existing representation of the world and then by changing that representation to accommodate this new piece of information. For Piaget, this process of adaptation is ongoing and dynamic, not passive. We reconstruct ourselves in an ongoing transaction with our environment. Another facet can be found in economist Kenneth Boulding's 1956 monograph entitled *The Image: Knowledge in Life and Society*. Here Boulding outlines an epistemology that links the personal to the social but preserves the individuality of the self. Boulding argues for an image (or representation) of the world which feeds on and grows organically through the messages it receives, messages filtered through the individual history of each image or self. Louise Rosenblatt, in *Literature as Exploration* (1983) and *The Reader, the Text, the Poem* (1978), has also made a powerful case, with particular respect to reading, for the transactional theory of knowledge, a theory strongly resembling Boulding's and Piaget's in its acknowledgment of both the personal and public dimensions of language and knowing. Rosenblatt insists on foregrounding the individual lived histories of students, and the way these lived histories shape student responses to literary texts. Janet Emig, in an essay entitled "Our Missing Theory" (1990), urges us to study learning theory, particularly what she describes as "Constructivism," emphasizing its personal dimension and characterizing it in terms that are consonant with the ideas of Boulding, Piaget, and Rosenblatt:

> Through their private and their school encounters with text, their creation, comprehension, and interpretation, our students have built constructs about what reading and writing are and about what roles these processes serve, or do not serve, in *their* lives. (92; italics mine)

We should begin with such personal knowledge, Emig argues, and one obvious way to do that, I would suggest, is through writing assignments that are personal and expressive in nature, at least in their initial phases, assignments that allow students to voice themselves and their location with respect to social authority and power in order to resist those forces which would explicitly or tacitly repress them.

Resistance

The fourth and final problematic term in my title—*resistance*—provides potential hope with regard to the subject, or self, and its capacity for liberatory struggle. If we can sensitize our students, make them aware of the ideology of the entrenched and empowered class and the way in which institutions often operate to maintain the status quo, we put these students in a position to fight back. Such retaliation might range from the minimal—essential recognition and articulation of their plight—to various forms of active resistance. We cannot, nor should we, choose for our students or pressure them into postures of resistance. Some, even after they recognize their disempowered condition, may prefer that condition to active resistance against it. To resist or not to resist: That choice is theirs alone. But if we can help them to recognize and voice their dominated condition, we will have served them well.

One way we might begin to raise the consciousness of our students is by *rejection*, the spatial metaphor of marginalization. Many of our students come to our classes feeling marginalized already, that is, out on the periphery, away from the center of power, so far out, in fact, that they bring with them attitudes of submission, helplessness, and indifference. The discourse of composition studies in recent times, as the discipline has become increasingly influenced by the ideological orientation of postmodernist theory, has been marked by a persistent reliance on the metaphors of marginalization and boundaries. Consider, for example, Mike Rose's excellent *Lives on the Boundary* (1989; a moving and *personal* account of how educational and economic institutions made powerless both Rose and the students he later worked with in literacy programs, and how sensitive teachers *can* make a difference). Consider, too, Carolyn Ericksen Hill's *Writing from the Margins: Power and Pedagogy for Teachers of Composition* (1990). Both books intelligently characterize the way in which disempowered students can be kept that way by ideological forces. But much as I agree with the overall "rightness" of their respective conclusions, I worry that the metaphor each uses can send the wrong message to student and teacher alike. In fact, the disempowered are not somewhere "out there," at the edge, far removed. They are, rather, at the center of power's corrosive processes. Paulo Friere makes this point in *The Politics of Education: Culture, Power, and Liberation* (1985b), arguing that

> In the light of such a concept [marginalization] . . . literacy programs can never be movements toward freedom. . . . These men [*sic*], illiterate or not, are not marginal. . . . They are not "beings outside of"; they are "beings for another." Therefore the solution to their problem is to become, not "beings inside of," but men freeing themselves; for, in reality, they are not marginal to the structure, but oppressed men within it. (48–49)

Illiteracy, for Friere, is a form of muteness in "the culture of silence" and literacy is tantamount to transformative action. If, he maintains, the illiterate can gain an awareness of how dominatory mechanisms work to oppress them, "they can 'have a voice,' that is, they [can] exercise the right to participate consciously in the sociohistorical transformation of their society" (50). He insists that the literacy process "must relate *speaking the word to transforming reality,* and to man's role in this transformation. . . . [Such learners] will ultimately recognize a much greater right than that of being literate. They will recognize that . . . they have the right to have a voice" (510). Friere clearly reinforces what I have been arguing in this essay about voice and human agency, but he is often too easily dismissed by critics who argue that the severe kind of illiteracy with which Friere has had to deal in third-world countries does not apply to conditions in this country. Though I agree with these critics in part, I suspect the conditions bear stronger similarities than most of us would like to admit. At any rate, let me turn to a few theoretical arguments that focus more directly on developed societies.

For those interested in the issues I have been exploring in this essay and in a pedagogy with a liberatory agenda, Henry A. Giroux's *Theory and Resistance in Education: A Pedagogy for the Opposition* (1983) is a good place to begin. In this book, Giroux sets out to assay the history of radical educational theory and its proponents—those who have regarded schools not merely as sites of instruction but also as sites of political and cultural struggle—in order to locate foundations upon which he might then construct a more contemporary theory of educational resistance. Giroux maintains that all too many of these educational critics are severely flawed because their theories do not contain an adequate view of human agency that would enable students to recognize and resist the sources of their domination. To supply what is missing from most radical educational theory, Giroux turns to the critical theory of the Frankfurt School—Adorno, Horkheimer, and Marcuse.

"The achievements of the critical theorists," Giroux stresses, "are their refusal to abandon the dialectic of agency and structure [state apparatuses, etc.] . . . and [their willingness to] treat seriously the claim that history can be changed, that the potential for radical transformation exists" (5). By human agency, Giroux essentially means that human beings create history rather than merely being prisoners of it. Students are not inevitably passive victims of prison-like schools which invisibly reproduce the interests of the ruling class. Vital to Giroux's outlook is that students are in some sense "selves," and that schools are sites of struggle where resistance and change can occur. In too much theory—educational or critical or literary—the concept of self has been erased, so Giroux turns to those theorists who attempt to preserve self, because, in one form or another, the capacity to resist depends on a theory of self.

The Frankfurt School, Giroux maintains, rejected the positivist rationality of science that had come to dominate in schools, and replaced it with the idea of "dialectical thinking." He defines this by quoting Fredric Jameson's (1985) definition:

> [D]ialectical thinking is . . . thought about thinking itself, in which the mind must deal with its own thought process just as much as with the material it works on, in which both the particular content involved and the style of thinking suited to it must be held together in the mind at the same time. (35)

Such dialectical thought—which, I might add, echoes strongly the ideas of James Britton—makes educators as well as students capable of what Giroux calls "critique," or the ability to think oppositionally. Such thinkers don't blindly accept the traditional narrative of progress and historical continuity; instead, they seek "the breaks, discontinuities, and tensions in history, all of which become valuable in that they highlight the centrality of human agency and struggle while simultaneously revealing the gap between society as it presently exists and society as it might be" (36). The socially oppressed—and I want to supplement Giroux's listing of the working class, women, African Americans, and other minorities by adding middle-class students—need "to affirm their own histories through the use of a language, a set of social conventions, and body of knowledge that critically reconstructs and dignifies the cultural experiences that make up the tissue, texture, and history of their daily lives" (37). This is a matter of great importance, Giroux insists, because

> once the affirmative nature of such a pedagogy is established, it becomes possible for students who have been traditionally voiceless in schools to learn the skills, knowledge, and modes of inquiry

> that will allow them to critically examine the role society has
> played in their own self-formation. . . . [I]t is important for stu-
> dents to come to grips with what a given society has made of
> them, how it is has incorporated them ideologically and materi-
> ally into its rules and logic, and what it is they need to affirm and
> reject in order to begin the process of struggling for the conditions
> that will give them opportunities to lead a self-managed existence.
> (37–38)

Here again we see Giroux's emphasis on human agency in the form of
critique as pitted in dialectical fashion against a dominant culture.
"[H]uman beings not only make history, they also make the constraints;
and needless to say, they also unmake them . . . power is both an enabling as well as a constraining force" (38).

After analyzing the concept of the "hidden curriculum"—"those
unstated norms, values, and beliefs embedded in and transmitted to
students through the underlying rules that structure the routines and
social relationships in school and classroom life" (47) in order to covertly undergird and reproduce the dominant society—Giroux insists
that we must see schools as "sites of *both domination and contestation*"
(62–63). Thus, we must recognize the dialectic tension between forces
of reproduction, on the one hand, and the concrete, lived experiences of
the students. Herein, Giroux suggests, lies a potent source of resistance,
for the concrete histories of students, when brought to consciousness
and placed in opposition to the cultural forces which have in part
produced these concrete histories and which attempt to perpetuate the
inequities there recorded, provide students with the necessary antece-
dent to resistance. Giroux ultimately says that the dialectic between the
actual experience of students and the ideological agenda of schools is a
far more complex matter than is generally granted by educational critics. Precisely because most of these critics omit any concern for human
agency or self as a resisting entity, one of Giroux's most important
contributions is his faith in the existence of human agency and his
location of it in the concrete lives of students (as well as teachers). The
self as Giroux conceives it may be ultimately socially constructed, but
the product of this construction is not pure victim; it is a potent force
for struggle, especially when the pedagogical environment is designed
to explore the dialectic nature of education. Giroux's message is an
affirmation of self and voicing as a tool for its growth. As such, it brings
us closer to a mediation between postmodernist claims and the Authentic Voice pedagogy.

Another useful starting point is Paul Smith's *Discerning the Subject*
(1988). In this book-length study, Smith also surveys a variety of social

theories (the Frankfurt School, various Marxist perspectives, postmodernism) as well as individuals (Althusser, Adorno, Marcuse, Derrida), and he too finds them flawed for their failure to include a workable concept of human agency. He believes "the calls to resistance made by such educational theorists as Henry Giroux are hampered by a view of subjectivity inherited from Fromm, Marcuse, and others" and he claims that an adequate theory of subjectivity and agency "must take account of what I call the mediating function of the unconscious in social life" (xxxi). Thus he proposes that Lacan's theory of the unconscious could provide the missing piece in assembling a viable theory of resistance. One problem, he notes, is the philosophic tradition of dualism, which has split the world into subject (or perceiver, or consciousness) and object (the material world, that which is perceived). Both Marx and Freud, Smith claims, have aided postmodernism by problematizing an oversimplified concept of the self, the former by rooting self in material reality, the latter by locating "true" self in the murky regions of the unconscious. Another problem, Smith argues, is that the majority of poststructuralist theories deal with the idea of Self at such an abstract level (a process which Smith labels "cerning") that they produce, in his words, "a purely theoretical 'subject,' removed from the political and ethical realities in which human agents live," and he concludes that "a different concept of the 'subject' must be discerned" (xxix), that is, the central and privileged Western concept of the self or subject must be negated if a more rich and accurate theory is to emerge. He also argues against versions of a monolithic process of interpellation, insisting that resistance "can be glimpsed as soon as the 'subject' is no longer theorized as an abstract or cerned entity" (xxx–xxxi).

Smith begins by establishing some definitions of terms, definitions useful for our purposes. He differentiates the terms "individual," "subject," and "agent." The individual, "that which is undivided and whole, and understood to be the source and agent of conscious action or meaning which is consistent with it," is essentially an illusion (xxxiii–xxxiv). The "subject" is not self-contained and is dominated by social formations, language, ideological apparatuses, and it is capable of many subject-positions in a specific, lived life. "The term 'agent,'" Smith says,

> [marks] the idea of a form of subjectivity where, by virtue of the contradictions and disturbances in and among subject-positions, the possibility (indeed, the actuality) of resistance to ideological pressure is allowed for, even though that resistance too must be produced in an ideological context [xxxv]. The main point in a sense is . . . that [a] person is not simply the actor who follows

ideological scripts, but is also an agent who reads them in order
to insert him/herself into them—or not. (xxxiv–xxxv)

In his concluding chapter, Smith reiterates "that the era of . . . poststructuralism has perhaps brought with it a tendency to problematize so much the 'subject's' relation to experience that it has become difficult to keep sight of the political necessity of being able to not only theorize but also *refer* to that experience" (159), and he contends that the specificity of experience—a rich source of resistance—has been severely debilitated by poststructuralist theories of language, representation, and subjectivity. "In other words," he says, "poststructuralism's skepticism, its radical doubt, about the availability of the referent has been canonized, even exaggerated, to the point that the real often disappears from consideration" (159).

After citing the failure of Marxism to provide an adequate account of the subject—mainly because this influential theory has, for the most part, ignored the individual dimension of the subject and stressed its collective nature—Smith poses what is the central issue for him and, to a certain degree, for Giroux as well: "how and under what conditions subjects/individuals simultaneously exist within and make purposive intervention into social formations" (5). An individual's concrete experience and personal history are not, Smith insists, determined by what class one belongs to or what set of economic conditions one must accept. Smith stresses this point in a more focused manner when he characterizes the individual existence as always at one level *solitary*, not interpersonal or social; although we *are* socially constructed, this construction takes place within specific historical and personal conditions, and resistance is made possible by a dialectic tension between the interpellation of dominant institutions and the subject, which is always in a process of evolving. Smith is not willing to posit some

> innate human capacity that could over-ride or transcend the very
> conditions of understanding and calculation—indeed of social existence. Resistance does take place, but it takes place only within
> a social context which has already constructed subject-positions
> for the human agent. The place of that resistance, has, then, to be
> glimpsed somewhere in the interstices of the subject-positions
> which are offered in any social formation. More precisely, resistance must be regarded as the by-product of contradictions in and
> among subject-positions. (25)

The personal history Smith repeatedly refers to as one half of the dialectic which makes resistance possible begins for him (and here he is influenced by Lacan) in one's engagement with language: "there is

no such thing as a 'subject-position' before the accession to language"
(31). This personal history is made up of an ongoing series of moments,

> a continuing series of overlapping subject-positions which may or
> may not be present to consciousness at any given moment. . . . A
> person's lived history cannot be abstracted as subjectivity pure
> and simple, but must be conceived as a colligation of multifarious
> and multiform subject-positions. (32)

So the problem, as Smith sees it, is that theorists too often simplify and
abstract the subject rather than recognize that each subject is the result
of a compilation of moments which constitute singular histories. Despite the difficult language in Smith's analysis, the careful reader can
begin to see connections between Smith's position and, for example,
those of Giroux and Rosenblatt.

Disagreeing with Althusser that the subject is identical to the concept
of individuality and at the same time the result of ideology, Smith
argues that "the state of being a 'subject' is best conceived of in something akin to a temporal aspect—the 'subject' as only a moment in a
lived life," the result being that interpellations don't automatically succeed. They can in fact fail, because what interpellation actually creates
is contradictions, "and through a recognition of the contradictory and
dialectical elements of subjectivity it may be possible to think of a
concept of the agent" (37). "A singular history," Smith insists, "always
mediates between the human agent and the interpellations directed at
him/her . . . each of us necessarily negotiates the power of specific ideologies by means of our own personal history" (37). "If this seems a
platitude," Smith continues (in what I think is a key reminder), "it bears
reiteration . . . [because] of the emphasis that has been placed, in contemporary discourse, on the subjection of the 'subject', usually to the
detriment of any consideration of the human agent's own historical
constitution" (37).

There is more and yet richer ground to cover in trying to recapitulate
Smith's subtle and at times difficult analysis of the failure of social and
critical theory to provide an adequate concept of human agency which
would make resistance possible. But I have, I think, given enough sense
of Smith's work for us to see the major outlines of his argument. What
is especially useful in both Giroux and Smith is that they recognize the
importance of postmodern theory and are not attempting to discredit
its contributions or argue for a return to a nostalgic theory of self. In
fact, both seek to define self in more complex ways than either neo-
Romantics or postmodernists have so far been willing to do. Both
Giroux and Smith seek to locate or articulate a concept of self that

allows for resistance, for opportunities for each of us to find our voice and enlist it in the struggle against oppressive forces. And as we have seen, both writers have explored new territory in this debate by their call for a more dialectical view of self. Before I conclude, I want to take a quick look at one final alternative to the limited concept of self against which I have arguing in this essay, an alternative found in what philosopher and political scientist Charles Taylor (1991) calls the *dialogical self.*

The very phrase itself, along with its opposite—*the monological self*—connects Taylor's perspective to the themes of voice and resistance I have been pursuing. Taylor considers the self to be essentially a modern and Western cultural phenomenon, at least in the sense that a concept of self goes beyond mere reflexivity, which earlier ages clearly possessed. It is a specific form of reflexivity that characterizes modern culture, a "radical reflexivity" that allows us to review and analyze our own thinking. Humans have always "devis[ed], or accept[ed], or have [had] thrust upon them descriptions of themselves, and these descriptions help to make them what they are" (305). And Taylor stresses the moral or ethical dimension of many of these descriptions: "A human being exists inescapably in a space of ethical questions; she or he cannot avoid assessing himself or herself in relation to some standards" (305). It is this sense of ethical space that truly defines our grasp of who we truly are, so our values serve as a compass for locating our selves in ethical space. This ethical space may be a defining feature of self, but the space itself changes; it is relative to one's time, place, and culture, and the "radical reflexivity," mentioned above Taylor cites as the central "ethical space" of the modern age. To do this, we "have had to discipline our thought to disengagement from embodied agency and social embedding. Each of us is called upon to become a responsible, thinking mind, self-reliant for his or her judgments" (307). This disengaged first-person singular "tends to see the human agent as primarily a subject of representations: representations about the world outside, [about] ends desired or feared" (307). This subject is a "monological" one because it operates on the basis of its own inner representations. Such a subject lives in an inner space, in effect cut off or separated from others.

This "stripped-down view of the subject" (307), this monological self, Taylor claims has permeated the social sciences and has been responsible for the privileging of individualism and rational choice making. And the near-hegemony of this concept of self "stands in the way of a richer and more adequate understanding of what the human sense of self is really like, and hence of a proper understanding of the real variety of human culture, and hence of a knowledge of human beings" (307). This monological view of self omits, says Taylor, two essential components of a fuller theory of self: the body and the other. Taylor notes that in the past two centuries some philosophers have tried to derive a fuller theory by conceiving of the human agent less in terms of a repository of representations and more in terms of someone engaged in practices, "as a being who acts in and on a world" (308). To be sure, Taylor does not deny that humans frame representations which *do* inform their actions; but many of our actions are undertaken "unformulated." That is, they originate "from an understanding that is largely inarticulate" and which is always there, like a great ocean, reducing our representations "to islands in the sea of our unformulated practical grasp on the world" (308).

This is where the body enters in. It doesn't simply execute our consciously framed goals: "[o]ur understanding itself is embodied. That is, our bodily know-how, and the way we act and move, can encode components of our understanding of self and world" (309). Such understanding obviously affects the way we place ourselves in the physical world, but it is more than that: "My sense of myself, of the footing I am on with others, is in large part also" affected and shaped (309). This bodily knowledge is not generally visible in our representations of the world and of others; it is most visible in our actions, which intuitively "sense" when they are appropriate or not. Here Taylor cites the work of Pierre Bourdieu, who has defined this tacit knowing as "habitus" (309). Since our actions are not played out like soliloquies on a stage empty of all "actors" but that of the solitary self, the "other" must invariably come into play, and this brings us to the heart of the dialogic nature of this unarticulated knowledge. Acts of a solitary agent Taylor labels "monological" acts; those of more than one he calls "dialogical" acts. Shared agency is the key to dialogical acts, which may be seen as a form of collaboration. Taylor concludes: "We cannot understand human life merely in terms of individual subjects, who frame representations about and respond to others, because a great deal of human action happens only insofar as the agent understands and constitutes himself or herself as integrally part of a 'we'" (311). Arguing against what he calls "a theory of introjection"—that is, the self is formed by simply internalizing the values and attitudes of others—Taylor rejects oversimplified theories of social construction because such theories leave no room for resistance. Indeed, suggests Taylor, the self draws from its social environment, but it must have within itself the capacity to say no, to refuse to conform, to set itself against the social world. Using conversation as his metaphor for the process he is advocating, Taylor says that the self "neither preexists all conversation, as in the old monological view; nor does it arise from an introjection of the interlocutor; but it arises within conversation, because this kind of dialogical action by its very nature marks a place for the new locutor who is being inducted into it" (312). We find our voice, in other words, among the voices of others, in a dialogic relation with them. We are not passive or silent in the conversation, nor are we rendered impotent by it. We are in effect empowered by the dialogue, and our voice is capable of resisting when resistance is required. As Taylor observes, "it is a matter of finding one's own voice as an interlocutor ... [in a] dialogue at the very center of our understanding of human life, an indispensable key to its comprehension" (313–14). We need the theoretical direction provided by Bakhtin, Taylor concludes, because human beings "are constituted in conversation; and hence what gets internalized in the mature subject is not the reaction of the other, but the whole conversation, with the interanimation of its voices" (314).

Conclusion and Questions for Further Study

We need to examine more deliberately the direction of composing pedagogy in light of what recent literary and social theory have claimed about language and knowing. It is obvious that we cannot simply cling to Romantic notions of self and Arnoldian concepts of culture and circle the wagons against Theorists, Philistines, and Barbarians. Nor should we, as it seems to me both Berlin and Faigley are inclined to do, sever our connections with teachers of the Authentic Voice school—teachers like Macrorie and Elbow and Coles—and the pedagogical practices they advocate and which have served us well. We might do well to listen to Peter Elbow when he says in a recent essay that "despite some recent critical theory, I'm not yet convinced we should give up talking in terms of selves and authors" (230).

Further study of the concept of self needs to be conducted. The extremes of the concept have been pretty well identified, but much remains to be settled about the way in which a self is constituted. The theory which derives from this further study will need to be a rich and more complex one, and it will need to continue to draw from a variety of disciplines for its evolving formulation. If we are to achieve the synthesis of old and new theory for which this essay has been arguing, we need to reexamine the pedagogical strategies associated with Expressionistic rhetoric and find ways of revising them that will promote the dialectic and dialogic features which Giroux, Smith, and Taylor have been advocating. Some of this work has already begun to develop in the form of collaborative writing assignments, electronic writing classes, computer conferencing and group work, and conversations in the form of electronic journals. Additional momentum can be seen in the essay by Barbara Henning which I cited earlier. To help basic writers, Henning has called for a dialogic pedagogy based on the work of Bakhtin, one which would involve "meeting and analyzing despair collectively, rather than accepting it as fate" (1991, 681). Such a pedagogy, she claims, can affect the consciousness of students and teachers "through rigorous dialogic interaction about issues of shared importance, and that small changes in consciousness (the internalized dialogue between human beings who are/were situated socially in worlds that are constantly changing) have the potential of the society we live in" (681).

Additional work as well needs to be done in making students aware of the omnipresence of ideology, particularly in theories of language and in forms of writing instruction. Teacher/researchers need to use the personal or autobiographical essay to explore the potential for political awareness and transformation this genre possesses. As the philosopher Sam Keen says, we must all learn to tell our own stories or have them told for us. Too many students at present do not realize that they have a unique story to tell, and that in the telling they can come to see something about their location with respect to power that, in a variety of ways, serves to effectively silence them. Journals, expressive writing, I-Searches, personal essays—all can be made consonant with a revitalized and expanded theory of voice. Much is at stake here. As members of a professional community whose theory is at the same time its practice, we must neither blindly reject nor simply accept the precepts of postmodernism. The latter option, an uncritical acceptance, is dangerous, because, as Giroux has pointed out,

> these perspectives are deeply pessimistic. By providing an "airtight" notion of domination and an equally reductionist notion of socialization, radical accounts provide little hope for social change or the promise of oppositional teaching within the schools. Consequently, they help to provide a blue-print for cynicism and despair, one that serves to reproduce the very mode of domination they claim to resist. (59)

That, of course, is not what we want. If we are to find a way out of this impasse, we must negotiate the extremes of traditional views of self and voice and the tenets of social construction. We must preserve a theory of human agency so that our students as well as ourselves can, like

Archimedes, seek a place to stand, a place from which to resist against a world so badly in need of change.

Works Cited

Barth, John. 1958. *The End of the Road*. New York: Avon.

Berlin, James. 1988. "Rhetoric and Ideology in the Writing Class." *College English* 50.5 (January): 477–94.

Boulding, Kenneth. 1956. *The Image: Knowledge in Life and Society*. Ann Arbor: University of Michigan Press.

Bowra, C. M. 1963. *Primitive Song*. New York: Mentor Books.

Britton, James. 1970. *Language and Learning*. Harmondsworth, Middlesex, England: Penguin.

———, Tony Burgess, Nancy Martin, Alex McLeod, and Harold Rosen. 1975. *The Development of Writing Abilities (11–18)*. London: Macmillan.

Camus, Albert. 1955. *The Myth of Sisyphus*. Translated by Justin O'Brien. New York: Vintage.

Coles, William E., Jr., and James Vopat. 1985. *What Makes Writing Good: A Multiperspective*. Lexington, MA: D. C. Heath.

Connor, Steven. 1989. *Postmodernist Culture: An Introduction to Theories of the Contemporary*. Oxford, England: Basil Blackwell.

Dobyns, Stephen. 1990. *Body Traffic*. New York: Viking.

Elbow, Peter. 1973. *Writing without Teachers*. London: Oxford University Press.

———. 1981. *Writing with Power: Techniques for Mastering the Writing Process*. New York: Oxford University Press.

———. 1989. "The Pleasures of Voice in the Literary Essay: Explorations in the Prose of Gretel Ehrlich and Richard Selzer." In *Literary Nonfiction: Theory, Criticism, Pedagogy*, edited by Chris Anderson, 211–34. Carbondale: Southern Illinois University Press.

Emig, Janet. 1990. "Our Missing Theory." In *Conversations: Contemporary Critical Theory and the Teaching of Literature*, edited by Charles Moran and Elizabeth F. Penfield, 87–96. Urbana: National Council of Teachers of English.

Faigley, Lester. 1989. "Judging Writing, Judging Selves." *College Composition and Communication* 40.4 (December): 395–412.

Freire, Paulo. 1985a. *Pedagogy of the Oppressed*. 2nd ed. New York: Continuum.

———. 1985b. *The Politics of Education: Culture, Power, and Liberation*. South Hadley, MA: Bergin & Garvey.

Gergen, Kenneth J. 1991. *The Saturated Self: Dilemmas of Identity in Contemporary Life*. New York: Basic Books.

Gilbert, Sandra. 1984. "My Name Is Darkness: The Poetry of Self-Definition." In *Poetics: Essays on the Art of Poetry*, edited by Paul Mariani and George Murphy, 98–110. Special issue of *Tendril* Magazine.

Giroux, Henry A. 1983. *Theory and Resistance in Education: A Pedagogy for the Opposition*. South Hadley, MA: Bergin & Garvey.

Henning, Barbara. 1991. "The World Was Stone Cold: Basic Writing in an Urban University." *College English* 53.6 (October): 674–85.

Hill, Carolyn Ericksen. 1990. *Writing from the Margins: Power and Pedagogy for Teachers of Composition.* New York: Oxford University Press.

Holden, Jonathan. 1980. *The Rhetoric of the Contemporary Lyric.* Bloomington: Indiana University Press.

———. 1986. *Style and Authenticity in Postmodern Poetry.* Columbia, MO: University of Missouri Press.

Jameson, Fredric. 1985. "Postmodernism and Consumer Society." In *Postmodern Culture,* edited by Hal Foster, 111–25. London: Pluto Press.

Kelly, Lou. 1972. *From Dialogue to Discourse: An Open Approach.* Glenview, IL: Scott, Foresman.

Kinnell, Galway. 1984. "Poetry, Personality, and Death." In *Poetics: Essays on the Art of Poetry,* edited by Paul Mariani and George Murphy, 67–84. Special issue of *Tendril* Magazine.

Macrorie, Ken. 1970a. *Telling Writing.* Rochelle Park, NJ: Hayden.

———. 1970b. *Uptaught.* Rochelle Park, NJ: Hayden.

———. 1974. *A Vulnerable Teacher.* Rochelle Park, NJ: Hayden.

———. 1986. *Writing to Be Read.* Rochelle Park, NJ: Hayden.

Rose, Mike. 1989. *Lives on the Boundary: A Moving Account of the Struggles and Achievements of America's Educational Underclass.* New York: Penguin.

Rosenblatt, Louise. 1983 [1938]. *Literature as Exploration.* 4th ed. New York: Modern Language Association of America.

———. 1978. *The Reader, the Text, the Poem: The Transactional Theory of the Literary Work.* Carbondale: Southern Illinois University Press.

Shor, Ira. 1987. *Critical Teaching and Everyday Life.* Chicago: University of Chicago Press.

Smith, Paul. 1988. *Discerning the Subject.* Minneapolis: University of Minnesota Press.

Stewart, Donald C. 1972. *The Authentic Voice: A Pre-Writing Approach to Student Writing.* Dubuque, IA: Wm. C. Brown.

Sypher, Wylie. 1962. *Loss of the Self in Modern Literature and Art.* New York: Random House.

Taylor, Charles. 1991. "The Dialogical Self." In *The Interpretive Turn,* edited by David R. Hiley, James F. Bohman, and Richard Shusterman, 304–14. Ithaca: Cornell University Press.

Turner, Alberta. 1980. "Not Your Flat Tire, My Flat Tire: Transcending the Self in Contemporary Poetry." In *A Field Guide to Contemporary Poetry and Poetics,* edited by Stuart Friebert and David Young, 135–46. New York: Longman.

Whitman, Walt. 1959 [1856]. "Song of Myself." In *Complete Poetry and Selected Prose of Walt Whitman.* Cambridge, MA: Houghton-Mifflin.

Wordsworth, William. 1965. *The Poetical Works of Wordsworth.* Edited by Thomas Hutchinson and Ernest De Selincourt. New York: Oxford University Press.

16 The Virtual Voice of Network Culture

Mark Zamierowski
Purdue University

Serendipity or misfortune, it just happened that my agreement to write an essay on voice from a poststructuralist perspective coincided with my introduction to electronic mail (e-mail) and wide-area networking (WAN); together they constitute a frame for this chapter's discussion of voice.

As those for whom e-mail has nearly replaced snail mail know, WAN is basically an electronic version of the sort of hand pressing and information sharing that academics call "networking" at regional and national conferences, along with the ability to gain access to library and other databases across the globe. The principal difference of WAN is, of course, that you only need to travel to the nearest computer terminal or dial up some organization's mainframe from your personal computer in order to do it. That stay-at-home capability and the ease with which you can obtain access to people and archives around the world make the whole process highly addictive. But the most interesting thing about computer-mediated communication (CMC) to me is the sheer novelty of it and the musings about the medium's capabilities which that novelty encourages.

J. David Bolter offers an especially instructive example of the sort of musing I have in mind. In *Writing Space: The Computer, Hypertex, and the History of Writing,* Bolter (1991) explains that more is involved in the ongoing displacement of the printed book by the computer as the principal source of information storage, retrieval, and distribution than a simple exchange of wood pulp for silicon. Bolter goes so far as to claim that "just as our culture is moving from the printed book to the computer, it is also in the final stages of the transition from a hierarchical social order to what we might call a 'network culture'" (232). What precisely "network culture" is or will become, it is still too early to say, if only because it is still too easy to write off such pronouncements as overestimations of a new technology's potential to transform perceived "standards" for operating procedures in the school, the workplace, the home, or the halls of government. Nonetheless, even the modest historical consciousness that we U.S. Americans are caricatured as having is enough to make Bolter's claims intriguing. I suspect few people believe the simultaneity of the Industrial Revolution and the American Revolution (to name but one of the great nationalist uprisings of the past three centuries) to be a matter of trivial coincidence, and I suspect, too, that every schoolchild is still at some time expected to know that Eli Whitney invented the cotton gin, even if they're seldom certain why they're expected to know that.

The fact of the matter is that Bolter's claim is warranted, even if it is still more a speculative than a descriptive claim. The concept of hierarchy understood as a rigid determiner of status, privilege, or opportunity has been under attack in various contexts and in various ways since the collapse of feudalism and the simultaneous developments of mercantilism/capitalism and Protestantism. Of course, we needn't go so far back to contextualize the dismantling of the concept of hierarchy. A simple thinking back to the social-political movements of the late 1960s and early 1970s is enough to recall the forcefulness of a liberatory ethos poised for change and demanding a reconceptualization of social arrangements and the empowerment of disenfranchised minorities.1 The very existence of minorities whose minority depends not so much on numerical or statistical invisibility as on their inability to secure economic and political power is a clear sign that hierarchy is alive and well, yet my ability to describe that situation as a signal product of the deleterious and negative effects of hierarchy is likewise a clear sign that hierarchical arrangements are no longer taken for granted. On a somewhat differently charged political level, we might refer to poststructuralist strategies of critique and a description such as Derridean deconstruction in which the concept of hierarchy and its vertical positioning of power are mapped as a system of asymmetrical binaries (i.e., either/or relationships in which one term controls or determines the nature of the other: masculine/feminine, being/nothingness, truth/falsity, subject/object, white/black, etc.) whose disguised ideological work is to preserve and protect a white, European, male prerogative.

Obviously, though, not everyone will greet a contestation of hierarchy as a happy occurrence. Hierarchies don't have to be (probably cannot be, given human diversity and quirkiness) perfectly rigid: vertical mobility makes fluid hierarchies by turns attractive and dangerous depending upon one's relative position. There's a fair bit of paranoia available at the top and just as much in the way of despair at the bottom. Nevertheless, there is a good deal of security and stability offered by fluid hierarchies: setting goals and making plans are a lot easier if you can count on things remaining pretty much the same and changes occurring reasonably slowly. It is much easier, too, to assess and evaluate events and phenomena if specific standards for judgment remain more or less permanently in place. It may also be the case that anti-authoritarianism, the breakdown of law and order, the disintegration of the family, the collapse of values, the failure of our schools, and the closing of the American mind are phenomena related to or effects produced by the dissolution of hierarchical schemes of order. Then again, these "effects" may well be constructed through negative if not downright nihilistic descriptions of a transformation that in and of itself isn't all that frightening. Or at least ain't necessarily so.

I say this primarily because the transition that Bolter adroitly and convincingly describes throughout his book, a transition *from hierarchy to network*, involves more of a shift of emphasis between competing strategies of arrangement than it does a hostile takeover of one entity by another. We can consider it a paradigm shift of sorts, as long as we bear in mind that ontological status of fictions or regulative ideas rather than that of actual, identifiable, and clearly articulated frameworks or rules of order. Paradigms are virtual entities, not hard and fast facts. Of course, that doesn't mean that we can't and don't speak of them as having real effects: a virtual entity is just as real as any idea or concept; what it lacks is the actual existence of an indicatable concrete thing. Hence, even though we can never give an exhaustive description of them or conclusively prove our adherence to them, paradigms do enable us to do things: to view phenomena from various perspectives, to privilege certain contexts-for-action or specific procedures for acting-alone or acting-with, to describe what we see and do using a preferred, shared vocabulary and syntax. The late French cultural historian Michel Foucault called them "discursive formations," arrangements of "statements" (call them beliefs, assumptions, rules, privileged attitudes or behaviors—anything but sentences) that delineate the field of the seeable and the sayable, the visible and the expressed. They are, basically, the virtual entities that establish the boundaries for acceptable discursive action.

Bolter and Foucault come together as well over a desire to articulate culture as, in Bolter's words, "a vast writing space, a complex of symbolic [or informating[2]] structures" (232); however, Bolter may press the case for the transition or displacement of one structure by another a bit dramatically. True, Bolter's talk of "final stages of transition" sounds much like Foucault's descriptions of discontinuity and rupture in the succession of historical epistemes, but Foucault's analyses at least had the security of historical distance on their side. In contrast, Bolter's analysis, positioned within and still under the influence of schemes of hierarchy, has a lot of utopian conviction driving it along. Which is not to say that Bolter's wrong. It is to say, rather, that hierarchical modes of arrangement aren't going to go away anytime soon—if, in fact, they go away at all.

Still, Bolter's distinction of hierarchy and network can be a very useful means of assessing our own discursive involvements as writers and as students and teachers of writing. This is especially true if we conceive of hierarchy and network not as mutually exclusive, warring realities poised on either side of a binary opposition (the Cold War, after all, is over), but as two different yet co-implicated modes or strategies of arrangement. Under this description pure hierarchy and pure network would have to be merely ideal states, distinctions made for the sake of analysis. The reality of the description would be that there are networking tendencies always and already within hierarchical arrangements and hierarchizing tendencies always and already within network. CMC itself shows the effects of these composite ordering operations. Although the ready availability of the microcomputer (the PC) has indeed ushered in a great decentralization of the means and methods of information distribution, those microcomputers can do precious little in the way of wide- or even local-area networking without tapping into some centralized corporate, university, or government mainframe supercomputer. In other words, to make networking possible, some centralization of both information and expertise (someone, after all, has to create the formats in which information is stored and transferred) is essential; a hierarchical arrangement of users, software, hardware, and even information itself is unavoidable. This does not mean that networking is covertly hierarchical; it simply means that an absolute decentralization would be tantamount to a dispersion or a dissipation and that networking would disappear into a chaos of digitized noise.

For the space of this essay, at any rate, hierarchy and network constitute the frame for a discussion of voice. Obviously, I will not have the luxury here to provide detailed historical material concerning either the rhetorical notion of voice or the various technological and theoretical developments which have made it difficult to take voice for granted as an innocent, natural fact.[3] I will, however, try to explain why taking voice for granted may be unwise, first by focusing on the ideology of voice in its hierarchical function, and then—to clarify the networking function of voice—by considering the curious practice of "flaming" and the tendency of networking to privilege voices that are ignored and excluded by hierarchical requirements for appropriateness and style.

The Ideology of Voice

As Alan France argues in "Assigning Places: Introductory Composition as a Cultural Discourse" (1993), the expressionist articulation of voice suggests that an advocacy of voice does indeed do disguised ideological work. That ideology is, in part, expressed by Jean-Francois Lyotard (1991/92) in the following few quick steps:

> [T]here is a voice, it belongs to someone; which is to say that this someone knows what he or she says by means of this voice; and this voice is addressed to someone—And by way of a complement that is no less ideological: that someone who has a voice also has a life which is recounted by that voice. (127)

It is this ideology which, in the experience of orality, takes us from voice to person, and it the strength of this ideology which encourages us to repeat that progression in our discursive operations. Lyotard's description of this ideology, of the fundamental assumptions which underwrite the privileging of voice and its status as a thing which goes without saying (particularly in discourse, it functions without truly saying), is accurate but limited (for our purposes) by (1) the conventions of philosophical critique which require the reduction of arguments to a portable set of fundamental claims and (2) his focus on Freud's acceptance and critique of this ideology in his psychoanalytic writings. Given that the focus of this essay is the operation of that ideology in the domain of rhetoric and composition, a somewhat different and far less portable set of claims needs to be assembled. The following is a list of what I take to be implicit predications of voice which function as unstated definitions in the expressionist discussions of voice. In these discussions of voice, voice is:

1. the inscription of authorial personality/presence in discourse;
2. the inexpungable effect of an autobiographical subject behind discourse;
3. an indicator of discursive authenticity, sincerity, honesty, etc.;
4. a condition of possibility for contact and identification between writers and readers;
5. a means of gaining recognition (from 1–4);
6. an indicator of discursive maturity, fluency, etc.;
7. the point of contact/continuity of orality and literacy (from 1, 2, 4, 5);

8. that which preserves humanity against/within technological appropriations of the Word (given 7);

9. an instrumentality of control and organization (given all of the above);

10. an operation of power in/over discourse (given all of the above);

11. a point of contact with institutional/academic power (given all of the above);

12. a real thing (assumed by all of the above);

13. a personal possession or effect (from 1–8); and

14. a dispensation of the institution/the social (from 7–11).

This may not be a complete list, and I doubt that all proponents of voice would accept all fourteen items with perfect equanimity. Nonetheless, I think that this arrangement helps to throw into relief a curious fact about the hierarchical functioning of voice. As commonly used, the metaphorical application of voice to writing exerts a controlling influence. Its reality goes uncontested; hence, the ideology which intimately connects voice and speaker places voice on the side of the consumption, closure, and formal integrity of texts. The integrity of the text—its fixed formal completeness—reflects and manifests the integrity of the text's author—his/her fixed, essential self-presence, identity, identifiability, or recognizability in print. Furthermore, formal and subjective integrity ensure the ethical integrity of both the writer and the written, and the degree to which a writer's voice promotes his unhindered recognition and the unhindered transmission of his messages marks the level of expertise ascribable to that writer and, hence, the "maturity" of his voice and the fluency of his writing: the less noise in the channel, the clearer the voice will be. If, then, the ideological intimacy of voice and speaker carries over into the medium of writing, the division of the oral and the literate is the product of an unimportant empirical distinction, for all their differences are once and for all safely grounded in the speaker-voice relation or, more specifically, in the privilege accorded to face-to-face exchanges by the ideology of voice. The literate is, in fact, merely the technological extension of the oral, and any subsequent technological extensions of the literate will necessarily be further extensions of the oral, by way of a simple association. As the oral controls the literate and all subsequent technological appropriations of the *logos,* so voice controls discourse and organizes the multiplicity of effects which could generate noise and interrupt the ideality and the power of voice.

The point that I'm trying to make about the hierarchical functioning of voice is this: When we talk about voice, we talk about a metaphorically extended term as if it had an independent discursive reality and clear ties to a parallel extradiscursive reality called self, subject, etc. When we talk about voice, we also talk about some "thing" that is indubitably real which is shared as a possession of an individual person and as a product of a hierarchical arrangement of social power relations. The problem seems to be that when we lose sight of the metaphorical or virtual reality of voice in discourse, we create a solid binary between the personal and the social where there should be a much more fluid relation. When we stabilize that binary, we pit authenticity (and the claims of ego psychology) against interpellation (and the claims of social constructionism and structuralist/poststructuralist Marxism), we pit the personal voice against academic discourse, and we privilege one or another on the basis of our own ideological, professional, and personal investments. Voice is either the voice of the person or the voice of the discourse community but never both at once, unless it is inflated into the Voice of History. Voice is not conceived of as a mere effect of discourse but as a thing to be possessed, as an accoutrement or symbol of power, and to the extent that it is, voice is deployed—as it is directly in Donald Stewart's textbook *The Authentic Voice* (1972), for instance—as a foundationalist gesture against the anti-foundationalist impulses—desires, emotions, the play of unbridled invention—which drive rhetoric and writing and which resist and defer the finality of closure as a matter more of formal constraint or temporal expedience than of the possibility of an end of discourse.

From Hierarchy to Network

It's taken me more time, space, and energy than I thought it would just to get to this point. In fact, the present version of this essay doesn't begin to include much of what I take to be central: an analysis of expressionist views of voice, as connected to hierarchy, aesthetics, and taste. An earlier version of this piece did include this history, weighing in initially at around sixty double-spaced pages. It sprawled and yawned, bitched and moaned, quickshifted from banality to bomphologia, and even ventured in an obscenity or two. The essay you have before you may be no well-wrought urn, but it's a far more comely conversation piece for polite company than it once was. The question I can't help asking, though, is, Why? Why was I encouraged to tone down, tune up, and try hard to be agreeable? Why do formal regularity and cohesiveness go hand in hand with demands for a consistent and socially acceptable voice? Whatever happened to the good-old, old-fashioned American jeremiad? Why do four-letter words get short schrift and the blue pencil from editors of academic discourse? The answer I'm prepared to give is that we've drunk deeply of the draught of hierarchy, so much so that those of us trained through trial and error in the appropriateness conditions of academic discourse no longer have to invent the university; we reproduce it everytime we open our mouths.

I bring these points up again because questions of appropriateness and a necessity of inventing are principal features of and spurs to activity within network culture. Let me put it this way. If academic discourse is easy to regulate, easy to identify, and even easy to lampoon, it is because it belongs to a discernible, visible power center, the academy/the university, and because it operates with a small palette of conventions. In the domain of network culture, the realm of cyberspace[4] or virtual reality, a decidedly different situation obtains. There are no clear landmarks, no visible centers of power, and no traditions of implicit understanding concerning what ought or ought not to be appropriate and what is or is not an actual convention. Most of the conventions, in fact, have to do with industry standards and formatting practices for manipulating one or another programming language— things, in short, that the great majority of PC owners, e-mailers, and networkers local or wide never have to know about anyway. Such a loosely regulated and recently invented sphere of action, networking is free to arrange itself horizontally rather than vertically, meaning that anyone who can get access can join in the conversation, and no university or corporation or governmental agency—no power center—needs to be invented before discourse can be produced or information disseminated. Which means, in effect, that discursive practices are both relatively unhindered and unprotected in cyberspace.

The open and unprotected nature of CMC brings with it two curiously related but seemingly opposite tendencies. The first is an almost smarmy affection for CMC that its staunchest advocates easily lapse into, but it is an affection that is directed not merely to either the medium itself or its potential egalitarianism *per se;* the affection proceeds from a recognition of the novel opportunities for sociality and community that CMC appears to provide: "The most surprising and consistent quality in e-mail communities is the human warmth they develop. They are a form of conversation" (Brand 1987, 24). But they are a form of conversation and peculiar kind of community which do not depend upon, do not privilege, and, in fact, seem to flourish precisely because of the absence of face-to-face communication. They are *virtual* communities, which, despite their technological constitution by virtue of a coming together of computers, telephone lines, modems, and computer conferencing programs, seem to deal in just as much actual affect as virtual group identity:

> A virtual community as they exist today is a group of people who may or may not meet one another face to face, and who exchange words and ideas through the mediation of computer bulletin boards and networks. In cyberspace, we chat and argue, engage in intellectual intercourse, exchange knowledge, share emotional support, make plans, brainstorm, gossip, feud, fall in love, find friends and lose them, play games and metagames, flirt, create a little high art and a lot of idle talk. We do everything people do when people get together, but we do it with words on computer screens, leaving our bodies behind. Millions of us have already built communities where our identities commingle and interact electronically, independent of local time or location. (Rheingold 1992 [3])

That description of virtual communities and of their rich affective life is typical in its enthusiasm for and commitment to networking and CMC. Affect rather than conventional and institutional restraint decisively differentiates the network arrangement from the hierarchy arrangement. So, too, does a stress on reciprocity and on a sort of gift exchange rather than a commodity—consumer economy. I take this idea directly from Howard Rheingold, editor of the *Whole Earth Review* and an early member of the San Francisco WELL, one of the first local-area networks in the U.S. I quote at length from Rheingold's on-line article "A Slice of Life in My Virtual Community" (1992) in order to clarify the economic base and social contract of virtual communities as well as to set the stage for a discussion of a virtual voice:

> This unwritten, unspoken social contract, a blend of strong-tie and weak-tie relationships among people who have a mixture of motives, requires one to give something, and enables one to receive something. I have to keep my friends in mind and send them pointers instead of throwing my informational discards into the virtual scrap heap. . . . The same strategy of nurturing and making use of loose information-sharing affiliations across the net can be applied to an infinite domain of problem areas, from literary criticism to software evaluation. It's a neat way for a sufficiently large, sufficiently diverse group of people to multiply their individual degree of expertise. . . . I think it works better when the community's conceptual model of itself is more like barn-raising than horse-trading, though. Reciprocity is a key element of any market-based culture, but the arrangement I'm describing feels to me more like a kind of gift-economy where people do things for one another out of a spirit of building something between them, rather than a spreadsheet-calculated *quid pro quo*.

I think one key difference between straightforward workaday reciprocity is that in the virtual community I know best, one valuable currency is knowledge, elegantly presented. Wit and use of language are rewarded in this medium, which is biased toward those who learn how to manipulate attention and emotion with the written word. Sometimes you give one person more information than you would give another person in response to the same query, simply because you recognize one of them to be more generous or funny or to-the-point or agreeable to your political convictions than the other one.

If you give useful information freely, without demanding tightly-coupled reciprocity, your requests for information are met more swiftly, in greater detail, than they would have been otherwise. ([34–39])

For Rheingold, then, the discursive practices of virtual communities emphasize reciprocity, free exchange, and a diversified conception of voice that depends far less on any connections to identity (how could it in a medium where, as Rheingold says, "identities commingle and interact"?) and far more on the style of reciprocity and the strategies of language manipulation evident in whichever posted message that a writer is using as a spur to her own response. The gift exchange economy and its call-and-response style of reciprocity place an emphasis upon what happens *in between,* upon maintaining the process and producing something between giver and receiver, rather than upon either one of the two discursive poles. In fact, given the nature of the reciprocating link between those two poles, they should actually have been named giver/receiver and receiver/giver, for in such a situation every giver is always already a receiver and vice versa. Voices are bound to commingle and interact, and they are bound to be multiplicities rather than unities in such a process. Even if wit and language manipulation are accorded a premium in this economy, they are so not simply because they establish identities and certainly not because they foreground the formal unity, regularity and beauty of a posted message, but because they diversify and multiply the voices of people posting messages in response. In this sense, network culture is a perfect medium for an education in the productivity and diversity of voice.

The second of the tendencies produced by network culture's open and unprotected nature also provides insight into the diversity of voice as well as support for Rheingold's claims regarding the free flow of affect in CMC. It also brings to the foreground a whole category of voices that are invariably dramatically conspicuous by their absence in any typical textbook (and I have in mind here not only the voice-based textbooks like Stewart's, but also current textbooks which may have a brief section on voice) treatment of voice: dysfunctional voices, voices that swear, rap, insult, badger, demean, intimidate, terrify, etc. Within the domain of cyberspace these constitute the voice of the flamer. A flamer is an e-mail participant who prefers to attack or inflame another participant, usually for the sake of defeating rather than sustaining a give and take on any topic of discussion. Why flamers flame, why they perceive disruption as a more congenial option than commiseration, is a question that people have been bandying about on electronic bulletin boards off and on for years now—and as yet no one is certain of what (if anything) to do about it.

What promotes or supports flaming? Is it the very telegraphic nature of the medium which encourages flaming? The distance involved and the lack of voice-face-body that Walker Gibson cautioned against pages (and years) ago? Is it the emphasis CMC places on language craft and wit? An emphasis that either naturally leads to or is unfortunately prone to being taken to extremes? Is flaming, then, a practice which is peculiar to computer networks, a practice which more recondite and sincere media such as writing or speech inhibit? There are, after all, USENET[5] groups dedicated to flaming and nothing but, where a sort of inverted version of the same call-and-response exchanging goes on day-in and day-out, one hurl after another. Could we disestablish flaming by dismantling the structures that support it, that seem to provide it a playful via media? Probably not. After all, congeniality and cooperation are nice, but they're not requirements for any and all language use. Flaming may be a nuisance, but a desire to eliminate it can too easily mutate into a paranoid desire to restrict access to information or to control and monitor pathways simply to maintain high seriousness. It short circuits the very process of exchange and production-in-between that Rheingold has described as characteristic of virtual communities, by redirecting the emphasis away from process and productivity and onto a sensitive and an insensitive discursive pole, a clearcut binary distinction and a clearcut incursion of identity and hierarchy into network culture. It shouldn't be too surprising, on this score, that the available means of dealing with a persistent flamer is to drop said person's name, moniker, or user I.D. into something called a "kill file," which suppresses any future messages with that name, moniker, or user I.D. from dirtying up your mailbox. If nothing else, it's a telling name for a file.

What may, in fact, be more interesting about flaming than either its causes or its consequences has to do with its unavoidability in network culture and the invisibility of analogous nasty voices in hierarchy. It is interesting that proponents of voice rarely take seriously a correspondence between something as unsavory as flaming, on the one hand, and authenticity or sincerity, on the other. Those who would claim that the persistence of what we might call voice in writing is the product of a person-specific effort to express deep-seated desires or utopic communitarian programs always seem to distance their claims from a recognition of the very real possibility that voice allows us not only to promote and engage in dialogue, but also to regulate, disrupt, and control it as well. I can provide no hard and fast evidence to either explain or explain away flaming; I have not researched it adequately, and I am not familiar with any such detailed research. I can, however, offer an explanation consistent with this essay's understanding of network and hierarchy. It seems likely that what keeps anything like flaming invisible in hierarchy and prominent in network has to do with the ethical predelictions of the former and the affective operations of the latter. The stress on rectitude, regularity, and correctness in hierarchy quietly eliminates not only the value but, more important, the reality of voices that don't fit, that don't fit the appropriateness conditions of discourse privileged in hierarchy. And if flaming tells us anything particularly interesting about network, it may be that a virtual community can be constituted on the basis of any call-and-response pattern of reciprocity, irrespective of the nature or content of the informational "gifts" being exchanged and regardless of the ethical character or *ethos* of the participants. That alone opens up the space of a dramatic difference.

A Virtual Voice

As I pointed out early in this essay, there are problems that plague the notion of voice, problems which need to be addressed at some time and at some level. Voice is not a concept (notion? thought? experience?) that can be innocently or immediately attached to such current lines of thought as social constructionism, social-epistemic rhetoric, cultural critique, Foucauldian analyses of power, Deleuzoguattarian diagrammatics of desire, semiotics, Derridean analyses of the closure of philosophy, or even process pedagogy, for that matter. Even Bakhtinian discussions of heteroglossia, polyphony, and the carnivalesque offer no safe home for voice, for there too voice is inexorably displaced through the echoes and sedimentations of other voices, which are in turn subject to the same regressive analysis. Voice without origin, identity, immediacy, or a community whose efficacity is strictly external to it is not obviously consistent with the commonsense claims we make when we talk about personal voice, our voices, yours and mine. Voice's hierarchical ties to Platonism, subjectivism, commonsense philosophies, ego psychology, phenomenology, and ontotheological concepts are not easily bracketed, and this is so at least in part because the ethical and political ramifications of these traditional lines of thought are embedded in our notions about citizenship, community, social institutions, political activism, and the State. All of this, all of these lines of thought and their interrelatedness, serves to screen off voice from any easy understanding.

In addition to these philosophical or theoretical problems, the steady growth of CMC brings additional pressures to bear on the articulation of voice. Much as one may like, following Ong or Eric Havelock, to classify CMC as a "secondary orality" along with other telegraphic, telephonic, and televisual media, CMC's technological extension of the human sensorium and its development of new communications media in the domains of cyberspace and virtual reality opened up in the computer age adumbrate an arena far different than a simple conflation of the oral and the literate. As Donald F. Theall (1992) puts it:

> Under the impact of electric communication, it is once again clear that the concept of the word must embrace artifacts and events as well. Writing and speech are subsumed into gesture, movement, rhythm, and all modes of sensory input, especially the tactile. To continue to speak about a dichotomy of orality versus literacy is a misleading oversimplification of the role that electric media play in this transformation, a role best comprehended through historical knowledge of the earliest stages of human communication where objects, gestures and movements apparently intermingled with verbal and non-verbal sounds. ([12])

In other words, an emphasis on either the oral or the literate or even both at once does short shrift to the possibilities within electronic media to construct a virtual reality with a multimedia or multisensual illusion of presence. Within the domains of cyberspace and virtual reality, voice loses its regularity and unity, and communication loses its grounding in the pure, abstract ideality of the self-present speaking subject addressing its mirror-image other. Voice in virtual reality is molecularized in "the flow of multidimensional, pansensory data" [Theall 1992 [2]]; it is lost among the " 'tactile, haptic, proprioceptive and acoustic spaces and involvements' " that transform communication in cyberspace [[3]].[6] Cyberspace and virtual reality, in short, return the body to CMC, but it is not the molar, organized, and individuated body of identity and identification; rather, it is the body as a site traversed by molecular effects and sensations, informing forces which the voice of discourse talks over and drowns out. Such a return of the body may offer interesting possibilities for a network function of voice, but that can be true only to the extent that voice is no longer conceived as an essential, personal voice, as the phonematic expression of an essential mind.

Let me back up here for a moment for the sake of clarity. The point that I'm struggling to make is not that the thought of a personal voice must be eliminated. That would be an absurdity given only my own experience, the hard fact of others, and the recognition of differences that emerges during encounters with others. There is no reason to deny either the personal or to reconfigure the interpersonal as impersonal. Furthermore, the acknowledgment of that absurdity leads me to suspect that no unbridgeable gulf exists between me and that which I produce. That is to say, what I produce must be an expression that I take part in some way, to some degree. That participation applies to all of my productions, regardless of the medium in which I work. That is not the issue.

What is at issue is the value of maintaining only that level of description to the exclusion of any others. To the extent that my body, for example, is a body continually in contact with and penetrated by other bodies (physical bodies, animate and inanimate—bodies of others, bodies of wood or metal or glass, bodies of water or air—but also abstract bodies—bodies of information, bodies of evidence, bodies of facts, laws, and precedents), it is a virtual body: a network of points of contact and a multiplicity of lines of exposure, exposition, or expression. To the extent that my body is a body continually traversed by effects, impulses, forces which have no need of conscious thought or recognition to realize effects, it is a virtual body: a dispersional field of forces and functions always in formation, always in flux. This does not mean that my body is not mine or that I am not recognizable or identifiable to myself and others as or by virtue of my body; it means that at some level(s) of description, my body's mine-ness escapes me, does not require the "me" of a molar personality in order to be the body (or bodies) it is (or is becoming). My point is that the same can be said of my voice if we bear in mind not only the effects and impulses which inflect my voice from the side of the body but also the multiplicity of other multiple voices that displace my voice toward the side of the community.

Voice need not be consigned to one side of a rigid either/or: either the sole possession of a sovereign subject (in which case it is "authenticated" out of reality as a means of regulating discourse from a pure position outside discourse) or the dispensation of an impersonal ideology (in which case it is relativized out of recognizability and absorbed into a pure immanence called Power). Given the already abstract, virtual nature of the thought of voice in discourse, it is eminently possible to acknowledge voice as a double-sided phenomenon that has more of event than entity about it. On a molar description, in its hierarchical function, voice faces on one side the personal and on the other the social/institutional. On a molecular description, in its network function, voice is better conceived as an aleatory point which circulates in two different series (call them affect and concept, nonsense and sense, process and product, etc.), causing them simultaneously to communicate and diverge. It faces both sides simultaneously and must do so, for the only reality it has is the reality of this double-facing of a double-sided surface or (mathematically conceived) of an aleatory point which causes two series, two domains, two bodies to converge and diverge simultaneously.

I borrow this language from Gilles Deleuze's *Logic of Sense* (1990), his erudite exploration into a paradoxical theory of sense as a non-existing entity, a virtual entity, which maintains special relations with non-sense (not the nonsense of insipidity, but that which is exterior to or exceeds that which can be expressed). I cannot offer here an extended discussion of Deleuze's demanding study of words and things; I can only steal the thought of this two-sided entity and offer the following brief quote in lieu of a lengthy summary:

> What are the characteristics of this paradoxical entity? It circulates without end in both series and, for this reason, assures their communication. It is a two-sided entity, equally present in the signifying and the signified series. It is the mirror. Thus, it is at once word and thing, name and object, sense and *denotatum*, expression and designation, etc. It guarantees, therefore, the convergence of the two series which it traverses, but precisely on the condition that it makes them endlessly diverge. (40)

With this in mind, though, what can be said of voice here can also be said (*mutatis mutandis*) of discourse in general. Discourse, too, can be thought as a double-sided entity facing on one side methodologies of production and on the other methodologies of consumption. Unlike voice, however, discourse is a real social entity, a means of communication, and its double-sided nature is merely a fact of its social function. Voice, on the other hand, virtual *not* actual, is a surface effect of discourse, an incorporeal "expressed" of discourse which traverses both domains of the personal and the social which it draws into communication but which also prohibits a relationship of either identity or simple unilateral hierarchy to obtain between them.

Why is this necessary? Why complicate something as seemingly obvious as voice by subjecting it to a reconceptualization that contradicts its obviousness and simplicity as a via media for the expression of person-specific information? The fact that the customary understanding of voice is embedded in an ideology shared by liberal humanism/education, aesthetic formalism, subjectivism, hermeneuticism, and Platonism forces us to do so because that ideology actually hinders what it claims to promote: the specificity of the productive agent's expressive action through language. It inhibits it by regularizing it as a matter of/for consumption. It is necessary because the aggregate movements of late twentieth-century theorizing and developments in information technologies encourage it. Finally, it is necessary simply because it is possible and simply because it is impossible to be satisfied with either a text-bound or a mouth-bound description of discourse at a time when electric media are adumbrating a future of hypertextual and hypermedial links, arrangements and assemblages which may thoroughly transform our accepted notions about writers, readers, and textuality.[7]

What, then, is a virtual voice? And what are its implications for teaching composition? Unfortunately, this is a difficult question, largely because it is nigh impossible to think pedagogical practice outside of the ideology of voice that compels us to think hierarchically in terms of identity, taste, and consumerism. My first guess, however, is that a virtual voice displaces the thought of closure more rigorously than the arguments hitherto advanced for a process pedagogy because it breaks with a notion of the ideal text which proceeds from demands for consumption. The virtual voice is unabashedly a voice of invention. But this cannot be construed as an invention determined before the fact by persuasion and a requirement to assemble arguments acceptable to a rigidly circumscribed (or caricatured) target audience. The invention in question here is an invention steeped in the available or imaginable means of inquiry: it is not one grounded on the reproduction of previously tested arguments, but on the production of novel arrangements.[8]

My second guess is that the possibility of a virtual voice would force student and teacher into more intricate and immediate exchanges, for the teacher could not (as those interviewed by Paula Gillespie), in good faith, fall back on a pallette of previously established voices in order to evaluate the efficacy of a student's productivity: the teacher would be forced into a position of negotiating that efficacy with the student, and in the process would be able to gather a thick description of that student's motivations, preliminary plans, and operational guidelines. Following Lester Faigley (1989), the procedures for judging texts and selves would instigate the need for a continual reassessment of the evaluator's own categories, whether the call for that reassessment ultimately issued from the teacher or the student.

My third guess is that Robert Boice's "neglected third factor" (1985) of productivity would necessarily eclipse concerns with linear argument, regulation, and correctness. To be honest, I am here arguing for a ground that would enable me as a teacher of basic or developmental writers to promote activity that could otherwise be stifled by a requirement that all texts should fully express the complex reality of their writer, a writer who must be in perfect control of his/her medium in order to advance claims, arguments, ideas in such a fashion as to determine in advance their destination in the preconceptions of a manufactured audience. Invention and the thought of productivity merge in the thought of a virtual voice to the extent that a virtual voice is itself always and necessarily a voice under construction, in process, in-between. I have seen far too many struggling basic writers freeze because they perceived themselves as having no right to a voice to call their own to believe that the traditional conception of voice enables either expression or productivity. The thought of voice for basic writers is a thought that they deny themselves simply because they are all too patently aware of the fact that they know too little about grammar, syntax, and discourse (not to mention belletristic culture and the conventions of propriety privileged in hierarchy) to be able to claim this voice. The realization that voice is no more than virtual could very well dispossess them of the idea that they are aliens in their own culture. Or to put it another way, if they have to invent the university, then they may as well be allowed to really invent it for themselves, in a way that they can live with and within.

As I said, this is largely a matter of guesswork. I hesitate to make any solid claims here simply because the possibility of a virtual voice is foreign to what we know about education. Nevertheless, the question remains: What is a virtual voice? The only answer that I can give is that it is nothing that you can put your finger on. Its virtuality keeps it from ever being fully realized as an evaluatable, discernible fact of discourse. A virtual voice is a matter of linkages and assemblages, arrangements that may not last beyond the space of their cooperation. A virtual voice is inherently a disputable fact. It should never *be*, but should always be a *becoming*-voice. It should never be thought of as existing except as a possibility and never be thought of as existing anywhere but in-between, in the very reciprocating structure of discourse itself. As such, a virtual voice cannot be the sole possession of anyone, nor the dispensation of any thing. In this respect, it is nothing more than a desire to express and invent, a desire that simply is expression and invention itself.

"I Want My CMC!"

As CMC makes its way gradually into becoming, if not a household word, at least a classroom word, I suspect the pedagogical value of a virtual voice, a network voice, will become easier to identify. I hasten to add that that process is already underway. As I finish the final revisions (actually, they might better be called negotiations between me, my earlier drafts, and the multiple-voiced comments I received from my editor) of this essay, I am sitting alone in a computer classroom complete with 30 Apple MacIntosh minicomputers loaded for bear with enough word-processing, spreadsheet, and graphics software (along with the availability of two hefty laser printers) to produce anything from a business card to a regional literary magazine. The machines are also connected to Purdue's mainframe computer, enabling access to electronic bulletin boards and computer conferencing services on several international networks. In short, the tools are in place in this room to bring the virtual voice of network culture to life; all that's missing are the students. They were here hours ago, packing the place during its open hours and forcing me to sneak back in with my key after midnight to polish up this essay that can do no more than announce the possibility of that virtual voice. In spite of the fact that I couldn't get at a computer, it was interesting watching them work and interact; anyone who fears the threat of network culture's elimination of face-to-face communication would have been hard pressed to make a case for that fear seeing five students pooled around two computers, animatedly clicking off options for completing a brochure assignment to meet a 9:30 a.m. deadline, or watching strangers peer tutoring other strangers in how to use the room's scanner. Yes, there were plenty of people working quietly alone, and, yes, access remains a problem—not only at access sites at Big Ten universities, but in homes and schools across the country. Nevertheless, the fact was clear that face-to-face exchanges and CMC are neither opposites nor antagonists; they are simply different means of communicating, and their co-presence in a classroom environment creates an invigorating, sometimes noisy, typically congenial, and almost invariably productive atmosphere for learning and exchange.

Whether the reason for that atmosphere rests largely with the novelty and openness of CMC or whether it can be ascribed to the loyalty and fervor of the instructors who hold memberships in any number of different virtual communities, I wouldn't hazard a guess. I do know, though, that the great majority of the classes that I've eavesdropped on have been informal, chatty, multitasking spectacles. And regardless of the reason, I'm happy to see that because it supports me in my belief that hierarchy is not a permanent and purely rigid state of affairs and that networking will not lead to anarchy and autistic rebellion from human interaction, that, in other words, voice can be rethought along lines of escape from the stranglehold of identity and ideality without dissipating into either noise or silence. We have for too long operated under the auspices of a voice that orders, organizes, and controls, for too long suppressed a voice that unsettles, destabilizes, and invents. The opportunity to think of voice as *both* a regulatory *and* a liberatory concept, both a matter of consumption and production at once enables us to think of voice as something virtual, something always in-between and never quite anywhere. In addition, we need to be circumspect when we talk about voice, for if we limit our conceptualization of voice to only those instances when discourse and a sincere desire to allow another voice to disclose itself discursively go hand in hand, then we are blinding ourselves to the distinct possibility that voice can be both a constraint upon and a customary means of silencing any discourse that calls into question (in whichever way, for whatever reason) the network of power relations which maintains a vigilant if not vital status quo. It is entirely possible that "voice," as personable and expressive as it sounds, may be little more than another name for the way in which discourse is sequestered from populations or possibilities which could derange or revolutionize communications media at present and in the future. Whether this is likely or not has to remain an open question.

To be accurate, however, my attempt to make voice a virtual event should come as no real surprise. Given the deployment of voice as metaphor (albeit an unexamined one) in rhetoric and composition, it is possible to claim that voice has never been as clearcut a matter of person-specific expression as it may have seemed to be. The fact of the matter is that voice has always been deployed extra-analytically as a name for the network of relations obtaining in any given rhetorical situation: all of the relations that obtain more or less clearly among writer, audience, message, medium, text, and world. In fact, there is good reason to believe that the thought of voice has always indicated a high level of activity and structural instability—the kind that could displace not only the technologies of writing but, more important, the technologies of its consumption and containment. My point is that the dispersion of the thought of voice has never been the problem. The problem has always been the sort of standardization and evaluation that the concept of voice could be made to legitimize. To the extent that a virtual voice is conceivable, it must be understood that such a capture is unconscionable because it can only be partial and can too easily be reduced to a desire for gate-keeping or for the safekeeping of a set of preapproved familiar voices.

Notes

1. It merits pointing out that the collapse of Camelot and the rise of social ferment are roughly contemporaneous with the rise and fall of voice-centered pedagogy in rhetoric and composition. An interesting starting point is Walter Ong's *The Barbarian Within* (1962), a text which Gibson's Persona is deeply indebted to, followed by Rohman and Wlecke's 1964 study *Pre-Writing*. I think, too, that a case can be made that Elbow's textbooks of the early to mid-1970s constitute something of the last solid achievements of a specifically voice-centered pedagogy in rhetoric and composition. For some funny reason, *ethos* outdistanced voice in the Reagan-Bush era. I can only look happily upon a resurgence of any interest in voice-centered pedagogy today. Unfortunately, not a great deal seems to have been done with voice within the past decade. Although voice is frequently mentioned in a variety of different contexts— particularly in discussions of evaluation, assessment, empowerment, and pedagogy—it is rarely examined as a singular, distinctive "fact" of writing. Its status as either concept or fact is generally taken for granted. In fact, I was able to locate only two recent discussions devoted exclusively to voice in the current literature: Toby Fulwiler's "Looking and Listening for My Voice" (1990) and Susan Wyche-Smith and Shirley K. Rose's "Throwing Our Voices: The Effects of Academic Discourse on Personal Voice" (1990).

2. I adopt this term from Shoshana Zuboff's fine study of the effects of CMC on middle managerial practice in American corporations, *In the Age of the Smart Machine: The Future of Work and Power* (1984). The term seems especially apt here because it suggests that active, dynamic, and productive effects proceed from these structures; in contrast, the phrase "symbolic structures" alone seems to suggest a sort of stable, static grid formation with meaning trickling down from some magisterial Above.

3. For a survey of perspectives on voice in rhetoric and composition, see Kathleen Blake Yancey's introduction to this volume. A good primer on the (roughly) current state of information technologies is Stuart Brand's *The Media Lab: Inventing the Future at MIT* (1987). An equally informative and intriguing document is "The Electronic Frontier Foundation's Open Platform Proposal" (EFF 1992), which recommends the deployment of a nationwide narrowband Integrated Services Digital Network (ISDN) as an economically sound first step toward providing national access to a "ubiquitous digital communications platform for information services."

4. Cyberspace is a term coined (as far as anyone seems to know) by cyberpunk (a sort of computer-science fiction) novelist William Gibson to designate a multimedia, usually computer-generated, environment of information that constitutes a virtual (not actual) reality or world. The term has been extended to refer to the "space"-in-common of CMC and all the existing and developing information technologies as well as their as yet unknown and unpredictable hybrids and mutations.

5. USENET, an acronym for User's Network, is a computer network mailsharing service used primarily by corporations and postsecondary schools.

6. The bracketed numerals in my citations of Theall, as well as those of Rheingold, refer to the numbered paragraphs of his essay. *Postmodern Culture* is an on-line journal; hence page references are impossible. In the bibliog-

raphical entry at the end of this essay, "THEALL 592" is the filename for Theall's essay. Also, for the sake of accuracy, the second of the two quoted phrases in the main-text sentence is actually Theall's quotation of Marshall McLuhan from *The Letters of Marshall McLuhan* (1987, 385).

7. For the sake of accuracy, I will offer a definition of hypertext from George P. Landow's *Hypertext: The Convergence of Critical Theory and Technology* (1992):

> *Hypertext*, a term coined by Theodor Nelson in the late 1960s, refers also to a form of electronic text, a radically new information technology, and a mode of publication. By "hypertext," Nelson explains, "I mean *nonsequential writing*—text that branches and allows choices to the reader, best read as an interactive screen. As popularly conceived, this is a series of text chunks connected by links which offer the reader different pathways." Hypertext, as the term will be used in the following pages, denotes text composed of blocks of text—what [Roland] Barthes terms a *lexia*—and the electronic links that join them. *Hypermedia* simply extends the notion of the text in hypertext by including visual information, sound, animation, and other forms of data. Since hypertext, which links a passage of verbal discourse to images, maps, diagrams, and sound as easily as to another verbal passage, expands the notion of text beyond the solely verbal, I do not distinguish between hypertext and hypermedia. (5)

Landow's fine book has not only fueled a fascination in me with computer hypertext systems; it has also affected my thinking about voice. Landow's book includes a helpful bibliography of printed and electronic materials, and it merits pointing out that Landow worked on the Brown University research team that developed the hypertext system Intermedia. Two other helpful sources of information which do not appear in Landow's bibliography are Stuart Moulthrop's "In the Zones: Hypertext and the Politics of Interpretation" (1989) and a collection of essays on hypertext, guest-edited by Moulthrop, for *Writing on the Edge* 2.2 (Spring 1991). A read-only diskette containing two hypertexts (*WOE* by Michael Joyce and *Izme Pass* by Carolyn Guyer and Martha Perry) was included in the issue.

8. I've taken the idea of an invention divorced from persuasion from Martin Rosenberg, specifically from one of his postings (see Rosenberg 1992) to Megabyte University (MBU-L). For the sake of fairly representing his point, I quote the first paragraph of his post:

> The fact that you've defined the canon/genre of literary, cultural and rhetorical theory as a repository of heuristic tools designed for varying forms of practice should clue all the rhetoric/comp folks that all theories can be thought of as coming under the rubric of invention: that is, if we change the definition of Invention ever so slightly from finding the available means of "inquiry," then we can use rhetoric as a way of understanding what the original innovators of contemporary theory "always" knew: "philosophy before linguistics" and "rhetoric before philosophy" were not just polemical expressions, but refer precisely to a sense of indebtedness to the one traditional discipline which as a matter of course embraced interdisciplinary thought-structures.

Works Cited

Bartholomae, David. 1985. "Inventing the University." In *When a Writer Can't Write: Studies in Writer's Block and Other Composing Process Problems*, edited by Mike Rose, 134–165. New York: Guilford.

Berlin, James A. 1987. *Rhetoric and Reality: Writing Instruction in American Colleges, 1900–1985*. Carbondale: Southern Illinois University Press.

Boice, Robert. 1985. "The Neglected Third Factor in Writing: Productivity." *College Composition and Communication* 36.4 (December): 472–80.

Bolter, J. David. 1991. *Writing Space: The Computer, Hypertext, and the History of Writing*. Hillsdale, NJ: Lawrence Erlbaum.

Brand, Stuart. 1987. *The Media Lab: Inventing the Future at MIT*. New York: Viking.

Deleuze, Gilles. 1990. *The Logic of Sense*. Translated by Mark Lester with Charles Stivale. New York: Columbia University Press.

———, and Felix Guattari. 1987. *Thousand Plateaus: Capitalism and Schizophrenia II*. Translated by Brian Massumi. Minneapolis: University of Minnesota Press.

Electronic Frontier Foundation. 1992. "The Electronic Frontier Foundation's Open Platform Proposal" (Version 4/June). The proposal is available from EFF as e-mail from archive-server@eff.org or through anonymous ftp to ftp.eff.org as 'eff/papers/open-platform-proposal.'

Faigley, Lester. 1989. "Judging Writing, Judging Selves." *College Composition and Communication* 40.4 (December): 395–412.

France, Alan. 1993. "Assigning Places: Introductory Composition as a Cultural Discourse." *College English* 55.6 (October): 593–610.

Fulwiler, Toby. 1990. "Looking and Listening for My Voice." *College Composition and Communication* 41.2 (October): 214–20.

Landow, George P. 1992. *Hypertext: The Convergence of Critical Theory and Technology*. Baltimore: Johns Hopkins University Press.

Lyotard, Jean-Francois. 1984. *The Postmodern Condition: A Report on Knowledge*. Translated by Geoff Bennington and Brian Massumi. Minneapolis: University of Minnesota Press.

———. 1991/92. "Voices of a Voice." Translated by Georges Van Den Abeele. *Discourse* 14.1 (Winter): 126–45.

McLuhan, Marshall. 1987. *The Letters of Marshall McLuhan*. Edited by Matie Molinaro, Corinne McLuhan, and William Toye. Toronto: Oxford University Press.

Moulthrop, Stuart. 1989. "In the Zones: Hypertext and the Politics of Interpretation" *Writing on the Edge* 1.1 (Fall): 18–27.

Nancy, Jean Luc. 1991. *The Inoperative Community*. Translated by Christopher Fynsk and edited by Peter Conner. Minneapolis: University of Minnesota Press.

Ong, Walter J., S.J. 1962. *The Barbarian Within*. New York: Macmillan.

Rheingold, Howard. 1992 (June). "A Slice of Life in My Virtual Community." Electronic Frontier Foundation On-Line Paper: 'eff/papers/cyber/life-in-virtual-community.'

Rohman, D. Gordan, and Albert O. Wlecke. 1964. *Pre-Writing: The Construction and Application of Models for Concept Formation in Writing.* East Lansing: Michigan State University Press.

Rosenberg, Martin. 1992. Posting to Megabyte University (MBU-L). 27 February/1600:28 MST.

Stewart, Donald C. 1972. *The Authentic Voice: A Pre-Writing Approach to Student Writing.* Dubuque, IA: Wm. C. Brown.

Theall, Donald F. 1992. "Beyond the Orality/Literacy Dichotomy: James Joyce and the Pre-History of Cyberspace." *Postmodern Culture* 2.3 (May): THEALL 592.

Wyche-Smith, Susan, and Shirley K. Rose. 1990. "Throwing Our Voices: The Effects of Academic Discourse on Personal Voice." *Writing on the Edge* 2.1 (Fall): 34–50.

Zuboff, Shoshana. 1984. *In the Age of the Smart Machine: The Future of Work and Power.* New York: Basic Books.

17 Concluding the Text: Notes toward a Theory and the Practice of Voice

Kathleen Blake Yancey
The University of North Carolina at Charlotte

Michael Spooner
Utah State University

. . . Voice. Self. Text. Context.

. . . It occurs to me that if this volume's demonstration of voice were irrefutable, or at least very persuasive, that if the loose ends were neatly bundled, then no final chapter would be needed. And a final chapter, I am advised, *is* needed.

. . . I wonder about the value of arguing again that voice exists: will those who want definitive persuasion even hear my voice on voice?

. . . I had hoped we could dispense with conclusions, could close this conversation with a chapter that, like the previous one, points us toward the future. In that way, the text wasn't going to end at all, was instead going to raise the prospect of the future and of how voice might be articulated then, thus creating the sound, and the sense, of voices departing in conversation.

In sum, I did not want the chapter to do the conventional end-of-the-book thing. I didn't want it to attempt "to make sense" of what had come before. It wouldn't pretend to answer questions or put issues to rest, wouldn't re-voice or voiceover the earlier arguments. And without such a "conclusion," the text spoke in chorus, although not without dissonance, through the contributors' voices—all of them. It was our text, our sense of voice, our collective textual presence.

. . . But in unconcluding the text, I was also hoping to avoid the subject both informing and haunting it, the subject of the self.

. . . So, I concede: A concluding chapter, then. But a "concluding" chapter whose purpose is to preclude closure, to summarize tentatively, under a kind of acoustic erasure defying dichotomies and certainty, arguing for possibilities beyond its own boundaries. It is a chapter that could be entitled "After-thought," or "Thoughts Afterward," or—for the Victorians among us—"Avoidance Avoided." For it is a chapter that finds it cannot avoid the unavoidable, the starting place, the central question of late twentieth century and a goodly number of centuries before that: the question of the self.

In the essays here, too, the self has been discussed. The writers of this text know that even finding the self in the postmodern era is no mean accomplishment—or quite a (vain) glorious illusion, depending on your point of view. As Randy Freisinger argues, in this era, the self per se—and its nature, even if one does exist—is precisely what's at issue. Or as another friend puts it to me[1]: <<I thought the unified self wasn't possible anymore.>>

<<But here,>> he continues, <<is where the argument between what we know as expressivism and what we know as postmodernism becomes tedious and unhelpful. Neither point of view seems aware of how invested it is in Western conventions, nor how limiting these might be. Expressivism, even in its revisionist form, depends heavily on an understanding of "authenticity" that defines experience in terms of the irreducible Western political/cultural entity—the individual self. On the other hand, postmodernism, in its critique of expressivist conventions, is silent about a need to reconnect the self with larger realities, focusing instead—in the time-honored Western mode of analysis by segmentation—on a need to atomize it.>>

And, of course, if there's no self, then there is no voice expressing or reflecting or representing the self. All the more reason, then, to begin this conclusion by exploring the nature of the self and its relationship to voice, before considering still-unresolved issues of voice: the nature of silence, of authority, of multivocality, of presence, of the self realized in the text (if indeed this is more than illusion), and the nature of text in which the self becomes.

The Nature of the Self

<<Luria (1982) says the key to human consciousness, if there is one, lies beyond the individual human organism. It is to be found ". . . not in the recesses of the human brain or in the depths of the human spirit, but in the external conditions of life. . ." (25). Luria is making a point about society, but when I look beyond the human organism, I'm impressed that we're embedded in external conditions of the physical world. The world of weather, the mysteries of geology, the inscrutable, retiring face of the forest. The symbiosis of the mite and leaf, the plankton and the whale. The microscope reveals even our own bodies as ineffable hierar-

chies interacting without our consent by codes we did not devise. Hormones, enzymes, antibodies, dense nets of neurons. DNA. The physical unity we understand as "self" retreats, the closer we look, among layers of oblivious networks. If our physical person replicates the structures beyond it, how can our consciousness be any different?

<<For me, the intellectual human is ultimately a projection of the physical universe. In one sense, this leads me to the postmodern dis-integrated self, but in a deeper sense it leads me toward non-Western views of solidarity—a communitarian self integrating the individual, the group, and nature.>>

In Western culture, as elsewhere, the self is formed through a kind of communitarian exchange, through its situation and the agents within that situation. As Charles Taylor (1991) explains it, the self is at once the repository and the vehicle, and yet also the transfiguration of the social experience: "Human beings are constituted in conversation; and hence what gets internalized in the mature subject is not the reaction of the other, but the whole conversation, with the interanimation of its voices" (314). Taylor calls such a self "dialogic," but a more thorough Bakhtinian reading might posit a self that is "multilogic."

Even the word "self" is a tease and misnomer, suggesting, almost promising, what is impossible for a living thing: a static, certain, secure entity. And yet there *is* some predictability attached to all of us, which is why our friends, our family, and indeed, even our adversaries know what to make of us. Defying the predictable can itself become predictable, as the works of William Faulkner, Anne Sexton, and Monty Python attest.

But predictable only to a point. And that point is our experience of the self, the person who is situated at a moment in time, in a specific place, reverberating with conscious and unconscious pasts, anticipating an immediate, if not long-term, future. A self both profound and ludicrous, complicated and complicating, complex, slippery. Historically and experientially, this self is not unitary but multiple, being composed of diverse, nonlinear senses:

- a sense of who—and also what—we have been to this moment (what's often described by people as a center or core or foundation or authentic self, depending on the metaphor);

- a sense of who we are in the immediate moment, in relation to multiple points of view/variables—in the culture, the scene, the other agents, the interaction;

- a sense of who we might have been, the potential but unrealized self articulated by Marlon Brando's fighter in *On the Waterfront* when he tells his brother that he "coulda been a contenda";
- a sense of who we will be, the self in process of becoming;
- a sense of who we might be still, the self that might be realized, particularly in another segment of life: the grandparent still dormant, the Grandma Moses we'd like to be, could still become.

Usually, what we experience isn't all of these selves concurrently, at least not consciously, although that combination, that intersection, is who we are. A poet who says that living well is living in the *fullness of the present tense* speaks to what current notions of the self suggest: multiple selves resonating one to another, through which we temporarily create and re-create a wholeness and oneness filling up, completing the present tense, as that tense is defined within specific cultures. For whatever kind of self we experience, it *becomes* within multiple contexts: the larger social structure, the local context, the personal. It relies on no single logic, but on a multilogic, expressed and created through a multivocality.

<<The closer we look, especially through the microscope of postmodern theory, the more layers of voices we discover within. We merely confirm a sense of disintegration.

<<Incredibly, this doesn't matter a whit. We do speak. That the unity of the organism is in some sense a fiction is, to the organism, a moot point. It doesn't change my relation to the tree to know that both tree and I are constellated of infinitely smaller physical parts (cells, molecules, electrons in orbit) whose spatial relations might make even the solar system seem crowded: I still must walk around the tree. Similarly, to know that both tree and I are deeply rooted in the community of the physical world—both projections of the earth—doesn't matter. I still walk around.

<<". . . and the table exists because I scrub it."

—W. H. Auden (1944, 195)

<<We experience ourselves as unities, I'm trying to say, in spite of our knowledge that we are both composed and extended. This is true in our physical selves, and no less true in our intellectual selves.>>

Self, Voice, and Silence

<<Voice testifies that self exists, just as self gives voice a body of content to express.>> But more precisely, what to make of this relationship? <<Doesn't one have to be careful about wrapping voice and self too tightly together? Presumably, there's no voice without *some* self (unified or multi), but there might be a self without voice. Olsen, Belenky . . . and plenty of others doing feminist theory want to make a point of silenced selves.>>

The notion of silence as *oppressive* finds its ideological underpinnings in Western thought. Even there and defined politically, however, silence and silencing are not monolithic. They take diverse forms, oppress various peoples. In the feminist tradition, Susan Carlton connects silence and women, but others have been stilled: Native Americans silenced by the Europeans, as Carr and Freisinger point out, African Americans silenced by their white neighbors, gays silenced by heterosexuals.

Even the most oppressive silencing, however, doesn't eradicate the self. Otherwise, there would have been no Ardienne Rich to find gendered margins, no Andrew Wiget to chart bilingual boundaries, no Emily Dickenson to write herself out of the ultimate paradox of a social silence, no Aleksandr Solzhenitsyn to record and narrate and protest—and voice—that which would not be silent.

And paradoxically, to have voice, in the West or elsewhere, requires silence, too. Voice we may hear; we may not. But its agency, its authority, its significance cannot be established without a context of silence. It is the silence that at once makes possible and counterpoints the voice. Silence is thus a necessary if not sufficient condition for voice to occur, even for the most voiced among us: the politician, the patriarch, and the artist.

In "The Aesthetics of Silence," for example, Susan Sontag (1989) argues that artists use silence as the dialectical collaborator of voice:

> A genuine emptiness, a pure silence, are not feasible—either conceptually or in fact. If only because the artwork exists in a world furnished with many other things, the artist who creates silence or emptiness must produce something dialectical: a full void, an enriching emptiness, a resonating or eloquent silence. Silence remains, inescapably, a form of speech (in many instances, of complaint or indictment) and an element in a dialogue. (367)

Bahktinian appropriation would, by this reasoning, include not just the words and voices of others, but their silences, too.

<<In this weeping season,
   nothing can exist
     without resistance;
       a word comes to its own
         only on the blankest page;
         gesture needs the eye;
      and voice, to be, must cry
       itself against a silence;
       and what I want to see from
        metaphysics most of all
       is the dialectic of
      a scarlet wing
     opposing grey
     and empty
     sky.>>*

So too for writers: the silence makes possible and accents voice, provides emphasis, sometimes even demonstrates power rather than victimization.

<<In some ways, isn't that what the expressivists know and the social constructivists don't always acknowledge: the role and the power of silence? If you focus on the empty page—its silence—then the writer's task becomes a lonely one, and you're drawn toward solitary conceptions like autonomy, authenticity, and the like.>>

Analogies to an oral rhetorical situation abound: the compulsive talker who marks the value of silence and her place in the social, verbal hierarchy even as she seeks to fill the empty space; the CEO who speaks to employees when *she* chooses; the wise man who chatters not.

An appreciation of silence and of the fullness and connectedness of voice, both oral and written, also informs non-Western cultures. Consider the case of the Native Americans, in whose culture all selves are speaking selves by virtue of their connection to, their expression of, and their contribution to the universe. As put by Leslie Marmon Silko (1989), speaking of the Paguate and Laguna, such an assumption is a matter of survival:

> The narratives linked with prominent features of the landscape between Paguate and Laguna delineate the complexities of the relationship which human beings must maintain with the surrounding natural world if they hope to survive in this place. Thus, the journey was an interior process of the imagination, a growing awareness that being human is somehow different from all other

---

*The poem "Winter," by Michael Spooner, first appeared in *The Spoon River Quarterly* 16.1/2 (1991): 39. Used by permission of the author.

life—animal, plant, and inanimate. Yet we are all from the same source: the awareness never deteriorated into Cartesian duality, cutting off the human from the natural world. (683)

In other words, in this culture no question about existence is begged: the self exists. It is communal, individual, social. It is real, felt, experienced. The tense and the voice tell a truth that is always recognized as relative. It was the case, as Freisinger suggests, "that Indian people were *silenced*, that they became voiceless" (my italics), not that *they* were silent. The idea that they were silent, as Tom Carr demonstrates in chapter 12, was not theirs, but the whites'.

<<Helen Fox, who works intensively with students from "world majority" cultures, likewise questions American readings of silence. She offers this from one of her students:

<Silence in my culture is the base for thinking. . . . In the U.S., I've <noticed that people are very nervous if there is silence for one <second. You must fill the silence; you must start talking quickly. <That seems a little immature, a little thoughtless to me." (Fox <1994 [in press])

<<We forget that our idea of silence as a mark of oppression, denial of self, dependency, or, at best, immaturity, is itself a cultural construct, a corollary of our obsession with individuality. And it's ironic that both of these constructs are imposed even by scholars like Belenky, et al., whose deepest wish is to liberate and empower. Fox complains that culturally unreflective theorizing like this "makes it all the more difficult to see the possibility of other routes to wisdom, other intelligent ideas of evidence, other valid ways of exploring human potential, other methods of learning and teaching.">>

It may be that Westerners, and English faculty particularly, have trouble valuing silence precisely because of who they are. Given their own verbosity, their own love affair with language and the imagination and the connections and promise they hold, they—like others who privilege a verbal mode of composing and interpreting the world—prefer verbal ways of knowing to the near exclusion of others. Inadvertently, they can victimize those who would be silent—in yet another form of oppression? As Jim Crosswhite (1993) suggests, in the classroom, silence is itself something to be honored:

<We have two goods in conflict here: equalitarian communication <and relishing diversity in communication. . . . If the commu-<nication is in some sense unequal, then we can criticize it on that <basis, and so decrease our adherence to the agreements it <produced.

<Does it make the same sense to criticize the results of
<communication in which people were not allowed to be silent
<when they were inclined to? That is, if we fail to recognize
<diversity in communicative style *even when the diversity*
<*produces unequal participation,* are we still liable to criticism to
<the same degree as we are when we fail to have equalitarian
<communication?>>

In such a case, the silence may be tentative and temporary, but in others, the silence can help prepare for a more profound voice. Janis Nark (1993), a nurse who served in Vietnam, maintained her silence on the experience for twenty years. She was, she says, "angry . . . because that's a lot safer than sadness. That doesn't hurt as much as sadness does. Sadness is where I am now, and that's the painful part."

Silence, then, does more than set the stage for and counterpoint voice. It is a part of voice itself, and voice(s) one means of self.

Developing Voice: The Oral Context, the Written Context

The oral context we speak and listen in provides many opportunities to see self, through the interpretations of others, the reactions of others, the power to influence both. It's a "natural" place to develop a notion of self, a chance to try out rhetorical strategies, the immediate response telling speakers how they are doing.

Perhaps that's why it's not strange to hear people say that a speaker's voice sounds funny, compared to the way the speaker normally sounds. For those familiar to us, there's a norm that provides a context for interpreting not just what is said, but how it is said—and thus what *is* said.

<<Interpersonal, face-to-face communication is a context of multiple cues—pausing, gestures, eye contact—that work together to add nuance.>>

Our ability to read the various cues helps us communicate; we speak "better" as we learn to read, interpret, and respond to those cues. Without direct instruction, speakers learn to vary volume, timbre, pitch, to modify and modulate voice to suit a rhetorical situation. Juggling multiple voices becomes normal.

Not so in writing, I think. Somehow in much writing, particularly in the writing of our students, this multivocality is as absent as the perceived audience itself. The story of James Britton, after all, is the story of students learning to write in the one voice for the one audience—first for the teacher as trusted adult, later for the teacher as teacher, finally for the teacher as examiner. There is always the rhetorical situation, to use Lloyd Bitzer's language, but to Britton's students as to ours, I think, each rhetorical situation appears as one classroom divorced from that which preceded it. Each successive classroom seems not only separate from the last, but more prestigious, too, perhaps even more correct or truthful or significant. The one where they will finally get it right.

Paula Gillespie's story confirms Britton's: the story of teachers deciding—without much reference to each other's definitions—what voice in writing is and how students can get it right, the story of definitions of voice that in their idiosyncrasy do not include or refer to each other. They presume a kind of special knowledge that the student often has to guess at or deduce. Margaret Woodworth's story is different, but even that—the one teacher seeking to understand and learn about voice with her students—is a special case of voice, one that fits well in the belletristic tradition, but that won't necessarily serve elsewhere.

A Pedagogy of Voice

<<I'm glad for the move toward pedagogy as we round the last turn. What does all this mean for how we teach? Do we analyze and explicate voice with our students? Or do we guide them more subtly? What does our view of silence imply for the writing conference or for dealing with international students?

<<I've been having trouble seeing how there is any way to reconcile the postmodern argument with the expressivist position on this question of voice. And I wish we could reconcile them better, because they both have implications for the way we help students write. They imply different pedagogies.

<<I'm browsing through two very different articles from expert writing teachers: "'My Own Voice': Students Say It Unlocks the Writing Process," by Zöe Keithley (1992), and "I Stand Here Writing," by Nancy Sommers (1993).

<<Keithley, a teacher and creative writer, reports the results of a formal research project in basic writing, and she concludes, if I may interpret, that without the expressivist attitude toward voice, you won't make any progress at all with a classroom of developing writers. Her project was to survey students to discover which genres of instructional methods and activities they found most helpful. Although some might question her methodology, here's what struck me about her conclusions: "Acceptance of the student's own voice is the key . . .", which is

to say that, in Keithley's view, a teacher absolutely needs the expressivist feel for voice.>>

Like John Albertini's deaf students, these hearing students find it valuable to identify and use their "own" voice—hearing it internally, accepting permission to use it, and whenever possible, reading it aloud.

<<Nancy Sommers (1993) too makes claims for an expressivist conception of voice, almost in spite of her own experience. "As I stand in my kitchen," she writes,

> <the voices that come to me come by way of a lifetime of reading,
> <they come on the waves of life, and they seem to be helping me
> <translate the untranslatable. They come, not at my bidding, but
> <when I least expect them, when I am receptive enough to listen
> <to their voices. They come when I am open. (425)

<<Personally, I can't identify with her mood on this matter, but her point is inarguable, right? And one can read it postmodernly: the self I am is composed of others and others. Yet when Sommers shows us her classroom, we see that she, like Keithley, teaches the uncomplicated self:

> <If I could teach my students one lesson about writing it would
> <be to see themselves as sources, as places from which ideas
> <originate. . . . I want them to know how it is always the writer's
> <voice, vision, and argument that create the new source. (425)

<<So, ultimately, Sommers talks the expressivist talk, too, and argues for teaching the autonomous self. But she also expects her students to bring judgment to bear, to examine "the voices that come" with a view toward controlling what they contribute to one's own voice. This seems congenial at least, though not identical, to a constructivist view. So she seems to promote a pedagogy not unlike others in your book (Fulwiler's, Elbow's, Minnerly's, your own); that is, one in the Romantic tradition, but influenced by dialectics. A dialectical expressivism? (An authentic self that talks to itself?)

<<So why would teachers as different as Sommers and Keithley gravitate toward the unified self/voice? I think it's because professional teachers understand what professional high theorists don't: that theory implies practice. And when we read these two as researchers—which they are, of course—we see in their conclusions an argument for a pedagogy of voice: that voice should be taught explicitly, explored thoroughly; that voice is key to a student writer's development into a mature writer. But we also see an implicit argument for an *expressivist* (or naïve realist) pedagogy of voice. Unfortunately, however, neither one really comes to grips with the implications of postmodern insight, so they leave as many issues unreconciled as the theorists do.

<<Not that this negotiation can ever be laid to rest.

<<But, just for fun, let's assume that both sides are right. Let's agree that voice is vital to pedagogy, admit that postmodern theory is rarely gracious in the classroom. On the other hand, let's agree that voice is multiple, that self is multiple, and that, in Lyotard's (1984) metaphor, we exist as "nodal points of specific communication circuits," posts in an infinite network of messages.

<<In fact, let's use another side of Lyotard's metaphor—it's "locality" if you will. Voice as place. Can we offer students the image of voice as a place where many voices intersect? If I am a node in a vast network, I can see that what seems "my" voice is composed of voices that reach me through the network. Yet I can also see that the place my voice inhabits is unique, since no other node has heard the same voices in the same order at the same time that I have. If you teach this to me, and then give me permission to explore the place my voice inhabits, I find I am not frustrated by the contradictions I hear. I am not bound to call one voice "authentic" and reject the rest. I begin to take liberties with my voices, to experiment, to manipulate the mix. I write in one voice or another; I write in multivoice. And as I write, I find myself relieved of the anxiety of authenticity that expressivism conjures, and also spared the weary insecurity of all things rootless and postmodern.>>

A pedagogy of voice? I think so. But let's qualify. I appreciate the insights of "creative" writers (though I am inclined to argue the term) as I do those of teachers; on the other hand, we all tend to think how *we* write is how others should write. Of course, these writers have helped us a great deal in demystifying their writing practice, and we learn from these accounts. How they write, though, is not necessarily how the rest of us write. Most of us, on reflection, recognize the inherent limitations of our own experience, recognize that different choices work for different writers and for different kinds of writing on different occasions. In sum, despite *that* generalization, I'm wary of generalizations.

But I want to pursue this proposed pedagogy of voice. Aren't we still in the same trap? Which version of voice do we mean here? I have used it variously, to mean the speaking voice and its relationship to writing, and also what it suggests about what we do when we write, and then on other occasions to mean the self and bringing that to the page for others to interpret. Other times, in class, I use it to refer to Wayne Booth's rhetorical stance, as in the stance of inspiration embodied by Martin Luther King in much of his writing. Sometimes I mean authority, and sometimes presence, and sometimes the rhetoric that is appropriate to a given situation, as in the voice used in biology. Saying that voice helps people learn to write only begins to raise questions, for me.

I think place as a way of locating voice is one promising metaphor. The class is to be a safe place to craft voice, to share it and to experiment with it, as you said, and to understand that experimenting with it will not only reveal a self but also perhaps construct it, perhaps change it. For altering the voice—changing it, adapting it to meet the needs of the audience—is, at the least, changing the presentation of the self, which can then lead to more profound changes. We see this in *Educating Rita*, and in our classrooms every day.

This rationale for a pedagogy of voice makes moot part of the student's allegiance to the one true voice, the authentic voice. Minnerly's voice changes yet stays authentic, and Cummins's authenticity derives from different sources both as she develops and as her rhetorical situations increase and enlarge. Speaking theoretically, Elbow cites authenticity as one of several features of voice. In other words, we see agreement here, practically and theoretically, on authenticity as variable, itself situated within a purpose, and audience, and a voice that, like Fulwiler's, has more than a single self inhabiting it.

Perhaps this is a part of it, too: the selves that inhabit voice. Students think, in large part because of what we tell them, that they are to bring to the page the one-selved, one voice—the voice *we* have sanctioned. And then we teachers confirm this. As Nancy Sommers (1993) and Robert Connors and Andrea Lunsford (1993) demonstrate, we provide the idealized and preferred reading through our own responses, which in turn encourage the student's adoption of the single, sanctioned voice, the uncomplicated self. What students don't realize—and what is very, very difficult to teach—is that many rhetorical situations, from the technical rhetorical situation of Bosley and Allen to the newsprint of Morgan, a voice inhabited by more than one self is not only acceptable but also desirable. It strikes me that even those who argue in favor of teaching the sanctioned voice first, like Bartholomae, do so in order that academic voice provide a place—a textual stage, if you will—for students to bring their other voices, to hear them, to orchestrate them. So place as a metaphorical connection to voice? Yes: a rhetorical situation as a place, a classroom as a place, voice itself as a place.

Voice in reading as well. Like Sommers, Carl Klaus, Laura Julier, and Tom Carr find that the voices they hear are those they allow, created from the fragments *they* recognize and legitimate. Our task in teaching students to read, too, is to help them learn to hear multiple voices, to move as writers and as readers from a familiar place to new, different, even uncharted places, to write in these new places in a voice that is inhabited by their many selves.

If we are to employ a pedagogy of voice, however, we may need to make other changes. For instance, how will assessment change? Shouldn't it reward the goals implied above—the goals of understanding the starting places of one's voice, of developing new voices, of using the language of voice to talk about this development and to account for achievement? Are these goals appropriate for writing classes? And what about applicability? I argued above that no one method or approach would work for all writers, and yet here we are almost suggesting that kind of uniform approach. We'd need to know, in other words, for whom this pedagogy would be suitable: individually, categorically. I wonder, for example, about the "helpfulness" of voice or the oral context for a shy student. And I wonder about "how much" of voice to include in any given course. Is it possible to bring the language of voice into the classroom without so diluting it that it's completely trivialized? Without turning it into a "content" course, on Voice? If we bring this language into the first-year courses, will sophomores complain, "Oh, not voice again. We did that last year!"

There are other questions, no doubt, but these come to mind readily. So trying a pedagogy of voice? Yes, cautiously, with planning, with review, with student insight.

Developing Voice: The Import of Medium

Our model of voice, however, is changing almost faster than the technology supporting it. As we move away from the technology of the pencil, toward the technology of the machine, and further toward the context of e-mail, we also move away from the hard copy of voice and are better able to conceptualize it from other perspectives and to observe what else might be possible.

Word processing and desktop publishing, for instance, change the nature of rhetoric and help make possible a voice that is "extra-verbal," one that includes but is not limited to words alone (see Wickliff, forthcoming). This preferred voice created through the new technology relies dramatically on what we might consider extra-verbal features—formatting, visuals, and document design. As the figures below suggest, the technology creates options, it makes what we teach and learn more complicated, and it problemizes assessment. Even as we learn to use it, it asks of us, "What do you make of me? How will you use me? What do *I* do to your notion of voice?" (See figures 1 and 2.)

E-mail, both in and of itself and as the place of a new rhetorical situation, also may change what's possible for voice and for self. That

> # Hello . . . Hello . . . Hello . . .
> *Is there anybody out there?*
> Just nod if you can hear me.
> *Now that I have your attention:*
> ## *LISTEN TO ME!*
> ### I have found my voice!
> I'm not joking
> *so read on, read on, read on . . .*

Fig. 1. Cover sheet from student's "voice" project.

is the argument made by Mark Zamierowski, that this new medium offers a new kind of locality, a place for a novel exchange, one unburdened by factors like age and race and gender. As such, it makes possible a rhetorical situation more democratic in nature, more networked than hierarchical, though one still subject to the prevailing aesthetic. Likewise, in the classroom, according to Gail Hawisher and Cindy Selfe: with the appropriate pedagogy, e-mail makes the class more democratic, less dominated by the patriarchy of the U.S. culture.

This is an argument I want to believe. I like e-mail, I write more frequently because of it, and I think—though can't prove—that I write differently because of it. The orality evoked in e-mail for me encourages me to bring different voices into contact, and I hear what happens, hear what response is created, and most importantly perhaps, hear who I become. Maybe that's what real correspondents always feel; I haven't been enough of a correspondent to know. But I do correspond on e-mail, routinely. I like the freedom, the three-dimensional feel of it, the sense that this isn't *just* a medium; it's a *place* with physical parameters and discourse conventions I can still help define. I like the freedom that implies, the opportunity, and the audience that seems always present. The exploration I've experienced there somehow has made its impact felt elsewhere, too. My hard-copy voice seems less like the paper voices of old, more like the fluid voices of e-mail.

I don't know that these observations are true, of course. What I do know is that because of e-mail I work differently now, and that working differently also contributes to voice. Charles Moran (1992) made just these points in beginning a review essay entitled "Computers and English: What Do We Make of Each Other?" Explaining that to write the review, he first began by "contact[ing] colleagues across the country,"

The Discovery and Cultivation of the Two Separate Aspects of
Karsen Palmer's Voice

(wait, wait, wait . . . no, you can't do that)

(What do you mean? How dare you just jump in my title sheet . . .)

(man, you can't write like that, it's so <u>serious</u> *and . . . yuck!)*

(Leave me alone. I'm trying to create and use a more formal voice, to
illustrate my growth as a writer.)

(But no one's going to read this thing if you don't put some <u>pizzazz</u> *in it!)*

(No, you are wrong; I'm trying to change and you're MESSING IT
UP!)

*(shhh, lower your voice, they'll hear you. But you can have it be fun too,
now can't ya?)*

(Well . . . I don't know.)

(let's try it and see . . .)

Karsen Palmer
Voice Portfolio
Dr. Yancey
Spring 1993

Fig. 2. Cover sheet from student's "voice" project.

he proceeds to talk about what that kind of instant access and connection signify:

> So in writing this review I am less the lone reviewer that I once
> was, speaking from the mountain or the garret; I am much more
> the voice of, yes, myself, but of others too, a corporate, collabora-
> tive, collective "self" that is more social and therefore more knowl-
> edgeable than the old. (193)

But these are claims that can evoke skepticism from others, from you,
in fact.

<<It's true that in other notes to you, I criticize certain claims for
e-mail—how it undermines hierarchy, how it makes the world safe for
discourse, how "in and of itself . . . it changes what is possible for
voice"—your own views of e-mail, in other words, and Zamierowski's,
and others'. I think e-mail simply changes what is convenient for the
writer.

<<But now in this from Moran, I can see a reading of e-mail at work that is notably more concrete and less utopian. At least in connection with this review project, Moran sees in e-mail *an opportunity*, even a place, to work out his interest in a new kind of voice. He chooses a *voice* "of others, too," a multivoice, and a collaborative *self*, to inform the *text* he's creating; e-mail is the *context* through which he chooses to accomplish this. And I'm saying ah, well—voice, self, text, context, if *that's* what you mean. . . .

<<Because that's what we're doing here: e-mail exchanges enabling a collective voice in the chapter. To some extent, I'm writing Sabine to your Griffin (though this implies that you may be mad and I may be your invention), i.e., as one autonomy sending postcards to another. But what's more interesting is that you're also playing Nick Bantock, *Griffin and Sabine*'s creator, who contrives and orchestrates a fictional correspondence for the sake of its unified effect. In this case, it's the Internet instead of the postal service that provides a context, but the text seems to carry no less a sense of unity; it does move the chapter toward what Moran might call a collaborated, "and therefore more knowledgeable," self. And though other collaborated texts express themselves in a single voice, this one is multivocal, composing its own voice by dividing it.>>

Yes, you've hit it—the issue of authority. Fish asked if there were a text in this class; we might ask what kind of text this e-mail is, and what kind of voice we find there, how the form of e-mail shapes our conception of both text and authority, how dividing the voice makes for unity.

<<But one can divide voice(s) forever, and then there really is no end to this chapter. Only a last page that precludes conclusion, eavesdrops on an unending conversation, reflects you back through itself and on into the book again. And I'm saying well, if *that's* what you mean. . . .>>

Yes: Context. Text. Self. Voice. Not a bad place to begin.

Note

1. This chapter was composed on e-mail by both authors.<<The brackets denote Michael Spooner's response to and discussion with the editor, throughout.>> We have chosen to represent the dialogue in this format in order to retain and express the multivocal conversation we experienced.

Works Cited

Auden, W. H. 1944. "For the Time Being." In *Collected Complete Poems*. London: Faber & Faber.

Bantock, Nick. 1991. *Griffin and Sabine: An Extraordinary Correspondence.* San Francisco: Chronicle Books.

Bitzer, Lloyd. 1968. "The Rhetorical Situation." *Philosophy and Rhetoric* 1 (Winter): 1–14.

Britton, J. N., T. Burgess, N. Martin, A. McLeod, and H. Rosen. 1975. *The Development of Writing Abilities (11–18).* London: Macmillan.

Connors, Robert J., and Andrea Lunsford. 1993. "Teachers' Rhetorical Comments on Student Papers." *College Composition and Communication* 44.2 (May): 207–23.

Crosswhite, Jim. 1993. Electronic communication. May.

Fox, Helen. 1994 [in press]. *Listening to the World: Cultural Issues in Academic Writing.* Urbana: National Council of Teachers of English.

Keithley, Zöe. 1992 " 'My Own Voice': Students Say It Unlocks the Writing Process." *Journal of Basic Writing* 11(2): 82–102.

Luria, Aleksandr Romanovich. 1982. *Language and Cognition.* Edited by James V. Wertsch. New York: John Wiley.

Lyotard, Jean-François. 1984. *The Postmodern Condition.* Translated by Geoff Bennington and Brian Massumi. Minneapolis: University of Minnesota Press.

Moran, Charles. 1992. "Computers and English: What Do We Make of Each Other?" *College English* 54.2 (February): 193–98.

Nark, Janis. 1993. As quoted in the *Charlotte Observer,* (31 May): A–1, A–7.

Silko, Leslie Marmon. 1989. "Landscape, History, and the Pueblo." Rpt. in *Women's Voices: Visions and Perspectives,* edited by Pat C. Hoy, Esther H. Schor, and Robert DiYanni, 677–87. New York: McGraw-Hill.

Sommers, Nancy. 1993. "I Stand Here Writing." *College English* 55.4 (April): 420–28.

Sontag, Susan. 1989. "The Aesthetics of Silence." Rpt. in *Women's Voices: Visions and Perspectives,* edited by Pat C. Hoy, Esther H. Schor, and Robert DiYanni, 363–80. New York: McGraw-Hill.

Spooner, Michael. 1991. "Winter." *The Spoon River Quarterly* 16.1/2: 39.

Taylor, Charles. 1991. "The Dialogical Self." In *The Interpretive Turn: Philosophy, Science, Culture,* edited by David R. Hiley, James F. Bohman, and Richard M. Shusterman, 304–15. Ithaca: Cornell University Press.

Wickliff, Greg. Forthcoming. "Portfolios and the Professional Writing Course." In *Portfolios in Practice: Voices from the Fields,* edited by Kathleen Blake Yancey.

18 An Annotated and Collective Bibliography of Voice: Soundings from the Voices Within

Peter Elbow
University of Massachusetts at Amherst

Kathleen Blake Yancey
University of North Carolina at Charlotte

We're very proud of this annotated bibliography. For a slippery and many-tentacled topic like voice, we feel that such a bibliography is needed and will be welcome. We wish we'd been able to consult one. We are pleased with the diversity of the titles. And we look forward to the additions that our readers will add to our beginning.

The history of the bibliography speaks to the quality of its voicing. Peter originally proposed the enterprise to Kathleen as a collaborative task for contributors—and primed the pump with a "messy monster bibliography." Peter also wrote the initial invitation to essayists in the book. Kathleen, as editor, agreed to take responsibility to coordinate and make it happen for most of the time of the collaboration: sending out successive versions to contributors, inviting, asking, badgering them to take titles to annotate, and to suggest titles of their own. And as the entries suggest, the writers brought their own knowledge and perspectives and tastes and values to the task.

But even though we feel this bibliography will be welcome, we also feel we better apologize a bit—or at least be diffident. For we've all done it "on the side" as it were. It is not complete, and many readers will complain of titles that ought to be here, perhaps of titles that seem too tangential. And these complaints may be valid. We experienced difficulty because we couldn't figure out what the "edges" of the topic were: "voice" leads to everything. Nor, probably, is the bibliography fully scholarly or completely objective. We invited people to emphasize description more than evaluation, yet also to permit a note of personal advice or appreciation to creep in around the sides. This means that in addition to their being qualitative, the annotations are anything but completely consistent.

Yet in the end, we're excited. We've made a start; perhaps it can lead to a better job down the road.

———————

Contributors to the bibliography are noted by their initials at the end of each entry—the initials standing for these names: Peter Elbow, Kathleen Blake Yancey, Deborah Bosley, Susan Carlton, Gail Summerskill Cummins, Randy Freisinger, Paula Gillespie, Gwen Gong, Laura Julier, Carl H. Klaus, and Meg Morgan.

———————

Aisenberg, Nadya, and Mona Harrington. 1988. *Women of Academe: Outsiders in the Sacred Grove.* Amherst: University of Massachusetts.

The authors identify two quests that women typically pursue—the marriage plot and the career plot—demonstrating with a small but illustrative sample that for most women, pursuing both is nearly impossible. More typically, pursuing a marriage plot has—for women but not for men—undermined chances for a rewarding career plot. In the chapter entitled "Voice of Authority," the authors provide a penetrating analysis of the difficulty in speaking with authority and in a new discourse when the terms of authority and the conventions of discourse are established by the other, in this case by men. In addition to identifying strategies that women might use, the authors recognize the underlying fear that as women assume authority, they threaten current patterns of social responsibility. (KBY)

Althusser, Louis. 1971. "Ideology and Ideological State Apparatuses." In *Lenin and Philosophy,* translated by Ben Brewster, 127–86. New York: Monthly Review Press.

An explanation of the power of dominant ideology to produce subjects who "answer" to the name and tasks assigned to them without critiquing the reigning mode of production. These subjects are simultaneously "hailed" by family, church, school, and state as occupying a particular space and function within the social order. The seamlessness of the various calls for participation reinforces the subject's belief in the inevitability of the continuation of the dominant social system. (SC)

Anzaldúa, Gloria, ed. 1990. *Making Face, Making Soul=Haciendo Caras Creative and Critical Perspectives by Women of Color*. San Francisco: Aunt Lute.

An anthology of fiction and nonfiction which presents the voices of rage, denial, silence, action, and hope of women of color. The book's aim is to "make accessible to others our struggle with all our identities." (GSC)

Aristotle. 1954. *Rhetoric*. In *"Rhetoric" and "On Poetics"* by Aristotle. Translated by W. Rhys Roberts (*Rhetoric*) and Ingram Bywater (*Poetics*). New York: Modern Library.

Treats *ethos* ("the personal character of the speaker") as one of three sources of persuasion (equal in importance to *logos* and *pathos*). Commentators quarrel as to whether by *ethos* Aristotle means the speaker's real character or his created *persona*—what has come to be called the "implied author." (PE)

Bakhtin, M. M. 1981. "Discourse in the Novel." *The Dialogic Imagination: Four Essays*, edited by Michael Holquist and translated by Caryl Emerson, 259–422. Austin: University of Texas Press.

An analysis of the novel as an artistic reorchestration of the dialogized heteroglossia which constitute social language exchange. The essay includes a general theory of language and its relationship to the novel, a series of close readings that show how novelistic strategies such as indirect speech coordinate the multiple social-ideological perspectives of a time and milieu, and a historical overview of novelized genres that shape the European novel. (SC)

Barfield, Owen. 1928. *Poetic Diction: A Study in Meaning*. London: Faber and Gwyer.

Although this book does present a theory of poetic diction, it is equally concerned with theories of poetry, of language, and of knowledge. A difficult book, nevertheless its various musings on the history of language, the origins of metaphor, and the nature of discourse—specific as well as poetic—provide a useful context for any inquiry into the concept of voice. (RF)

Barthes, Roland. 1977. "The Grain of the Voice." In *Image—Music—Text*, translated by Stephen Heath, 179–89. New York: Hill and Wang.

Barthes locates a dimension of music which "escapes the tyranny of meaning" (185), a dimension which is not communicative, nor expressive, nor stylistic, nor interpretive, nor representational. This dimension corresponds to gesture in the body, grain in the voice, metrics in language. Its materiality aligns it with the fluidity of the signifier, and though it cannot be assigned a qualitative essence, it can be apprehended through an image of the body that it makes available to a listener. (SC)

————. 1985. "From Speech to Writing." In *The Grain of Voice*. New York: Hill and Wang.

Barthes writes, "It should be understood after these few observations that what is lost in transcription is quite simply the body—at least this exterior (contingent) body which, in a dialogue, flings itself toward another body, just as fragile (or frantic) as itself, messages that are intellectually empty, the only function of which is in a way to hook the Other (even in the prostitutional sense of the term) and to keep it in its state of partnership." (PE)

Belenky, Mary Field, Blythe McVicker Clinchy, Nancy Rule Goldberger, and Jill Mattuck Tarule. 1986. *Women's Ways of Knowing: The Development of Self, Voice, and Mind*. New York: Basic Books.

Linking metaphors of sight with a male stance toward knowledge acquisition and manipulation, the authors deploy the metaphor of voice to ground a typology of the strategies women use to position themselves as knowers, a typology ranging from silence to the most productive stance, that of integrating the voices of self and others. Voice also grounds the text methodologically: the typology is drawn from the authors' analysis of interviews with 135 women. (SC)

Bialostosky, Don H. 1991. "Liberal Education, Writing, and the Dialogic Self." In *Contending with Words: Composition and Rhetoric in a Postmodern Age*, edited by Patricia Harkin and John Schilb, 11–22. New York: Modern Language Association of America.

A Bakhtin-inspired reflection on demands placed on undergraduate writers, who are too often encouraged to meet disciplinary discourse norms instead of placing their own voices in contestatory proximity to authoritative academic voices. In the writing classroom, where no one disciplinary standard of behavior need reign, the undergraduate can develop "ideological consciousness" through a struggle with conflicting disciplinary perspectives. (SC)

Bolinger, Dwight. 1986. *Intonation and Its Parts: Melody in Spoken English.* Stanford, CA: Stanford University Press.

A distinguished linguist describes in great detail all the ways in which speech has intonation or melody—and the relations to meaning. Somewhat technical, but written in a clear and lively voice of its own. (PE)

Booth, Wayne C. 1982. *The Rhetoric of Fiction.* 2nd ed. Chicago: University of Chicago Press.

Classic work that establishes the "implied author" as an important concept in criticism: everything the author writes in a text—whether written seemingly in his own voice or through a highly ironic persona—and indeed all rhetorical choices—serve to establish an image of this implied author: not the actual author, but the kind of person who would write this work. See also his essay on Bakhtin, "Freedom of Interpretation: Bakhtin and the Challenge of Feminist Criticism," in *Critical Inquiry* (9 [September 1982]: 45–76). (PE)

———. 1988. *The Company We Keep: An Ethics of Fiction.* Berkeley: University of California Press.

Booth talks here about how there is no such thing as a self—yet he wants to talk about mind and spirit. Booth would have to be one of the most humane persons around to deny self. See Booth's earlier works *The Rhetoric of Fiction* (above) and *Critical Understanding* (University of Chicago Press, 1978), in which he is more or less inventor of the concept of the implied author. See also his essay on Bakhtin *Critical Inquiry.* (PE)

Bowden, Betsy. 1987. *Chaucer Aloud: The Varieties of Textual Interpretation.* Philadelphia: University of Pennsylvania Press.

A study of interpretation as voicing, exploring Chaucer's poems in terms of how they are read out loud. (The book comes with a cassette.) Bowden compares readings by noted Chaucer scholars and, among other things, finds more blandness than expected in contested passages and more variation than expected in traditionally uncontested passages. (PE)

Brooke, Robert E. 1991. *Writing and Sense of Self: Identity Negotiation in Writing Workshops.* Urbana: National Council of Teachers of English.

Brooke shows how learning is influenced more by the roles provided by schools than by the content being taught; therefore, negotiating roles, identities, is key to both teaching and learning. He also explains how students find their voices through negotiating identity. (GSC)

Brower, Reuben. 1962. "The Speaking Voice." In *The Fields of Light: An Experiment in Critical Reading*, 19–30. New York: Oxford University Press.

A classic statement of the New Critical principle that any text is really an instance of a "speaker" "addressing" someone. In this chapter Brower devotes loving attention to the myriad ways poets add to the voice resources of written language. He is influenced by Frost's dictum that "A dramatic necessity goes deep into the nature of the sentence. . . . All that can save them [sentences] is the speaking tone of voice somehow entangled in the words and fastened to the page for the ear of the imagination." (PE)

Brown, L. M., and Carol Gilligan. (1990) "Listening for Self and Relational Voices: A Responsive/Resisting Reader's Guide." *Literary Theory as a Guide to Psychological Analysis*, 1–16. M. Franklin, chair.

A paper presented at a symposium conducted at the annual meeting of the American Psychological Association. The authors describe a method for reading and interpreting interviews with people: reading the transcripts four times, each time listening for a different voice—as a way to see the multivocal nature of people's experience—e.g., they listen for "care" and then for "justice" in the development of moral judgment. (PE)

Brownmiller, Susan. 1984. "Voice." In *Femininity*, 103–27. New York: Fawcett/Columbine.

Although noting the range of scientific study on the biology of voice, Brownmiller argues that sexual differentiation in voice is socially conditioned: Woman the Communicator has had her capacity to speak, acquire, and transmit knowledge squelched, hindered, restricted, and scoffed at in every age, in the name of "the feminine ideal." Final sections of the essay detail the characteristics of "speaking in feminine" and "writing in feminine." (LJ)

Buley-Meissner, Mary Louise. 1991. "Rhetorics of the Self." In *Balancing Acts: Essays on the Teaching of Writing in Honor of William F. Irmscher*, edited by Virginia Chappell, Mary Louis Buley-Meissner, and Chris Anderson, 29–53. Carbondale: Southern Illinois University Press.

How do students negotiate the difference between the self writing and the self being written? Students' selves often try to reflect either a transparent self through which the reader knows the author, or an opaque self which knows only what the reader will find acceptable. For Buley-Meissner, knowledges are similar processes, too complex to be accounted for by social construction theories of discourse and stifled by a mere introduction to academic discourse. (PG)

Chang, Hui-Ching. 1992. "From Words to Communication: Some Philosophical Implications for Chinese Interpersonal Communication." Paper presented to the Speech Communication Association. Chicago, Illinois. October.

This essay begins with a clear survey of three of the most fundamental philosophies contributing to the development of East Asian voice: Confucianism, Taoism, and Buddhism. In each case, Chang identifies the propositions and principles that characterize the philosophy and discusses their implications for understanding Chinese communication practices. Based on the summary of philosophical principles, the second part of the essay describes several features of Chinese cultural character, including its spirit of humanism, ethical consciousness, emphasis on the integration of theory and practice, and its belief in the unity of humanity with the rest of the universe. (GG)

Coles, William E., Jr. 1978. *The Plural I: The Teaching of Writing*. New York: Holt, Rinehart & Winston.

According to Coles, we make ourselves with voices. (For help in glossing, see Joseph Harris 1987.) A novelistic account of a writing course in which the goal is to help students achieve a style and voice that is "theirs," but which fights the idea that we have an essence of static self and that "own style" is a picture of it. Rather, Coles contends, it is gradually forged, flexible, but still one's own, resistant. (PE)

Crismore, Avon. 1989. *Talking with Readers: Metadiscourse as Rhetorical Act*. New York: Peter Lang.

Crismore shows how metadiscourse is almost always a heightening of voice—more direct address from writer to reader. (Metadiscourse: discourse about the discourse itself rather than about the topic, e.g., "In my third paragraph" or "In conclusion" or "Nevertheless".) Lots of analysis of textbook prose and studies of how students seem to pay better attention and remember more when there is more metadiscourse. (PE)

Dasenbrook, Reed Way. 1988. "Becoming Aware of the Myth of Presence." *Journal of Advanced Composition* 8: 1–11.

Poststructuralist critique which sees an emphasis on voice as an example of logocentrism, "the privileging of the *logos* of spoken word over the written word" (1). Dasenbrook feels students operate too unthink-

ties of speech and writing and focus more on the presence/absence distinction. (PE)

Di Mare, Leslie. 1990. "*Ma* and Japan." *Southern Communication Journal* 55: 319–28.

This essay focuses on the Japanese concept of *ma*, which, according to Di Mare, refers to a natural and necessary pause in the progress of events. It emphasizes the interval between things and is used to account for why Japanese have greater tolerance for conversational silence, empty space in the visual arts, extended periods of time required for business transactions, and even the lack of extensive decoration in Japanese homes. As such, acting on the concept of *ma* appears to be a major contributor to the development of a distinctively Japanese voice. (GG)

Doi, L. Takeo. 1973. "The Japanese Patterns of Communication and the Concept of *Amæ*." *Quarterly Journal of Speech* 59: 180–85.

Doi claims that the concept of *amæ* is an important key to understanding the distinctive nature of Japanese culture (and therefore voice). Described as a sense of "sweet dependency"—such as a child feels for a parent—*amæ* forms the center of a large number of other concepts that emphasize and institutionalize the notion of mutual dependence among people. With its emphasis on *amæ*, Japanese culture (and especially its communication patterns) differs in numerous ways from Western cultures, which tend to emphasize the role of the independent individual. (GG)

Donaghue, Denis. 1984. *Ferocious Alphabets.* New York: Columbia University Press.

Donaghue distinguishes two opposing ways or styles of reading: reading where you favor hearing, voice, and presence ("epireading") and reading where you favor sight, distance, and coolness ("graphireading"). He works hard at doing justice to both, but clearly his heart is in his ear. It is a witty, learned, and allusive book that examines the prose and the methods of a more than a dozen central literary figures of this century (e.g., Burke, Poulet, de Man, Derrida). Donaghue pursues the same issues in his "The Question of Voice." (PE)

Elbow, Peter. 1985. "The Shifting Relationships between Speech and Writing." *Conference on College Composition and Communication* 36.2 (October): 283–383.

From the conclusion: "I have argued three contrary claims: writing is essentially unlike speech because it is indelible; writing is essentially unlike speech because it is ephemeral; and writing is essentially like speech. My goal is to stop people from talking so much about the inherent nature of speech and writing and start them talking more about the different ways we can use them. In particular I seek to celebrate the flexibility of writing as a medium." (PE)

————. 1989. "The Pleasures of Voices in the Literary Essay: Explorations in the Prose of Gretel Ehrlich and Richard Selzer." In *Literary Nonfiction: Theory, Criticism, Pedagogy,* edited by Chris Anderson, 211–34. Carbondale: Southern Illinois University Press.

Elbow argues that voice is a complex term when applied to writing. He proposes three senses: audible voice (text which we hear), dramatic voice (the implied author or character), and "one's own voice" (a connection with the actual writer). This essay is Elbow's attempt to pay better attention to the misgivings and disputes about voice in literary, critical, and composition theory—that is, to complicate his account of voice in two chapters devoted to the subject in *Writing with Power* (Oxford University Press, 1981) where he distinguished between "voice" and "real voice"—the latter transcending personal or sincere voice. In these two chapters he argues that teaching for voice in writing can be a particularly direct way to help students get more power and command in writing. (PE)

Eliot, T. S. 1957. "Three Voices of Poetry." In *On Poetry and Poets*, 89–102. London: Faber & Faber.

Eliot asserts that "The first voice is the voice of the poet talking to himself—or to nobody. The second is the voice of the poet addressing an audience, whether large or small. The third is the voice of the poet when he attempts to create a dramatic character. . . . In every poem, from the private meditation to the epic or the drama, there is more than one voice to be heard. If the author never spoke to himself, the result would not be poetry, though it might be magnificent rhetoric. . . . But if the poem were exclusively for the author, it would be a poem in a private and unknown language. . . . And in all poetic drama, I am inclined to believe that all three voices are audible." (PE)

Ellsworth, Elizabeth. 1989. "Why Doesn't This Feel Empowering? Working through the Repressive Myths of Critical Pedagogy." *Harvard Educational Review* 59.3 (August): 297–323.

A critique of the "voice as empowerment" agenda often advocated by Henry Giroux. Ellsworth describes her experience teaching an anti-racist course and argues—from an explicitly political, feminist point of view—that the "critical pedagogy" of empowering voice gives rise to repressive myths. (PE)

Emerson, Caryl. 1983. "The Outer Word and Inner Speech: Bakhtin, Vygotsky, and the Internalization of Language." *Critical Inquiry* 10 (December): 245–64.

Extended, scholarly exploration of language and consciousness from someone interested not only in the two figures of the title but also in Foucault, Saussure, Freud, Lacan. The focus is on how outer word becomes inner speech; the theme is dialogue. A full, rich, clear, learned essay. (PE)

Enos, Theresa. 1992. "Voice as Echo of Delivery, *Ethos* as Transforming Process." In *Composition in Context: Essays in Honor of Donald C. Stewart*, edited by W. Ross Winterowd and Vincent Gillespie, 180–95. Carbondale: Southern Illinois University Press.

Enos argues that voice is central to rhetoric, that *ethos* emerges from voice and not vice-versa; that actual delivery or the speaking of one's words helps create the real self that is in or behind a text. (PE)

Faigley, Lester. 1989. "Judging Writing, Judging Selves." *College Composition and Communication* 40.4 (December): 395–412.

Faigley is troubled by how often writing teachers seem "interested in *who* they want their students to be [rather than] in *what* they want their students to write" (396). He believes that all judgments as to who the person is behind the text are completely suspect—since there is nothing but language, a shifting slippery medium, by which to make these judgments. (PE)

Finke, Laurie. 1993. "Knowledge as Bait: Feminism, Voice, and the Pedagogical Unconscious." *College English* 55.1(January): 7–27.

Uses Lacanian psychoanalytic theory to reveal the problems and potential of examining more closely what is meant by voice in feminist pedagogy. (LJ)

Genette, Gérard. 1980. *Narrative Discourse: An Essay in Method.* Translated by Jane E. Lewin. Ithaca: Cornell University Press.

Genette presents a systematic theory of narrative using Proust's *Remembrance of Things Past* as his model. His section on voice deals with the relationship between the speaker and the narrating instance. Because Proust is his model, he focuses on temporality. He asserts that "person," (first, third, and the like) are fictions, since all narration must be in first person, ultimately. A very good source of definitions, except for his definition of voice. (PG)

Gergen, Kenneth J. 1991. *The Saturated Self: Dilemmas of Identity in Contemporary Life.* New York: HarperCollins.

This book examines the ways in which traditional assumptions about the self have been challenged by changing concepts of truth posed by postmodernist thought. Gergen asserts that rapid technological changes have radically altered our exposure to one another, resulting in a state of "social saturation." Coherence has vanished, and relativity reigns. Gergen argues that beneath the apparent pessimism of this saturated state lies the potential for hope by "playing out the positive potentials of this postmodern erasure of the self." Gergen's study provides a thorough and accessible analysis of the problem of self in postmodern times. (RF)

Gibson, Walker. 1966. *Tough, Sweet, and Stuffy: An Essay on Modern American Prose Styles.* Bloomington: Indiana University Press.

He sees these three styles as central in American culture: the "tough guy" voice (as in Hemingway); the "sweet talker" seductive voice (as in advertising—but not only that); and the stuffy impersonal voice (as in academic writing and some journalism). Gibson says that he can describe the voice of any piece of prose by looking at the mix of these three features—by a kind of triangulation. Enormously sophisticated and elegant. (PE)

―――. 1969. *Persona: A Style Study for Readers and Writers.* New York: Random House.

A textbook application (and simplication) of the distinctions that Gibson makes in *Tough, Sweet, and Stuffy* (see above). Beginning with a basic contrast between "talker style" (informal, "loose, idiomatic") and "writer style" (formal, "traditionally bookish"), Gibson shows how an awareness of the voices created by different lexical and syntactic choices can be used in reading and writing a variety of both fictional and nonfictional prose. (CHK)

Gillam, Alice. 1994 [forthcoming]. *Voices from the Center: Peer Tutoring in Theory and Practice.* New York: Oxford University Press.

A history and evaluation of current writing center practices. Drawing from the work of Derrida and Elbow, Gillam stresses the human tendency to trust the human voice; the writing center is the locus of the "talking cure" for writing challenges. It is also a place where voice is fostered in student writing. (PG)

Gilligan, Carol. 1990. "Joining the Resistance: Psychology, Politics, Girls, and Women." *Michigan Quarterly Review* 29.4 (Fall): 501–36.

Describes longitudinal research on a group of girls moving through adolescence. Gilligan discovers a strong, confident, gutsy voice at the onset of adolescence (not just "voice" as confidence about one's opinions but literal, physical sounding voice)—and a hesitant, breathy, unconfident voice as the girls get older. She hypothesizes a story of resistance going underground and becoming unavailable. (PE)

Giroux, Henry A. 1983. *Theory and Resistance in Education: A Pedagogy for the Opposition.* New York: Bergin & Garvey.

This is a learned but reasonably accessible argument for a pedagogy of resistance. Examining a rich variety of theories of resistance, Giroux offers critiques of most with the intent of finding a workable theory grounded in the concrete realities of the oppressed and in a satisfactory concept of human agency. He believes teachers have a crucial but necessarily limited role to play in the creation of an equitable world. Emancipation against the forces of domination is possible, asserts Giroux, but radical pedagogy needs "a discourse that illuminates the ideological and material conditions necessary to promote critical modes of schooling and alternative modes of education for the working class and other groups that bear the brunt of political and economic oppression." Giroux's writings are essential reading for teachers seeking to understand the political pressures and potentialities of education. (RF)

Gubar, Susan. 1985. "'The Blank Page' and the Issues of Female Creativity." In *The New Feminist Criticism: Essays on Women, Literature and Theory,* edited by Elaine Showalter, 292–313. New York: Pantheon.

An analysis of how British and American women writers from the late nineteenth century to the present have confronted and reconfigured the metaphor of woman as the page to be written on or the object to be written of. Tracing metaphors of blood that attend these writers' descriptions of coming to voice, Gubar claims that to women poets and fiction writers, "the creation of female art feels like the destruction of the female body" (302). (SC)

Hall, Donald. 1978. "Goatfoot, Milktongue, Twinbird: The Psychic Origins of Poetic Form." In *Goatfoot, Milktongue, Twinbird: Interviews, Essays, and Notes on Poetry, 1970–76*, edited by Donald Hall, 117–19. *Poets on Poetry* Series. Ann Arbor: University of Michigan Press.

Hall examines voice in a poetic or "vatic" context and links voice with "the sensual body of the poem," a sensuality separate from message or meaning. This sensual body originates in infantile pleasures of orality (Milktongue), movement (Goatfoot), and resolution of contradictions (Twinbird). This essay illustrates a radical form of expressionism, locating poetic voice in the preverbal urges of the human psyche. See also Hall's "The Vatic Voice" in the same collection. (RF)

Hancock, Emily. 1989. *The Girl Within*. New York: Ballantine.

Working from the epistomelogical stance articulated by Carol Gilligan, Hancock identifies what she considers a pattern of successful women. Perceiving themselves as androgynous until the pre-teen years, girls think they can compete evenly with boys—until upon entering puberty, they "hear" otherwise. In order to be healthy and successful, women thus have to carry forward with them this pre-adolescent girl "within," or—more likely—recover that girl as an adult, usually in the context of a crisis. Although the book observes the conventions of the popular press and works from a too-small and tidy sample, the thesis is powerful in locating a possible source of woman's voice. (KBY)

Hanson, Melanie Sarra. 1986. *Developmental Concepts of Voice in Case Studies of College Students: The Owned Voice and Authoring*. Ann Arbor, Michigan: University Microfilms International.

By looking at the intellectual and ego development of college students, Hanson construes a five-stage developmental construction of voice which culminates not in "finding one's own voice," but in owning one's voice. (GSC)

Harris, Joseph. 1987. "The Plural Text/The Plural Self: Roland Barthes and William Coles." *College English* 49.2 (February): 158–70.

Writing from a social constructionist stance, Harris shows that it's not a question of self/no self or individuality/no individuality, but of how people create an individual self and style out of language: "how to forge something new out of a language never wholly our own, that always comes to us secondhand" (164). Clear, sophisticated, and helpful by cutting through stereotyped positions. (PE)

Harris, Maria. 1988. *Women and Teaching: Themes for a Spirituality of Teaching.* New York: Paulist Press.

Harris outlines a "spirituality of pedagogy" characterized by five generative themes: silence, remembering, ritual mourning, artistry, and birthing. Of particular interest to scholars interested in voice is Harris's transformative and plural conception of silences: silence in the curriculum, responses to silence, and silence as healing power. (KBY)

Havelock, Eric. 1986. *The Muse Learns to Write: Reflections on Orality and Literacy from Antiquity to the Present.* New Haven: Yale University Press.

A brief, lucid summary written at the end of his career of Havelock's explorations of the transition from orality to literacy in Greece. He argues that this transition carried with it a change in thinking—and in particular made logic and abstract thinking more possible. (He stresses, by the way, how the Phoenician-Greek alphabet made possible the rendering of the sound of syllables—unlike many other alphabets.) However, in "Orality, Literacy, and Star Wars" (*Written Communication* 3 [1986]: 411–20), he argues eloquently for the value of orality in present-day schooling or literacy training in general, and in the teaching of writing in particular. (PE)

Hawkes, John. 1970. "The Voice Project: An Idea for Innovation in the Teaching of Writing." In *Writers as Teachers: Teachers as Writers*, 89–144. New York: Holt, Rinehart & Winston.

Hawkes describes an extended and ambitious project in the first-year writing course at Stanford in the late 1960s to teach writing by "attempting to make the word 'voice' meaningful and useful for the student." Lots of experimental practices centering on reading out loud and speaking into and listening to tapes. The group was trying to heighten students' sensitivity to language, both literary and everyday, and to "see behavior, physical gesture, and vocal gesture as forms of expression related to verbal language." Hawkes described the project at greater length in "Voice Project: Final Report." (Stanford University, 1967, ERIC ED 018 442.) (PE)

Hazlitt, William. 1845 [1821/22]. "The Familiar Style." In *Table Talk: Opinions on Books, Men, and Things.* New York: Wiley and Putnam.

In this classic essay, Hazlitt defines, defends, and explains how "to write a genuine, familiar or truly English style," which is "to write as any one would speak in common conversation, who had a thorough command and choice of words, or who could discourse with ease, force, and perspicuity, setting aside pedantic and oratorical flourishes." Though Hazlitt's appeal to "common conversation" might seem to legislate a colloquial, informal essayistic voice, he goes out of his way to make clear that the familiar style does not give one "liberty to gabble on at a venture without emphasis or discretion, or to resort to vulgar dialect. . . . You must steer a middle course. You are tied down to a given and appropriate articulation, which is determined by the habitual associations between sense and sound. . . ." (CHK)

Hickey, Dona J. 1993. *Developing a Written Voice*. Mountain View, CA: Mayfield.

In this textbook, which reflects the influence of Walker Gibson (see above), Hickey pays special attention to syntax—"It all happens at the sentence level." Illustrating her discussion with both professional and student writing, she devotes extensive space to showing how various grammatical and rhetorical structures, as well as tropes and schemes and lexical choices, can be used to create a range or mix of different voices on "the formality ladder," ranging from "high" to "high-middle," "middle," "low-middle," or "low." (CHK)

Hoddeson, David. 1981. "The Reviser's Voices." *Journal of Basic Writing* 3.3 (Fall/Winter): 91–108.

In a rich and suggestive essay about "the semiotics of spoken and written codes," Hoddeson argues that speech has more semiotic channels than writing; that the problem with basic writing is often that it is too close to the qualities of speech; yet that basic writers will benefit from learning to use voice in a more conscious and sophisticated way. Hodeson claims that "the ability to revise language from the flow of inner and outer voices to the written page" is central to "the entire process of writing." (PE)

hooks, bell. 1989. *Talking Back: Thinking Feminist, Thinking Black*. Boston: South End Press.

An autobiographical account of how bell hooks learned to "talk back," to find her voice. (GSC)

Ihde, Don. 1976. *Listening and Voice: A Phenomenology of Sound*. Athens, OH: Ohio University Press.

A personal and autobiographical, yet densely philosophical, exploration of just what the title says. Here are some apposite phrases from a review in *Human Studies* (quoted as cover blurb): "articulates the claim of sound—against the hegemony of visualism in the history of Western thought"; "patient phenomenological description and reflection on the character of the auditory dimension in perception, hearing, and auditory imagination in vocal utterance." (PE)

Jaynes, Julian. 1976. *The Origins of Consciousness in the Breakdown of the Bicameral Mind.* Boston: Houghton-Mifflin.

Jaynes argues a radically new way to think about human consciousness. He believes that ancient civilizations from Mesopotamia to Peru had no consciousness as we normally construe that term. Instead, as a result of right hemispheric dominance, they heard "voices," auditory hallucinations, which they believed to be gods instructing them about what to do. Humans lost this bicameral brain roughly 3,000 years ago, but it still manifests itself residually in schizophrenia, religious ecstacy, and poetic inspiration (cf. Hall's essay on the vatic voice, above). This is a challenging and groundbreaking source for scholars interested in voice. (RF)

Jensen, J. Vernon. 1987. "Rhetoric of East Asia—A Bibliography." *Rhetoric Society Quarterly* 17: 213–31.

Presents an extensive bibliography of articles related to understanding East Asian communication and culture. Although the bibliography contains articles on rhetoric in the narrow sense, it ranges broadly to include references that would be helpful in understanding the background of East Asian communication in all of its aspects. In addition to a section on East Asia in general, the bibliography includes specific sections on Japan, Korea, China, Vietnam, Laos, Indonesia, Malaysia and Singapore, Thailand, Burma (Myamar), and the South Pacific. (GG)

Johnson, Barbara. 1986. "Metaphor, Metonymy, and Voice in Zora Neale Hurston's *Their Eyes Were Watching God.*" In *Textual Analysis: Some Readers Reading,* edited by Mary Ann Caws, 232–44. New York: Modern Language Association of America.

A deconstructive critic celebrates the relationship of voice to self-division: "The sign of an authentic voice is thus not self-identity but self-difference." Johnson starts out using "authentic" in question marks and then drops them. Johnson's essay celebrates writing that doesn't mix the inside and outside—that renders incompatible forces. (PE)

Johnson, Nan. 1984. "Ethos and the Aims of Rhetoric." In *Essays on Classical Rhetoric and Modern Discourse,* edited by Robert J. Connors, Lisa Ede, and Andrea A. Lunsford, 198–214. Carbondale: Southern Illinois University Press.

Identifies two major traditions in classical rhetoric: Plato and Quintilian (and others), who treat *ethos* as the real character of the rhetor; and Aristotle and Cicero (and others), who treat *ethos* as something the rhetor can adopt or achieve or even pretend. Learned, elegant, clear; an Olympian view. (PE)

Joos, Martin. 1962. *The Five Clocks*. New York: Harcourt, Brace and Company.

A short, lively, classic study of five ranges of register that characterize speech and writing in English—from "frozen" to "intimate." (PE)

Jordan, June. 1985. "Nobody Mean More to Me than You: And the Future Life of Willie Jordan." In *On Call: Political Essays*, 123–39. *Boston: South End Press.*

An eloquent account of a course in which Jordan taught Black English. She taught the principles—linguistic, psychological, and ideological—and taught students to translate into and out of Black English. Jordan explores many complex effects of this process on various black college students. (PE)

Juhl, P. D. 1980. *Interpretation: An Essay in the Philosophy of Literary Criticism*. Princeton, NJ: Princeton University Press.

Juhl's work demonstrates that a philosopher can make a trenchant and sophisticated case against the idea of intentional fallacy—that is, for the idea that we can indeed find the writer's actual intention in the text. (PE)

Katz, Steven. 1994 [in press]. *The Epistemic Music of Rhetoric: The Temporal Dimension of Reader Response and Writing*. Carbondale: Southern Illinois University Press.

An extended, subtle, learned, and remarkable argument that one fears to summarize—but wants to share. Katz argues that reader-response criticism is an attempt to get away from the lurking positivism ("right answers") in most modern criticism, especially New Criticism. However reader-response criticism itself carries implicit positivism in its premises—especially in its emphasis on interpretation and its assumption of a visual-logical paradigm of knowing. As a remedy for this problem, Katz turns to the Sophists (insisting that this is a next step forward) for their emphasis on performance and their assumption of an oral-hearing paradigm of knowing. This study contains powerful explorations of visual and oral/aural modalities and the phenomenology of music. (PE)

Kinkaid, D. Lawrence, ed. 1987. *Communication Theory: Eastern and Western Perspectives*. San Diego: Academic Press.

Although this collection of articles also includes essays on Western communication theory, the thirteen essays of part I provide an excellent introduction to Asian communication and voice. After an introductory essay drawing together the findings in the subsequent essays, part I contains three essays on Chinese philosophy, narrative, and political communication; three on Korean philosophy and the history of Confucianism in Korea; three on the characteristics of Japanese communication, indirect speech acts, and communication within Japanese business organizations; and three on communication in India. (GG)

Klaus, Carl H. 1990. "Montaigne on His Essays: Toward a Poetics of Self." *The Iowa Review* 20: 1–23.

In this analysis of Montaigne's wide-ranging reflections on his writing, which appear in 27 of his 107 essays, Montaigne is shown to have been painstakingly self-conscious about his style and voice, striving in particular to be "natural," "simple," "ordinary," "plain," or "free"—to "speak to my paper as I speak to the first man I meet"—in order to create "a style attuned to the freedom of his mind." Yet he is also shown to have been increasingly aware that "his elaborately contrived attempts at 'free writing' . . . were not so free and natural as they might seem" and, therefore, that he was also conscious of a problematic and unstable relationship between his voice and himself. (CHK)

Kneale, J. Douglas. 1986. "Wordsworth's Images of Language: Voice and Letter in *The Prelude*." *PMLA* 101.3 (May): 351–61.

Kneale asserts that writing, for Wordsworth, is the consummation of voice; he sought a writing as immediate as breath—"men speaking to men." Yet this impulse competes with a more durable "insistence of the letter." The poem is intersection of voice and letter. (PE)

Kristeva, Julia. 1986. "The System and the Speaking Subject." In *The Kristeva Reader*, edited by Toril Moi, 24–33. New York: Columbia University Press.

A call for a theory of meaning that combines the formalization techniques of structural linguistics with a theory of the speaking subject, always traversed by psychic-physiological processes and social-cultural constraints. Such a subject, unlike the Western transcendental unified subject, engenders practices that renew social exchange by producing meaning constituted through its reception by addressees, and not through a finalized system of semiotics that cannot apprehend "play, pleasure, or desire" (26). (SC)

Lanser, Susan Sniader. 1992. *Fictions of Authority: Women Writers and Narrative Voice.* Ithaca: Cornell University Press.

Lanser's study explores both the "incompatible tendencies" and "fruitful counterpoints" of the concepts of voice used by feminist and narrative theorists. Her hypothesis, linking social identity and narrative form, is that "female voice . . . is a site of ideological tension made visible in textual practices." Includes sections on authorial, personal, and communal voice, in British, French, and U.S. fiction from the eighteenth to twentieth centuries. See especially the initial essay, "Toward a Feminist Poetics of Narrative Voice." (LJ)

Lerman, Claire L. 1983. "Dominant Discourse: The Institutional Voice and Control of Topic." In *Language, Image, and Media,* edited by Howard Davis and Paul Walton, 75–103. New York: St. Martin's.

Lerman's premise is that institutions are always trying to maintain power; the treatment of voice becomes a covert way of doing it. (PE)

Lewis, Magda, and Roger Simon. 1986. "A Discourse Not Intended for Her: Learning and Teaching within Patriarchy." *Harvard Educational Review,* 56.4 (November): 457–72.

A dual account, by a male professor and a female student, of how women were silenced in a graduate seminar—one focused on language and power and taught by the male author—and on how the women struggled to create a space for themselves. The authors conclude at the outset that they could not write in a single voice, and they argue in the end for "a pedagogical project that allows a polyphony of voices," though they were unable to effect this polyphony themselves. A provocative essay that speaks to its purpose both unintentionally and consciously. (KBY)

Linklater, Kristin. 1976. *Freeing the Natural Voice.* New York: Drama Book Specialists.

A trainer of actors gives an extensive and sophisticated program of exercises to help develop the physical voice. She argues that this involves getting not only the body behind the words but also harnessing the self. (PE)

Mairs, Nancy. 1990. "Carnal Acts." In *Carnal Acts,* 81–96. New York: HarperCollins.

In this confessionally detailed essay, occasioned by an invitation to deliver a talk "on how you cope with your MS disability, and also on how you discovered your voice as a writer," Mairs challenges the "Western tradition of distinguishing the body from the mind and/or the soul," in order to make a case for the "interdependent" relationship between her physical "disability" and her "voice." In an elaborately developed metaphor that extends throughout the essay, Mairs conceives of the relationship as being so intimate as to constitute an "erotic connection." Thus she refers to both speaking and writing as "carnal acts," profoundly erotic in the root sense of the impulse to join or connect—voice with body, speaker/writer with listener/reader, the "I" with the "other." (CHK)

Mellix, Barbara. 1989. "From Outside, In." In *Essays on the Essay,* edited by Alexander J. Butrym, 43–52. Athens, GA: University of Georgia Press.

In this personal account, Mellix tells not only about how she "grew up speaking what I considered two distinctly different languages—Black English and standard English," but also about how that sense of "doubleness" became "something menacing, a built-in enemy" when she found herself "face to face with the demands of academic writing . . . Whenever I turned inward for salvation, the balm so available during my childhood, I found instead this new fragmentation which spoke to me in many voices. It was the voice of my desire to prosper, but at the same time it spoke of what I had relinquished and could not regain: a safe way of being, a state of powerlessness which exempted me from responsibility for who I was and might be." (CHK)

Moffett, James. 1981. "Writing, Inner Speech, and Meditation." In *Coming On Center,* 133–81. Upper Montclair, NJ: Boynton/Cook.

Moffett explores the uses of meditation to escape obsessive, repetitive inner speech and instead finds creativity and surprise in the composing process. See also his "Liberating Inner Speech" (*College Composition and Communication* 36.2 [October 1985]: 304–8) for a short, direct, and practical introduction to the other longer, more complex essay. (PE)

Morson, Gary Saul, ed. 1986. *Bakhtin: Essays and Dialogues on His Work.* Chicago: University of Chicago Press.

A compilation of essays that appeared originally in *Critical Inquiry,* as well as excerpts from Bakhtin's essay "The Problem of Speech Genres." Critics concur that Bakhtin rejects a synchronic linguistics of "langue" and instead argues for a theory of the unfinalizable, temporal utterance as an instrument for understanding situated discourse in general and literature in particular. (SC)

Olson, Charles. 1966. "Projective Verse." In *Selected Writings*, edited by Robert Creeley, 15–26. New York: New Directions.

Olson pushes connections between the poetic line in projective verse and the human voice, and calls for verse which honors the "full relevance of human voice. The beginning and the end [of verse] is breath, voice in its largest sense." (LJ)

Ong, Walter J. 1967 *Presence of the Word: Some Prolegomena for Cultural and Religious History.* New Haven, CT: Yale University Press.

———. 1982. *Orality and Literacy: The Technologizing of the Word.* New York: Methuen.

Both studies are extended explorations of the profound effects on mentality and even on perception itself of orality and literacy (and also print literacy and "secondary orality"). Ong is eloquent on the differences in our relationship to language and to the world depending on our relation to literacy. Much of the rest of his prolific output explores these issues. (PE)

Parenti, Michael. 1986. *Inventing Reality: The Politics of the Media.* New York: St. Martin's.

Parenti likens the voices in the news to "many voices, one chorus" as he examines what he sees as the control of the news by corporations. He maintains that any news that challenges the mainstream ideology— that is, the ideology that endorses corporate interests—is suppressed. He also notes that the press itself is a large corporation and therefore protects its own interests by following and promoting this ideology. (MM)

Park, Clara Clairborne. 1989. "Talking Back to the Speaker." *Hudson Review* 41: 21–44.

Park, in a piece of detective work, traces the history of the practice in criticism of insisting that it is a "speaker's voice in the text and not the author's voice." She notes that Brooks and Warren never made it as rigid a doctrine as their followers came to do. Park's main point pertains especially to teaching: "Our gain in subtlety [of reading] is a loss in human community if we succeed in detaching the utterance from the uttering tongue and mind and heart" (42). A witty, sophisticated, and passionate essay. (PE)

Randall, Margaret. 1991. "Reclaiming Voices: Notes on a New Female Practice in Journalism." In *Walking to the Edge: Essays of Resistance,* 67–78. Boston: South End Press.

An essay on the role of feminism in understanding new ways of hearing women's voices in *testimonio* and oral history: "it has created a body of voice and image, a new resource literature—much of it from the so-called Third World and much of it from and about women." (LJ)

Rich, Adrienne. 1979a. "When We Dead Awaken: Writing as Re-Vision." In *On Lies, Secrets, and Silence: Selected Prose 1966–1978,* 33–49. New York: W. W. Norton.

A germinal essay on how women must negotiate within patriarchal culture for voice, for freedom from "the specter of . . . male judgment," and for models of what they will write and how they will speak. (LJ)

————. 1979b. "Women and Honor: Some Notes on Lying." In *On Lies, Secrets, and Silence: Selected Prose 1966-1978,* 185–94. New York: W. W. Norton.

Beginning with "the terrible negative power of the lie," this essay explores the ways using one's voice or withholding one's voice may be lying, and the ways women are taught to lie, especially among themselves. (LJ)

Rodriguez, Richard. 1981. *Hunger of Memory: The Education of Richard Rodriguez.* Boston: D. Godine.

Well-known narrative about the growing up of a Hispanic "scholarship boy" whose immersion into mainstream culture necessitated his emotional departure from his family, his home, his native voice. Rodriguez also argues, on the basis of his experience, against bilingual education. (KBY)

Sacks, Oliver. 1985. "The President's Speech." In *The Man Who Mistook His Wife for a Hat: And Other Clinical Tales,* 76–80. New York: Summit Books.

A medical clinician describes the amusement of patients in the aphasic ward listening to a U.S. president's speech. Being unable to understand the propositional content of speech, "they have an infallible ear for every vocal nuance, the tone, the rhythm, the cadences, the music, the subtlest modulations, inflections, intonations, which can give—or remove—verisimilitude to or from a man's voice. In this, then, lies their power of understanding—understanding without words what is authentic or inauthentic." (PE)

———. 1990. *Seeing Voices: A Journey into the World of the Deaf.* New York: Harper Perennial.

This book chronicles the history of the deaf as they struggle for acceptance in a world of sound. Sacks examines the importance and extraordinary nature of American Sign Language and the impact ASL has had on the lives of the deaf *and* the hearing. Finally, he tells the story of Gallaudet University, the only university for the deaf in the U.S., where protests were raised when a hearing person was nominated as president. With their "collective voices," the students successfully urged trustees to withdraw the nominee. He shows us the "soundless" world of the deaf who nevertheless have the means to make their voices heard. (DB)

Sanders, Scott Russell. 1991. "The Singular First Person." In *Secrets of the Universe: Scenes from the Journey Home,* 187–204. New York: Beacon.

As his title suggests, Sanders conceives of the personal essay as "a haven for the private, idiosyncratic voice in an era of anonymous babble." Correspondingly, Sanders maintains that "it is the *singularity* of the first person—its warts and crotchets and turns of voice—that lures many of us into reading essays, and that lingers with us after we finish." Given this special emphasis on voice in the personal essay, Sanders maintains that the essayist "had better speak from a region pretty close to the heart or the reader will detect the wind of phoniness whistling through your hollow phrases." Yet he also acknowledges that "the first-person singular is too narrow a gate for the whole writer to squeeze through. What we meet on the page is not the flesh and blood author, but a simulacrum, a character who wears the label 'I'." (CHK)

Schultz, John. 1977. "The Story Workshop Method: Writing from Start to Finish." *College English* 39.4 (December): 411–36.

Describes an experimental, experiential method of teaching writing developed by Schultz and a few others. "The two essential Story Workshop terms are *seeing* and *voice.*" Central activities are exercises in reading and speaking out loud—one's own words and those of published writers; and exercises in visualizing and seeing. (Also exercises in memory.) One of the few groups of teachers of writing who make a central practice of publishing the student writing—and it is impressively voiced. These teachers insist on making a powerful link between voice and seeing—whereas so many people interested in voice want to downplay seeing for hearing. See also Betty Shiflett's "Story Workshop as a Method of Teaching Writing" (*College English* 35.2 [November

1973]: 141–60) and Schultz's *Writing from Start to Finish: The "Story Workshop" Basic Forms Rhetoric Reader* (Portsmouth, NH: Boynton/Cook-Heinemann, 1982; concise edition, 1990). Additionally, see two videotapes distributed by Boynton/Cook-Heinemann, "The Living Voice Moves" and "Story from First Impulse to Final Draft." (PE)

Shen, Fan. 1989. "The Classroom and the Wider Culture: Identity as a Key to Learning English Composition." *College Composition and Communication* 40.4 (December): 459–66).

An examination of the way the author, as a Chinese communist, had to construct a Western self—and be that self—before he could write in a Western manner. An explanation of the way communism affects the individual's understanding of the word "I," a word with negative connotations in Shen's culture, but one demanded of composition students in the United States. (PG)

Shudson, Michael. 1978. *Discovering the News: A Social History of American Newspapers.* New York: Basic Books.

Shudson links the emergence of news and the changes in news to the changes in the social, political, and economic conditions of this country. He suggests that the modern newspapers arose out of a need to know— a need to be literate—fed by a rising middle class that was increasingly commercial and entrepreneurial. He notes that the ideal of objectivity arose only after World War I, when the separation of facts from opinions and values became part of the popular culture. (MM)

Shweder, Richard, and Robert A. Levine, eds. 1984. *Culture Theory: Essays on Mind, Self, and Emotion.* New York: Cambridge University Press.

Anthropologists and social scientists, even extreme relativists, admitting continuity of sense of self. The book starts with a roundtable discussion that lays out the territory. (PE)

Smith, Paul. 1988. *Discerning the Subject.* Minneapolis: University of Minnesota Press.

This important, though at times difficult, book examines the differences between various concepts of the human subject and of human agency. Smith surveys perspectives on the subject in the humanities and social sciences in order to free the term from limiting definitions. Like Giroux, Smith believes that theory has made the notion of subject too abstract, divorcing it from "political and ethical realities in which human agents actually live." Smith asserts that a different concept of the subject is required if meaningful resistance to dominatory forces is to be made possible. In combination with Giroux, Smith's book provides a thorough introduction to the concepts of subject and resistance. (RF)

Sommers, Nancy. 1992. "Between the Drafts." *College Composition and Communication* 43.1 (February): 3–31.

Sommers describes her own coming to voice: resisting her home voice as spoken by her parents, imitating the voices of her professors, hearing her voice in the voices of her children. She argues that we find our voice "between" drafts as opposed to on them. (KBY)

Stoehr, Taylor. 1968. "Tone and Voice." *College English* 30.2 (November): 150–61.

Stoehr defines tone as "an author's attitude toward his audience" and voice as a "reflection . . . of an author's character." He explores tone and voice through a series of comparisons: Thoreau and Henry Adams; Paine and Jefferson; Clemens and Twain. "Writing is not the same as speaking," Stoehr asserts, "but the whole Anglo-American literary tradition—from Chaucer and Shakespeare to Samuel Johnson and from Wordsworth to Whitman and Twain and James—shows that the greatest writing is always in touch with the human speaking voice." (PE)

Tannen, Deborah. 1983. "Oral and Literate Strategies in Spoken and Written Discourse." In *Literacy for Life: The Demand for Reading and Writing,* edited by Richard W. Bailey and Robin Melanie Fosheim, 79–96. New York: Modern Language Association of America.

A linguist takes a kind of anthropological approach to describe the contrasting linguistic characteristics of spoken and written discourse. Tannen notes briefly at the end that literary writing seems to be an exception to the generalizations she has made: that it has more of the features of orality than most writing. It is this theme, then, that she takes up at length in her book *Talking Voices: Repetition, Dialogue, and Imagery in Conversational Discourse* (Cambridge, MA: Cambridge University Press, 1989). This is an extended "poetics of talk" in which she argues that there are a myriad ways in which "ordinary conversation is made up of linguistic strategies that have been thought quintessentially literary. . . . I call them 'involvement strategies' because, I argue, they reflect and simultaneously create interpersonal involvement." (PE)

———. 1990. *You Just Don't Understand: Women and Men in Conversation.* New York: Ballantine.

Tannen delineates the differences between how men and women communicate among their own gender and across gender. It is Tannen's contention that because women and men grow up with widely divergent views on the purpose and means of communication, conversations between them are often fraught with misunderstanding and frustrations. Filled with anecdotal examples, Tannen shows how men and women use language and cultural differences in an attempt to communicate with each other. (DB)

Taylor, Charles. 1991. "The Dialogical Self." In *The Interpretive Turn: Philosophy, Science, Culture,* edited by David Hiley, James Bohman, and Richard Shusterman, 304–15. Ithaca: Cornell University Press.

Taylor argues against what he calls the "monological self"—one forming its own representations of the world. The "dialogical self" Taylor offers as an alternative provides readers with a compromise between self as pure romantic reflexivity and self as socially constructed. Taylor, influenced by Bakhtin, views self as an ongoing tension between a capacity for resistance against social construction and a necessary collaboration with such forces. See also Taylor's *Sources of the Modern Self: The Making of Modern Identity* (Harvard University Press, 1989) and *The Ethics of Authenticity* (Harvard University Press, 1992). (RF)

Trilling, Lionel. 1972. *Sincerity and Authenticity.* Cambridge, MA: Harvard University Press.

A historical study of the origins of interest in sincerity in the Renaissance and especially in the eighteenth century ("the honest soul"), and similarly for authenticity in the nineteenth and twentieth ("the authentic unconscious") centuries. A learned, allusive work that does justice to the slipperiness of these terms. (PE)

Trimbur, John. 1987. "Beyond Cognition: The Voices in Inner Speech." *Rhetoric Review* 5 (Spring): 211–21.

About the conflict between Piaget-based and Vygotsky-based models of development. The first posits a private self and language moving gradually toward socialization; the second views inner and early speech as being already socialized. Trimbur stresses the Vygotskian idea that inner life is socially constructed; that writing builds in social inner dialogue. (PE)

Tuchman, Gaye. 1978. *Making News: A Study in the Construction of Reality.* New York: The Free Press.

Tuchman's study shows how news is socially constructed; in fact, she takes the position that new forms of news are quite impossible because the act of news gathering depends upon a cultural ideology that prohibits new forms of news and new ways of looking at the search for news. At the same time that news "imposes a frame for defining and constructing social reality," it also "blocks inquiry." The news ideology we have embraced—of which the "objective voice" is one tenet—in fact limits citizens' "access to ideas." (MM)

Warhol, Robyn R. 1986. "Toward a Theory of the Engaging Narrator: Earnest Interventions in Gaskell, Stowe, and Eliot." *PMLA* 101.5 (October): 811–18.

Warhol argues that narrative theory has neglected to describe texts in which the author invites readers to identify the author explicitly with the narrator and the reader with the narratee. She sees a link between this narrative stance and nineteenth-century women writers—hence, perhaps, an issue in gender criticism. (PE)

Welty, Eudora. 1984. "Finding a Voice." In *One Writer's Beginnings*, 77–114. Cambridge, MA: Harvard University Press.

The three chapters of the book are entitled "Listening," "Learning to See," and "Finding a Voice." This final chapter explores the way memories, including the memories of others, form and give substance to creativity. As she begins her publishing career, Welty "finds her voice" when she creates a character who speaks for her, expresses her need to share her art. "In the making of [my] character out of my most inward and most deeply feeling self, I would say I have found my voice in my fiction" (101). (PG)

Wiget, Andrew. 1992. "Identity, Voice, and Authority: Artist-Audience Relations in Native American Literature." *World Literature Today* 66 (2): 258.

Wiget articulates a theory of the relationship among authority, authorship, and audience, focusing specifically on the dual worlds inhabited by Native American writers. He focuses on the ability of the audience to influence what writers can compose, and on "whether it is possible to write as an Indian apart from the Anglo-authored discourse of Indianness." Wiget's conclusion is that Indian writers can write in multiple voices, drawing on the literary resources of both voices and on two "distinct fields of action, of meaning making." (KBY)

Wolfe, Tom. 1973. "Like a Novel." In *The New Journalism*, 10–22. New York: Harper and Row.

In this personal account, Wolfe explains the stylistic and narrative "experimenting in non-fiction" that led him during the early 1960s to reject the "century-old British tradition in which it is understood that the narrator shall assume a calm, cultivated and, in fact, genteel voice." That "pale beige tone" led readers, according to Wolfe, to regard the journalist as having "a pedestrian mind, a phlegmatic spirit, a faded personality." To counter such impressions, Wolfe "would try anything ..." feigning the tones of various characters, shifting "back and forth between points of view continually," getting "into the eye sockets, as it were, of the people in the story," so as to give readers something that they "always had to go to novels and short stories for: namely, the subjective and emotional life of the characters." (CHK)

Wolff, Geoffrey. 1989. "Introduction: An Apprentice." In *The Best American Essays 1989*, xiii-xxxv. New York: Ticknor & Fields.

In this animated and vividly detailed personal account, Wolff chronicles the changing quality of his protean voice, which he describes at first as having been characterized by the "puffed-up gravitas" of his graduate school days at Cambridge University, but which then became "increasingly intimate, almost thrustingly candid," then "willing to lighten up, to giggle, to play the fool," then inspired by the "sassy voices" as well as the "high-voltage, high-pitched, bully great ruckus" of the sixties," and more recently willing to be "less cocksure, I think, more sociable (on the page)." (CHK)

Woolf, Virginia. 1953 [1925]. "The Modern Essay." In *The Common Reader*. New York: Harcourt, Brace, Jovanovich.

In this review essay, occasioned by Ernest Rhys's five-volume collection *Modern English Essays*, Woolf reflects on the changing style and voice of the English essay: "some time in the 'nineties, it must have surprised readers accustomed to exhortation, information, and denunciation to find themselves familiarly addressed by a voice which seemed to belong to a man no larger than themselves. ..." Now once more the conditions have changed, resulting in a personality that "comes to us not with the natural richness of the speaking voice, but strained and thin and full of mannerisms and affectations, like the voice, of a man shouting through a megaphone to a crowd on a windy day." (CHK)

———. 1970 [1942]. "Professions for Women." In *The Death of the Moth and Other Essays*, 235–42. San Diego: Harcourt, Brace, Jovanovich.

About the "need to do battle with a certain phantom," which Woolf calls the "Angel in the House": a personification of the cultural prohibitions and prescriptions about voice which women (particularly women writers) internalize, and which interfere with what they may say and how they may say it. (LJ)

Yum, June Ock. 1988. "The Impact of Confucianism on Interpersonal Relationships and Communication Patterns in East Asia." *Communication Monographs* 55: 374–88.

Surveys the consequences of Confucianism in Korean communication concepts and practices. Yum discusses the Confucian emphasis on the importance of proper social relationships as the basis of society, describes the philosophical concepts that were developed during the over 500 years that Confucianism was the official philosophy of the Korean court and schools, and explores the impact of Confucianism on interpersonal relationship patterns. (GG)

Zweig, Paul. 1983. "A Voice Speaking to No One." In *In Praise of What Persists*, edited by Stephen Berg, 281–89. New York: Harper and Row.

Zweig's autobiographical meditation on voice in his life: about his greater identification with stammering immigrant grandparents who didn't know English than with careful speakers like his father and his teachers; his loss of sense of a Native American voice after living at length in France; about the influence of various literary voices in achieving a voice that felt his own in his writing. See also *Departures* (Harper and Row, 1986), the book he wrote under the awareness of his impending death, in which he continued his autobiographical reflections, which emphasized a tension between his sense of voice as central to identity and his perplexity as to whether he had a center, voice, or identity. (PE)

Index

Editor

Kathleen Blake Yancey is assistant professor of English at the University of North Carolina at Charlotte, where she teaches courses in writing, pedagogy, and writing assessment. Her first collection of essays is *Portfolios in the Writing Classroom: An Introduction.* She initially came to voice by working with graduate students at Purdue and observing that the first-year students were being asked to write not only on several assignments, but in several voices. She was encouraged in this project by several colleagues, among them Michael Spooner and Peter Elbow; by her UNC–Charlotte students, especially those in expository writing; and by David, Genevieve, and Matthew, whose voices also inhabit hers.

Contributors

John A. Albertini, associate professor at the National Technical Institute for the Deaf at the Rochester Institute of Technology, received his doctorate in linguistics from Georgetown University. He has taught ESL to high school students in Iran and to adults in Washington, D.C; since 1976, he has taught writing to deaf students. In 1987, he received a Fulbright to conduct research on the teaching of writing to German deaf students.

Nancy Allen is assistant professor in the English department at Eastern Michigan University, where she teaches graduate and undergraduate courses in written communication. She specializes in professional writing and recently designed the English department's Macintosh classroom for upper-division writing courses. She received her Ph.D. in rhetoric and composition from Purdue University, where her research included a study of the characteristics, such as voice, in collaboratively written documents. An article describing results of this study appeared in a recent issue of the *Technical Communication Quarterly.*

Deborah S. Bosley is assistant professor of English at the University of North Carolina at Charlotte, where she teaches courses in technical communication and composition theory to undergraduates and graduate students. She has published articles in *Technical Communication Quarterly, Technical Communication,* the *ABC Bulletin,* and the *Journal of Business and Technical Communication.* She won an award for "outstanding article" from STC in 1992. In addition to her research in collaboration and gender and technology, she has been a technical communications consultant to such firms as Hoechst Celanese, IBM, and Royal Insurance among others. She is a member of both the NCTE Committee on Instructional Technology and the Committee on Scientific and Technical Communication.

Susan Brown Carlton is assistant professor of English at Pacific Lutheran University, where she teaches composition and critical theory and directs the writing center. Her first published essay appeared in *Writing Theory and Critical Theory,* edited by John Clifford and John Schilb. She makes presentations frequently at conferences of the Conference on College Composition and Communication, Rhetoric Society of America, and the Midwest Modern Language Association. Her research interests include the poetic/rhetoric relation, feminist theory, and contemporary issues in rhetorical invention. In 1992, she was awarded the CCCC's Outstanding Dissertation Award. She currently serves on the CCCC's Outstanding Dissertation Committee.

Tom Carr is a graduate student in anthropology at the University of Colorado at Boulder. His research will focus on early Native American migrations and settlement in North America. He is also a professional photographer, and enjoys synthesizing the communication aspects of various disciplines. His essay in this volume represents his first contribution to a professional publication.

Gail Summerskill Cummins is director of the Writing Center and director of Writing Across the Curriculum at the University of Kentucky. She previously taught at the Maryland Institute's College of Art, and the Friends Middle School, both in Baltimore. She has given papers at the Penn State Conference on Rhetoric and Composition and the Institute for Writing and Thinking at Bard College. As a member of the Maryland Writing Project and the Baltimore Area Consortium for Writing Across the Curriculum (BACWAC), she has helped coordinate writing programs for a variety of institutions and organizations. A published poet, her works are found in several journals.

Peter Elbow is professor of English at the University of Massachusetts at Amherst. He has taught at M.I.T., Franconia College, Evergreen State College, and SUNY at Stony Brook, where for five years he directed the writing program. He is author of *Oppositions in Chaucer, Writing without Teachers, Writing with Power, Embracing Contraries, What Is English?* and (with Pat Belanoff) both a textbook, *A Community of Writers,* and a pamphlet to help students give peer responses, *Sharing and Responding.* He has published numerous essays, and won the Braddock award in 1986 for "The Shifting Relationships between Speech and Writing."

Randall R. Freisinger is professor of rhetoric, literature, and creative writing at Michigan Technological University. He has served as director of the Missouri Writing Project and co-director of the Upper Peninsula Writing Project. He was one of the original founders of Michigan Technological University's Writing-Across-the-Curriculum Program and has directed or co-directed faculty WAC workshops at a number of colleges and universities across the country. He has regularly given papers at the CCCC, MLA, and NCTE. His essays and poems have appeared widely in scholarly and literary journals. He has two books of poems, *Hand Shadows* and *Running Patterns,* the latter of which won the 1985 Flume Press National Chapbook Competition. He teaches writing courses in literary nonfiction, fiction, and poetry, as well as courses in nineteenth-century British and twentieth-century American literature and serves as a poetry editor for *The Laurel Review.*

Toby Fulwiler has directed the writing program at the University of Vermont since 1983. Before that he taught at Michigan Tech and the University of Wisconsin where, in 1973, he also received his Ph.D. in American literature. He conducts writing workshops for teachers across the disciplines and teaches classes in first-year composition as well as upper-division courses with titles such as "Personal Voice" and "Writing *The New Yorker.*" His most recent book is *The Blair Handbook,* co-authored with Alan Hayakawa. He has also written *College Writing* (1992) and *Teaching with Writing* (1986) and numerous professional articles on teaching writing; he has edited *The Journal Book* (1987) and co-edited *Programs That Work* (1990), *Community of Voices* (1992), and *Angles of Vision* (1992).

Paula Gillespie directs the Writing Center at Marquette University and has presented at various conferences, including the CCCC, the National Writing Center Association, and the East Coast Writing Center Association. In addition to her work in rhetoric, she is completing a study of voice in the narrative of James Joyce's fiction.

Gwendolyn Gong, who received her Ph.D. from Purdue University, is associate professor of English at Texas A&M University. She served as the director of Freshman English Studies and is a consultant for the Center for Executive Development at Texas A&M as well as for various colleges and universities. She has taught writing and reading courses at the Institut Teknologi Mara in Shah Alam, Malaysia, and is currently on a research leave in Hong Kong. Her *Editing: The Design of Rhetoric* (1989), co-authored with Sam Dragga, received the 1990 NCTE Achievement Award for Technical and Scientific Writing in the category of "Best Book of the Year." Gong and Dragga are currently completing two books focusing on academic writing and reading abilities: *A Writer's Repertoire* (1995) and *A Reader's Repertoire* (1996).

David P. Harris recently retired as professor of linguistics from Georgetown University. He obtained his doctorate in linguistics from the University of Michigan. From 1963–1965 he served as the first program director of TOEFL (Test of English as a Foreign Language), and he was president of TESOL (Teachers of English to Speakers of Other Languages) from 1969–1970. After directing the American Language Institute at Georgetown for nineteen years, he returned to full-time teaching in 1980. He has published primarily in the areas of ESL teaching and testing.

Laura Julier does not suffer from migraine headaches, except in March when she writes her papers, which are usually on literary nonfiction and writing pedagogy, for the annual convention of the Conference on College Composition and Communication. Her most recent work on Didion's literary nonfiction appears in *The Critical Response to Joan Didion,* edited by Sharon Felton (1993). She is on the faculty of the Department of American Thought and Language at Michigan State University, where she teaches writing and women's studies.

Carl H. Klaus is professor of English and director of the Nonfiction Writing Program at the University of Iowa, where he previously served as director of the NEH/Iowa Institute on Writing. Currently at work on a book about the personal essay, he has authored, edited, or collaborated on several books about writing and the teaching of writing: *Composing Adolescent Experience, Courses for Change in Writing* (co-winner of MLA's Mina Shaughnessy Prize), *Elements of the Essay, Elements of Writing, Fields of Writing: Readings Across the Disciplines, In Depth: Essayists for Our Time,* and *Style in English Prose.*

Bonnie Meath-Lang, professor at the National Technical Institute for the Deaf at the Rochester Institute of Technology, received her doctorate in education from the University of Rochester. She has taught writing since 1972 to deaf, nonnative-English-speaking, and adult students, and has done research on the relationship of journal and biographical writing to curriculum and teaching. In 1988, she spent a semester consulting and teaching in a new bilingual deaf education program at the University of Leeds, West Yorkshire, England.

Doug Minnerly is assistant professor of theatre at Queens College, Charlotte, North Carolina, with a specialty in theatrical design and technology and an interest in almost everything else. The interdisciplinary thrust of the Queens' curriculum has recently rekindled an interest in writing, both his own and his students'. Along with his interest in *voice*, he is also interested in writing assessment and, with missionary zeal, has presented to the faculty of Queens College on the subject of portfolio assessment.

Meg Morgan, assistant professor at the University of North Carolina at Charlotte, teaches journalism, technical communication, composition, and graduate courses in composition theory, history, and pedagogy and also coordinates the journalism program. Her articles have appeared in the *Journal of Business and Technical Communication, Journal of Advanced Composition, Technical Communication,* and the *Bulletin of the Association for Business Communication.* She has also written chapters in *Effective Documentation: What We Learn from Research* (edited by Stephen Doheny-Farina); *Collaborative Writing in Industry* (edited by Mary M. Lay and William Karis); and *Professional Communication: The Social Perspective* (edited by Nancy Roundy Blyler and Charlotte Thralls).

John H. Powers, who received his Ph.D. from the University of Denver, is associate professor in the Department of Speech Communication and Theatre Arts at Texas A&M University. In addition, he has also taught reading and writing courses at the Institut Teknologi Mara in Shah Alam, Malaysia. Currently, he is on a two-year leave to conduct research and teach communication studies at Hong Kong Baptist University. Powers is the author of *Public Speaking: The Lively Art* (1994) and is completing another book focusing on human communication theory.

Michael Spooner is director of the Utah State University Press. He was formerly senior editor for publications at the National Council of Teachers of English and has worked in scholarly publishing for several years. He has taught classes in editing, word processing, and writing, and has published articles on writing and education, as well as essays, poems, and reviews in a number of publications. He is the author of *A Moon in Your Lunch Box* (1993) and has two other books for children forthcoming.

Margaret K. Woodworth, assistant professor of English and director of the Writing Center at Hollins College, is a former Fulbright Scholar in American literature and linguistics. After establishing a graduate program in composition and rhetoric at Virginia Tech, Woodworth came to Hollins in 1988, where she established a writing center and a faculty write-to-learn program. She teaches advanced grammar, advanced expository writing, and American literature, as well as graduate courses in American literature and rhetorical theory. Her scholarly interests include writing pedagogy, classical rhetoric, the lives of older Appalachian women, and Southern American writers, especially Eudora Welty and Flannery O'Connor. Her stories, poems, and essays have appeared in a variety of publications including *The American Poetry Review, Sparrow,* and *The Greensboro Review.*

Mark Zamierowski is a doctoral candidate in the English and philosophy program at Purdue University. By the date of publication of this volume, he hopes to have his dissertation complete, its focus at present, a Deleuzean approach to text production in antebellum America.